Crime–Terror Alliances and the State

This book examines the trans-border connections between militant and criminal networks and the relationship between these and the states in which they operate.

"Unholy alliances" is a term used to describe hybrid trans-border militant and criminal networks that pose serious threats to security in Europe and elsewhere. Identity networks provide the basis for militant organizations using violent strategies – insurgency and terrorism – for political objectives. To gain funds and weapons militant networks may establish criminal enterprises, or align with existing trans-border criminal and financial networks.

This book extends the concept of unholy alliances to include the trans-state criminal syndicates that arise in failed and dysfunctional states, exemplified by Serbia and Bulgaria during their post-Communist transitions. To deal with this complex and unconventional subject, the authors develop a theoretical framework that looks at four kinds of factors conditioning the interaction between the political and the criminal: trans-state identity networks, armed conflict, the balance of market opportunities and constraints, and the role of unstable and corrupt states. The volume also examines actors at two levels of analysis: the structure and activities of militant (and/or criminal) networks, and the policies of state actors that shape and reshape the interaction of opportunities and constraints.

This book will be of much interest to students of terrorism, insurgency, transnational crime, war and conflict studies, and IR in general.

Lyubov Grigorova Mincheva is Associate Professor of Political Science at the University of Sofia, Bulgaria. She earned her Ph.D. from the University of Maryland and has published extensively in English and Bulgarian languages on ethnopolitics, spillover crisis, peacekeeping, crime, and terrorism. She is a member of the European Standing Group in International Relations.

Ted Robert Gurr is Distinguished University Professor, Emeritus, at the University of Maryland, USA. He founded and consults on the Minorities at Risk project at the University's Center for International Development and Conflict Management. Among his books are *Why Men Rebel*, *Violence in America*, and *Peoples vs. States*. He also established and coedits the biennial global report *Peace and Conflict*.

"Both criminologists and political scientists have found it difficult to find adequate conceptual tools to address political crime and criminal politics. Here then, at long last, is a study that provides a sophisticated theoretical framework and new conceptual tools to understand the complex interaction between kleptocratic public officials, trans-border organized crime syndicates and identity-based international terrorist networks. It has been said that nothing is as practical as a good theory. In this sense, this path-breaking volume with its six in-depth case studies should be an eye-opener for national law enforcement agencies as well as Europol and Interpol."
– Alex P. Schmid, Editor, **Perspectives on Terrorism** *and Fellow,*
International Centre for Counter-Terrorism,
The Hague, The Netherlands

"This pathbreaking book by Gurr and Mincheva addresses one of the issues that transcends traditional academic disciplines – cross-border networks of criminals and terrorists. With rich case study material from the Balkans, the Middle East, and North Africa, the authors explore the intersection of organized crime and terrorism with stunning insight. The book is a must-read for scholars of organized crime, terrorism, and money laundering, regardless of the disciplines with which they identify."
– Peter Grabosky, Australian National University,
Canberra, Australia

"The academic disciplines of political science and criminology have long kept political and criminal issues in artificially isolated silos. Mincheva and Gurr break through these silos by examining the violent intersection of organized crime and terrorism. Using six carefully selected case studies they scrutinize the trans-border militant and criminal networks that currently pose a major security threat to many parts of the world. The result is an important look at how politics and crime sometimes bleed into each other."
– Gary LaFree, University of Maryland, USA

Contemporary security studies
Series Editors: James Gow and Rachel Kerr
King's College London

European Security in a Global Context
Internal and external dynamics
Edited by Thierry Tardy

Women and Political Violence
Female combatants in ethno-national conflict
Miranda H. Alison

Justice, Intervention and Force in International Relations
Reassessing just war theory in the 21st century
Kimberley A. Hudson

Clinton's Foreign Policy
Between the Bushes, 1992–2000
John Dumbrell

Aggression, Crime and International Security
Moral, political and legal dimensions of international relations
Page Wilson

European Security Governance
The European Union in a Westphalian world
Charlotte Wagnsson, James Sperling and Jan Hallenberg

Private Security and the Reconstruction of Iraq
Christopher Kinsey

US Foreign Policy and Iran
American–Iranian relations since the Islamic revolution
Donette Murray

Legitimising the Use of Force in International Relations
Kosovo, Iraq and the ethics of intervention
Corneliu Bjola

The EU and European Security Order
Interfacing security actors
Rikard Bengtsson

US Counter-terrorism Strategy and al-Qaeda
Signalling and the terrorist world-view
Joshua Alexander Geltzer

Global Biosecurity
Threats and responses
Edited by Peter Katona, John P. Sullivan and Michael D. Intriligator

US Hegemony and International Legitimacy
Norms, power and followership in the wars on Iraq
Lavina Lee

Private Security Contractors and New Wars
Risk, law, and ethics
Kateri Carmola

Russia's Foreign Security Policy in the 21st Century
Putin, Medvedev and beyond
Marcel de Haas

Rethinking Security Governance
The problem of unintended consequences
Edited by Christopher Daase and Cornelius Friesendorf

Territory, War, and Peace
John A. Vasquez and Marie T. Henehan

Justifying America's Wars
The conduct and practice of US military intervention
Nicholas Kerton-Johnson

Legitimacy and the Use of Armed Force
Stability missions in the post-cold war era
Chiyuki Aoi

Women, Peace and Security
Translating policy into practice
Edited by Funmi Olonisakin, Karen Barnes and Ekaette Ikpe

War, Ethics and Justice
New perspectives on a post-9/11 world
Edited by Annika Bergman-Rosamond and Mark Phythian

Transitional Justice, Peace and Accountability
Outreach and the role of international courts after conflict
Jessica Lincoln

International Law, Security and Ethics
Policy challenges in the post-911 world
Edited by Aidan Hehir, Matasha Kuhrt and Andrew Mumford

Multipolarity in the 21st Century
A new world order
Edited by David Brown and Donette Murray

European Homeland Security
A European strategy in the making?
Edited by Christian Kaunert, Sarah Léonard and Patryk Pawlak

Transatlantic Relations in the 21st Century
Europe, America and the rise of the rest
Erwan Lagadec

The EU, the UN and Collective Security
Making multilateralism effective
Edited by Joachim Krause and Natalino Ronzitti

Understanding Emerging Security Challenges
Threats and opportunities
Ashok Swain

Crime–Terror Alliances and the State
Ethnonationalist and Islamist challenges to regional security
Lyubov Grigorova Mincheva and Ted Robert Gurr

Understanding NATO in the 21st Century
Alliance strategies, security and global governance
Edited by Graeme P. Herd and John Kriendler

Crime–Terror Alliances and the State

Ethnonationalist and Islamist challenges to regional security

Lyubov Grigorova Mincheva
and Ted Robert Gurr

LONDON AND NEW YORK

First published 2013
by Routledge
2 Park Square, Milton Park, Abingdon, Oxon, OX14 4RN

Simultaneously published in the USA and Canada
by Routledge
711 Third Avenue, New York, NY 10017

Routledge is an imprint of the Taylor & Francis Group, an informa business

© 2013 Lyubov Grigorova Mincheva and Ted Robert Gurr

The right of Lyubov Grigorova Mincheva and Ted Robert Gurr to be identified
as authors of this work has been asserted by them in accordance with
sections 77 and 78 of the Copyright, Designs and Patents Act 1988.

All rights reserved. No part of this book may be reprinted or reproduced
or utilised in any form or by any electronic, mechanical, or other means,
now known or hereafter invented, including photocopying and recording,
or in any information storage or retrieval system, without permission in
writing from the publishers.

Trademark notice: Product or corporate names may be trademarks or
registered trademarks, and are used only for identification and
explanation without intent to infringe.

British Library Cataloguing in Publication Data
A catalogue record for this book is available from the British Library

Library of Congress Cataloging-in-Publication Data
Grigorova, Lyubov, 1962–
    Crime–terror alliances and the state : ethnonationalist and Islamist
    challenges to regional security / Lyubov Grigorova Mincheva and
    Ted Robert Gurr.
    p. cm.—(Contemporary security studies)
    Includes bibliographical references and index.
    1. Transnational crime—Case studies. 2. Criminals—Social
    networks—Case studies. 3. Terrorism—Case studies.
    I. Gurr, Ted Robert, 1936– II. Title.
    HV6252.G75 2013
    364.106—dc23
    2012024286

ISBN13: 978–0–415–50648–9 (hbk)
ISBN13: 978–0–203–07750–4 (ebk)

Typeset in Baskerville
by Swales & Willis Ltd, Exeter, Devon

Printed and bound in the United States of America by Publishers Graphics,
LLC on sustainably sourced paper.

Contents

	List of figures, maps, and tables	x
	Preface and acknowledgments	xi
1	Unholy alliances: a theoretical framework for analyzing trans-border crime–terror networks	1
2	Crime, political violence, and governance in Kosovo: a triple alliance?	24
3	Kurdish nationalists and criminal networks: the PKK in Turkey, the Middle East, and Europe	41
4	Militant Islam and Bosnia's civil war 1991–1995	68
5	Greed, grievance, and political Islam in the Algerian revolutionary war of the 1990s	87
6	Serbia in the 1990s: militant nationalism and the criminalized state	103
7	The state and crime syndicates in post-communist Bulgaria	122
8	Militants and money: the political economy of communal rebels in post-communist Europe and the Middle East	143
9	Conclusions: responding to ethnonational and Islamist crime–terror networks	159
	Notes	179
	Select bibliography	215
	Index	219

List of figures, maps, and tables

Figures

1.1	Unholy alliances explained	2
3.1	Determinants of strategic choices and actions of hybrid crime–terror networks: the Kurdish PKK	43
7.1	Phases, structural elements, and international factors in state criminalization	127
7.2	Bombings in Bulgaria by year, 1991–2006	128

Maps

0.1	Countries with crime–terror alliances in South-East Europe	xvi
0.2	The heroin pipelines to Western Europe through countries with crime–terror alliances. Heroin flows in metric tons, 2008	xvii

Tables

1.1	Politically active minorities with kindred in neighboring cross-border regions, c. 2005	9
1.2	Transparency International's ratings of 2010 public sector corruption in host states of militant/criminal networks	18
8.1	Criminal activities by communally based organizations in the Middle East, 1980–2004	153
8.2	Criminal activities by communally based organizations in the post-communist states, 1980–2006	154
9.1	Unholy alliances comparisons: the impact of conflict, identity and opportunities on criminal/political linkages	163

Preface and acknowledgments

The Kosovo Liberation Army (KLA), which formed in the mid-1990s to resist harsh Serbian rule, was based on the traditional clans of rural Kosovo but had ethnonational aims to create a greater Albania. The clans were also the basis of long-established trans-border smuggling networks that expanded rapidly during the decade, gaining control of 40 per cent of the West European heroin market. As Serbs' retaliation against the Kosovars escalated, NATO unleashed a bombing campaign in 1999 that compelled Serbia to withdraw. Nearly 20,000 UN and European personnel, military and civilians, were posted to Kosovo to maintain peace and build new institutions. The leaders of the clans that ran the criminal networks and organized armed resistance became key figures in a new government that has high marks for corruption. Hashim Thaqi of the Drenica clans, the incumbent prime minister in 2011, was so adept at melding nationalism, enterprise and political influence that his countrymen admiringly called him "The Snake."[1] Entrepreneurs meanwhile laundered some crime proceeds by establishing hotels and brothels, staffed with women they trafficked illegally from the East, to service international personnel.[2]

The clan-based networks of Kosovar Albanians exemplify what we call an "unholy alliance" between militants and criminals. The details of this narrative, most of them reported in chapter 2, make a good journalistic account. But what analytic framework can be used to find and analyze comparable cases? Conflict analysis is relevant but provides no conceptual tools for dealing with trans-border criminal activity. Criminologists focus on the market opportunities, constraints, and networks that shape international crime networks but do not analyze the political context or conflicts that breed crime networks. Specialists in conflict management and peace-building are mostly practitioners and, in Kosovo at least, had little purchase on the country's trans-border networks. One international official reportedly said that trafficking was just a matter of Kosovars taking along some heroin in their luggage on visits to relatives in West Europe. The accompanying maps show the six countries that host unholy alliances (p. xvi) and trace the heroin trafficking routes that provide much of their illicit income (p. xvii). Only Algeria is not affected by trafficking.

The theoretical framework we devised for studying such networks, summarized in chapter 1, was shaped and then reshaped by the results of our comparative case xii *Preface and acknowledgments*

studies. We began by focusing on contemporary trans-state identity movements in conflict situations. These movements, and more specifically their trans-state identity networks, are our two-level units of analysis. The key question is how and why movements such as the Albanian and Kurdish nationalists give rise to hybrid criminal-militant networks. Identity networks provide the basis for militant organizations using violent strategies – insurgency and terrorism – for political objectives. To gain funds and weapons militants may establish criminal enterprises or align with existing criminal networks. Two sets of factors determine the establishment of militant-criminal networks: the endogenous factors of domestic politics and the exogenous factors of regional politics. These hybrid networks can only be fully understood in terms of the interaction between these endogenous and exogenous factors. They command both economic and political resources that can be used to broaden support and to suborn officials wherever their communal networks extend. And we came to recognize that corrupt officials of weak, unstable, and criminalizing states also can become active participants in trans-border crime networks.

Unholy alliances are best thought of as networks, not unitary actors. They are highly resilient and adaptive actors on the contemporary world scene and not well understood. Cells and networks of members carry out criminal enterprises partly to fund their political agendas and partly for personal gain – they are driven by complex interactions between collective identity and self-interest. And sometimes there are agenda shifts in which material interests displace political objectives. Commentators on this project have asked whether there are contrasting cases in which criminal enterprises have developed a political agenda. Undoubtedly so, especially at the local level – for example, in municipal "machine" politics in United States history. Contemporary African warlords, like the leaders of the notorious Revolutionary United Front in Sierra Leone, may be predators in the early stages of their movements and then evolve into militants who use political ideology to legitimate their profit-seeking activities. Most conspicuously, the Mexican drug cartels have emerged as criminal actors whose rapidly expanding business has demanded the establishment of security forces and encouraged them to seek alliances with state and other non-state actors to expand their power and profits. But the authors do not focus on militant identity networks that may have evolved from criminal enterprises. Trans-state identity networks are our beginning point, not the end point.

In one sense "unholy alliances" is a metaphor for the convergence between two global bads, international terrorism and crime. Most actors in this comparative study are "unholy alliances" in two more exact senses. Some militant networks work in consort with separate criminal organizations as a matter of mutual convenience – these are alliances in the conventional meaning of the word. In other situations militants run their own criminal activities, either directly or through what might be called subsidiaries drawn from their own identity groups. In the latter case – the operations of the Kurdish PKK in Europe are a good example – there is a convergence, or loosely an alliance, of political and economic motives and activities in entities within the same larger identity group.

In common usage the criminal-militant networks are "terrorists," and we have used that term in working papers for this project as well as in this book's title. But the label can be misleading. Their violent tactics are part of larger and shifting strategies that usually aim at fundamental political change. They may seek to carve out new trans-border political entities, or to establish autonomous regions in existing states, or to subvert existing states – all by some combination of coercion and persuasion. Money and coercion are means to those ends: money is necessary to sustain the movements, violence and its threat are essential strategic tools. So we usually refer to the movements in this study as militants, a more inclusive term than terrorists.

Some of our six cases are in the Balkans, others in the Islamic world proximate to Europe. All the criminal-militant networks in these cases have operated in and across Europe and thus are of major concern for European regional security. State actors add another layer of complexity to the analysis. Criminal-militant networks, or alliances, command a potent combination of political and economic resources that can be used to subvert state officials. In some situations there are no clear boundaries between state institutions, criminal networks, and militant identity politics. Serbia during the wars of Yugoslav secession shows some of these processes at work. In post-Communist Bulgaria substantial elements of the state became criminalized not directly because of identity politics but because of economic opportunities provided by ethnonational warfare beyond its borders.

This project is an exploration of borderlands in two ways. First, we are dealing mainly with trans-state networks rather than state or domestic actors. Second, we are working at the intersection of identity politics, conflict analysis, criminology, and international politics. To deal with this complex and unconventional subject we develop in chapter 1 a theoretical framework that looks at four kinds of factors conditioning the interaction between the political and the criminal: trans-state identity networks, armed conflict, the balance of market opportunities and constraints, and the role of unstable and corrupt states. We also look at actors at two levels of analysis: the structure and activities of militant (and/or criminal) networks as such, and the policies of state actors that shape and reshape the interaction of opportunities and constraints. The relevant actors in the European space include the European Union, the Organization for Security and Cooperation in Europe, and individual states. Their counter-terrorism and crime control policies are the subject of our concluding chapter.

The six case studies are supplemented by a broader comparative study of criminal activities by ethnoterritorial and religious communal groups in the Middle East and the post-Communist states. This is incorporated in chapter 8's analysis of militants' fund-raising strategies and how they might be controlled. The information was collected as part of the Minorities at Risk Organizational Behavior (MAROB) project at the University of Maryland's Center for International Development and Conflict Management. The MAROB project coded all organizations spawned by each identity group in the MAR universe of analysis from 1980 to the mid-2000s. A total of 383 communally based organizations have been profiled in these two regions, 112 in the Middle East and 271 in the Soviet and Yugoslav successor states. The authors designed MAROB coding indicators to tap such variables as the

xiv *Preface and acknowledgments*

organizations' transnational goals and networks; transnational violent behavior; criminal activities; and cooperation with criminal networks and security personnel.

Whereas the cases in the MAROB study are inclusive, our choice of case studies of unholy alliances is strategic. A significant body of literature focuses on connections between crime and terrorism in general and narco-terrorism in particular.[3] We focus more narrowly on militant trans-state identity networks and how criminal economic activity shapes and sustains them. There is also considerable evidence and commentary on the ethnically based drug and commodities trade across porous state borders in Southeast Asia's "Golden Triangle." In Afghanistan the Taliban's growing reliance on extracting rents from opium production and transit has attracted much international attention.[4] We focus specifically on networks that operate in or on the periphery of Europe and directly affect governance, security, and society in European states. Our cases are by no means exhaustive of this limited set, and others, in Europe and elsewhere, can be analyzed with similar theoretical questions in mind.

Islam is a factor in four of the six cases but Islamist political doctrine is central to only two of them, Bosnia and Algeria. In Algeria the political-criminal network, or rather interacting networks, have pursued militantly Islamist objectives at home and in Western Europe. In mid-1990s Bosnia two different brands of Islamic politics were active, the quasi-secular nationalism of the Bosnian state and the militant Salafist doctrine of foreign mujahedeen fighters who came to Bosnia's aid. Among the Kosovar Albanians, identity networks are based on shared clan membership and nationality, with Islam playing at most a secondary role. The Kurds of Turkey define themselves by national identity and political objectives, not religion – their Islamic faith is a distinguishing identity trait only for the Kurdish diaspora in Europe.

The ideas that led to this project emerged out of discussions and papers prepared for the Economics Working Group of the International Summit on Democracy, Terrorism, and Security convened in Madrid in March 2005. The second author chaired the Working Group, the first author was one of the participants. Comments from Alex Schmid and Jeroen Gunning helped shape our initial ideas.[5] Five of our subsequent case studies were prepared as papers for annual meetings of the International Studies Association: Kosovo (2006), Bosnia (2007), Kurdish nationalists in Turkey (2008), Bulgaria (2009), and Serbia (2010). Our understanding of the topic and our theoretical framework has evolved over time, and all the ISA papers have been substantially revised for this book.[6]

We thank the many scholars and institutions that have contributed ideas, information, and support to the Unholy Alliances project. Alex Schmid, formerly at the UN Office on Drugs and Crime in Vienna and at St Andrews University, has given us encouragement, information, and constructive criticism from our Madrid beginnings. The support of our home institutions has been essential: the University of Sofia's Graduate Program in International and Security Studies and the University of Maryland. Institutional assistance has been provided by the University of Sofia's Dialogue Europe Institute, directed by Prof. Kostadin Grozev. At

Preface and acknowledgments xv

Maryland the Center of International Development and Conflict Management, directed by Jonathan Wilkenfeld, and the National Center for the Study of Terrorism and Responses to Terrorism (START), directed by Gary LaFree, provided critical grant support. We are also indebted to associates of the MAROB project at the University of Maryland, especially Amy Pate and Victor Asal. Other supporting institutions have included the Human Security (HUMSEC) project of the European Commission and the Academic Fellowship Program of the Open Society Institute, Budapest. As important as this support has been, for the most part our work over the last seven years has been unfunded, fueled by our shared fascination with a new and little-understood subject.

In Europe scholarly advice and information have been provided by Tihomir Bezlov of the Center for the Study of Democracy, Sofia, Bulgaria; Anton Parvanov of the University for National and World Economy, Sofia, Bulgaria; Alison Pargeter of Cambridge University; Wolfgang Benedek of the European Human Rights Center, Gratz; Christopher Daase, Goethe-Universität, Frankfurt am Main; and Iztok Prezelj of the University of Ljubljana, Slovenia. The ISA panelists and discussants at ISA presentations have also provided a wide range of helpful comments and leads, most recently Michael Johns. Research assistants and graduate students who contributed substantially to the case studies include Major Sean Cosden, US Air Force and Olmstead scholar at the University of Sofia; Captain Daniel Rueth, also of the US Air Force and an Olmstead scholar; and Marzena Orlowska, Polish Erasmus student at the University of Sofia. Majid Shirali, PhD student at the University of Nevada, Las Vegas, helped substantially with the case studies of Kosovo and Algeria, and gave a final reading to the completed manuscript. Others who have read and commented on our case studies are thanked in notes to those chapters.

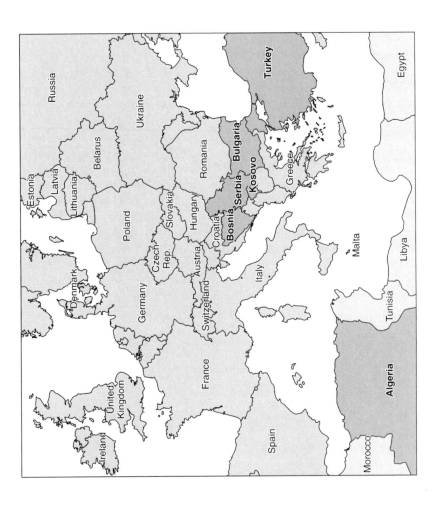

Map 0.1 Countries with crime–terror alliances in South-East Europe

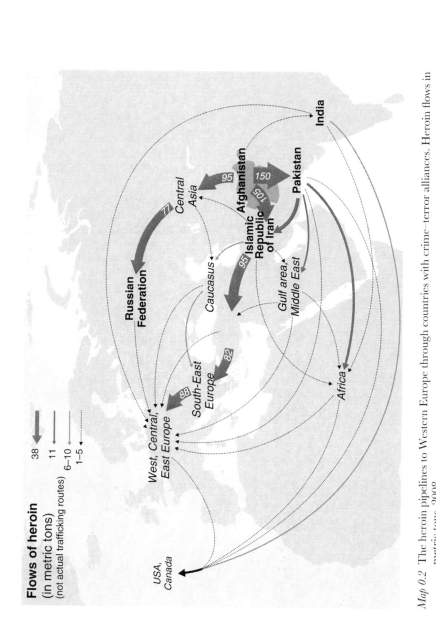

Map 0.2 The heroin pipelines to Western Europe through countries with crime–terror alliances. Heroin flows in metric tons, 2008

1 Unholy alliances

A theoretical framework for analyzing trans-border crime–terror networks

"Unholy alliances" is our term for hybrid trans-border militant and criminal networks that pose serious threats to security in Europe and elsewhere. Identity networks provide the basis for militant organizations using violent strategies – insurgency and terrorism – for political objectives. To gain funds and weapons militant networks may establish criminal enterprises, or align with existing trans-border criminal and financial networks. The nationalist movements of Kosovar Albanians and Turkish Kurds have been the basis for profitable and durable militant and criminal networks that operate from Asia Minor to the Balkans and Western Europe. The joint political and criminal activities of Jihadist Muslims in Bosnia and Algeria are recent instances of unholy alliances based on a political-religious ideology. Weak and corrupt states, ungoverned areas, and regional conflicts provide opportunities and lootable resources for trans-border criminal networks with material objectives as well as for political militants. We extend the concept of unholy alliances to include the trans-state criminal syndicates that arise in failed and dysfunctional states, exemplified by Serbia and Bulgaria during their post-Communist transitions.

When do militant and criminal networks form and align, and under what conditions? This chapter develops theoretical arguments about the complex conditions that provide the incentives and opportunities in which unholy alliances are established and persist. The accompanying figure shows the major concepts and principal linkages that are explored below.

A major challenge in building an explanatory model is its complex dependent variable that demands explanation for the *interaction* of two conceptually distinct motives for joint action. In the first section below, "Power, Profits, and Violence," we sketch a typology of interactions, thereby operationalizing our dependent variable. Then we develop an explanatory model. Five major factors are proposed to condition militant-criminal interactions. A strongly disposing condition is the existence of trans-state nationalist, ethnic, and religious *movements*. These provide settings conducive to joint political and criminal action based on shared values and mutual trust. A second condition is the occurrence of armed conflict, which often provides incentives and opportunities for interdependence. Trans-state identity movements and violent regional conflicts are

2 Unholy alliances

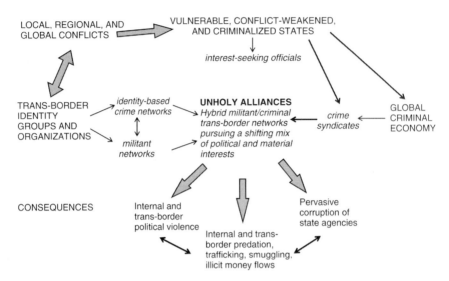

Figure 1.1 Unholy alliances explained

the subject of the second major section of this chapter, "Identity Conflicts across Borders." The third set of conditions comprises the criminal markets, networks, opportunities, and constraints that facilitate joint action by criminals and militants. These conditions are the subject of "Criminal Markets and Networks," a section that incorporates perspectives from criminology, conflict analysis, and international economics. Fourth is the role of weak states in conflict zones, ungoverned areas ("black holes"), as well as states in transition whose corrupted agencies create and profit from illicit market opportunities and cooperate with hybrid trans-border networks. This factor is the subject of the fourth section of this chapter, "Weak States, Failed States, Corrupted and Criminalized States." We also mention narco-states as examples of states corrupted by their involvement in trans-border drug networks, though most such states are outside the scope of an analysis that focuses on identity-based movements. Lastly, we discuss briefly the effects and limitations of the "Policies of Supra-national Institutions" in Europe that are designed to rebuild dysfunctional states and contain trans-border crime and terrorism.

Power, profits, and violence: the complex dependent variable

We define and describe the complex dependent variable, the *interaction* between two distinct motives, by focusing on actors. The actors whose behavior and driving motivations are to be explained are criminalized rebels who cooperate in or conduct illegal enterprises in pursuit of radical political goals. Rebels' main objective is to attain power but economic gain is also on their agenda. Power and profit are frequently mutable, with power taking the lead. In some situations, as we show in some of our case studies, economic gain displaces political objectives.

Our assumption that the violent pursuit of power (by insurgency or terrorism) and illicit material gain (criminal enterprise) are different purposes may seem obvious. It is not just a definitional point but a difference that helps explain actors' choices of strategies and their organizational structures. However, international conventions conflate crime and terrorism: from a legal perspective, terrorism *is* criminal behavior. Both militant and criminal enterprises engage in illegal violence whether in pursuit of power or profit.[1] The United Nations Secretariat has characterized terrorism as the most visible and openly aggressive form of transnational organized crime.[2] Martin and Romano, following other writers, have introduced the general concept of *multinational systemic crime* to denote the "collective behavior" of groups engaged in terrorism, espionage, and trafficking in drug and arms.[3] A fashionable economic theory of rebellion deals with political motivations by ignoring them. Collier and Hoeffler posit that rebellion is "an industry that generates profits from looting. . . . Such rebellions are motivated by greed."[4]

If we accept these premises as a beginning point, there is little to explain. Social movement and conflict theories would be irrelevant, or at best secondary, to the explanation of linkages between militant movements and crime. In our view the essential differences are these. Profit maximization and risk reduction are the motives that shape the behavior of international criminal groups. In contrast, the ideologically driven pursuit of social and political goals motivates militant political movements. They seek to influence political processes and ultimately to exercise state power. Strategically, criminal groups use violence to establish and maintain control over the supply, shipment, and distribution of illicit goods and services. Political militants, by contrast, use violence mainly to publicize their objectives and to demonstrate the weakness of their opponents – usually states, sometimes rival groups. Organizational differences follow. International criminal enterprises need regular access to suppliers, transit routes, and markets, implying a relatively high degree of coordination. Their profits are usually large and can be used to buy immunity from security and judicial officials. Militant movements, by contrast, are more likely to function as cells or networks, capable of carrying out episodic attacks on political targets but otherwise flexible and mutable. Their survival depends more on evading and weakening security forces than on buying them off.[5]

This dualistic approach to analyzing militancy and crime is affirmed in different contexts. European experts point to "symbiotic partners from arms trades and narcotics" as a connection that straddles the schism between the two spheres.[6] "Narco-terrorism" is widely used to describe the activities of Latin American narcotics traffickers in collusion with revolutionary movements in Peru, Colombia, and elsewhere. The term can mask very complex and mutable interactions among traffickers, revolutionaries, and security agencies, as it has in Peru[7] and Colombia.[8]

Pragmatic considerations bring these two types of actors together in hybrid "unholy alliances." Militant political movements require resources for arms, logistics, and sustenance and shelter for militants. Consequently they frequently engage in criminal activity to finance their activities, relying on robbery, kidnapping for ransom, extortion, and trafficking in drugs and humans. Joint action between militants and criminal enterprises potentially provides more opportunities for profit and political impact than either group enjoys when acting alone. But there are barriers to joint action. Cooperation depends on a common basis of trust. Ethnonational and sectarian identifications seem especially important to establishing trust that transcends international boundaries because they imply cultural cohesion, group loyalty, and shared antipathy toward states and other social actors.[9]

It has been suggested that militant movements gradually lose interest in establishing alliances with crime networks as basic sources of funding. Where such alliances do exist they usually are transitory rather than essential for the political economy of militant movements. The general pattern seems to be that successful militants become self-funded, at the risk of an agenda shift in which they evolve in the direction of "fighters turned felons."[10] Their chances for political survival and success increase as they run criminal enterprises themselves. In doing so their political agenda may remain central. Or they may shift away from political objectives to profit-seeking.

Militant groups also have incentives to skip intermediaries in their business operations because most lines of trans-border exchange of illegal commodities become increasingly complex. Being driven by demand alone, narcotics and arms sales do not necessarily have a symbiotic relationship. However, conditions that promote one type of trafficking more often than not promote the other as well. Narcotics and arms thus often become items of exchange in complex deals involving third and fourth parties. Within this setting few partners could expect to be "end recipients" of precisely what they were seeking from the market, with no collateral transactions.[11] This presents contemporary militants with the need to increasingly think as businessmen to whom profits will be available if they are pragmatic, while loss will follow if they remain doctrinaire.

As this discussion suggests, the interaction of militant and criminal objectives can take various and changing forms. Below we develop further our dependent variable, "unholy alliances," by looking at actors and motivations. Our actors are trans-state networks based on some combination of identity and interest. Some are *cross-border* networks that link adjacent groups. Others are extraterritorial *trans-state* networks that link together groups and organizations across regions.

The mix of motivations driving interaction between criminal and militant networks varies. We sketch three patterns by which militants may operate or cooperate with illegal enterprises, and examine their cross-border and trans-state networks. Three types of interaction are evident from our cases and the literature. The first pattern is characterized by a mix of *opportunistic* and *pragmatic* objectives. It offers the clearest examples of what we term "unholy alliances." Militants who initially engage in illegal enterprises in pursuit of radical political objectives simultaneously become self-interested "felons." These Janus-faced militant/criminal networks stretch across borders and are especially likely to emerge when local conflicts spark cross-border regional crises. In the second pattern militants are driven by *ideological* objectives, and illegal enterprises are kept subordinate to their political objectives.

Networks of the third type are almost wholly *predatory*. Here we deal with criminals and criminal syndicates that build and use trans-state networks for purposes of profit maximization and risk reduction. They may make use of trans-border identity networks but only or mainly to pursue material gain. As our case studies show, these patterns of motivation can change during a movement's lifespan.

Patterns of militancy–crime linkages: opportunistic interdependence

The opportunistic pattern of terrorism-crime connections is one in which political goals and material gain coexist on a more or less equal footing. Actors shift easily from one to another. Analysts have called this pattern a political-criminal hybrid. What is distinctive about it is the simultaneous pursuit of political and criminal objectives. Two of our case studies of cross-border networks exemplify this pattern: the clan-based cross-border networks of Kosovar Albanian nationalists and the nationalist and fundraising network of the Kurdish Workers Party (the PKK) in Europe. These instances of *opportunistic interdependence* evolved within cross-border networks. Territorial cross-border communication and action is key here. Based on territorially adjacent identity groups, these networks mobilize support across the border. The real political-criminal agents are in fact paramilitary/criminal units or cells. They profit immensely as they commute across adjacent territories and interact with their more distant diasporas. They simultaneously promote political violence in neighboring areas and earn money from their trans-state brethren.

The clan-based Kosovo Liberation Army (KLA) waged insurgency in the 1990s against the Serb authorities in Kosovo and later promoted insurgencies across borders to south Serbia and Macedonia. Simultaneously the clan networks exploited the West European market for drugs. Criminologist Xavier Raufer said of the Albanian political-criminal syndicate that it was impossible to distinguish between liberation fighters and drug traffickers. A Serbian analyst reported that 15 leading Albanian family clans (*fis*) established complete control over criminal activity in Albania in 1997 during the collapse of the Albanian state into anarchy. Motivated by fear of inter-*fis* blood feuds over the limited Balkan criminal turf, the 15 *fis* allegedly made a deal to accept a common paramilitary enforcement unit, the KLA, in order to incite violence in Kosovo with the dual objectives of making money and financing wars to unify all Albanian-inhabited areas of the Balkans.[12]

Closely related is the *pragmatic* pattern in which a militant organization's agenda alternates between political and material objectives, depending on circumstances. Cross-border networks and external opportunities are here again in play. The PKK – the Kurdish Workers Party in Turkey – is our case in point. The group was established in 1978 with an ideology that blended Marxism-Leninism with a war of terror aimed at national self-determination of the Turkish Kurdish people. From 1984 to 1999 the organization carried out brutal campaigns of terrorism throughout Turkey and in some European countries that claimed the lives of more than 37,000 victims, including Turkish security forces, rival political groups,

6   Unholy alliances

as well as fellow Kurds. To sustain its insurgency the PKK sought support from states, other terror movements, and the Kurdish diaspora in Europe. Over the past thirty and more years the group evolved into a criminal enterprise involved in drug production and trafficking as well as in money laundering of the profits. Curtis and Karacan observe that "regional criminal organizations parallel terrorist and political cells and have common membership."[13] Not surprisingly the PKK become intertwined with organized crime networks in Europe and elsewhere.[14]

The pragmatic characterization of the PKK was evident from its activities between 1999 and 2004. During these years the PKK insurgency largely subsided due to the arrest of its leader Abdullah Öcalan and his call for an end to armed struggle. But the supportive structure of its criminal activities remained in place. Analyzing the group's activities in the course of those years, it has been observed that the PKK adopted a pattern of behavior very similar to that of the Philippine-based Abu-Sayyaf group. It eschewed civic and cultural activities and concentrated on criminal activities to sustain a small but threatening military presence.[15]

Patterns of militancy–crime linkages: ideological movements

Some militants give primacy to their ideological and political objectives, and undertake illicit economic activities mainly or exclusively to fund their political program. We examine two case studies exemplifying *ideological* interactions within trans-border identity networks: Bosnia and Algeria. The Muslim government of the newly independent Bosnian state, facing an international arms embargo, sought collaboration in the early 1990s with trans-state Islamic identity movements to survive the challenges of interethnic strife, as well as nearly all-out interstate war with Yugoslavia and Croatia. Territorial discontinuity between the Bosniak movement and its international co-religionists was not important as a factor. Instead the Bosnian Muslim government was supported with money, arms, and fighters, in contravention of the international embargo, by Islamic endowments, states, and individual sponsors from across the Middle East and the Persian Gulf. This support made use of the trans-state Islamic identity networks that existed long before the outbreak of the Bosnian war. Once the war was over the Bosnian government sought to distance itself from Islamists and ousted most fighters. But connections and local institutions established during the war secured the Islamists a presence in Bosnia that the government never succeeded in eliminating. Weakened Islamist networks are said to be still in place along which money, ideas, and activists move from the Middle East to Bosnia and beyond to Western Europe.

Islamists in Algeria began their 1990s resistance to the military-controlled government as an ideological movement. They first relied on domestic and international contributions, then a country-wide campaign of kidnappings, extortion, and robbery. Government repression, and European efforts to stop the flow of money from Islamist sympathizers, left the remaining bands of armed Islamists in Algeria to rely on banditry for survival. By 2000 ideology provided little more than a rationale for predation. This exemplifies one of the ways in which "unholy alliances" established for ideological goals can shift to opportunism and then predation.

Patterns of militancy–crime linkages: predatory networks

The third pattern is one in which material gain becomes the group's principal objective. Predatory trans-border alliances have two kinds of origins. In some, changing circumstances divert militants away from political objectives toward material gain, as in Algeria. "Social bandits" are a recognized object of historical analysis – marginalized rural groups for whom banditry displaced explicit political objectives. According to E.J. Hobsbawm, the Sicilian Mafia, for example, originated in nineteenth-century political resistance to foreign rule.[16]

The political transitions in South-Eastern Europe gave rise to predatory networks very different from those in Algeria. The Serbian network, for instance, was based on the Serb trans-border movement that was promoted, armed, and financed by the Milošević regime. Its paramilitary units fought the irredentist wars in Croatia and Bosnia. In parallel, however, these units engaged in looting and smuggling. Journalist Ron Haviv observed that the Serb paramilitary units fighting in Croatia were also acting as thugs, and their activities were in fact large-scale robbery disguised as nationalism.

In neighboring Bulgaria the networks that emerged at the same time were solely profit-driven. In the early 1990s the Bulgarian state lost control over its legitimate monopoly of coercion. State security and judicial institutions were paralyzed due to speedy reformation and democratization. Thus the predatory networks emerged out of the power vacuum. They comprised experienced former state security employees and economic managers, who collaborated with corrupt officials to drain state resources.[17] The transition to a market economy opened up opportunities for the theft of state property and the emergence of a new kleptocratic elite. International pressures aimed at the speedy replacement of central economic planning and at establishment of free markets on the liberal model. But while Western observers were focused mostly on the politics of post-communist transitions, predation and criminalization became one of the most distinctive features of Bulgaria's transition. Former state security officials established private banks and privatized the national capital. Their subsequent abuse of financial power, including the establishment of financial pyramids and the provision of "bad credit," led in 1996–7 to country-wide bank failures and hyperinflation. The financial loss of all banks monitored as of 31 May 1996 amounted to more than 33,600,000,000 BG levas. The period was notorious for the emergence of the so-called "credit millionaires," that is, bank officers and customers who profited from the collapse of the banking system and speedily exported their gains to Western banks. Official reports testify to packages worth $352,000,000 that left the country through the Customs Office at Sofia Airport about this time.[18]

In summary, the three patterns discussed above identify different actors and illustrate different degrees of interdependence between the actors' political and material objectives. Actors include cross-border hybrid militant/criminal networks; trans-state identity-based networks; and trans-state interest-based criminal networks. To explain how these types of global bad make common cause we need to develop a model of the circumstances under which trans-border militant and

8 *Unholy alliances*

criminal networks emerge and join forces. In the next section we discuss the trans-border identity conflicts that provide the groundwork for the formation of hybrid militant-criminal alliances.

Explaining unholy alliances: identity conflicts across borders

Trans-state insurgency and terrorism have been widely used to pursue ethno-national, religious or revolutionary objectives in the Balkans, Central and South Asia, the Caucasus, the Middle East, Central Africa and elsewhere. Their actors are trans-state nationalist, ethnic, and religious movements. Some pursue ethno-territorial separatist objectives for themselves and sometimes for segments in adjoining countries. Here we review some evidence about their dynamics and frequency, beginning at the regional level.

The expansion of violent country-centered conflicts from their core creates larger zones of what Monty Marshall calls "protracted conflict regions." Actors in these regions develop a pervasive sense of insecurity; coercion and violence are increasingly used in political relations throughout the region; and state resources are shifted from social and economic development to building up coercive capacities. Armed conflicts in such regions both diffuse and persist. Marshall uses comparative data to profile six such regions that developed between the 1940s and the 1980s, in East, Southeast, and South Asia; Southern Africa; the Middle East; and Central America.[19]

The Balkans became a protracted conflict region in the 1990s because of the violent contestation that accompanied the disintegration of the Yugoslavian federation. This process was propelled by spill-over crises, the term Lyubov Mincheva uses for conflict regions created by the diffusion of conflict among segments of cross-boundary kindred groups.[20] Our case studies of Serbia, Bosnia, and Kosovo show in depth how conflict diffused among trans-border identity groups – Serbs, Croats, Bosnian Muslims, and Albanians. Cross-border or trans-state identities provide the combustible materials that movement elites use to mobilize political action against one state. Once underway their collective actions aggregate and diffuse across borders from more mobilized to less mobilized segments and often draw on support from more distant diasporas.[21]

Cross-border movements are most often concerned with territorial changes that provide greater autonomy. Depending on circumstances they may seek secession, unification with kindred across borders, or regional autonomy within existing states. Their specific demands vary as movement leaders respond to shifting political circumstances. Trans-state movements whose segments are not territorially adjacent may raise alternative claims such as power devolution, power sharing, regime change, or global revolution.[22] And changing opportunities determine strategies of collective action, transforming it from political into military, or the reverse.

Local conflicts inflamed by cross-border identity groups are not a new phenomenon. Trans-state identity groups have been involved in many of the armed conflicts fought in the last half-century. A global survey in 2005 identified 71 ethnically based separatist movements that had fought wars against the states that governed them at some time in the previous 50 years. Half of them had politically active kindred in neighboring states, many of them sources of sanctuary and material support.[23] Another study surveyed the 26 armed conflicts of all kinds being fought in 2006. Half of them were based on ethnic minorities seeking autonomy or independence, and eight of these 13 were cross-border insurgencies supported by external kindred, including Armenians in the Nagorno-Karabakh enclave in Azerbaijan, Tamils in Sri Lanka, and the Karen in Myanmar (Burma).[24] It is clear from these studies that many if not most insurgencies of the past half-century were ethnically based, and half or more of them had support from kindred in neighboring states.

There is a major potential for new conflicts by trans-state identity groups in every world region. Of the 281 in-country identity groups tracked by the Minorities at Risk project all but 35 have kindred groups in neighboring countries. In many cases there is no direct regional basis for joint political action because the kin groups are dispersed in larger populations, for example, indigenous peoples in Bolivia and Brazil, or Roma in Slovakia and Romania. The opportunities for trans-border networking are greatest in the 124 instances in which a politically active identity group has kindred in contiguous areas of adjoining countries. The accompanying table shows the regional breakdown and some examples.[25]

Since the 1990s Islamic jihad has provided the idiom for a new kind of trans-state identity conflict, based on shared faith rather than territorial linkages. Islamist doctrine was the rationale for militants in nine of the 26 major armed conflicts of 2006, sometimes reinforcing separatist aims. These internal wars were not part of a global al-Qaeda-led conspiracy against the West, as Reveron and Murer point out in their comparative analysis of country and regional terrorist movements in the Islamic world. Rather most of them grew out of resistance to local and regional conditions such as Russian dominance over Muslim-majority Chechnya and corruption in the nominally Islamic, military-dominated government of

Table 1.1 Politically active minorities with kindred in neighboring cross-border regions, c. 2005

Region	Bi-sected Kin Groups	Examples
Western Europe	7	Basques in Spain and France
Latin America	12	Indigenous Mayans in Guatemala and Mexico
Post-Communist States	35	Ossetians in Georgia, Crimean Russians in Ukraine, Slovaks in Czech Republic
Sub-Saharan Africa	24	Acholi in Uganda and Kenya, Bakongo in Angola and Congo, Tuareg in Niger and Mali
Middle East and North Africa	18	Baluchi in Iran and Pakistan, Arabs in Iran and Iraq, Berbers in Algeria and Morocco
Asia	28	Tajiks in Afghanistan, Nagas in India, Turkmen in China

10   *Unholy alliances*

Algeria.[26] In the Islamic countries of Central Asia Omelicheva shows that support for radical Islam has been greatest among Uzbek and Tajik minorities who have been subject to religious persecution and discrimination.[27] In these and other instances Islamic identity provided the basis for mobilization and justifications for resistance against oppression; the global Islamic Umma offered moral and material support.

Religious faith often is one of the markers of identity groups. The 281 politically significant minorities profiled by the Minorities at Risk project (see note 24 above) include 125 groups who differ in both ethnicity and belief from dominant groups in the countries where they reside. More than half are Muslim minorities that live around the contested perimeter of the Islamic world. When these groups are drawn into minority/majority conflicts there is always the potential that conflict will be redefined or reinforced by Islamist doctrine.

In protracted conflict regions, especially those based on a trans-border ethnic or religious identity group, criminals have good reasons to cooperate with insurgents. Regional conflicts provide opportunities for profit making and risk reduction at the same time. Arms supply is a highly profitable business, for example, and in times of regional instability the potential profits increase as risks go down. When armed conflict is based on a trans-border identity group its networks make for easy movement of supplies, munitions, and fighters – as well as trafficking in consumer goods and drugs. And risk decreases as militants establish control in border areas or "black holes" (see below) that become havens for smugglers and bases for rebels.

Explaining unholy alliances: criminal networks and markets

Organized crime is a global phenomenon whose proceeds were recently estimated by the UN Office on Drugs and Crime at $130 billion per year.[28] By contrast most militant movements are local or regional. In order to connect to the world of global crime networks militants must accept and comply with the implicit rules guiding criminal enterprise. No generally accepted definition of organized crime exists. However, three approaches to criminal enterprise have shaped public and professional thinking for much of the past century. One is to analyze organized crime in terms of activities such as racketeering and other predatory aspects of domestic criminal enterprise. Crime has also been discussed in terms of actors seen as centralized Mafia-type underworld power structures that exercise control over illegal domestic markets. This image of criminal actors has evolved into a conception of international criminal conspiracies as multiple crime cartels, often ethnically based, engaged in drug trafficking, money laundering, and related illegal activities.

Contemporary studies of organized crime integrate and simultaneously depart from previous traditions. Organized crime nowadays is interpreted as profit-driven "*illegal collective behavior,*"[29] shaped by the interaction of the criminal *market's opportunities and constraints*, and performed within *fluid criminal cooperatives*.[30] In short, *"illegal collective behavior,"network*, and *market* are the three pillars that guide most contemporary analysis of criminal business.

Illegal collective behavior

From the perspective of criminology and organization theory, criminal enterprise can be interpreted as collective action based on what Klaus von Lampe calls "criminally exploitable ties." They are the basic ingredient of any form of criminal cooperation and are defined by two main characteristics. First are similar or corresponding criminal dispositions, meaning that actors have similar criminal interests and preferences. They may include cigarette and liquor smuggling, drug trafficking, arms trafficking, or trafficking in women, illegal money transfers, etc. Second is the availability of a common basis for trust, a basis that could be provided by kinship, ethnicity, childhood relations or any other social affiliation. These affiliations help guarantee the relative predictability of actors' behavior and thus minimize the risks of discovery and betrayal. Research findings suggest that where strong social links underpinning working criminal networks do not exist, criminal cooperation is ephemeral.[31] "Criminally exploitable ties" are an important analytical category because they help establish niches in which criminal enterprise can flourish. They also suggest that some degree of security is necessary for those involved in common business; they imply at least a partial overlap in social affiliation of interacting groups and individuals.

Criminal networks

Criminal enterprise as collective action takes place within *criminal networks*. Currently, criminal enterprises are conceived as webs of "social networks" or "criminal cooperatives." Their efficiency is assessed according to various criteria. The social affiliation of networks' membership is arguably most important. As suggested earlier, "social ties, much more than business relations or formal command structures, form the basis for criminal cooperation."[32] The common social affiliation of the criminal networks' membership keeps the number of successfully performed operations high; while fluid criminal networks only provide occasional "nodes" for successful operations.[33] Another important criterion in networks assessment is "the overall network size." This sets the limits for a criminal undertaking. Locally centered networks are used for purposes of domestic criminal activities. Cross-border and trans-state criminal networks are increasingly likely to be embedded in trans-state identity groups or diasporas – locally and abroad. They have become key components of international organized crime.[34]

The success of criminal enterprise is further conditioned by the mobilization and control of resources. In order to control resources a criminal enterprise must either find the suppliers or establish itself as such, and protect itself against interdiction by authorities. Criminal networks distinguish themselves depending on their activities. Some networks engage in *illegal* production and distribution of *legal goods* and services. Alternatively, other networks offer *illegal goods* and services for

12 *Unholy alliances*

free market exchange between suppliers and willing customers.[35] The first group, consisting of legal goods and services produced or distributed illegally, is mainly of interest for domestic profit-driven crime. The availability of those commodities and services depends on "the criminogenic properties of the industry and its regulatory environment," which create a "twilight zone where crime and business interact, often to their mutual benefit."[36] Criminal networks involved in the illegal provision of legal goods and services are especially active in societies in transition. We examine them in our case studies of Bulgaria and Serbia. The second group of resources – illegal goods and services – is mostly of interest to international criminal enterprise. Among various illegal commodities and services provided by transnational crime groups nowadays illegal drug production and distribution is unquestionably the first. Its emerging crime cartels in the 1980s have displaced "traditional organized crime" and have become a primary concern of the US and European Union policy makers, leading to the opening of America's war on drugs in the first case; as well as to development of EU legislation in the area of freedom, security and justice, in the second case.

Market opportunities and constraints

Criminologists also analyze opportunities for illicit activities by rational actors. The strategic making of successful criminal enterprise is achieved by knowledge and calculation; it depends on how well actors respond to criminal market opportunities and constraints. And the latter have greatly expanded via globalization of trade and finance, and global transportation and communication networks. Global communication networks help buyers and sellers locate each other, identify points of common interest, and establish cooperation. It is especially helpful at times when the transnational exchange of commodities has become increasingly complex. *Ad hoc* interactions with third parties may lead to profit; however, they may also incur loss. The expanding global communication network arguably reduces the risk of *ad hoc* interactions.

Criminal and armed organizations also have discovered and used the wide range of opportunities to share the international/global economic and financial infrastructure. Subsequently they also have engaged in the building of an illegal economy with global reach. Though a relatively recent phenomenon, this alternative economy has become a strong and independent global financial actor. In the late 1990s the Gross Criminal Product was estimated to be between $600 billion and $1.5 trillion or between 2 and 5 percent of the world's Gross Domestic Product.[37] It represents the value of illegal capital movement plus the profits of international crime in the alternative global economy. This alternative economy provides multiple opportunities for illicit business and imposes relatively few restraints.

Building on a study by Loretta Napoleoni,[38] we identify three branches within the global illegal economy. Each of them provides profitable business opportunities and is the source of streams of illegal money extracted from multiple sources. The first branch consists of capital flow from unreported and undetected money moving illegally across countries. Those who extract profits from this flow include the financial manipulators and smugglers who perpetrate frauds such as tax evasion, customs documents fraud, and falsified transfers unrelated to any real transnational commodity import/exports. In many circumstances they are assisted by corrupt state agencies such as customs services and financial police.

The illicit funds generated by the second branch come from the global money laundering of the illegal profits of transnational criminal networks. The globalization of finance is the strategic factor that has made this process possible. As David C. Jordan points out,

> [T]he development of unregulated global financial markets facilitates a system where crime syndicates based in Americas, Europe, the Middle East, Africa, the Pacific Basin, and Russia launder money throughout the world and reinvest in legitimate business.[39]

A more thorough consideration of the emergence and the functioning of global money laundering would identify the diverse means and actors responsible for "primitive accumulation" in the global illegal economy.

Beginning in the 1970s the Bretton Woods system of international monetary management, which once kept international capital flow subordinated to the individual interests of member states, gave way to the liberalization of the international financial system and released international capital flow from state control. This liberalization has elevated the power of the central and international private banks vis-à-vis nation-states so that domestic economies are now subject to international rules and restraints. And national economies are forced to seek means to survive and stay competitive in the international capital market.

The global shadow banking system simultaneously emerged as the hub of unregulated global finance. It flourishes within a network of offshore zones in countries with less stringent banking regulations such as Aruba, the Bahamas, Barbados, Bermuda, the British Virgin Islands, Cayman Islands, Costa Rica, Cyprus, Gibraltar, Guernsey, Hong Kong, the Isle of Man, Jersey, Liberia, Lichtenstein, Nauru, the Netherlands Antilles, Nevis, Panama, Switzerland, Turks and Caicos, and Vanuatu.[40]

Criminal banks are primary actors in the global money laundering process. It is not uncommon for legal banks to do the same. Banks frequently succumb to the temptation to "don't ask, don't tell" policies where transnational customers deposit large sums of questionable origin. Bank officials have been quoted as saying that more often than not they are aware of the illegal origin of some large incoming deposits, but they tend to turn a blind eye because the deposits have gone through multiple transfers before arriving at the end recipient bank.[41] Illegitimate from the perspective of strategic bank management, these policies signal the beginning of the process of criminalization of the global financial system. They make it possible for criminals to accumulate dirty money and then reinvest it in legal enterprises.

So the global money laundering and the shadow banking system have expanded opportunities for profit maximization and risk reduction for international crime and terror networks alike. Global money laundering has blurred the divide

14 *Unholy alliances*

between legal and illegal bank deposits. More importantly, deposits of this kind have changed the profile and also the configurations of actors behind these illicit transfers. Money laundering helps former criminals and narco-barons establish themselves as financial oligarchs and also as managers of large trans-national non-transparent holding companies. Therefore they have not only recurring access to offshore zones and banking facilities but they gain long-term influence over banks' governing bodies, as well as their strategic decision making process. Once they have gained such a foothold they can realign strategic bank policies with their private interests.[42]

Roth, among others, observes the devastating consequences of the admission of criminal lobbies to the banking sector. He echoes Jordan's warning that the global criminal and especially the narco business "buy off" advanced democracies and societies in transition and corrupt their financial institutions. So, some banks come to pursue adventurous policies not necessarily grounded on sound risk estimates: some embark upon irresponsible investment policies, others may adopt ruinous credit policies. And ironically, bank credit frauds are at times presented as leading policy innovations in global finance. Roth would argue that these were among the most significant sources of the 2007–8 global financial crisis. And evidence suggests that the crisis has further multiplied profit opportunities for the international Mafiosi. Their wide control of financial resources has turned them into valued partners to banks facing bankruptcy during the crisis. The United Nations Office on Drugs and Crime has thus reported that due to the lack of instant liquidity in 2008, the only available funds for many banks was money earned in drug business and that some banks evaded bankruptcy thanks exclusively to deposits received from the drug trade.[43]

The third branch in the illegal global economy is the so-called new economy of terror. Loretta Napoleoni defines it as "an international network linking the support and [the] logistical systems of armed groups." This is substantially the economy of global Jihad. But the economics of regional and local conflicts, including guerrilla, commercial and predatory wars should also be discussed in this context. The perpetuation of such conflicts is frequently an end in itself. These conflicts are fought by armed groups, or "state-shells," that is, entities created around the economics of armed conflict and sustained by terror groups.[44] The economics of global wars and local conflicts are bound; they are not isolated. They thereby expand the windows of opportunities for profit maximization and risk reduction for militants, securing weapons and ammunitions for conflict maintenance. The Revolutionary United Front (RUF) in Sierra Leone, an ethnically based alliance of rebels-turned-predators, exchanged "blood diamonds" for arms and munitions, but by the end of 1990s, the trade in precious stones reportedly expanded to include members of the bin Laden network among their commercial partners. The RUF's "blood diamonds" became highly liquid assets used by al-Qaeda for laundering its drug money.[45] Overall, war economies add substantially to the amount of illegal money earned within the alternative global economy.

The illicit/alternative global economic system now brings big money into the hands of criminals and entrepreneurs operating in gray and unregulated economic sectors. The sources include flight of capital from country to country, global money laundering by criminal and legal banks in offshore zones, establishment of criminal lobbies in the banking sector and in legal business, and the new economy of terror. However, the illicit markets appear to have weak powers to foster unholy alliances with revolutionaries and terrorists. With the spectrum of illegal business obviously vast, and with global financial regulations so loose and badly enforced, profit maximization and risk reduction are easy to achieve and are not necessarily dependent on alliances with militant partners. On the other hand, the same range of opportunities in the illicit global economic system is open to revolutionary and terrorist movements, if they have the skills and interest to take advantage of them.[46]

Explaining unholy alliances: weak states, failed states, corrupted, and criminalized states

In liberal economic theory governments have been called "stationary bandits," entities with political objectives who establish a system for extracting rents from a population, fixed in a particular territory.[47] States and proto-states – stationary bandits – can facilitate the formation of unholy alliances and even actively participate in their criminal undertakings. The interaction between states and unholy alliances can take on various forms. Most often states are only indirect partners with trans-border militant movements or criminal networks. For instance, *state weakness* provides as a rule low risks and high opportunities for criminals and insurgent challenges. Similarly, states crippled by armed conflict, that is, *failed or collapsing states*, frequently are unable to exercise their theoretical monopoly of power over the entire territory of the state. Thus ungoverned spaces can open up opportunities that offer a hospitable environment to criminal enterprises and cross-border insurgencies. In such situations the state is a background condition while trans-border violent networks remain the main actor. The Unholy Alliances project analyzes four cases in which networks have made use of state weakness and ungoverned spaces: Algeria, Bosnia, the PKK of Turkey, and Kosovo.

Other cases show that trans-border networks are not necessarily the principal actors in unholy alliances. State officials on their part have sometimes entered into joint criminal enterprises, thereby making a long-term commitment to illicit economic ventures. Some states thus become thinly disguised protection rackets whose leaders use power to pursue their private interests and those of their supporters, clan, or ethnic group. In these predatory states collusion is easy between officials and criminals, and sometimes with militants. We call these *criminalized states* and give special attention to the factors responsible for their growing numbers – including the globalization of banking and finance (discussed above), the neoliberal deconstruction of state socialist economies, protracted internal conflicts, and the rising power of cartels in the narcotics trade. Our case study of Serbia shows how state officials can align with criminals and militants, first in pursuit of political and ethnonational objectives; and second in pursuit of purely criminal and predatory goals. And our case study of Bulgaria reveals various corruption schemas

16   *Unholy alliances*

aimed at the privatization of state property. It also shows how police, judiciary and criminal networks can establish collaborative relationships in the protection and promotion of drug trade networks.

Weak states

A number of states, especially in less-developed regions, have limited capacities for effective governance. Their police and judicial systems lack the means and will to resist political challenges or to control organized crime. These weaknesses are especially common among newer states of Africa and Central Asia. A recent world survey of weak states by the Brookings Institution defines them as

> countries that lack the essential capacity and/or will to fulfill four sets of critical government responsibilities: fostering an environment conducive to sustainable and equitable economic growth; establishing and maintaining legitimate, transparent, and accountable political institutions; securing their populations from violent conflict and controlling their territory; and meeting the basic human needs of their population.[48]

All the countries in our "unholy alliance" case studies score relatively well on the weak state index as of 2011. Algeria is relatively the weakest among the 141 states rated, but ranks 57th from the bottom, whose bottom-dwellers are Somalia and Afghanistan, ranked 1 and 2. The others are all above the median, from Turkey at 98th to Bulgaria at 127th – in other words, none are weak by a world standard.

We accept the Brookings Institution criteria for weak states but question some of their ratings. While scored relatively well, Algeria, Bosnia, and Turkey hosted for a long time sustainable transnational criminal networks and violent movements. Therefore these countries do not match condition three, specified as "security of populations from violent conflict and the state's control over state territory." These countries should score low on a scale measuring capacities for meeting basic state and government responsibilities. Algeria, Bosnia, and Turkey are in fact weak states on some of the proposed criteria, or *vulnerable states*, as we call them. The Unholy Alliances project examines these cases to show among all else how vulnerable states provide opportunities for the establishment and the functioning of trans-border crime and terror networks.

State failure and instability

Political upheavals[49] were the immediate antecedent of the unholy alliances in all six of our case studies. All the states in which unholy alliances were formed – except Turkey – underwent abrupt and fundamental political changes that provided crucial incentives and opportunities for political/criminal alliances. In South-Eastern Europe they formed in the immediate aftermath of the breakup of the Yugoslav federation and the end of one-party rule. In Algeria they were a reaction to the military government's reversal of the process of democratization. The

PKK's survivability has depended on instability in Iraq from the 1990s to the present, which has given the militants a more or less secure territorial base in Iraqi Kurdistan.

Black holes

Failed and unstable states particularly interest us because they often harbor sovereign-free zones in which criminal activities can flourish. Stanislawski and Hermann call them "criminal enclaves" or "black spots."[50] And quoting Korteweg and Ehrhardt, Farah provides a more detailed definition: "A black hole is a geographic entity where, due to the absent or ineffective exercise of state governance, criminal and terrorist elements can deploy activities in support of, or otherwise directly relating to criminal or terrorist acts, including the act itself."[51] Four of our case studies of hybrid networks show the role that the criminal enclaves play in their trans-border operations. In northern Iraq, the Bahara Valley has reportedly hosted PKK-run cannabis farms as well as provided sanctuary for PKK fighters and supporters. Kosovo's border areas with Macedonia and south Serbia have been extensively used by militant networks for staging violent cross-border attacks; and by criminal networks running trans-border illicit business. The mountainous areas of the Central Bosnia have reportedly hosted training camps of international Islamist networks. And the Algerian Islamists operated crime–terror networks from large rural areas, though they were subsequently displaced by military action to remote parts of the Sahara.

The amount of harm posed by sovereign-free areas to hosting and neighboring states varies. Some analysts talk of the "black hole syndrome," arguing these geographic areas cultivate hybrid political-criminal gangs whose initial political insurgency evolves into orgies of crime and violence. Post-Cold War local conflicts – runs the argument –are not ideologically driven. They are "fought for criminal interests and they are secured by terrorist tactics."[52] States that have been particularly threatened by the "black hole syndrome" include Moldova, Georgia, Afghanistan, Pakistan, the Democratic Republic of Congo, and Sierra Leone, among others.

In general, however, the global or regional threat potential of "black holes" for political violence seems to be modest. Evidence suggests that locally thriving crime and terrorism only occasionally intersect. An expert analysis of the Triborder Area between Brazil, Paraguay, and Argentina suggests that "There is no indication . . . of any significant organizational overlap between the criminal and terrorist groups. Their cooperation, when it exists, is *ad hoc* and without any formal or lasting agreement." And, "[T]there is no evidence that their long term goals converge in this environment, which suggests that their interaction did not go further than a nexus form."[53] It is important to note that some of the so-called ungoverned territories are in fact administered by self-proclaimed autonomous governments. We analyze some of these autonomous regions in chapter 8's overview of the loci of political criminality in the Middle East and post-Communist Europe and the Caucasus. The leaders of these regions may fight the nominally sovereign state

18 *Unholy alliances*

in defense of their own interests; but they may equally well cooperate with it – or with neighboring states – wherever criminal business or political insurgency offer mutual advantages.[54]

State corruption and organized crime: the criminalized state ascending

In corrupt states officials are able to pursue their material interests without being much constrained by the rule of law, democratic checks or the countervailing power of competing groups. They may demand kickbacks on government-awarded contracts, pocket some of the proceeds of export and import trade, sell or operate public enterprises for personal profit, direct public funds to people in their patronage networks, or in myriad other ways act as "stationary bandits." Corruption is particularly likely in states that are new, weak, and on the periphery of the world economy. Ratings of public sector corruption have been compiled by Transparency International (TI) (www.transparency.org) since the mid-1990s, based on the independent judgments of country experts and business leaders from ten other organizations such as the World Bank. Table 1.2 summarizes the 2010 rankings and scores of the host countries of the hybrid militant/criminal networks in this study. The least and most corrupt states are shown for comparative purposes, along with an indication of changes in a country's rating since it was first included in TI's surveys, 1995 at the earliest. The unholy alliances existed long before 2010; on the other hand TI's corruption scores and rankings change relatively little over time for most countries.

It is consistent with our case study evidence that militant/criminal networks are most likely to take root and persist in countries with high levels of public sector corruption. Kosovo's low ranking fits our evidence that its clan-based alliances persist and now involve its government. Algeria's low rating suggests that the public corruption that prompted the Islamist revolution continues, despite an improving trend. The corruption scores and rankings in the other three South-East European states are significantly higher than Kosovo but much lower than those of West European countries. The implication is that the conditions for reemergence (or persistence) of militant/criminal networks and hybrid alliances remain. Turkey is

Table 1.2 Transparency International's ratings of 2010 public sector corruption in host states of militant/criminal networks

Country	Score in 2010	Rank in 2010	Direction of change from earlier TI reports
New Zealand	9.3 (least corrupt)	1 of 178	none
Turkey	4.4	58	slight improvement
Bulgaria	3.6	73	slight decline
Serbia	3.5	78	slight improvement
Bosnia	3.2	91	none
Algeria	2.9	105	slight improvement
Kosovo	2.8	110	not previously rated
Iraq	1.5 (most corrupt)	175	none

the highest-ranked country but, as pointed out above, the PKK has survived not because Turkey is a hospitable environment for criminal/militant alliances but because of its bases in neighboring Iraq, one of the world's most corrupt states.

It is evident that state corruption provides a hospitable environment to emerging and active trans-border criminal-militant networks. But more than that, state corruption is likely to give birth to a *criminalized state* in which state institutions and public officials participate directly in economic crimes. In such states criminal activities are carried out at all levels of economics, politics and public administration. And state facilities are used for purposes of private gain.[55]

The criminalization of the state is an ongoing and accelerating process. David C. Jordan shows that the *criminalized state* emerges not exclusively in structurally weak societies and that its criminal base is not necessarily confined to drug production and drug trafficking.[56] Many factors increase states' vulnerability to criminalization, including transitions from state socialist to market economies, protracted internal wars, governmental weakness, and penetration by transnational organized crime. However, the globalization of economics is likely the most common and most general of these factors. It has set new principles in the functioning of the national economies that facilitate increasing state corruption.

Analysts have written extensively on this issue. Thus, for instance, Tremonti and others observe that the interaction of nation-states with the global economy has encouraged the transformation of national wealth into financial capital. The latter – unlike material wealth – flows so easily across national boundaries that it is no longer a national possession. Tremonti suggests that the worst consequence of this process has been the severe disruption of the linkage binding *state, territory*, and *wealth*. Specifically, a state's control of its territory no longer guarantees the state control of its wealth.[57] The domestic decision-making process in economics thus has been distorted and susceptible to new influences, some of them out-of-state. This mix of internal and external factors severely challenges the nature and the mechanism of transparency and democratic accountability. Members of the ruling elite have come to seek compensating and even explicitly alternative mechanisms for decision making and implementation. The overall outcome has been the increase in levels of government corruption, noticeable as much in democratic countries as in authoritarian ones.[58]

Of course criminalized states do not necessarily emerge in all corruptible societies. Its sufficient condition arguably is the availability and persistence of *structural corruption*. The latter implies long-standing and efficiently functioning linkages between the government and organized crime. The structured corruption has been metaphorically referred to as the *Mafia Borguesse*.[59] It is a network of bank managers, tax advisers, attorneys, notaries, economists and politicians, connected to the world of organized economic crime, and in particular to drug production and narcotics commerce and consumption. They assist in legalizing illicit business activities of criminal networks and powerful crime syndicates. They also help in the money laundering process.

The criminalized state and structural corruption flourish in different economic settings. Peaceful transitions to market economies in East Europe provide an

20 *Unholy alliances*

instructive perspective on how state structures and government officials succumb to criminalization. A look at Bulgaria is telling in this respect. Launched under the banner of the self-regulating free market, the Bulgarian transition soon degenerated into market fundamentalism. Writing on a related issue, Giulio Tremonti has introduced the more precise concept of *marketism* to explain the essence of the new ideological paradigm of capitalism.[60] *Marketism* is market fundamentalism and it flourished following the collapse of communism. It has become as doctrinaire as was the Marxist-Leninist doctrine positing state control over the economy. *Marketism*, he suggests, is a totalitarian-like economic doctrine that in practice denies the principle of economic freedom and ignores the rules and institutions of liberal democracy. Organized criminal groups in Bulgaria and state officials soon colluded to establish the rules and mechanisms of structural corruption, motivated by the new economic elite's determined pursuit of its own priorities. Enjoying access to state assets and using their control of the pace and direction of the privatization process, government officials, former state security employees, and former managers of large socialist enterprises showed envious criminal ingenuity in developing various corrupt schemes for financing and crediting privileges in super-profitable economic areas. So with good reason a recent report by the Sofia-based Center for the Study of Democracy has concluded that all East European/Balkan transitions were to varying degrees criminalized.[61]

The criminalized state and structural corruption also flourished in societies where the post-communist transition was carried out during ethnic/civil unrest. Here again the rules of neoliberal transition undermined the role of the state, giving primacy to the free market in economic development. Yet market conditions were not conductive to big social and economic change. The starting point of the economic transitions in Eastern European and the Balkans was low. In Yugoslavia, for instance, the formal economy had collapsed in the 1980s as a result of Yugoslavia's failure to implement externally inspired neoliberal international structural adjustment programs. From the macro structural point of view this transition scored low; Yugoslavia was a "peripheral economy," marginalized by global capitalism. The concurrent spread of violent conflict was an additional complicating factor. The political economy of war and sanctions imposed at the onset of the 1990s Balkan wars contributed to the emergence of illiberal economies in Serbia and the Yugoslav successor states. They rested upon informal/traditional ties and were managed by kleptocratic economic elites. And the criminal policies of the ruling elites in peripheral and conflict ridden societies inevitably led to the corrosion and the criminalization of the state.[62]

The criminalized state and structural corruption are especially likely to take root in states that host trans-border drug networks. Officials in a narco-state become accomplices in regional or global narcotics production, trafficking, and international money laundering in a process that Jordan characterizes as *narcostatization*. His central argument is that narcostatization "undermines weak democracies and transforms consolidated and transitional democratic regimes into pseudo-democracies, or anocracies."[63] Narco-trafficking is the driving economic engine of transnational organized crime. More than 80 percent of the annual income of transnational crime, or $105 billion, is generated by international heroin and cocaine trafficking, according to the UN Office on Drugs and Crime.[64] Side payments from this huge sum lead increasing numbers of states to succumb to narco-criminalization. Jordan points out that officials are ever more likely to cooperate with drug networks and narco-cartels because they "depend on the monetary surpluses provided by narcotics trafficking to service debts, limit taxes, subsidize constituencies, buy off power contenders and project state power into other states and societies."[65] Moreover increasing numbers of drug consumers worldwide guarantee a long-term increase in drug profits and payoffs. Mexico offers a tragic illustration of the interaction between the state and drug networks. It is not a case study in the Unholy Alliances project, because the traffickers have no militant political agenda, but provides a well-documented example of how structural corruption emerges.[66] Map 0.2 (p. xvii) shows the heroin flow in metric tons streaming from Asia to Western Europe. Five of our six case studies relate to this traffic. Situated at the European periphery, these crime–terror alliances open up many opportunities for militant fundraising and corruption.

Explaining unholy alliances: policies of supra-national institutions

How much of the threat posed by the political and the criminal activities of unholy alliances might be contained by the policies of supra-national organizations? How much of the power vacuum in failed states can be filled by the work of international organizations? And, to what extent can the administrative and commercial relations within a nation-state distorted by criminal activities be corrected by out-of-state regional institutions? There was much trust in capabilities of regional and international organizations in the aftermath of the Cold War. In peacekeeping, for instance, practitioners developed third- and fourth-generation peacekeeping missions for situations in which international organizations had to work in a local vacuum of power and take on overall responsibility for rebuilding dysfunctional states. Likewise, practitioners also embarked upon post-conflict development projects that targeted civil societies – not nation-states – as recipients of development aid, seeking the speedy establishment of liberal market economies.

In this book's concluding chapter 9 we examine the counter-terrorism and crime control polices, as well as the post-conflict development strategies, of the European Union. We look more briefly at the conflict management diplomacy of the Organization for Security and Cooperation in Europe. We also discuss the policies and circumstances that lead to transitions in the activities of unholy alliances – which sometimes shift into conventional politics and the licit economy.

Our research is not confined to the borders of the EU. We also consider the applicability of European counter-terrorism and crime policies to the EU accession countries, the EU neighborhoods, and the Euro-Mediterranean partnership as well as to other EU partners. International and supra-national organizations do have capacities to establish control over trans-border violence and crime; and they do have capacities to assist in post-conflict development areas. In principle these

22 *Unholy alliances*

organizations can crack down on the illicit predatory and commercial activities of trans-border networks. They can also promote conflict management and long-term societal peace-building, and can help states rebuild their institutions of order, justice, and security.

However, their capacities are not unlimited. The European Union is a relatively new entity whose structures have changed significantly over the years. The EU's counter-terrorism and crime policies have evolved out of the joint activities of many institutions – some intergovernmental, others supra-national. Policy strategies are developed by one set of institutions, legislation is launched by a second set, and the enforcement process is undertaken by yet others. And the EU member states are major actors in these processes. We share the view of critics that the EU continues to function on the principle of a union of states, rather than the state of a union. This hampers the development and implementation of efficient supra-national policies to counter terrorism and control crime, especially when carried out by trans-border networks.[67]

The EU's member states can and do crack down on the local activities of illicit trans-border networks. They also have operating responsibilities for initiating and implementing the Union's interstate counter-terrorism and anti-crime strategies and regulations. What European institutions and states are less effective in doing is managing global and regional crises. The emergence of war economies and the persistence of corrupt governments and illiberal economies on the world peripheries, and closer to home on the periphery of Europe, are challenges less amenable to control that demand coordinated, long-term strategic thinking and action.

From the theoretical framework to case studies

Trans-border identity networks, political instability, criminal market opportunities, and state weakness and corruption provide the matrix in which trans-border alliances between criminals and militants are likely to form. Since there are comparative global data on three key variables, it should be possible to identify high-risk situations. The Minorities at Risk project profiles trans-border identity groups in every world region, as we have seen above. Transparency International rates public corruption and highlights countries with the greatest short-term changes. Current research by Joseph Hewitt uses empirical analysis to identify countries in each world region that are at greatest risk of future instability.[68] Cross-comparison of these data on cross-border identity groups, risks of instability and high and increasing corruption should direct attention to the places where criminal/militant alliances are likely to form and persist.

No such risk analysis is done here. Instead we turn now to six case studies that illustrate the dynamics of trans-border alliances in which political violence is joined to criminal enterprise. Our theoretical framework directs attention to the role of trans-border identity groups and their ideological commitments, armed conflict and state failure, opportunities for material gain, and supra-national institutions. The cases were selected not because they are a sample of a well-defined universe of analysis but because they allow us to explore the different ways in which these hybrid trans-border networks originate and decline. All the alliances analyzed here developed in or on the periphery of Europe, and all of them have had major impacts on European security. We chose them based on our own interests and knowledge, hoping better to understand the dynamics and diversity of a network-based trans-border phenomenon that is not well understood, and not well controlled. The final two chapters review some of the findings and provide the basis for an analysis of strategies for improving local and regional security in Europe, strategies that may have applications elsewhere.

2 Crime, political violence, and governance in Kosovo

A triple alliance?[1]

Albanian-ruled Kosovo is Europe's newest state, with some two million people in an area of 4212 square miles in the uplands of the western Balkans between Albania to the southwest, Serbia to the north, and Macedonia to the south. It was born in terrorist resistance by the Kosovo Liberation Army (KLA) to Serbian rule (1996–9), midwifed by NATO military intervention that ended a Serbian campaign of ethnic cleansing (March–June 1999), and nurtured from 1999 to 2008 by the UN Mission in Kosovo (UNMIK) whose administration has been called "a sorry exemplar of institution building."[2] Western powers acceded to the Kosovo government's declaration of independence in February 2008 over the opposition of the Serbian and Russian governments, and in the face of Belgrade-inspired resistance from its 120,000 to 150,000 minority Serbs.[3]

Kosovo now has "supervised independence" under the tutelage of the European Union's Rule of Law Mission in Kosovo (EULEX). Kosovo's legal economy is the weakest in Europe, with persistent 50 per cent unemployment, and depends heavily on European subsidies. Its greatest financial resources are those of the illiberal or black economy. International administration produced no coherent political strategy to support investment or development.[4] Its political institutions are imported from and supported by international actors. Western hopes for establishing the rule of law and reform of Kosovo's dysfunctional criminal justice system depend on European money, military and civilian personnel, and the carrot of eventual membership in the European Union. Effective reform surely will require active participation by Kosovar stakeholders from the emerging civil society sector.

Kosovo also sits at the crossroads of a major drug trafficking route from the Middle East to West European markets. During the wars of Yugoslav and Kosovo secession Kosovar Albanians used their clan-based criminal networks to smuggle arms and consumer goods. In the 1990s and thereafter the clan networks became the main agents in trafficking and distribution of drugs, and smuggling thousands of East European women each year for prostitution in Kosovo and West Europe. According to the FBI, Albanian criminal networks also have become significant actors in the US. The proceeds of this shadow economy have enriched many Kosovars, pay for the cooperation of public officials, and have reportedly attracted a few UN personnel into lucrative and illicit partnerships with Kosovar entrepreneurs. The new country is arguably a criminalized state, and the challenge for European and domestic reformers is enormous.

This chapter analyzes the transformation of Kosovo from Yugoslav control to criminalized state in the framework of the "Unholy Alliances" project. We look first at the Albanian identity group, with special reference to particular characteristics of Kosovar society, then at the role of armed conflicts and the opportunities and incentives they provided for criminal activity, and last at the lack of effective regional and international governance that has facilitated Kosovo's criminalization.

Albanian people and traditions

The nine million people who call themselves *Shqiptarë* have an enduring tradition of clan and extended family networks that survived in their Balkan homeland across centuries of Ottoman governance and decades of Communist rule. In addition to Kosovo's Albanian population, 3.5 million live in Albania itself plus an estimated 850,000 in contiguous areas of Macedonia (275,000), Greece (482,000), Montenegro, and Serbia proper. There also are as many as 1.3 million people of Albanian descent in Turkey and 438,000 in Italy, as a result of historical and contemporary migration to those countries. In Western Europe (other than Italy) and North America the Albanian diaspora numbers about three-quarters of a million, with 100,000 or more in Italy, Switzerland, Netherlands, Germany, and the United States. Ethnic networks tie many in these Albanian communities to their homeland in the Balkans.[5]

The rural-based clan networks, called *fis*, and the cultural traditions that sustain them enabled Albanian society to survive centuries of oppressive rule.[6] They also are key to understanding the symbiotic connections of the last two decades between political movements, terrorism, and international crime and the emergence of an intransigent culture of government corruption. Emil Giatzidis writes that "the Balkans [are] a world of kinship, clan and ethnicity, of family loyalty, intense friendship networks and ethnic solidarity, with codes of conduct based on honour and brotherhood."[7]

Albanian society is broadly divided between Ghegs and Tosks, speakers of two different dialects. Almost all Kosovars are Ghegs, who are reputed to be more traditional and many of whom identify with the precepts of the fifteenth-century Kanun of Lek Dukagjini, a codification of customary law that emphasizes honor, hospitality, and the subordination of women – and countenances vengeance and honor killings in defense of these principles. The persistence of these principles in much of Albanian society is in sharp contrast to Western value systems that condemn violent self-help. Blood feuds have been a threatening feature of Albanian society since the fall of Communism. In 2002 the World Health Organization reported that in the late 1990s neighboring Albania had the world's fifth highest reported homicide rate, at 28 per 100,000 people.[8]

This background helps account for the leading role that Kosovars took in violent nationalism beginning in the 1990s. In Albania under Enver Hoxha's regime

26 *Crime, political violence and governance*

every effort was made to eliminate civil and traditional institutions that might intervene between state and individuals – clan identities were suppressed and Albanian society was largely atomized. In Kosovo, by contrast, Tito's Yugoslavia was more tolerant of Albanian society, and the province had significant political and cultural autonomy from the late 1960s until 1989. Hence the Kosovo clan networks were largely intact, a natural basis of opposition to the Milošević government's new policies of exclusive Serbian nationalism, and a basis for criminal activity in support of militant nationalism. Bardos says that "given Kosovo's social structure, the line between organized crime groups trafficking in arms, drugs, and human beings and 'legitimate politicians' is blurred."[9] Sorensen contrasts the Albanian networks with Serbian and other South Slav crime networks, pointing out that

> The Albanian mafia . . . is tightly knit through extended family and clan relations. This makes it particularly difficult to infiltrate and to obtain witness statements against it. Like the code of silence in the Sicilian Cosa Nostra, the Albanians have their code of how to solve disputes between families or clans. In this sense the term "mafia" . . . is particularly appropriate.[10]

During the 1990s the Kosvars' international networks both competed and cooperated with criminal networks of the Kurds, Calabrians, Croatians, Serbians, and Montenegrins.[11]

The Albanian ethnoterritorial separatist movement and the war for Kosovo's independence

At the local level the clans were historically the social basis for political control, criminal entrepreneurship, and organized violence in Kosovo and Albania. Transcending the clans, Albanians have a long twentieth-century history of separatist politics. The 1990s war against Serb control of Kosovo was only one episode, and not the last. The Albanian ethnoterritorial separatist movement bridges the ethnic Albanians of Kosovo and their kindred in border areas of west Macedonia, south Serbia, and Montenegro. The movement activated in the late 1960s when its most active segment – the Kosovars – began to raise claims for self-governance. They ranged from autonomy, to secession, to unification with mother state Albania, or at least with kindred groups across the (former) Yugoslav republican borders. Kindred groups echoed these claims.

The movement became intensely active in the early 1990s. In 1989 the Yugoslav government, then dominated by Slobodan Milošević's Serbian ultranationalists, terminated Kosovo's long-standing status as an autonomous region in an effort to regain control over the Serbs' traditional homeland. Heavily repressive policies were imposed to implement the policy. The Kosovars responded by establishing a shadow state, the Republic of Kosova, headed by moderate Ibrahim Rugova and his Democratic League of Kosovo.[12] It was backed by a nascent national army, the FARK (the armed forces of the Republic of Kosovo), organized by Albanian officers who had served in the Yugoslav National Army, the JNA. The Republic and the FARK were financed in substantial part by a 3 per cent income tax on Kosovar émigrés, evidence that networks linking Kosovars with their diaspora were already well established and politicized.[13]

The negotiations that led to the US- and European-sponsored Dayton Accords in December 1995, which ended the wars of Bosnian and Croat independence, ignored the status of Kosovars. The principals at Dayton thought, probably with good reason, that if they added Kosovo's autonomy to their demands on the Serbian government, it would be a deal-breaker.[14] But this undercut the Rugova government's policies of nonviolent resistance to Serbian repression and provided a rationale for armed resistance. The first armed unit of the Kosovar separatist movement is usually said to be the Kosovo Liberation Army (KLA). It had a direct predecessor, however, a clandestine paramilitary organization that aimed at the creation of a Greater Albania, founded by young militants in Macedonia in 1992.[15]

The KLA was a paramilitary network that operated a dispersed guerrilla movement closely tied to the clans. The first KLA armed groups in the Drenica region, for example, were reportedly led by Adem Jashari, their membership "mainly composed of his close and distant relatives."[16] This was not a unique situation. Rather, as Yoshihara writes, the KLA was "framed along the lines of local clans" and "operated in dispersed cells and did not have a rigid, hierarchical structure."[17] KLA operations were decided by councils of clan elders who agreed on the best courses of action. The Serbian Security Information Agency says that cooperation among clans was sometimes coerced. "Organized in so-called 'troikas,' the extremists visited the heads of the clans and threatened to liquidate some of those who had refused to send members to KLA units."[18]

The political entity that helped fund the KLA was the People's Movement of Kosovo (LPK), a rival underground movement to Ibrahim Rugova's DLK.[19] A growing portion of the KLA's funding, especially their arms, came from the clans' own criminal activities. Drugs smuggled and distributed through the Albanian diaspora in Western Europe either provided funds for arms purchases or were exchanged directly for weapons that were then smuggled back to Kosovo.

The KLA's strategic claims were equivocal. KLA's radical left and right wings argued "over whether to carry the fighting to the pockets of ethnic Albanians who live in Western Macedonia and neighboring Montenegro." The wings agreed only "on the need to liberate Kosovo from Serbian rule," while all else was left to be decided later.[20]

The KLA began a terror campaign in 1995 when it launched a few attacks on Serbian police in Kosovo. One year later, in June of 1996, the KLA assumed responsibility for a series of acts of sabotage committed against Kosovo police stations and policemen.[21] In 1997 the KLA benefitted from the spring uprising in Albania that followed the collapse of a financial pyramid scheme there in which government, political parties, and criminal networks were all implicated.[22] Large numbers of weapons looted from Albanian police and army posts found their way to Kosovo, many of them trafficked by Kosovar clan networks through connections with allied clans in the Republic of Albania.[23]

28 *Crime, political violence and governance*

In early 1998 KLA escalated its violent attacks on agents of the Belgrade regime. This prompted a campaign of retribution carried out by local Serbian militia with the support of regular Serbian forces that gained international attention and prompted new condemnations of Serbian policies. Western observers characterized the campaign as ethnic cleansing, and scholars counted it as the world's latest episode of politicide, that is, political mass murder.[24] The Serb strategy was to target Kosovars, especially those suspected of KLA sympathies. The killings included a widely publicized massacre in Raček in January 1999, mostly aimed at members of the Jashari clan. Serb violence had its intended effect of causing one million Kosovars to flee, some to Albania but most to Macedonia, which initially tried to prevent their entry. It was later estimated that 11,000 people died, most of them Albanians killed by Serb militias but also some Serbs and Roma, victims of KLA revenge killings.[25] An international effort to get the Milošević government to accept restoration of Kosovo's autonomy and permit stationing of UN peace keepers – the Rambouillet Accords of March 1999 – was rejected by the Serbs, and the killings and expulsions continued. This triggered a three-month NATO campaign, relying mainly on air strikes against Serb targets in Kosovo and in Serbia proper, including Belgrade.

Serb attacks also prompted the KLA's mobilization of many more fighters. Whereas the KLA had an estimated 500 members in 1998, by the time of the NATO bombing campaign it numbered between 12,000 and 20,000. Yoshihara observes that the United States supported the KLA in its opposition to Serbian forces, first by removing it from the US list of terrorist organizations in 1998. She adds that "coordination of NATO airpower and KLA ground forces forced Serbian troop withdrawal in June 1999."[26] Ibrahim Rugova's parallel government, the Republic of Kosova, was succeeded by a new administrative structure established by the UN Interim Administration Mission in Kosovo (UNMIK).

During the early years of the UNMIK protectorate the KLA insurgency of 1995–9 evolved into campaigns of terrorism aimed at the speedy attainment of Kosovo's independence and resolution of the all-ethnic-Albanian issue. While many KLA members and commanders were incorporated in the new Kosovo Protection Corps (KPC) under international supervision, militants continued their terror campaign. Some challenged international attempts to help Kosovars build provisional institutions of self-government as defined within the April 2001 Constitutional Framework UNMIK devised for Kosovo. Terrorist attacks increased in 2001 in protest against closer links established between NATO and Belgrade. During the next several years militants targeted peacekeeping units, the office of the federal Yugoslav government in Pristina, and ethnic Serbs living in the province. Attacks intensified in the summer of 2005 as talks on Kosovo's status were to begin. Other attacks were aimed at the UN mission, the provincial parliament, the European Agency for Reconstruction and Development in Pristina, and OSCE headquarters.[27] One militant group was the National Unification Front (NUF), which described the UN mission in the Kosovo province as occupier. The Front demanded immediate recognition of Kosovo's sovereignty and merging of south Serbian areas with independent Kosovo. Its counterpart in south Serbia was another new terrorist organization called The Black Shadow,[28] no doubt sponsored and armed by KLA militants.

The Kosovars' minimum demand for independence for Kosovo was attained in February 2008, accepted by most European states but rejected by Serbia and Russia, among others. Unresolved is the larger issue of whether and how to incorporate all Albanians in a single political entity. The Albanian nationalist movement evolved considerably after the establishment of Kosovo as a United Nations protectorate. Most important has been the movement's factionalization. All elements of the larger Albanian ethnoterritorial separatist movement – new organizations included – are radical in their political objectives. However, not all of them have been extremist in their tactics. The intensification of ethnic Albanian militancy in the first decade of the twenty-first century is a significant change within the movement's evolution. Although virtually no political terrorism has occurred since early 2008 (see below), the separatist political ambitions of nationalists remain a serious threat to long-term interethnic peace and stability in Albanian-populated areas in the Balkans.

The threat is exemplified by the export of Kosovo terrorism across borders. Soon after the UNMIK takeover militants from the KLA gave birth to new paramilitary organizations adjacent to Kosovo. The first paramilitary offshoot of "mother" KLA was the Liberation Army of Preshevo, Bujanovac and Medvedja (UCPMB), which was activated in 2000. UCPMB militants used the NATO-established buffer zone around Kosovo as a base for exporting the Kosovo insurgency to the south Serbia municipalities of Preshevo, Bujanovac and Medvedja – home of some 70,000 Albanians. Arms smuggling and cross-border incursions from Kosovo into Preshevo Valley recurred throughout the year, culminating early in 2001 with a local Albanian uprising that was suppressed by Serb authorities. The political objective of ethnic Albanian leaders was to extend Kosovo's protectorate status to south Serbia, an objective that ultimately failed because of opposition from both the UN and Belgrade.[29] Its successor was The Black Shadow, cited above.

Cadres of the former KLA also moved to western Macedonia where a new paramilitary unit – the National Liberation Army (NLA) – was established. The NLA staged a rebellion against Macedonian authorities in early through mid-2001. They gained temporary control of Albanian-inhabited areas, causing many Slav Macedonians to flee, and seized a suburb of Skopje, the country's capital. The conflict dynamics were clearly regional. The precipitant of the spread of armed conflict to that country was the Macedonian parliament's ratification of a long-awaited border treaty with Serbia. There also were reports of renewed fighting of ethnic Albanian insurgents against Yugoslav police in the Preshevo Valley in south Serbia and against Macedonian forces in Brest.[30]

The Macedonian crisis of 2001 was the result of the interaction of domestic and international factors. They included the arrival of Kosovo insurgents who claimed they fought to end a decade of oppression against ethnic Albanians by the Slav-dominated Macedonian government; and the political leadership of the Macedonian Albanians, who complained about the lack of progress on their

30   *Crime, political violence and governance*

political rights and used the NLA's presence to press their case: reform or war. Concerted and persistent international pressure on the Macedonian government and its legal Albanian political parties led to negotiations that culminated in the Ohrid Agreement of 13 August 2001, in which the government committed itself to long-term improvements in the status of the Albanian minority. The NLA dissolved but before returning to Kosovo, NLA paramilitary cadres established (or reestablished) the Albanian National Army (ANA) that, like its predecessors, urged the creation of a Greater Albania.[31] In 2002 the Macedonian Interior Ministry said that the leadership of the ANA was involved in drug smuggling, carried out along the Balkan drug route, and used the money to finance its activities in Macedonia.[32] In the meantime the US blacklisted the ANA and in 2003 the head of UNMIK, Michael Steiner, branded it as a terrorist organization in reaction to a new wave of attacks in northern Kosovo, southern Serbia, and northern Macedonia.[33] In broader perspective, the cause of Albanian separatism has been and continues to be pursued by any number of metastasizing militant organizations. They differ in leadership, tactics, and territorial base but share a Kosovar origin and a general objective: the liberation of all Balkan Albanians from non-Albanian rule.

Terror attacks in Kosovo declined after UNMIK intervention in 1999 to a low in 2000 but then increased, averaging about 10 per year between 2001 and 2004 with a peak of 60 deaths in 2002. Some of this violence was directed at the Serbian minority. Other targets included government officials, police, and religious figures.[34] Clan rivalries led to some killings, for example, a dispute that came to a head in 2000 between the Musaj and Haradinaj clans "caused by political differences and an attempt of the Musaj clan to take over the arms and narcotics trafficking business from the Haradinaj clan." Sinan Musaj was murdered and soon thereafter Ramush Haradinaj was wounded.[35]

Since Kosovo's contested independence in February 2008 separatist political violence has largely ended in Kosovo and surrounding Albanian-populated regions. A handful of subsequent news items refer to arrests and prosecutions for political violence and plotting in Macedonia and Montenegro for activities that occurred prior to February 2008. A Kosovo police spokesman in September 2009 mentioned nine terrorist cases in the country since 2008 but added that on investigation most or all did not fit the legal definition of terrorism, that is, they were criminal rather than political acts.[36] The most serious episode occurred on August 2009, when the EULEX mission (see below) was subject to violent protests organized by the *Vetevendosja* (Self-Determination) political group in reaction to EULEX's police cooperation with Serbia. A EULEX member and three police officers were injured and 28 EU vehicles damaged.[37]

Moreover Albanian Kosovar violence against Serbs, Jews, Roma, and other minorities has been common since the late 1990s. Most serious was episodic conflict in the multiethnic northern city of Mitrovica. In 2004 interethnic rioting in Mitrovica, initiated by ethnic Albanians against ethnic Serbs, resulted in 20 fatalities, 800 wounded, and damage to 32 Orthodox Christian churches and monasteries. The pogrom was condemned by a NATO commander as "ethnic cleansing." The embattled Serb minority maintains its own local government institutions in parts of north Kosovo with encouragement, finance, and (clandestine) security personnel from Belgrade. Repeated UN and European efforts to bridge the ethnic gap with common institutions have had little success. The divide between Kosovo's Albanians and Serbs is the country's greatest immediate challenge to security and remains a likely flash point for future violence.[38]

War and Kosovo crime networks

The wars of Yugoslav succession provided enormous incentives and opportunities for trans-border crime. A Balkan-wide network of criminal networks was activated, based largely on the Kosovo Albanian clan networks. The UN-imposed embargo on the Yugoslav successor states created a large market for fuel and consumer goods that had to be smuggled across international borders. Our chapter on Bulgaria shows how this trade was organized. The blockade also disrupted the long-established "Balkan route" by which heroin from the Middle East transited Bulgaria and Yugoslavia to Western Europe. In the 1990s trafficking shifted to the southern Balkans and the Kosovars became ever more closely involved. Their clan networks had long been involved in smuggling licit goods across borders to avoid taxation. Now, as Strazzari observes, "the routes that were initially opened for cigarettes and petrol soon saw the flow of drugs and weapons, and then all sorts of goods, from stolen vehicles to human beings. All of this happened with the complicity of part of the existing or aspiring state authorities."[39] Fleets of speedboats operating out of Montenegrin ports smuggled cigarettes and then drugs in 150-mile night-time runs to the Italian coast near Bari with the tacit approval of Montenegrin authorities.[40]

Intelligence reports from Germany and NATO in 1999 helped show how profits from Albanian drug trafficking and prostitution rings in German cities had reached the KLA. Some funds evidently were laundered by expatriate Kosovars in the form of donations to the KLA, others by transfers through private banks and currency exchange offices. According to one intelligence report, half of the 900 million Deutschmarks that had reached the KLA between its founding and the Serb withdrawal in 1999 was drug money.[41] Some of the drug-dealing profits were used directly to purchase arms – and in 1999 some KLA supporters diverted weapons for sale on the West European black market.[42]

The ruling Bosniak party in Sarajevo, the *Stranka Demokratske Akcie* (SDA), also gave military assistance to the KLA. Bosnian President Alija Izebegovic tasked ethnic Albanian members of his military to provide weapons and advisers to the KLA in 1998. A deputy brigade commander named Haili Bijac "arranged gunrunning from Bosnian Muslim caches, under control of the Cengic family, to Kosovar militants." Caches of Bosnian weapons in transit to Kosovo were later found by NATO troops in both countries.[43]

As we noted at the outset of this chapter, the clans are deeply rooted elements of Kosovar society. They were closely linked to Rugova's shadow government of the 1990s and provided the basis for the organization of the KLA. Their preexisting networks extended to Albanian communities in Macedonia, Montenegro,

32 Crime, political violence and governance

Albania, and the Albanian diaspora in Western Europe and North America, so they were well positioned to take advantage of the opportunities for profitable activity created by the wars of Yugoslav secession. The *fis*'s clan linkages and smuggling networks transcended borders and helped in establishing the KLA's presence in neighboring Albania and Macedonia. Some KLA units reportedly trained in Albania, for example. In another, more grisly example, a 2010 report to the Council of Europe showed that in 1999 clan networks enabled the transfer of captured Serbs from Kosovo to rural locations in Albania proper where they were killed and their organs sold abroad for transplantation.[44]

At the same time the highly competitive and aggressive clan networks came to dominate drug trafficking and markets throughout Central and Northern Europe. Afghan-cultivated opium is obtained from Turkish (likely Kurdish) criminal organizations. The EU reports that in the mid-2000s some opium was being grown in Kosovo and processed into heroin in several major KLA-run laboratories in the Urosevac area.[45] Albanian production of marijuana for export also was increasing.[46] According to the US State Department in 2009, though, "Neither the KPS [Kosovo Police Service] nor UNMIK have found any direct evidence of narcotics refining laboratories or synthetic drug production in Kosovo. There have been reports of seizures of small quantities of precursor chemicals in Kosovo."[47] In view of UNMIK's and the KPS's hands-off approach to the crime networks – "no direct evidence" – the EU report is more credible.

The *fares*' networks at first were transmission belts but in the second half of the 1990s the Kosovars established close connections with Italian criminal networks, fought an underground war against challengers from Albania, and came to dominate local sales of drugs throughout Central and North Europe. By the end of the decade European law enforcement agencies reported that Albanians had become the second biggest community after Turks detained in Europe for narco-trafficking.[48] A Western intelligence official in Kosovo observed that "[t]he rebels in Macedonia, former KLA freedom fighters in Kosovo, and extremist Albanians in southern Serbia are all part of the network of Albanian and Kosovar Albanian families who [currently] control criminal networks [even] in Switzerland, Austria, Germany and elsewhere."[49]

By the middle of the first decade of the twenty-first century Albanian groups were said to be "direct distributors of an estimated 40 per cent of heroin in West European markets and may have an indirect role in as much again."[50] More recently, however, their market share seems to be shrinking. According to a 2008 report from the United Nations Office on Drugs and Crime, Kosovars and other ethnic Albanians now supply only 10–20 per cent of West Europe's heroin, while arrests of ethnic Albanian drug dealers in Germany and elsewhere have trended sharply downward. "In short, the single most notorious Balkan organized crime phenomenon – the role played by ethnic Albanian traffickers in West European heroin markets – appears to be in decline."[51]

Market shares aside, beginning in the mid-1990s the Kosovar clans became the basis of political-criminal syndicates with an international reach. French criminologist Xavier Raufer describes it as follows:

> In the Albanian world – you have clans and in those clans you have a mix of young men fighting for the cause of national liberation, . . . belonging to the mafia . . . driving their cousins . . . into prostitution. . . . It is . . . impossible to distinguish between them. . . . The guys are liberation fighters by day and sell heroin by night and vice versa.[52]

Bozinovich adds further details about the connections between the clans in Albania and Kosovo: "Claims are made that 15 leading family clans in Albania (*fis*) . . . during the collapse of the Albanian state into anarchy in 1997 . . . established complete control over the criminal activity in Albania including arms smuggling." Motivated by fear of inter-*fis* blood feuds over the limited Balkan criminal turf, the 15 *fis* reportedly made a deal to accept a common paramilitary enforcement unit, the KLA, in order to incite violence in Kosovo with the dual objectives of making money by financing the war and incorporate Albanian-inhabited areas of the Balkans.[53]

Serb sources provide details on the criminal activities of three major clans and nine lesser ones. One major clan is the so-called Drenica group in west-central Kosovo, led by Adem Jashiri and loyal to Hashim Thaqi, former political leader of the KLA, later head of Kosovo's second largest political party, and now prime minister. This network connected with Macedonia and Montenegro, dealing mainly in "arms trafficking . . . in stolen vehicles, in human beings, excise goods, and, above all, cigarettes and fuel." Further north is the Metohija or Dugagjini group, led by another national political figure, Ramush Haradinaj. This family "is mainly oriented toward the illegal trade of weapons, drugs, excise goods and stolen cars, but also toward the racketeering of the Albanian population." This group handled illicit trade with south Serbia, Macedonia, and Montenegro. A third clan, based in the northern Lab area, specialized in drug trafficking. Its chief is Rustem Mustafa, aka "Remi," formerly a KLA and Kosovo Police Corps commander. Remi, like Thaqi and Haradinaj, have used their official connections to protect their kindred's economic activities and safe transit across international borders.[54] The territorial and functional divisions among the clans are to some degree fluid and the subject of rivalries "whose origins lie in the political differences between them and the attempts of the groups to acquire more power in the respective region." Some of these rivalries have culminated in political killings.[55]

During the mid-1990s some proceeds of smuggling and drug trafficking were reinvested in weapons commerce aimed at arming KLA and its affiliated groups, as documented above. No doubt the smugglers and distributors drew income from crime and so did KLA militants. During the decade of UNMIK administration, from 1999 to 2008, the war market was considerably reduced and the Kosovar crime networks put their earnings to other uses. Conspicuous consumption seems to be a universal practise among criminal entrepreneurs in the Balkans and elsewhere – high-end automobiles, luxury goods, trophy mistresses, gated villas, and holiday properties. In January 2000 UNMIK police raided the apartment of Hashim Thaqi's brother and discovered DM 500,000 in cash, proceeds of racketeering activities.[56]

34 *Crime, political violence and governance*

Some illicit funds are channeled to Kosovo's public sector. Michaletos remarks that "former UN employees have made joint companies in Kosovo in collaboration with figures related to organized crime."[57] A former senior official of UNMIK, Steven Schook, was one of the main promoters of "Kosovo C.," a large coal-fired power project, in collaboration with crime-linked government ministers.[58] Kosovar crime groups also have invested profits in businesses in Kosovo, including construction firms, petrol stations, hotels, and brothels. Brothels are staffed with women trafficked from Albania and the East, notably Moldova and Ukraine, and include international personnel among their main patrons.[59] Other funds are invested outside Kosovo, for example, in Albanian resorts on the Adriatic and properties in southern Italy, where the Kosovar networks developed close links with Calabrian crime groups. Ilir Gjonir, a former Albanian defense and interior minister, provides this overview:

> Albanian organized crime groups operating outside Albania usually transfer their capital to the country of origin i.e. Albania, Kosovo or Macedonia, where they purchase property, real estate and business and do the same activities in the target countries. Thus, according to the Italian Anti-Mafia Investigation Directorate (AID), the Albanian organized crime groups "reinvest directly in their motherland, and in purchasing real estate in Italy, to be used as operations bases or havens."[60]

War and militant Islam in Kosovo

War in Kosovo and UNMIK's post-war administration provided not only criminal opportunities but, as in Bosnia (see chapter 4), gave Islamists an opening to establish a foothold in Kosovo. Osama bin Laden reportedly set up a terrorist training camp for Albanian nationalists in a north Albanian town in the 1990s. Some Kosovars trained there and then with jihadists in Afghanistan before returning to Kosovo.[61] In May–June 1998 a mujahedin unit called "Abu Bekir Sidik" operated in the Drenica region. A dozen of its 115 members were Saudis and Egyptians and its arms reportedly were provided by Islamist organizations. It was later disbanded.[62] No permanent jihadist presence seems to have been established because secular Albanian nationalism trumps Islam. "Albanian nationalism is secular," writes Yoshihara "and the Albanian practice of Islam is largely subsumed into cultural and national identity."[63] Schindler comes to the same conclusion. Despite Bosniaks' support for Kosovars, mentioned above: "the heavily secular Kosovar Albanians proved to be poor fodder for the global jihad, showing minimal interest in political Islam."[64] Religion played almost no role in the mobilization of Kosovar Albanians.

During UNMIK's administration Saudi Arabian humanitarian and religious entities sought to establish a cultural foothold in Kosovo. They built or rebuilt mosques and, according to Bardos, set up 98 primary and secondary schools in rural areas. Yoshiara, though, observes that the Saudi focus on education "was limited to Wahhabi instruction, and radio broadcasts were in Arabic and propagated fundamental Islam."[65] Even this cultural intrusion was resented by Kosovar Albanian leadership. Their *Kosovapress News Agency* warned, in December 1999,

> we now see attempts not only in Kosovo but everywhere Albanians live to introduce religion into public schools. . . . Supplemental courses for children have been set up by foreign Islamic organizations who hide behind assistance programs. . . . It is time for Albanian mosques to be separated from Arab connections and for Islam to be developed on the basis of Albanian culture.[66]

Islamists, in short, gained little by engaging in Kosovar Albanian society. A few Kosovars may be attracted by Islamist preaching but most are secular nationalists. Criminal networks have a traditional basis in Kosovar society and their participants and clients have reaped substantial material gains from them. Militant Islam has no similar resonance for Kosovars.

Governance in Kosovo: weak obstacle to organized crime

Conventional Western views about the state's responsibility for controlling crime are largely irrelevant to contemporary Kosovo. The flourishing crime networks based on the *fis* are a durable and thriving legacy of recent Balkan history, as we have shown. Albanian separatism provided the immediate setting for the growth of the networks. The larger context was the decay of state power throughout the larger region. The end of Communist rule in Yugoslavia's republics and in neighboring Albania made it possible for clan networks to flourish. As Cilluffo and Salmoiraghi observe, "The *fares'* success illustrates the extent to which the state [Albania] has slipped into ungovernability."[67] The post-communist governments of every state in the region were more or less quickly corrupted by self-serving officials and people associated with the old regimes who looted state properties and took advantage of new market opportunities, both licit and illicit.[68]

Before Serbian nationalists suppressed its autonomy in 1989 Kosovo had a civil law-based judicial system with many Albanian officials and staff. After Serbs largely banned Albanians from the system, "ethnic Albanians returned to using traditional alternative dispute resolution mechanisms and Reconciliation Councils. These were essentially a form of arbitration overseen by village elders." The councils were credited with solving some 1000 blood feuds during the 1990s.[69] Traditional clan authority inevitably gained strength and legitimacy.

UNMIK's administration attempted to create a new criminal justice system that had little connection with any Kosovo traditions, old or new. The institutional design was a dense thicket of agencies, plans, organizational units, and objectives designed and mainly staffed by international personnel and, of course, entirely funded by international actors. Public security was the responsibility of a (temporary) international civilian police force tasked with building an indigenous Kosovo Police Force (KPF, later KP) and the Kosovo Protection Force (KPF), an international contingent of 16,000 military personnel. The Kosovo Liberation Army

(KLA) was dissolved but many of its members, including most of its command structures, were incorporated into the Kosovo Protection Corps (the KPC, later renamed the Kosovo Protection Service) with 3052 active duty and 2000 reserve duty troops. Many in these units were later blamed for maintaining links with political violence and crime – not surprisingly since the clan ties of KLA members carried over into the new institutions. Paralleling the security agencies was a new criminal justice system – courts, prosecutors, defense counsel, witness protection programs, prisons.[70]

The corruptability and limited effectiveness of these institutions is amply documented in reports by scholars, international agencies, and non-government organizations such as Human Rights Watch. Strazzari says that "UNMIK governed for a long time by issuing 'regulations'," and cites NATO commander Fabio Mini who tried to take more effective action. Mini was "one of the most stringent critics of the ease of money laundering in Kosovo," and was instrumental in prosecutions of KPC members for such offenses, for example a ten-year prison sentence given to Sali Veseli. "As the list of arrested KPC officers grew longer, the KPC command showed signs of unrest. Mini declared that all members of the KPC were criminals" but held back from a purge.[71] UNMIK reports made very few references to organized crime and political corruption. A Kosovo NGO activist, Avni Zogiani, said in 2008 that

> the UNMIK has tolerated these organized crime structures in Kosovo and their connection to politics. One of the reasons is that if you have politicians who have police files, you can control them easier. . .the other reason is that these structures had the potential to derail the stability of Kosovo.[72]

The Brussels-based Commission of the European Communities issued a *Kosovo: 2008 Progress Report* that contains these highly critical "key findings":

- "corruption is still widespread and remains a major problem in Kosovo. This is due to insufficient legislative and implementing measures and a lack of determination and the weakness of the judicial system" (p. 15)
- "the Kosovo Police [successor to the Kosovo Police Service] has only a limited degree of control on the movement of persons into and out of Kosovo" (p. 51)
- "The KP lacks the skills and equipment. . .to effectively tackle drug trafficking. . . .Overall there has been no progress to report" (p. 52)
- "there is neither a strategy nor an action plan to combat organized crime. . . . The police tend to focus on maintaining order. . . . The motivation of public prosecutors and judges to tackle organized crime is further undermined by the lack of adequate working conditions, salaries and social protection"[73] (p. 53).

The last phrase is a coded reference to the fact that most Kosovar justices and prosecutors are reluctant, for whatever mix of reasons, to take action against fellow

Albanians. Michaletos says that in Kosovo "the unresolved court cases reach up to 300,000."[74] Arrests may be made and charges brought, but there is no carry-through. Human Rights Watch pinpoints another factor: "Inadequate witness protection remains a major impediment to justice, especially for organized crime, war crimes, and attacks on minorities . . . cases of witness intimidation and harassment are widespread."[75]

The Kosovo Police are a relative success story. Early during UNMIK's administration training courses were established whose international instructors provided intensive instruction to successive cadres of KP officers. The Kosovo Progress Report is no doubt correct that they have little capacity to deal with trafficking and border controls. They concentrate instead on ordinary crime and public safety issues and, according to a recent survey, have high marks from Kosovars for their performance of these duties.[76]

When Kosovo declared independence in February 2008 the capacity of its institutions of public security and criminal justice to deal with trafficking and corruption had long been seriously compromised. The explanation lies in the way in which Kosovo was governed. A number of prominent KLA commanders shifted to conventional politics. Ramush Haradinaj headed the center-right Alliance for the Future of Kosovo and served as prime minister of the provisional government in 2004. Hashim Thaqi led the rival Democratic Party of Kosovo, won a plurality of the popular vote in November 2007 elections, and was the prime minister who led Kosovo at independence. They and their peers brought into democratic politics the web of connections among clan and crime networks, and they politicized some long-standing interclan rivalries.

An inside view of how criminal networks penetrate politics and the state comes from John Rosenthal's 2008 interview with Avni Zogiani, a former journalist and co-founder of a Pristina-based NGO that focuses on links between organized crime and politics. According to Zogiani:

> The organized crime that has been connected to political parties has been chiefly financed from public funds, whereas the part of organized crime involved in human trafficking and drug trafficking has represented a sort of independent structure that time after time was protected by political parties, but not necessarily directly connected to them. They have often been found to enjoy protection also from the judicial system.

He adds that all three of Kosovo's biggest political parties "have had their parallel structures and intelligence services: gangsters basically, who control part of the economic resources in Kosovo."[77]

Kosovo's economy is paradoxically both poor and thriving. Official unemployment hovers around 50 per cent, but a great many Kosovars benefit from the shadow economy, including the laundering of international crime profits that are invested in Kosovo. UNMIK has estimated that organized crime contributed 15–20 per cent of the Kosovo economy. Aside from crime, the sources of the money for Kosovo's private and public economies are mainly external. Official estimates from

38   *Crime, political violence and governance*

2002 are that only 20 per cent of Kosovo's Gross Domestic Product was internally generated; remittances made up another 30 per cent and foreign aid 50 per cent. In 2008, when the European Union Rule of Law Mission in Kosovo (EULEX) replaced UNMIK, the country was receiving two billion Euros annually from the EU.[78]

The EULEX team aims to reform Kosovo's security and criminal justice system but with a lighter touch than UNMIK. It is committed to "supervised independence," meaning that its 2000 members are to work "inside the offices of the Kosovar police, prosecutors, and judges whom they are mentoring in a hands-on way that UNMIK never attempted." Kosovars are being given "ownership" of the reforms with the long-range objective that Kosovo will be able to join the European Union.[79]

It would be a mistake to assume that all Kosovars are complicit in crime and corruption. The urban and civil society segments of Kosovo society are growing. Strazzari observes that "[t]he sustained process of urbanization represents a challenge for the rural, clan-based structure of most groups active in criminal structures."[80] More than 4600 civil society organizations were registered with the Ministry of Public Services in 2008, 280 of which "have public benefit status and are entitled to financial support from the Kosovo consolidated budgets."[81] Many urban Kosovars are disenchanted with the thuggery and corruption that has followed from the clan networks' economic and political power. Zogiani can be said to speak for Kosovo's new civil society when he observes that, under UNMIK administration, "the 'strong figures' in the political parties acquired total impunity and society fell into a kind of lethargy." But under the EU mission there is some hope of curbing their dominance.[82] Pond suggests that gradual reform is precisely what EULEX leaders have in mind. Kosovo's criminalization will be pursued not by showcase trials of high-profile crime bosses:

> the more modest tactic will be to hope that economic growth; social evolution, as more Kosovar Albanians who have studied and worked in Germany and Switzerland come home; and increasing transparency and accountability work together to constrict the space for major crime through gradual maturing processes.[83]

Conclusion: A theoretical overview

The Kosovar Albanian case demonstrates vividly how armed conflict, criminal opportunities, and the lack of effective domestic or international controls led to the establishment of a "criminalized state" in Kosovo. The Kosovar Albanian clan networks were a traditional instrument of social control and the basis of illicit trade before the ascendancy of the Albanian ethnoterritorial separatist movement in the 1990s. The clans, along with their Albanian kindred and diaspora, provided what criminologists call "criminally exploitable ties" and, we would add, politically exploitable ties. Huge economic opportunities opened up, notably the international embargo on the warring Yugoslav successor states and the need for alternative transit routes for Middle East narcotics destined for West European markets. The political opportunities were equally great. The post-communist Balkan states were virtually powerless to deal with organized crime, not least because many of their officials participated in it. Albanian separatism provided another kind of political opportunity: most Albanian Kosovars opposed Serbian control by supporting the Rugova government in the early 1990s and, after 1995, the insurgency organized by the KLA.

The KLA exemplified the type of convergence between political terror and international crime that we labeled *opportunistic interdependence* in chapter 1. The clans pursed power and profit simultaneously, though by different means. Power came eventually from the political struggle against Serb control, facilitated by international intervention. Profits were generated by the market expansion of Albanians into the West European drug trade and, in parallel, human smuggling. During the insurgency some profits were repatriated as arms for the KLA. Now crime profits, some of them, are laundered by reinvestment in "legitimate" businesses in Kosovo and elsewhere.

The attainment of the KLA's political objectives was greatly facilitated by international actors. When the Serbs responded to the KLA's strategy of terror with a strategy of killings and mass expulsions, sympathy for the Kosovars increased in the West, and particularly among officials in NATO countries. They saw another Serb-perpetrated genocide in the making and feared its destabilizing regional consequences.[84] Once NATO decided on a bombing campaign its military commanders cooperated with KLA, and as noted above, after the Serb withdrawal many KLA members and most of its command structure were incorporated in the internationally sanctioned Kosovo Protection Corps. Senior KLA and clan leaders formed political parties and through them became elected leaders of the Kosovar government. They brought with them the clan and criminal ties that allowed them to exploit both government and economy for their own purposes. UNMIK officials mostly turned a blind eye to the endemic corruption that followed.

International actors also contributed inadvertently to the perpetuation of international criminal activity. The Albanian clan networks, working through the diaspora, became for a while the most successful criminal entrepreneurs of modern Europe. UNMIK largely ignored this business, not surprisingly since Kosovo was a transit zone, not the principal locale of crime. The European Community, meanwhile, was slow to develop policies for controlling international terrorism, trafficking, and crime on a regional scale – as we show in chapter 9. Community-wide EU policies were not formulated and put in place until well after 2000.

The risks of Albanian terrorism have abated, partly to the credit of UNMIK and its successor, the Kosovo Force (KFOR) but mainly because independence has satisfied the immediate interests of Albanian ethnonationalists. A potential for terrorism in other Albanian-inhabited lands remains. Not all Albanians are pragmatists nor likely to be satisfied by devoting their energies to institution-building in Kosovo. Others may resume militant campaigns in Macedonia and south Serbia on behalf of a Greater Albania. Instability elsewhere in the region, not only in Albanian-inhabited areas but in Bosnia, where interethnic accommodation remains fragile, would likely trigger new violence by militant Albanian separatists.

40   *Crime, political violence and governance*

The corruption of the Kosovo political system and economy are the most durable and troublesome legacies of the Kosovo war of independence and everything that went with it. Corruption is no longer a clan-based phenomenon, though it operates through informal social and political networks that are derived from the clans. Income from international crime may be declining as Albanian traffickers lose market share and are increasingly constrained by European-wide policies. In any case we do not know to what extent the one-time clan leaders who now dominate Kosovo politics can count on income from international crime. Most likely not much, because those who run the crime networks probably use most of the profits for their own advantage. Rather, as Avni Zogiani suggests, most political corruption now is financed by diverted public funds.

So what is the future of those who operate and benefit from the international crime networks? Ilir Gjonir, one-time Albanian official, lays out three possibilities that are worth quoting at length:

> One [is] that there will be a gradual legitimization of criminal capitalists . . . although the first generation of capitalists [in post-communist societies] are more concerned with capital accumulation rather than with the means of achieving it, they will want their sons and daughters to be legitimate, with the result that there will be a gradual transition from illicit to licit business. . . . [Another] school of thought suggests that organized crime could become the dominant force. Once criminal organizations have consolidated their positions within the society then it is very difficult to remove them, especially when symbiotic relationships have been established with the political and economic elites. In essence the idea is that instead of the legitimization of criminal capitalism and criminal organizations by the licit economy, the process is marked by corruption . . . leading ultimately to a collusive relationship between the state and organized crime. The third school of thought . . . is that organized crime can be fought successfully once its root-causes are identified and clear strategies are put in place.[85]

Criminal entrepreneurs, by investing in Kosovo businesses, may be following the first track. EULEX officials seem committed to the third course via their focus on the reform of Kosovo's institutions of public security and criminal justice. But institutional reform can only go so far. Good long-run outcomes will depend on active participation of Kosovars themselves. Civil society and reformist political movements will gradually have to displace corrupt officials and reduce the symbiotic connections between crime and politics. The Kosovar Stability Initiative (IKS), an independent think tank based in Pristina, is one example of a civil society organization that aims to break those connections. It carries out policy-relevant research based on the principle that "evidence-based public debates stand at the core of democratic decision making."[86] International institutions can do little more than encourage and facilitate this process, holding out the prospect of accession to the European Union as an incentive.

3 Kurdish nationalists and criminal networks

The PKK in Turkey, the Middle East, and Europe[1]

One chilly fall night in 1978, a small group of university drop-outs and their friends gathered behind blacked-out windows in Turkey's southeast to plan a war for an independent Kurdish state. Driven by their revolutionary zeal and moral certitude, the young men and women did not see any serous barriers to their success. But outsiders might have been forgiven for thinking otherwise. Turkey's military had hundreds of thousands of experienced soldiers. A NATO member, its government was a close ally of the United States. . . . It was no wonder that those who tracked radical groups dismissed the newly founded Kurdistan Workers' Party (PKK) as nothing more than thrill-seekers or brigands.[2]

The PKK, the Kurdish Workers Party, is known as the iron fist of the larger Kurdish liberation movement in Turkey. Founded in 1978 by Abdullah Ocalan, a charismatic Stalinist-like leader, the organization has fought a three-decade-long insurgency against Turkey aimed at Kurdish national liberation and a better social order for the impoverished southeast, where most Turkish Kurds live. Blending Marxism and theories of class struggle on the one hand, with the romanticism inherent in national self-determination movements on the other, the PKK has shifted its political objectives over time. Its goals have ranged from the establishment of an independent Kurdish state, to an autonomous Kurdistan, to a truly democratic Turkey in which the Kurds would have equal rights and freedoms.[3] The PKK's internal discipline, as well as members' uncontested subordination to its leader, might have secured it success on the battleground. Indeed, the PKK- and PKK-related fighting has claimed from 1984 through 2007 more than 37,000 victims, both Turks and Kurds.[4] However, the organization has achieved little in the long run, alienating friends and allies by its flagrant dogmatism and provoking tough and uncompromising resistance by state authorities and the military in response to its recurring violent campaigns. The bloody war that lasted from 1984 through 1999, and which temporarily subsided through 2004, is now on again. It provokes Turkish military raids across the border into neighboring Iraq, where the PKK has sanctuaries in territories controlled by the Iraqi Kurds. Labeled as a terrorist organization by the United States and the European Union, the PKK is also prosecuted for being involved in criminal activities in EU states, such as drug and human trafficking, the facilitation of illegal immigration, credit card skimming, money laundering, and fraud to fund terrorist and related support operations.[5]

All of the facts outlined above would suffice for an outside observer to qualify the PKK as an opportunistic movement, that is, a hybrid terror-crime network in which political and economic objectives count almost equally, and – depending on circumstances – would easily convert from one to another. The methodology of the Unholy Alliances project, and specifically our typology of crime–terror networks,[6] suggests that this assessment is correct.

However the Unholy Alliances project also builds on the Minorities at Risk project, one that monitors the status of 283 minority groups across the globe and focuses specifically on groups that suffer collective discrimination and have the capacity for collective action in defense of their self-interests.[7] MAR data show that the Kurds in Turkey comprise approximately one-fifth of the country's population. The Kurds are denied autonomy; but, even more importantly, they face serious discrimination, including sharp restrictions on their language and any expression of Kurdish culture, as well as suppression of non-violent political organizations. These restrictions are enforced at times by mass arrest. From this perspective attention also should be paid to the grievances of the Kurdish population; it highlights the motivations that underlie and sustain the PKK's fight, though they provide no excuse for terror campaigns.[8] However, due to the organization's extremist ideology and its near-exclusive reliance on terrorist tactics, in combination with Turkey's persisting rejection of any demands for Kurdish collective rights, the PKK degraded into a terrorist-criminal organization seeking to secure funds in dirty business for ongoing and prospective terror campaigns.

We analyze the PKK as an opportunistic movement, blending ideological sectarianism with the pragmatic objectives of profit maximization and risk reduction in illicit trans-border business activities. The PKK is a hybrid terror-crime network, one of few that currently operates across Europe, for which political and economic objectives count equally, especially in its most recent activities. Drawing on the theoretical model developed in chapter 1, we show that crime–terror hybrids emerge: (1) within a larger regional ethnoterritorial separatist movement, such as the Kurdish ETSM, which we analyze hereafter. Crime–terror hybrids emerge: (2) as the result of protracted violent conflict;[9] (3) they make use of an ETSM's cross-border identity networks to export violence and terrorism across the border; (4) crime–terror hybrids are opportunistic networks because they use indiscriminately various revolutionary and funding strategies. Their elites' strategic choices are largely devised *ad hoc* in view of a complex regional institutional setting, and shift in keeping with dynamically changing political opportunities, both internal and external. The mix of possible revolutionary strategies we observe among the Kurdish segments include group self-reliance; cross-border identity alliances; group–state alliances; and intra-group contention, with or without state backing. Funding strategies illustrated by the PKK include state-sponsored terrorism, diaspora funding, and cross-border criminal entrepreneurship (see Figure 3.1, p. 43).

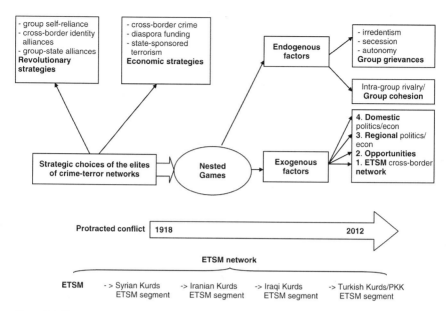

Figure 3.1 Determinants of strategic choices and actions of hybrid crime–terror networks: the Kurdish PKK

The Kurdish people and traditions: the Kurdish ethnoterritorial separatist movement

Kurdish people populating Middle Eastern countries are frequently referred to as regional diaspora. Expert assessments suggest that they constitute about 22 percent of the population in Turkey; 11 percent of the population of Iran; 23 percent of the Iraqi population; and about a tenth of Syria's population.[10] "Diaspora," however, is an inaccurate term for a "people without a country," as the Kurds have been called.[11] Unlike other regional diasporas, ethnic Kurds have had no independent state or homeland, rather their segments constitute a loose trans-border ethnic movement. Here, as elsewhere, we call it an ethnoterritorial separatist movement (ETSM), defined as a non-state trans-border regional actor comprising identical ethnic groups, or segments, populating adjacent areas of neighboring countries. This section surveys the elements of the Kurdish ETSM. It constitutes the regional ethnopolitical context within which the hybrid crime–terror network, the PKK, emerged, consolidated, and has devised and carried out its strategies.

Ethnoterritorial Separatist Movements are a species of social movements.[12] We develop the concept of ETSM by drawing on Sidney Tarrow's conception of social movement,[13] but also incorporate elements from other research.[14] ETSMs emerge out of bi-sected identity groups. The latter form the movements' local segments and are bound within sustainable trans-border identity networks. The ETSMs raise mutable territorial claims that, depending on circumstances, can range from autonomy to separatism to irredentism. The movement's internal dynamics may draw the entire movement into the pursuit of any one of its segment's specific territorial objectives. This makes ETSMs dangerous, semi-excited, non-state actors whose unpredictability poses threats to regional security, especially in regions that are already unstable. Most commonly, however, only one ETSM segment activates. So, trans-border violence and a major spillover crisis are uncommon. Large-scale regional instability should only be expected where a segment's territorial objective is sought by radical ideologies and violent means. In such instances, the export of conflict across borders mobilizes the territorially contiguous trans-border identity network. The process is described as the aggregation and diffusion of violence, or contentious action, from a more mobilized to less mobilized segments.[15]

The ETSMs are relatively recent non-state trans-border actors, born out of the post-1945 and post-Cold War realities. They can be seen as a "new volcano" erupting out of the crater of movements for national liberation and unification (MNLU).[16] Before World War I the MNLU were the political agents of the ethnic nationalities comprising the multicultural societies of the Russian, the Ottoman, and the Habsburg empires. In their quest for self-determination they staged insurgencies against their host empires that mobilized *en masse* support. Like their predecessors, the ETSM also are driven by the quest for ethnic self-determination. However, they do not necessarily enjoy *en masse* support. More often than not contemporary ETSMs act through paramilitary or terrorist groups that are largely responsible for the trans-border export of violence and crime.

Tarrow has suggested that movements only emerge out of sustained interaction with political opponents. So, isolated contentious acts should not be seen as proof of durable ethnopolitical movements. Time is an important factor in the evolution of a movement. But so too are the available opportunities. Recurring cross-border activities of small paramilitary/terrorist groups keep the cross-border network alive. And the more persistent the group's contentious activities, the more likely that a fully developed ETSM will come about.

Sources and objectives of the Kurdish ETSM

The Kurdish ETSM is composed of four segments including the Kurds in Turkey, Syria, Iraq, and Iran, whose common root is Kurdish nationalism. A twentieth-century construction, Kurdish nationalism provides a common ground for identity to a population of some 30 million. It evolves out of ideas of a common culture, myths of common origin, and shared faith in Islam. It builds on the idea of a common homeland, currently divided among contiguous areas of four states. It also builds on a history of centuries-long resistance against the Ottoman and the Persian empires, the original homelands for many Kurds. Another source of Kurdish nationalism is the Kurdish language. It is however not uniform. Kurds in southeast Turkey and northern Iraq speak Kurmanji; Kurds in Iran and those residing in the rest of Iraq speak Sorani. Although both languages are related to Farsi they make communication among the ethnic Kurds problematic.[17]

The most problematic issue with the evolution of Kurdish nationalism, however, is the fact that it has no economic root. Unlike most nations in the contemporary world, which have developed along ethnic but also along economic lines, the Kurdish nation seems to have had very sporadic relations with the capitalist market. So the strongest source of modern nationalism, that is, its connection to the emerging capitalist market,[18] was largely absent in the Kurdish case. Kurdish society was therefore missing one crucial structural capacity for the successful implementation of its nation-building process.[19] It remained pastoral even in the twentieth century, and its leaders were mostly rural-based tribal chiefs. Not surprisingly, the Kurdish ETSM confined its political objectives to autonomy and separatism. Trans-border unification was never widely advocated or planned as a possible objective.

Protracted conflicts and cross-border identity networks

Each Kurdish group has fought its own battles to establish itself as a separate entity. The Kurds have fought mainly to secure respect for their cultural and political rights as well as to establish autonomous or independent regions governed by the Kurds themselves. The Kurdish rebellions that we review in the post-World War II period were hard-fought and persistent but their accomplishments were usually small and short-lived. Yet the Kurds have gained something out of this process: more than half a century of struggles for self-determination have given the Kurds a solid sense of group identity, as well as expanding identity networks across borders and providing a setting for future collaboration. And some Kurdish groups have gained more than that. We provide a short overview of the conflict history of the Syrian, Iranian, and Iraqi segments of the Kurdish ETSM. This provides essential background for our more detailed analysis of the Turkish Kurds and their hybrid crime–terror network, the PKK.

The Syrian ETSM

The Syrian branch of the Kurdish ETSM is least developed. Until the 1980s the Syrian government did not officially acknowledge the existence of a Kurdish ethnic group. Recurrent violations of the human rights of ethnic Kurds have being reported including stripping Syrian Kurds of Syrian citizenship, a policy that has been officially pursued since 1962. It also included discrimination through land expropriation; prohibition of the use of the Kurdish language and publishing in Kurdish; and policies aimed at internal resettlement. The only Kurdish political party in the post-World War II period was the Kurdish Democratic Party of Syria whose goals were limited to the promotion of Kurdish cultural rights, economic progress, and democratic change. Despite its moderate objectives the party was never recognized by the Syrian authorities. Instead, several of its leaders were arrested, imprisoned, and charged with separatism.[20]

The Syrian Kurds became politically more active in the early 1980s. Demonstrations and riots, followed by mass arrests, torture, and ill treatment, have become common. In 2006 the Kurdistan National Assembly of Syria, an out-of-state body, was established to represent Syrian Kurds but confined its goals to the establishment of democracy for Syria, as well as to granting rights to Kurds and other minorities. In 2011, with the onset of the Arab Spring, the Kurds in Syria were among the first to organize protest against the lack of basic rights. However, their long-term strategy again is moderate, limited to securing their basic human and political rights.

The Syrian branch of the Kurdish ETSM is also significant for our project in another respect. It is worth speculating on the strategic decision making process, that is, on the strategic choices made by the Syrian Kurdish elite in view of the opportunities opened up by the 2011 Arab Spring uprisings. It should be generally applicable to analyses of the strategic revolutionary choices made by ETSM elites within a complex regional institutional setting, itself subjected to dynamic changes. Here we integrate George Tsebelis' conception of "nested games" into our ETSM model.[21] From this theoretical perspective ETSM elites make strategic choices in view of the opportunities provided by two sets of factors. One set comprises endogenous factors, including the group's grievances and political objectives. The other set is the exogenous factors, that is, those related to domestic and regional politics and economics. The endogenous factors determine the selection of the elite's revolutionary strategy. However, the elite's final strategic choice is actually shaped by the constraints imposed by the exogenous factors.

We observed above that the Syrian Kurds have been cautious regarding the selection of a long-term strategy. This is a consequence of multiple factors, some of which relate to their grievances and objectives. Grievances are mostly related to the Syrian Kurds' basic rights. Their more ambitious objectives reportedly include the establishment of independence of West Kurdistan.[22] The endogenous factors are multiple. One of them is the Syrian National Council (SNC), the government in exile formed in 2011 by the Syrian opposition to the government of Bashar al Assad. Known as an Arab-dominated body, it aggregates various political and religious interests and pursues its own political agenda.[23] Still another factor is Turkey's support for the Syrian Arab opposition movement.[24] Turkey's policy toward the Arab Spring processes, as well as her leading regional role, are a concern for the Syrian Kurdish players. Other relevant factors include the policies of other Kurds in the Middle East, and in particular the strategy to be pursued by the Kurdish Workers Party of Turkey, the PKK.[25] Also relevant to the decision process are the politics of regional powers, that is, Iran, as well as some Western states. Obviously there is no simple answer to the question as to what should be the Syrian Kurds' optimal strategic choice.

We suggest that the choice to be made by the Syrian branch of the Kurdish ETSM would be the end result of what Tsebelis has termed "games in multiple arenas."[26] These not only include the game in the actor's principal arena, but also a game about the rules of the game. The actors here are presented with different and complex choices within a "web of multiple games." The interaction of endogenous and exogenous factors reveals the actual web of multiple games. It enables us to understand each actor's pay offs and constraints, as well as the final selection of an actor's strategy. And the latter obviously cannot be overly ambitious. Instead an actor should pursue pragmatic, realistic, and principally achievable objectives.

And indeed, the Syrian Kurds have limited their central strategic choice to collective self-preservation and to securing the protection of their basic rights. This choice is minimalistic. It is likely based on a worst-case scenario,[27] and aims at preempting the risk of all-out repression.[28]

The Iranian ETSM

The Iranian branch of the Kurdish ETSM has had greater success, though its point of departure was also low. From the 1920s to the 1940s the Kurdish identity was denied in Iran, while the Kurds were encouraged to assimilate into Iranian society. And while the pressure to assimilate was not intense, the Kurds responded to pressures and opportunities by staging two uprisings since the 1940s. Both were led by tribal chiefs and aimed at the development of indigenous institutions of self-governance. Neither had enduring success. Both were characterized by rebellion that was repressed, then recurred.

The Iranian Kurds have suffered and still suffer severe discrimination and government repression, including executions of political prisoners. Activists who seek to draw public attention to human rights abuses reportedly risk further human rights violations.[29] The 1990s have seen riots, protests, and demonstrations, some of them about local issues, others on cross-border kindred politics. In most cases the government has responded with arrests, closures of Kurdish newspapers, and physical violence. The fight of the Iranian Kurds has had, however, one serious achievement. The presidency of Mohammad Khatami, from 1997 to 2005, accommodated some Kurdish demands related to the recognition and use of the Kurdish language; the presence of Kurdish representatives in the Madjlis, the Iranian parliament; as well as their presence in local governance.

The case of the Iranian Kurds is instructive in several aspects. First, it shows how over the years and as the result of protracted conflict the Iranian ETSM has consolidated. Thus, when in 1946 the small Republic of Mahabad was established, it failed even to secure the support of all Iranian Kurds. Born out of the World War II Soviet and British occupation of Iran, the Republic lasted less than an year, largely owing to challenges against its leaders by fellow Kurds and tribal chiefs. A subsequent attempt to establish control over the Iranian Kurdish area began in early 1979, when after the fall of the Pahlavi Dynasty a wave of nationalism engulfed eastern Kurdistan. The composition of the contending Kurdish elite included the Democratic Party of Iranian Kurdistan as well as the leftist Komala (Revolutionary Organization of Kurdish Toilers). By the spring of 1980 the Kurdish armed factions were crushed by government forces. However, the Kurdish elite showed more cohesion than in 1946, maintaining unity against the new government.

The Iranian Kurdish ETSM has also strengthened its cross-border alliances due to the spillover effects of local conflicts. The Republic of Mahabad, for instance, survived, however briefly, because of assistance from Mustafa Barzani, the leader of the Iraqi Kurds. Barzani was in fact appointed commander of the Kurdish army in the Republic and controlled some 3000 troops. ETSM networks also strengthen where cross-border organizations emerge. An instance is the Party of Free Life of Kurdistan (PJAK), formed in 2004, which is a sister organization of the Kurdish Workers Party of Turkey (PKK). These organizations share leadership[30] and logistics, and both also belong to the Kurdistan Democratic Confederation, an alliance of outlawed Kurdish groups led by an elected Executive Council.[31] Both have bases in the Kandil mountains in Iraq. PKK leader Cemil Bayik has said that "the PKK is the one who formed PJAK, who established PJAK and supports PJAK," and Ahmedi, the PJAK's leader, has conceded that PKK's Ocalan has defined PJAK strategy.[32]

The Iraqi ETSM

The Iraqi branch of the Kurdish ETSM is politically most advanced. The Iraqi Kurds received official recognition of their separate identity in the 1920s, recognition that was embodied in the 1954 Iraqi Constitution. The official recognition of a separate Kurdish identity, however, has not saved the Iraqi Kurds from battles for their actual establishment. Iraq – a state only established in 1932 – was to undergo a series of regime changes, coups, wars, and foreign interventions. Recent Iraqi political history, following the overthrow of the monarchy and the establishment of the republic in 1958, has seen two coups, one in 1963,[33] another in 1968;[34] three large-scale and devastating wars – in 1980,[35] 1990,[36] and 2003;[37] and a large-scale campaign against rebellious Kurds that began in 1982 and ended after the genocidal *al Anfal* campaign in 1989. The Iraqi Kurds have sought to protect their collective identity and interests during this violence-wracked process and also have sought to benefit from the dynamics of domestic and regional politics to advance the cause of an autonomous Kurdistan. The KDP – the Kurdish Democratic Party, founded in 1946 – has been the major actor in Iraqi Kurdish politics for nearly 30 years. A faction of it – the Patriotic Union of Kurdistan (PUK) – split and established itself in 1975.

The fight of the Kurdish liberation movement over the past 50 years has employed myriad revolutionary strategies. A brief overview of the Iraqi Kurds' political agenda follows, organized by decade. The 1960s seemed promising for the Iraqi Kurdish liberation movement: the Iraqi government had promised them regional autonomy; the Soviet Union provided backing; and Kurdish rebellions staged over unfulfilled government concessions were successful. But in the 1970s there were setbacks. In 1972 officially established ties between the Soviet Union and the regime in Bagdad cut off the Iraqi Kurds from their external supporter. Iran, a potential new international ally of Iraqi Kurdistan, signed with the Ba'athist government the *Algiers* agreement in 1975, thereby securing a comprehensive settlement of all points of disagreement between the two states. Subsequently, all sources of external support for the resistance of Iraqi Kurds dried up. On top of all that, official campaigns of deportation and resettlement undertaken by the Baghdad regime aimed to reduce the scope of Kurdistan and strengthen government claims to oil fields in the Kirkuk region.

The one significant achievement of the Iraqi Kurdish liberation movement of the decade was the establishment of the Kurdish Autonomous Region in 1971, based on the Autonomy Accord between the Iraqi government and Kurdish leaders. A largely formal undertaking, it did recognize the Kurdish people and Kurdish language, and it provided autonomy for their region in northern Iraq. The actual meaning of the "true recognition" of the Kurds' separate identity became clear in the early 1980s, with the beginning of the war between Iran and Iraq, and later on with the launching of the *al-Anfal* campaign in 1986. Rebellious Iraqi Kurds were subject to genocidal repression, including all-out military operations, forced relocation, and massacres, partly implemented by the use of chemical weaponry. An estimated 2000 villages were reportedly destroyed and between 50,000 and 100,000 noncombatants killed. It was only in the early 1990s that the Iraqi Kurds gained protection. UN Security Resolution 688 secured the establishment of a safe haven, while the US and British governments established a no-fly zone over large parts of northern Iraq.

The 1990s brought another set of challenges. Since 1991 the Kurds have controlled their region, with Baghdad letting them function almost entirely independently. But those Kurds who survived the repression of the 1980s now suffered from severe economic deprivation. The Kurdish region was placed under a dual economic embargo, one imposed by the UN on Iraq, the others imposed by Iraqi President Saddam Hussein on the Kurdish region. So, with few resources at hand – though in formal control of their politics – the Iraqi Kurdish parties, the KDP and PUK, were sharply divided against each other and fought battles for control over power and resources. It was only in the late 1990s that the *Washington* agreement[38] put an end to this intra-group conflict. So the Iraqi Kurds entered the first decade of the twenty-first century with brighter prospects. Having played an important role in the 2003 war led by the coalition forces against the regime of Saddam Hussein, the Iraqi Kurds have consolidated their power in Iraqi Kurdistan by establishing a well-institutionalized, representative government and have also significantly contributed to the establishment of the central institutions of post-invasion Iraq. They have also established themselves economically, turning Iraqi Kurdistan in a prosperous region based on local production and trade with Iraqi and Turkish markets. Indeed, since the fall of Saddam Hussein Iraqi Kurdistan has become the safest place for foreign investments in the country, attracted in part by development of the region's vast oil fields.

So the Iraqi Kurdish ETSM has emerged out of a protracted conflict with authorities in Baghdad. The group now seems more cohesive; its leadership has matured. Now that Iraqi Kurdistan has secured its autonomy within post-2003 Iraq, the Kurds can shift their attention from issues of independence to corruption, bad governance, imperfect democracy, black marketing, and oil smuggling. These issues appeared on the Iraqi Kurds' policy agenda at the time of the 2011 Arab Spring. Not without good reason, policy analysts have called Iraqi Kurdistan a "success story on moving sands."[39]

However, our discussion of the Iraqi Kurdish ETSM should provide more than a chronology. It also illustrates how elites make strategic choices "playing games within complex and dynamically changing multiple arenas." The strategies of the Iraqi Kurds illustrate what we call "nested games within spillover crises." Indeed,

50 *Kurdish nationalists and criminal networks*

the most conspicuous episode in the recent history of the Iraqi Kurdish movement is the contentious relationship between the KDP and the PUK. Another is the controversial relationship between the Iraqi Kurdish parties and the Turkish PKK. While the two "national" branches have long been bound within a cross-border identity network they did not necessarily cooperate. Instead, for most of the time their relationships have been strained. The conflict between the two Iraqi Kurdish parties was based on rivalry over power and resources. Alternatively, the PUK/KDP controversy with the PKK arose from the latter's presence in northern Iraq. In pursuit of gain in this intra-group fighting, the Kurdish organizations have employed various strategies, including (1) group self-reliance; (2) establishment of cross-border identity alliances; (3) group–state alliances; (4) intra-communal rivalry and fighting; (5) and intra-communal rivalry provoked or supported by the state.

Group–state alliances

In the past, as well as currently, the PKK bases in northern Iraq have been crucial for the success of the PKK insurgency against Turkey. Symptomatically, for various considerations related to domestic and regional politics, as well as to the dynamics of internal power struggles, the Iraqi Kurdish organizations have not necessarily been inviting hosts. Ocalan twice managed to secure authorization to settle in northern Iraq, once in 1982, when he received permission to do so from KDP's Barzani,[40] and later in 1988, when he negotiated this issue with PUK's Talabani. However, the PKK presence was looked upon with suspicion, and neither of the PKK's hosts seemed to have planned to extend their hospitality for long. The 1982 PKK accommodation with Barzani began to unravel by 1986. And when negotiations were subsequently sought with Talabani, he insisted that the PKK should be admitted to northern Iraq only on the condition that it first renounce terrorism. To avoid dependence on either of the groups Ocalan approached the Iraqi government and received permission for establishing the PKK in northern Iraq, shortly after which Talabani agreed to cooperate.[41]

Intra-group rivalry; intra-group rivalry involving state backing

The intra-group rivalry within the Iraqi Kurdish ETSM has been a persistent issue in Iraqi Kurdish politics. It has been especially topical since the 1990s when the KDP and PUK emerged as the major political actors of the newly established autonomous KRG. Inter-personal rivalry between Barzani and Talabani was one of the bones of contention. More importantly, the civil war that broke out between the KDP and PUK was fought over control of power and resources at the time of the double economic embargo mentioned above. Paradoxically, Turkey, Iraq, and Iran all were involved as allies of the two organizations during this internecine warfare. In the 1996 the PUK–KDP battles were largely supported by government forces, the Iranians supporting the PUK while Barzani invited Iraqi government forces to assist the KDP.

Another instance of intra-group contention involving state backing has been the ambivalent relationships between the two Iraqi Kurdish parties and the PKK since 2003. The KDP and PUK essentially let the PKK live and train unimpeded in northern Iraq. However, in 2007 Iraq and Turkey signed a Memorandum of Understanding (MOU) to jointly combat terrorism, including the PKK. And the MOU demands that all parties in Iraq shall observe it, the KRG included. The KRG authorities have nominally supported the MOU and occasionally skirmished with PKK forces, and tolerated Turkish military incursions into PKK safe havens, but in most circumstances continue to tolerate the PKK presence, likely because of the Iraqi Kurds' sympathy for their Turkish kindred.

For an outside observer the motivations driving the Kurdish elite choices in decision making might seem incomprehensible. Obviously in the Kurdish case the trans-border and domestic identity networks do not necessarily determine compliant and collaborative intra-group behavior. Other factors also are relevant. Background factors concern the significant differences between the Turkish PKK on the one hand and the Iraqi KDP and PUK on the other. The PKK is widely regarded as a terrorist organization based on its strategic choices. The PUK and the KDP are not. In early 1991 the PUK's Talabani himself labeled the PKK a terrorist organization, indicating PUK's willingness to distance itself from its Turkish counterpart. Another difference is that the KDP and PUK have not resorted to drug trafficking for financing their fight. The PKK has done so and increasingly relies on this source of funding. Iraqi Kurds historically have smuggled goods across the Iraq–Turkish border, but since 2003 they are heavily engaged in licit trade. Other factors determining strategic elite choices should be sought in the existing institutional setting, others in emerging political and economic opportunities; and still others in the *interaction* between *the institutional design and opportunities*. This interaction illustrates what we understand by "nested games within spillover crises." The games are nested because the institutional design is complex, while the games within it multiply and/or overlap. And, the crises are defined as spillover crises because they break out not least as the result of the export of violence across international borders.

Factors of institutional design in the larger region that have shaped Kurdish decisions include the authoritarian politics of most countries in the region; the prevalence of political repression against opposition movements; and the widespread practice of human rights violations. The factors that establish and reshape institutional design also include regional politics and rivalries among states; their foreign and defense policies; and their geostrategic concerns. And political opportunity factors also abound. They include the 2003 Coalition war against Iraq and the follow-up strengthening of the KRG, both regionally and in its role in the Baghdad government. Economic opportunities follow from increasing Turkish investment in Iraqi Kurdistan. Almost 80 per cent of reconstruction investment in northern Iraq in recent years has been made by Turkish firms. And the new airports in Irbil (the KDP capital) and Sulaymaniya (the PUK capital), worth a combined $650 million, were constructed by Turkish companies.[42] Economic opportunities should be expected to increasingly determine the Kurdish elites' strategic choices. Still other regional opportunity factors include the 2011 Arab Spring and the resurgence of nationalism throughout the Kurdish ETSM. And perhaps there are many more.

In sum, this discussion of the Iraqi ETSM has introduced various strategies in network research. We have shown how an ETSM can provide a regional setting in which cross-border identity networks emerge, and have seen the importance of protracted conflict in shaping opportunistic revolutionary strategies. We turn now to the Turkish Kurdish branch of ETSM, and specifically to the PKK, showing *inter alia* how artificial is the divide between political and economic opportunism. The PKK elite choices have been in some sense most creative, combining legal with illegal strategies in pursuit of political objectives; and blending licit with illicit economic activities to secure funding for recurring yet not necessarily politically meaningful campaigns of violence and terrorism.

The Turkish ETSM and the Kurdistan workers party (PKK): violent protracted conflict with the Turkish state

The Kurdistan Workers Party, the PKK, is the most radical political organization of the ethnic Kurds in Turkey. The party was founded on 27 November 1978, and has fought two brutal campaigns against Turkey in defense of their rights. There is a complex explanation behind the PKK's radicalism. It rests with the history of the Turkish state, as well as with the plight of the ethnic Kurds populating its territory. Established in 1922 from the disintegrated Ottoman Empire, the young Turkish state received international recognition with the Treaty of Lausanne in 1923, and its leaders sought to establish a modern and democratic state in the Middle East. Its guiding ideology was developed by its first president, Mustafa Kemal Ataturk, a modern, secular, and democratically minded politician. Turkey's way toward the establishment of modern nation state was uneasy, marked by international and internal threats to security and progress.

Since end of World War II Turkey has experienced four military coups – in 1960, 1971, 1980, and 1997 – each aimed at stabilizing the state and correcting various failures in democratic governance, including corruption and high treason; poor economic performance; and tension in domestic politics instigated from outside. Moreover Turkey faced the challenge of accommodating the identity conflicts sparked by its large Kurdish minority, a challenge for which the Turkish state showed no adaptive capacity. The ethos of the Turkish state was and is modern nationalism, which accentuates the central importance of Turkish identity for all citizens, regardless of their ethnic or religious backgrounds. Ataturk's nationalism insisted that all citizens of Turkey share a common history, language, and value system; it stressed the importance of being a Turk.[43] And so from 1924 through the 1990s the Kurds of Turkey were denied any symbols or expression of separate identity despite their large numbers,[44] and despite their concentrated residence in southeast part of the country.

The Turkish Kurds had little choice about how to respond. From the mid-1920s through the late 1930s they staged serious rebellions across Kurdistan but achieved nothing in terms of official recognition of their rights or political representation. Turkey's official policy toward the Kurds was one of turkification, mainly by suppressing any manifestation of Kurdish culture or collective interest and by means of mass population resettlement.[45] In the 1960s, the Turkish state launched a new project for solving the problem of Kurdish separatism and underdevelopment. The Turkish State Planning Organization was established, aiming to devise a plan to diffuse Kurdish separatism in the southeast by encouraging ethnic mixture through migration.

Turkey liberalized its policy toward its ethnic Kurds only in the 1990s. By that time the Kurdish Workers Party was well established and had launched its first rebellion. The PKK's insurgency was not the only manifestation of Kurdish ethnopolitics. Kurdish political action from the 1990s onward was a collaborative and a joint project of many political parties that sought expression through official politics. Most were short-lived, soon to be banned and replaced by others. HEP, the People's Labor Party, was founded in 1990 and banned in 1993. The DEP was then established in its place but existed only for a year before it too was disbanded. Three years later DEHAP was established and operated for the next six years. In 2002 Turkey started easing restrictions on the Kurdish language and culture. However, its politics toward the Kurdish political organizations remained tight. In 2003 HADEP was banned on the ground that it had maintained connections with the PKK and had become a center of illegal activities.[46]

In 2004 the Democratic Society Movement (DTH) was formed, and one year later merged with DEHAP and establish the Democratic Society Party (DTP). The DTP was active from 2005 through 2009, and took part in the 2007 general elections, as well as in the 2009 local elections. The policy of the Democratic Society Party indicated shifting priorities within intra-Kurdish politics. Soner Cagaptay observes that "The growing prominence of the DTP in Turkey suggests that while previously Kurdish nationalist political parties, such as HADEP, were secondary to the PKK, now the political party is the main body of the organization with the military wing working for its sake."[47] Turkish intelligence, however, claims to have tracked linkages between the DTP and the terrorist PKK. In 2009 the Constitutional Court voted to ban the DTP, ruling that the party had links to the PKK and was guilty of spreading "terrorist propaganda." The DTP was succeeded by the Peace and Democratic Party (BDP), which has been active since then.

Unlike other Kurdish political organizations, the PKK's strategy toward Turkey has relied almost entirely on violence. The PKK insurgency against Turkey is 34 years old at the time of writing, and is embedded in more than 90 years of resistance by the Turkish Kurdish ETSM against the Turkish state. From our theoretical perspective it illustrates how a protracted identity conflict can give birth to an opportunistic hybrid crime–terror network.

The PKK is the most potent organization within the Turkish Kurdish ETSM. Its political objectives are not surprisingly mutable. Most have been territorial, others have been more moderate and aimed at acquiring basic political and civil rights for the Turkish ethnic Kurds. Initially the PKK fought Turkey for the revolutionary overthrow of the Turkish government in southeastern Turkey and for the establishment of an independent Kurdistan in Turkey under "Stalinist" socialism.[48] As the PKK's battle against the Turkish state unfolded its major objectives shifted. The establishment of an independent Kurdistan, carved out of Turkey, has gradually been abandoned for the softer objective of an autonomous Kurdistan within Turkey's southeast. And most recently, that is, since 1999, the PKK has been fighting for a "Democratic Republic" – a democratic Turkey under which the Kurds should have equal rights and freedoms.[49] Also, the PKK's initial strong commitment to Marxist-Leninism has softened over the years, especially after the downfall of the Soviet Union at the end of the 1980s and the more recent increase in the influence of Islamic movements.

The PKK is a mass political and military organization with between 10,000 and 15,000 fighters. Turkish government sources suggest that as of 2004 the number of the PKK fighters was less, between 4000 and 5000, numbers that were said to have increased by 2007. The PKK's leader Murat Karayilan claimed more recently that the organization has between 7000 and 8000 active fighters across the region.[50] The organization has employed various tactics in the pursuit of its political objectives. As a Marxist-Leninist organization it has employed generic Party techniques mostly for purposes of eliminating like-minded rivals. When the PKK was officially founded in 1978, there were at least eight other illegal Kurdish organizations in Turkey. There were also a number of socialist and communist groups. Instead of cooperating with these like-minded organizations, the PKK's leader Ocalan dedicated much of his time and energies to cleansing his movement of those who dared to contest his authority.[51] Ocalan was willing to kill his fellow leftists, as well as other Kurds whom he believed to disagree with the PKK's plan for the immediate communist revolution in Kurdistan.[52] Brutality took place even inside the ranks of the PKK itself.

The PKK's revolutionary war against Turkey was grounded on the Maoist theory of the people's war, which should unfold in three stages. The first stage of the PKK's insurgency lasted from 1978 to 1984. Its major objective was to build up its organization and fight the rival Kurdish organizations as well as to gain supporters among the Kurdish population. The PKK's mechanism of party building was essentially a Stalinist policy aimed at eliminating those whom Ocalan viewed as rivals. At this first stage of the PKK's insurgency the organization's activities were largely restricted to minor skirmishes between fighters and the Turkish security forces. The PKK tactics also included riots and demonstrations as well as sabotage and ambushes.

The second phase of the PKK's insurgency was a guerrilla campaign that sought to undermine Turkish authority throughout the region. Lasting from 1984 through 1999, it was known as an extremely bloody war. The insurgency began with a process of internal party consolidation. In 1985 the People's Liberation Army of Kurdistan – the ARGK – was established as the military wing of the PKK. In the same year the National Liberation Front of Kurdistan – the ERNK – was also founded as the propaganda and the legal arm of the organization. The primary targets of the PKK insurgency were Turkish military and security forces. But the PKK also attacked the "temporary village guards." The latter were progovernment Kurdish militias who were paid and trained to defend against the

PKK insurgents.[53] Civilians of Turkish and of Kurdish origin were also targeted, including Kurds believed to be disloyal to the organization.

As the insurgency evolved the PKK's activities increased tremendously. Rural insurgency in the southeast was fought alongside urban terrorism, a strategy used on a front that could only be fought by terrorist means. Major protests called *Serhildan* broke out in the 1990s throughout the Kurdish cities. The PKK justified the use of techniques such as roadside bombs and anti-personnel mines, claiming it was fighting a war of independence. And at the 4th National Congress of the PKK in 1996 Ocalan even authorized the use of suicide bombers.[54] Civilians have also been a target of brutality and violence. This has sometimes been undertaken in the pursuit of minor political objectives. Thus in an effort to coerce support from neighboring villages the PKK in 1987 reportedly killed the entire population of the Kurdish town of Pinarcik.[55] The PKK is also known for recruiting children as soldiers. In 1998 3000 children were said to be incorporated within its ranks, about one-tenth of them girls. Recruitment was taking part in Turkey and Europe alike; and it was notorious for being an involuntary process.[56]

In 1991 the PKK established bases in northern Iraq. Turkey responded by staging counter-insurgency raids between 1992 and 1995. In 1993 Turkish President Turgut Özal attempted to establish a dialogue with the PKK's leaders, intending to solve the conflict by peaceful means and signaling his willingness to compromise on a number of issues. However, Özal's death later in the year brought this initiative to an end. The conflict escalated to reach its peak of violence in the mid-1990s.[57] In 1998 PKK's activities subsided because of the withdrawal of external support for the organization, as we discuss in the next section. Then in 1999 the PKK insurgency nearly ended following the capture of the PKK's leader Abdullah Ocalan in Kenya, his return to Turkey, and his subsequent trial and imprisonment.[58] Ocalan's arrest and trial changed the course of the war. Communicating through intermediaries, Ocalan called in 1999 for a unilateral ceasefire and ordered the PKK to evacuate Turkey for Iraq and give up armed struggle.[59]

From 1999 to 2004 some small-scale terrorist attacks were carried out by different groups claiming loyalty to Ocalan. Apo's Revenge Hawks, the Nationalist Kurdish Revenge Teams, and Apo's Youth Revenge Brigade launched attacks in 1999, killing at least 14 people. It is common that once guerrilla warfare is suspended, dissident factions continue to stage attacks beyond the control of the central organization. However, in this case it remains unclear whether these groups worked independently or did in fact operate under Ocalan's direct guidance.[60]

Overall, from 1999 through 2004 the PKK sought to transform itself into a pseudo-political entity, working through Kurdish political parties. The 7th extraordinary Congress of the PKK met in 2000 in northern Iraq and upheld the authority and decisions of Ocalan. Initially, the venture looked promising. The organization renamed itself twice in 2002–3, taking respectively the names Congress for Freedom and Democracy in Kurdistan (Kongreya Azadi Demokrasiya, or KADEK), and Kurdistan People's Congress (Kongra Gele Kurdistan, or KONGRA-GEL). In 2003 the PKK/KADEK even announced that it would dissolve to form the Kurdistan People's Conference and seek peaceful negotiations with Turkey.

56   *Kurdish nationalists and criminal networks*

However, in mid-2004 the organization resumed terrorist activities, partially because of Kurdish frustration with the lack of any meaningful reforms by the Turkish government; partially because of the 2003 war in Iraq; and not least, owing to the establishment of the autonomous Kurdistan Regional Government (KRG) in northern Iraq. Ocalan renounced the ceasefire with Turkey in mid-2004, and the organization changed its name back to PKK. According to the Maoist theory of people's war, the PKK insurgency against Turkey had entered its third phase. In theory, the phase is characterized by conventional fighting aimed at seizing cities, overthrowing the government and taking control of the country. In practice, the PKK insurgency at this stage has showed increasing complexity. First, it combines guerrilla warfare with urban terrorism.[61] Second, it is fought by different splinter groups of the PKK that are not necessarily internally coordinated. Third, this insurgency has aimed to destabilize the Turkish economy and tourist industry. As a matter of fact, Ocalan said already in 1993, in an interview published in *Ozgur Gundem*, that the Turkish economy remained one of the PKK's prime targets.[62] Since then the PKK has actively targeted Turkish commercial interests, both at home and abroad. However, the PKK's attacks on economic infrastructure have intensified recently even further. Last but not least, this insurgency has become more complex because it is in effect a regional spillover crisis, being intensely fought by the PKK out of safe havens it controls in the autonomous Kurdistan Regional Government (KRG) area of northern Iraq. It has led to the mobilization of Turkish troops along the Turkish–Iraqi border and incites frequent incursions by Turkish troops into Iraqi territory in hot pursuit operations against the PKK insurgents. The insurgency has become entwined with the politics of the Iraqi Kurdish Regional Government, thereby dragging into the PKK–Turkish war a number of regional players.

One of Turkey's biggest concerns with the current phase of the PKK insurgency is that it is being fought by new splinter groups of the PKK, which seem to be operating autonomously from their original organization, while sometimes staging joint attacks with it. One of these groups is the Kurdistan Freedom Hawks (or TAK), also known as the Kurdistan Freedom Falcons (Teyrebazen Azadiya Kurdistan). Created in 2004, the group operates as an urban terrorist arm of the PKK. It is unclear if TAK is a part of the PKK. While there is evidence that TAK was created by disaffected PKK members, the PKK denies that it controls this organization.[63] TAK targets tourist and urban areas. On 10 July 2005 TAK exploded a bomb in the resort town of Cesme in which 20 people were injured. Shortly thereafter a minibus explosion in Kusadasi, another tourist center, killed at least five people.[64] On 28 August 2006 three coordinated PKK attacks occurred in Antalya and Marmaris that injured 20 people. On 22 May 2007 the group detonated a bomb in Ankara that killed at least six people and wounded one hundred.[65] Attacks by TAK and PKK were also reported through the end of the decade. In a further effort to destabilize the Turkish economy the PKK has staged attacks on the Iraqi pipeline transporting oil from Iraq into Turkey. As observed by analysts, it was not the first time that the PKK has targeted Turkey's energy sector, but it was the first time that the group has set ablaze Iraq's oil.[66] Another splinter

Kurdish nationalists and criminal networks 57

organization of the PKK, the People's Defense Forces, has been attacking mainly military and paramilitary targets. So from 2006 through 2008 the violence perpetrated by the PKK, the TAK,[67] the People's Defense Forces and others claimed hundreds of Turkish lives and an economic loss of millions of dollars.

The PKK insurgency on Turkey was from its onset a conflict that spilled over inter-state boundaries. This became increasingly obvious following Ocalan's capture and PKK's subsequent evacuation to northern Iraq, where the PKK had established bases in 1991. Then, more than a decade later, taking advantage of the chaos in Iraq that followed the US-led invasion in 2003, the organization gained safe havens there with the aim of relaunching its campaign of violence against Turkey.[68] And so when, in 2004, the PKK renounced the 1999 ceasefire, the PKK–Turkish conflict speedily escalated and turned into a large-scale spillover crisis. The military records of this regional crisis have abundant information of large-scale, cross-border violence. In response to the PKK's cross-border attacks the Turks mobilized troops on their side of the border in 2006. In 2007 a law was passed allowing the Turkish military to take action inside Iraqi territory.[69] Turkish forces have since launched a number of cross-border incursions in hot pursuit operations against PKK paramilitaries. In February 2008 a ground operation launched by the Turkish forces in northern Iraq claimed 657 PKK members killed; 161 were said to have been captured or surrendered in skirmishes throughout the year.[70] In 2009 violence temporarily subsided following the announcement of the government's Kurdish Democratic Initiative.[71] But in 2010 there was an escalation of violence after the perceived failure of the initiative. Indeed, in an interview for the *Firat News Agency* Murat Karayilan, the head of the PKK's Executive Committee, declared on 5 June 2010 that the PKK's insurgency had entered a new era, that escalation of violence should have to be expected, and that the PKK's attacks would target economic and military infrastructure in the west of the country.[72] A year later Ankara announced that 22 battalions, or nearly 10,000 soldiers, were taking part in operation in northern Iraq and southeast Turkey.[73]

This extended overview of PKK's wars on Turkey provides ample evidence that the PKK–Turkey conflict is driven by both ideology and political objectives. As this discussion suggests, the PKK's collective grievances, its long-term strategy including the defense of the Kurdish cause at home and abroad, its mutable territorial objectives, where the margins separating autonomy, separatism, and irredentism are unclear and constructed *ad hoc* – all this shows that the PKK is the heart of the Turkish Kurdish ETSM. And the PKK's organization, its leadership structure, its long-term strategy including the spread of leftist ideology, and not least, the PKK's blows to the Turkish economy are the hallmarks of an integrated revolutionary strategy, driven by ethnopolitical identity and a communist vision. Clearly, the PKK is a nationalist-leftist movement, born out in sustainable interaction with political opponents, a movement that has proven its strategic capacities to secure resources for its long-term political and revolutionary survival.

"And who is siding with it?" – this crucial question determines the success or the failure of any significant revolutionary venture. We show below that the PKK has had a large number of friends and allies. Their long-term support has allowed

58 *Kurdish nationalists and criminal networks*

the organization to switch easily among various political objectives; to flirt with different "partners in arms"; and to cooperate with all "partners in crime" who in diverse times and places have been interested in supporting terrorism, national liberation movements, and people's revolutions at large.

The political economy of the PKK's revolutionary war on Turkey

International support for the PKK

> [A]ll counter-terrorism is aimed at dealing with the armed threat as and when it arrives. . . . [T]he emphasis in counter-terrorism is always on the arrest or killing of terrorists. . . . [B]ut this is obviously not enough to counter those organizations which have managed to cross the economic divide and appear to prosper no matter what is done to reduce their numbers by conventional methods. . . . Jail or kill some terrorist leaders while leaving their economic base intact and the organization will simply change direction and grow once again. . . . Destroy the economic base and the terrorist group will wither and die.[74]

Who were the PKK's allies and how did they contribute to its origins and persistence? We examine separately three types of allies: states, other terrorist groups, and the Kurdish diaspora in Europe.

States as allies

Many of Turkey's neighbors have supported the PKK at different points in time with money, weapons and training, safe haven, or with intangible moral and political support. State support for terrorist groups helps them survive and evolve into larger, better-trained, and well-equipped groups. Some states, notably Syria, Iran, and Iraq, have provided substantial material support. Others, such as Greece and the USSR, also are suspected of helping the PKK but supporting evidence is either anecdotal or controversial. And finally there are states such as Denmark and the Netherlands that have "passively" facilitated the PKK's activities, as we shall see.

Syria, one of the first and main supporters of the PKK, helped from the early 1980s through 1998. PKK members sought refuge in Syria and the Bekaa Valley in Syrian-controlled Lebanon after fleeing Turkey, following the coup d'etat in 1980. PKK rebels trained with other terrorists in Syrian camps under different identities,[75] though Syria denied Turkish accusations of providing such assistance.[76] Tensions between the two states came to a head in 1998 when Turkish President Suleyman Demirel warned Syria of pending use of military force and started massing troops along the Syrian border. The Adana Memorandum signed thereafter between the two states obliged Syria to recognize PKK as a terrorist organization and cease all support for it. In addition Syria closed down all PKK camps and deported Ocalan. No further PKK attacks from Syria were reported.[77]

Iran has also been a long-time supporter of the PKK, extending assistance throughout the 1980s and 1990s. Tehran reportedly provided bases for 1200 PKK activists at 50 different locations in Iran, while Iranian security officials facilitated their travel elsewhere in the region. In return, the PKK was expected to provide intelligence about Turkish and US military installations.[78] Turkey also accused Iran of providing weapons, training, and funding to the PKK. In July 2004 the two countries signed a security cooperation agreement by which Iran agreed to recognize PKK as a terrorist organization, after which Iranian support significantly decreased.[79] Moreover, by battling the PJAK – the Kurdish Free Life Party, which is the main Iranian Kurdish rebel group – Iran is in effect helping its Turkish neighbor.[80]

Under Saddam Hussein's regime, from 1980 to 2003, Iraq also played a role in PKK activities. Speaking about Iraqi support, Aliza Marcus observes that "the relation was fairly informal . . ., more so than the PKK's relations with Iran."[81] The PKK was interested in base areas in Iraq for many reasons, not least for dealing with kindred Kurdish groups. Saddam on his part was seeking allies around the region and believed that the PKK might provide intelligence on Turkey and Iraqi Kurds. While the 2003 war in Iraq terminated direct Iraqi support for the PKK the latter remained in the country, setting up offices in Baghdad and Kirkuk.[82]

However, the PKK is not necessarily safe on Iraqi territory. In September 2007 Iraqi Prime Minister Nouri al-Maliki and Turkish Prime Minister Erdogan signed a Memorandum of Understanding to combat terrorism, including PKK, though the two countries failed to reach agreement on issues of border security.[83] The Turkish Parliament voted on 17 October 2007 to authorize military intervention in Iraq to quell PKK cross-border incursions, and a major incursion was carried out in February 2008.[84] The tacit support the PKK receives from the Iraqi Kurdish Regional Government is analyzed in greater depth in a later section.

Because of its adherence to Marxism-Leninism, the PKK has likely attracted support from ex-communist states, though little evidence exists of supplies. All we know is that Ocalan briefly received sanctuary in Moscow when he was ousted from Syria.[85] And captured PKK members have mentioned the occasional presence of Soviet, Bulgarian, and Cuban personnel in Syrian PKK training camps during the 1980s. Alternative views exist on Russia's post-communist policies toward the PKK. Some believe that Russia has remained ambivalent, others speculate that Russia could be interested in supporting PKK in a quest to engage Turkey in battles at home, thereby preventing it from expanding its influence in the Caucasus and Central Asia. Nur Bilge Criss has reported that the Russian Duma's Committee on Geopolitical Problems had circulated a report stating that support for the PKK would help bring about Turkey's disintegration, thereby eliminating a security threat in the Black Sea and Caucasus region.[86] It is also the case that in November 1994 Moscow allowed the establishment of the "Confederation of Kurdish Organizations of the Commonwealth of Independent States (CIS)." During its meetings delegates displayed pictures of Ocalan and openly called for Russian support for the PKK. However, none of this demonstrates that Russia has a committed engagement in the PKK's war with Turkey.

60 *Kurdish nationalists and criminal networks*

Greece, Turkey's western neighbor and long-time antagonist over the status of Cyprus, also has been identified as a PKK supporter. Turkey has raised the issue of Greece's alleged support for Kurdish rebels a number of times. And, while it may be "difficult to substantiate [all Turkish accusations] . . . perception[s] may be as important as reality."[87] Thus the Turkish Ministry of Foreign Affairs has claimed that PKK members have received permission to use as a training base the Livron refugee camp outside Athens. Then in June of 1998, after the arrest of eight PKK terrorists with explosives and plans to attack the Istanbul metro, Turkish police said one of the members had been trained in Greece.[88] Greece has denied any state support for the PKK, but has acknowledged that perhaps some private individuals might have provided occasional support.[89]

At least three facts justify suspicions that Greece sympathizes with the PKK, in addition to the long-standing eastern Mediterranean rivalry of the two countries. One is certainly the fact that in 1999 Ocalan was captured in Kenya in possession of a Greek Cypriot passport.[90] This gave Turkish politicians reason to demand that "Greece . . . be added to the list of countries that support terrorism and harbor terrorists."[91] Next, Ocalan himself has made public statements about Greece's support for his organization. He reportedly said that "Greece has for years supported the PKK movement. They even gave us arms and rockets."[92] It is true that this statement appeared in the Turkish *Hurriyet* after Ocalan's arrest and might have been paraphrased. But some actions and statements of Greek politicians do imply they gave at the minimum moral support to this organization. Third, Deputy Parliamentary Chairman Panayiotis Sghouridhis, a deputy from the Pan-Hellenic Socialist Movement, admitted in 2000 that he had met Ocalan twice, once in 1995 in Damascus and later in 1998 in Rome.

So what is the role of Greece in the making of the economics of PKK's war on Turkey? The easiest answer would be, "ambiguous." Support means interaction, and interaction must be twofold. It would be fair to recall that after Ocalan's eviction from Syria Greece twice denied him asylum. And some evidence suggests that Greece may have aided in Ocalan's capture. But, more importantly, there are no accusations of Greek support of the organization after 1999. Ocalan's arrest became a pretext for reconciliation between the two neighbors, who later pledged cooperation in the fight against terrorism.

Two other European states have also been mentioned as having *de facto* facilitated some of the PKK's revolutionary activities. One is Italy, which extended its hospitality to Ocalan by providing him with asylum after he was expelled from Turkey. Indicatively, neither the Greeks nor the Russians would offer asylum but Italy, headed by Massimo D'Alema, a former communist. Ocalan enjoyed warm hospitality from many Italian citizens, and while in the country had no problems maintaining communications with his fighters in the Middle East. Moreover, Italy resolved to ignore an Interpol Red Notice for a pending arrest warrant in Germany and refused to extradite Ocalan to Germany.[93]

The other country is the Netherlands whose liberal legislation has played into the hands of PKK terrorists. For example, PKK members have acknowledged in interviews that their officials would rent a farmhouse in an isolated area that then would be used for political training and indoctrination. Some trainees later would be employed by the PKK as fighters in Turkey.[94]

Foreign terrorist organizations as allies

States can be important ideological and economic allies to terrorist groups. However, the role of other terrorist organizations should not be overlooked. The Turkish Ministry of Foreign Affairs claims that the PKK has maintained connections with the Palestine Liberation Organization (PLO), the Armenian Secret Army for the Liberation of Armenia (ASALA), and the Red Army Faction.[95] What was their role in the making of the PKK as an effective and durable terrorist organization? Joint activities included both training and joint terrorist operations. PKK members trained with several Palestinian groups – including Arafat's Fatah – while living in the Bekaa Valley in Lebanon and in Syria.[96] The PKK also had a "fruitful collaboration" with ASALA, according to a 1980 statement issued by the two groups following a joint operation aimed at bombing the Turkish Consulate in Strasbourg, France.[97] But this seems to have been a one-time caper in which each group sought publicity. The PKK has also received support from the Hawks of Thrace – a Greek terrorist organization that has expressed solidarity with the PKK based on shared antipathy toward the Turkish authorities.[98] Support from these sources does not seem to have had much effect on the PKK's capacity for action in its early years, and less than what the PKK developed from friendly states and other Kurdish groups, especially the Kurdish diaspora in Europe (see below). Lastly, the Turkish government has claimed that PKK is linked to al-Qaeda,[99] but without any solid evidence. It seems doubtful that Islamist al-Qaeda would support the Marxist-Leninist PKK.

The trans-border Kurdish ETSM: the Kurdish European Diaspora

State sponsorship might have been a reliable source of support for terrorist groups during the Cold War period. It is nowadays decreasingly likely that states would make long-term commitments to the terrorist activities of paramilitary groups. Very few states that support terrorist groups can still be mentioned as potential allies. On the other hand, terrorist organizations and insurgency groups do have incentives to cooperate with one another. However, this collaboration is arranged *ad hoc*; it is situational and not durable. The strongest explanation of why intra-terrorist collaboration is short-lived lies perhaps with the fact that neither insurgency groups nor terrorist organizations are likely to compromise on their strategic political objectives. The Kosovo and the Bosnia insurgencies clearly support this conclusion. The Chechen case is another in point. So militants may join hands, but when they do it is mostly for the sake of a short-term success. In the long run, however, each organization pursues its own agenda. Who would then remain as the strongest and the most reliable ally of a militant organization in the long run? We have argued that militants are most likely to receive long-term support on behalf of their kindred fellows. The Kurdish ETSM is such a political and economic ally.

62 *Kurdish nationalists and criminal networks*

Our overview of the Kurdish (Turkish) ETSM at the outset of this chapter is missing one important element. These are the Turkish Kurds who live and work in Western Europe. They are large in numbers and their European settlement is well established. With their various organizations and propaganda machines they constitute a legitimate segment within the Turkish Kurdish ETSM. Their legal and illicit business activities nourish the PKK's funds on a regular basis.

Political organizations of the European Kurdish Diaspora

Many Kurdish organizations have operated freely in Europe over the last three decades. They avail themselves of the liberal laws of the European Union and its strong support of the freedom of press and speech. Kurdish cultural information centers, organizations, websites, and propaganda institutions have been engaged in dissemination of information about the Kurdish struggle in Turkey. The PKK makes use of them. According to Francois Haut of France's Departement de Recherche sur les Menaces Criminelles Contemporaines, the PKK's guiding idea is "to control and exploit the Kurdish Community as well as Europe's wealth using all its system's weakness and joints: political activism based on major mafios [*sic*] methods."[100] The PKK views the Kurdish community as a never-failing resource for various insurgency-related activities. The PKK has sought recruits among the Kurdish populations in Europe. But, more importantly, it tried to gain legal recognition for the work of its branches in European societies as well as in rich European fundraising centers. The best strategy to the attainment of this goal is to establish PKK- related organizations and build up a pro-PKK propaganda machine.

Prominent among the pro-PKK organizations is the Kurdish Parliament in exile, established on 12 April 1995 in The Hague, the Netherlands. The parliament has gained acceptance by European governments and has met throughout Europe, including in Vienna, Moscow, Copenhagen, Rome, and Oslo. Other pro-PKK Kurdish organizations include the Officio d'Informazione del Kurdistan in Italy, which explicitly solicits donations. Another PKK-related organization is the Cologne based "Freedom-for-Ocalan.com." Still another is "Kurdishinfor.com," based in Brussels and considered by counterterrorism experts to be "one of the most effective pro-PKK organizations in Europe."[101]

The Kurdish Diaspora-based PKK propaganda machine

The PKK has built an influential and widely based propaganda machine across West Europe, which helps the organization disseminate information about its activities and also solicit donations. The most popular pro-PKK channel, Roj TV, is located in Denmark. In view of Ankara's harsh restrictions on Kurdish and PKK communications the latter has found satellite television to be one of the most effective media to reach the Turkish Kurds. Roj TV is the third attempt to broadcast PKK-inspired television in Turkey, and it remains a matter of contention between Turkey and Denmark.[102] Its general manager, Manouchehr Tahsili Zonoozi, has acknowledged that Roj TV has had contacts with the PKK, though it is not controlled by the organization.[103]

The European Kurdish-based PKK donation and business activities

The Kurdish community in West Europe is not only the host network for PKK political activities. It is also a major source of financial support. According to Bruce Hoffman of the RAND Corporation, "one-half of the [PKK's revenue comes] from the Kurdish Diaspora in Europe."[104] These funds come from a mix of legal and illegal activities. The major sources of the PKK's legal income are the Kurdish cultural centers throughout Europe. They raise funds for the PKK through festivals and shows as well as from the sale of publications. It is reported that the annual revenue coming from the Kurdish cultural centers approximates $20 million. It would be fair to note that only some of these organizations work for the cause of the PKK. Others are independent and dislike PKK's tactics. Another $30 million comes from donations from Kurdish families in Europe. Former PKK operatives say they solicit donations once a month.[105]

Max-Peter Ratzel, Director of Europol, also mentions the establishment and management of small companies as sources of terrorists' in come.[106] The PKK is said to "tax" such enterprises, sometimes using threats.[107] The PKK has helped the establishment of many Kurdish businesses in London. Once established the PKK extorts protection money from the shop owners. Interestingly, many local Kurds and Turks speak favorably of this "alliance of convenience." They feel safer and protected against the "Mafia."[108] And when discussing the recent growth of Kurd-created trading companies in the UK and Belgium, Francois Haut observes that these businesses provide greater infiltration for the PKK into Kurdish commercial community.[109]

The PKK relationships with Kurdish and Turkish businesses throughout Europe are comparable to the collaborative relationships between the FARC – the Marxist Revolutionary Armed Forces of Colombia – and drug producers and traffickers. The latter decided to locate processing facilities in FARC-controlled areas and relied on guerrillas to maintain order and security, in exchange for paying protection taxes.[110] The resurgence of the Taliban in Afghanistan since 2005 is reportedly based on a similar relationship.

The political economy of the PKK's revolutionary war on Turkey: PKK involvement in international crime

In both politics and economics numbers matter. The broader a trans-border identity network – the better. But networks alone are of little help if strong units within them do not assume the major responsibility for putting networks in action. So, what role for the PKK itself? To sustain insurgency for more than 30 years an organization obviously needs more than influential international allies and broad trans-border identity networks. The organization itself should have the capacities to think and act as business enterprise, even if its economic activities lie exclusively within the grey and black market sector. The theoretical model developed in chapter 1 has identified potential sources of terrorist funding. They should be

64 *Kurdish nationalists and criminal networks*

sought within the different branches of the global illegal economy. As our theoretical chapter has suggested, the spectrum of global illegal business nowadays is vast, while global financial regulations are loose and badly enforced. So profit maximization and risk reduction are theoretically easy to achieve. The following review of the PKK's illegal economic activities provides substantiating evidence.

Drug trafficking

How did the PKK evolve into a criminal group, self-funding its revolutionary and terrorist activities? The PKK's largest source of financing is its involvement in drug trafficking and the money laundering of the profits. In 2010 about 80 per cent of Europe's heroin supply flowed through Turkey, according to the UN Office on Drugs and Crime, and many of those arrested for drug trafficking in European countries were Turks – in statistics that do not distinguish between Turks and Kurds.[111] The UN does not estimate the PKK's share in this trade, but the Turkish Ministry of Foreign Affairs claims that the PKK is involved in all phases of drug trafficking, including production, storage, transportation, and marketing.[112] In view of this Curtis and Karacan call the PKK "a multilevel business organization." And Frank Cilluffo testified before the US House of Representatives that "the Kurdish Workers Party . . . has financed their separatist movement by . . . engaging in the trade themselves. The PKK is heavily involved in European drug trade, especially in France and Germany."[113] According to French law enforcement, 80 per cent of the heroin in Paris is brought in by the PKK.[114] The British National Service of Criminal Intelligence estimates that 70 per cent of heroin in the country is smuggled in by Turkish gangs.[115] The German Daily *NRZ* reported in March 1993 that the narcotic trades of Hamburg, Essen, Bremen, and Frankfurt were all under the control of the PKK. Bavarian Minister of the Interior Gunter Becktein concluded in July 1995 that the PKK had taken over control of the European drug market.[116] The total percentage of all European drug trafficking that has been attributed to the PKK varies from 40[117] to nearly 80 per cent.[118]

How much has the PKK earned annually? Estimates vary greatly. According to the British National Criminal Intelligence Service, the PKK in 1993 earned about $75 million from the illicit drug trade, amounting to 44 per cent of their total annual budget.[119] The Turkish press estimated that in 2003 the PKK received about $40 million annually from the drug trade.[120] Capagtay in 2007 estimated that half the profits of the European heroin trade went to the PKK.[121] We can assume from this scrum of mostly speculative statistics that the PKK had at least $40 million in annual revenue from illegal drug trade at the beginning of the 2010s. This compares with an older estimate of $50 million annually from Kurdish cultural centers, businesses, and families in the European diaspora.

Collaboration with international organized crime networks

It is also worth noting that because of its involvement in the drug trade, the PKK has become intertwined with organized crime networks in Europe. Curtis and

Karacan observe that in Europe, "regional criminal organizations parallel terrorist and political cells and have common membership."[122] The PKK is known to be linked to other Kurdish and ethnic Turk criminal clans. Interpol, for instance, followed the narcotic smuggling activities of several Kurdish clans in the 1990s. They were based in Germany, the Netherlands, Italy, and Spain, and they all had links with the PKK. Moreover there are at least a dozen criminal clans in Turkey. One of them is the Sakik clan, which has high-ranking members in the PKK. Moving eastward, along the Syria/Lebanon/Turkey border, an illegal trade triangle exists. There luxury cars, stolen from Europe, are exchanged for heroin, which in turn is traded for cash and arms.[123] So due to the level of its involvement in the drug market, the PKK has become a European organized crime syndicate itself. The Turkish Ministry of Foreign Affairs claims that the PKK "is a clear example of the interconnected nature of terrorism and transnational organized crime."[124] And Hayri Birler argues in the *Turkish Daily News* that "the PKK has ceased to be merely a terrorist organization, and has become part of the international organized crime network whose tentacles engulf the globe."[125] Members of Kongra-Gel, a PKK splinter group, reportedly were arrested in 2008 and 2009 across Europe, from France to Cyprus, on various charges, but most importantly on drug trafficking.[126]

Specialized reports on narco-trafficking observe that given the complex and mixed PKK/Turkish/Kurdish structure of criminal interaction, the PKK's true share of the narcotics market cannot be precisely identified.[127] However, experts agree that the PKK profits immensely from its location at the cross-roads between the major narcotics sources in South and Central Asia and Western Europe.

Drug production

Kurdistan is not only located on a natural trade route. It is also a place where illegal drugs are cultivated. Turkish police reports say that Turkish operations in northern Iraq have discovered large farms of cannabis near a PKK camp in the Bahara Valley, where the drugs captured exceeded 4.5 tons. Drug production facilities are reported by PKK militants as being available in Iran, where Ocalan's brother Osman is reportedly in charge of PKK narcotics production. In 2007 and 2008 Turkish law enforcement seized a number of drug shipments and drug laboratories that belonged to the Kongra-Gel, a PKK splinter group, operating in south Turkey, and designated as a significant narcotics trafficker. The organization is also reported to collect money from drug traffickers.[128]

Other profit centers

There is evidence that the PKK is also involved in other profitable illegal activities. The Turkish Ministry of Foreign Affairs says that the organization is involved in arms smuggling, abduction of children, and human trafficking.[129] Curtis and Karacan's report confirms the arms smuggling activities of the PKK, with the qualification that this information is mostly relevant for the 1990s. Anecdotal evidence suggests that the PKK supplied arms to other Kurdish terrorist groups and also to the Tamil Tigers of Sri Lanka.[130] Cagaptay's research confirms PKK's involvement in human trafficking.[131] A Romanian daily newspaper, *Adevarul*, reported in 2005 that a PKK-affiliated human smuggling ring was transporting people through Turkey, Romania, Hungary, Austria, Britain, and France.[132] And Curtis and Karacan identify major smuggling networks for refugees and illegal migrants more broadly. The three routes most frequently used by Kurds are Istanbul–Milan; Istanbul–Bosnia–Milan; and Turkey–Tunisia–Malta–Italy.[133]

Money laundering

Drug production and trade generate illegal profits whose laundering is the next stage in PKK illicit business activities. Operation Sputnik provided evidence.[134] In February 1996 a Canadian businessman admitted that he had been contracted by PKK-front Med TV to launder money for the organization. In September of that year British and Belgian agents raided Med TV, elements of the "Kurdish parliament in exile," and homes of Kurdish activists. About $11 million had been deposited into the accounts of Med TV. Police claimed that the proceeds came from drugs, arms, and human trafficking.

Curtis and Karacin also say that the group's scope of interest was significantly reduced after Ocalan's arrest in 1999. However, the supportive structure of its criminal activities remains in place. And Haut suggests that the PKK has adopted patterns of behavior similar to the Philippine-based Abu-Sayyaf group, eschewing civic and cultural activities to concentrate instead on criminal activities to sustain its military presence.[135]

To recapitulate, this overview of the PKK's illicit economic activities has shown that the group has been especially successful in criminal activities. In fact, it has evolved into a criminal syndicate that has used multiple economic strategies in the making of money. It has also collaborated with other criminal networks, and has itself given birth to multiple criminal organizations.

Instead of a conclusion: nested games in spillover crises

As this discussion has suggested, an active ETSM itself should not be held responsible for episodes or patterns of political violence and crime. Rather, the agents of the two bads are instead the hybrid terror-crime networks, such as the PKK, that emerge and persist in protracted conflict with opponents. Hybrid networks, in particular the more durable ones, have learned to make strategic choices in view of shifting opportunities and constraints. They choose from wide repertoires of revolutionary and funding strategies.[136] Can we anticipate which strategies a hybrid crime–terror network is likely to employ in an emerging political and economic conjuncture?[137] The answer to this question is indicative of the actor's current status, as well as the long-term impact of its activities on domestic and regional politics and economics. If the revolutionary and economic strategies chosen are predicated on group capacities alone, the group risks weakness in the face of its opponent(s). However, if the group selects a revolutionary strategy predicated on the support of segments of an ETSM, or if it attracts a major state sponsor, then it gains strength and its insurgency has long-term implications.

Multiple factors affect strategic forces, factors that can only be understood in separate and multiple case studies. The elites of hybrid crime–terror networks (as well as of the ETSMs' segments) make their choices within a "web of multiple games" where endogenous and exogenous factors interact. The Syrian ETSM was mentioned as an example of an actor selecting its strategies very cautiously within a "nested game."[138] The process by which the PKK leadership has made strategic choices is another example with very different outcomes. The factors that have shaped the PKK elite's strategic choices are more numerous and complex: the relevant exogenous factors operate at multiple levels. The first analytic point is that the exogenous factors in the Kurdish case are necessarily related to recurring and large-scale spillover crises that, in effect, change the rules of the game.

The PKK insurgency has been a spillover crisis from its beginning. No surprise: the ETSM's extended cross-border networks facilitated the export of group violence and crime into the adjoining neighborhood. And Middle Eastern politics have added one important element to otherwise communally incited cross-border violence; and states have frequently joined in. We have identified six major spillover crises that have shaped and reshaped the PKK's activities and summarize them once more:

1. Support from the Syrian state to the PKK, 1980–1998
2. Support from the Iranian state to the PKK, 1980–1990s
3. Support from the Iraqi state to the PKK, 1991–2003[139]
4. The intra-group conflict between the PKK and the Iraqi Kurdish groups, the Patriotic Union of Kurdistan and the Kurdish Democratic Party, 1991–2003[140]
5. The support provided by the Kurdish Regional Government of Iraq (KRG) to the PKK in its insurgency against Turkey fought out of northern Iraq, 2003–2012[141]
6. The insurgency of the Iranian Kurdish group, the Party of Free Life (PJAK), fought against Iran from northern Iraq, 2005–2012. The PJAK is claimed to be a PKK splinter group.[142]

When examined through the prism of the PKK elite's strategic choices, each spillover crisis illustrates the concrete meaning of "nested games in spillover crises." In the cases of Syria, Iran, Iraq, and the KRG all "nested games" factors have been at work, the full range of endogenous as well as exogenous ones. Nested games are being played and strategic decisions made in a four-dimensional space. Thus the PKK has navigated opportunistically among the possibilities and risks inherent not only in Turkish politics but in larger spheres, which include other segments of the Kurdish ETSM, states in the region, and the Kurdish diaspora and its host states in Western Europe. We have characterized the PKK as an opportunistic hybrid terror-crime network. It could not have adapted and survived otherwise.

4 Militant Islam and Bosnia's civil war 1991–1995[1]

There are two narratives about the civil war in Bosnia between the Sarajevo-based government of the Party of Democratic Action (the *Stranka Demokratske Akcie*, SDA) and the rival Bosnian Serb government based in Banja Luka. The dominant narrative is that radical Serb nationalists, backed by the Milošević regime in Belgrade, initiated a genocidal war against a secular and multicultural Bosnian state. The besieged Sarajevo government of necessity accepted funds and mujahedeen fighters from sympathetic Muslims elsewhere. The alternative narrative, which gained credence during the American-led war on terror that began after September 11, 2001, was that the SDA, its leadership dominated by Islamists, was in close alliance with international jihadists from the beginning and sought to establish a non-secular Islamist state in Bosnia. The linkages established during the war persist, and Muslim Bosnia is a jihadist threat to European security.[2]

We do not have to accept either narrative – both have some plausibility – to find detailed evidence about how complex unholy alliances emerged in wartime Bosnia, based on foreign funding, militant Islamists, corrupt officials, and black marketers. Which of these conditions persist is key to assessing Bosnia's future.[3]

In terms of our theoretical framework, in Bosnia as in Kosovo and Serbia the interaction of trans-border identity networks, ongoing armed conflict, and illegal market opportunities gave birth to criminal-terror networks. *Militarized conflict* and *market constraints* opened the way for political-criminal alliances in Bosnia. The international portrayal of Bosnian Muslims under attack prompted Islamic countries and charities to provide material and ideological assistance. Mujahedeen, many of them veterans of the civil war in Afghanistan that overthrew its Soviet-backed regime in 1992, worked closely with Islamic charities to import money and to establish a trans-state Islamic advocacy network. Virtually every entity involved in providing money and arms to the Bosniaks profited from the transactions, including Bosnian officials. Smugglers and black marketers who supplied the warring parties also profited from illicit trade, usually in collusion with local officials of all ethnic groups and, sometimes, with international peacekeepers.[4]

After the Dayton Peace Accords of December 1995 secular Bosniaks, encouraged by international actors, sought to contain the Islamization of the Sarajevo-based Bosnian state. The black marketing networks that flourished during the war with the complicity of officials were no longer necessary, though some smuggling operations continue. The constraints on international Islamist activities imposed by the Bosnian authorities, in grudging compliance with the international requirements of the war on terrorism, marginalized but did not eliminate the wartime connections among some officials and Bosnian branches of Islamist charities. In short, once armed conflict ended, *illegal market opportunities* dried up but the influence of the *trans-border Islamist identity network* persisted. A few mujahedeen with Bosnian citizenship stayed behind. Elements of the Islamist infrastructure also remained: new Saudi-financed mosques, madrassas, youth groups, and publications. Their activities are kept under close scrutiny by Bosnian, European, NATO, and US intelligence and security services.

Militarized conflict: background to civil war

On 7 April 1992 the EC recognized Bosnia-Herzegovina as an independent state. Of the new state's 4,270,000 million inhabitants 44 percent had identified themselves as Muslims in the 1991 census, 31 percent as Serbs, and 17 percent as Croats.[5] It was governed by the Party of Democratic Action (SDA), a Muslim party established in 1989 by Alija Izetbegović and a cadre of Islamic activists. Eight of its 40 founding members had been members of the Young Muslims, a group with long-standing ideological ties to the Muslim Brotherhood in Egypt that had been nurtured by travel and study. Some of them, including Izetbegović, had been tried in 1949 and again in 1983 by Tito's government, and had served prison terms for their advocacy of an Islamic state. The *Islamic Declaration*, written by Izetbegović, during the Communist period but not published until 1990, said that

> The struggle for an Islamic system, and a thorough rebuilding of Muslim society, can only be successfully carried out by hardened personalities, forming a strong and homogenous organization. This organization is not a political party from the arsenal of Western democracy; it is a movement based on Islamic theology.[6]

The key to the SDA's electoral success in 1990–1 was its support from Bosnia's Muslim villages and small towns, where traditional Islam was stronger than in multi-ethnic Sarajevo. Secular Muslims also were represented in the SDA's leadership, but a number of them resigned as the Islamic orientation of the party came to the fore.

It was not entirely clear from Itzegebović's often Delphic and contradictory pronouncements just what kind of state he envisioned for Bosnia-Herzegovina. In his discourse with Westerners, in contrast to the *Islamic Declaration*, he used the language of multiculturalism. It is clear, at least in retrospect, that he hoped to establish an Islamic state in Bosnia but not necessarily an Islamist one. His ideal seems to have been the Ottoman Empire, an Islamic state in which non-Muslim *dhimmis* were tolerated. The Bosnian Serbs were both alienated by the SDS's Islamic emphasis and attracted by the militant pan-Serbian nationalism of Slobodan Milošević's government in Belgrade. When the Bosnian parliament declared independence in October 1991 with the support of both Muslim and

70 *Militant Islam*

Croat delegates, Serbian representatives walked out. The Bosnian Serbs established their own assembly and soon after the autonomous Republica Serpska.

On 20 May, 1992 the UN General Assembly admitted the new sovereign state to membership. A number of regional and international efforts were made to broker the differences among the country's three constituent communities, especially the widening split between the SDS government and the Bosnian Serb authorities. In the most promising of such efforts the European Community convened a meeting in Portugal of the Bosniak, Serbian, and Croat leaders in early 1992. They agreed in principle that Bosnia would be a single state organized on the basis of ethnic regions, or cantons, with substantial local autonomy, a plan that foreshadowed the settlement concluded in Dayton after four years of war. But after Izetbegović's return to Sarajevo he publically rejected the agreement, reportedly with the encouragement of the US ambassador.[7]

Meanwhile both Bosniaks and Serbs were preparing for war. Already in late 1991 the SDS had established the Patriotic League, a paramilitary force separate from the Bosnian army, and its agents were buying arms for it in Vienna from former Warsaw Pact members. During early 1992 SDA representatives also visited a number of Muslim countries, including Iran, seeking diplomatic and, as it later became evident, more substantial support for a war that had not yet begun. The Bosnian Serbs got substantial military assistance from the Serb-dominated Yugoslav National Army (the JNA). In early 1992 the intelligence branch of the JNA estimated that there were 100,000 paramilitary forces in Bosnia – Muslim, Serb, and Croat.[8]

Militarized conflict: war by atrocity

Violent clashes between Muslims and Serbs in late 1991 had escalated to large-scale fighting by April 1992. The course of the war has been described in detail elsewhere,[9] but it had several features that are relevant to our analysis. First, because the Muslim population was widely dispersed, much of the fighting focused on the defense or enlargement of Muslim enclaves besieged by Serb forces – including Sarajevo itself. Second, the Bosnian Serbs occupied more cohesive territory, which extended from northeast to west across central Bosnia, and had a more effective military, thanks to the JNA's support. The Serbs' control gradually expanded from about 50 to nearly 70 percent of the country's territory. Third, Muslim and Serb-held areas both endured scarcities that could not be met by local production or humanitarian assistance. This provided market opportunities for entrepreneurs of all ethnicities to trade across battle lines, profiting from highly inflated prices.[10]

Fourth, "ethnic cleansing" was practiced by all sides. Many of the estimated 55,000 civilians killed during the war were victims either of sieges or of Serb, Croat, or Muslim massacres in mixed areas where locally dominant forces sought to expel civilians of different ethnicity.[11] Atrocities were common, widely publicized – especially when carried out by Serbs – and issues of culpability and severity were intensely debated for years afterward, not least at the Yugoslav war crime trials in den Haag.

For example, Croats and Bosniaks were supposedly allies but in early 1993, in the mixed Croat–Muslim areas of central Bosnia, Croat and Bosniak units carried out competing atrocities aimed at expanding their territorial control. Schindler writes that at least 1500 Croat civilians were killed in the fighting, many of them massacred, and many HVO (Croat) soldiers were executed by the Muslims. Units with foreign mujahedeen were said to be particularly vicious. "In the village of Milerici, the massacre of five civilians was videotaped, while the slaughter of thirty-six Croats in Majine a few weeks later by 'holy warriors' killed women and the elderly as well as disarmed HVO prisoners."[12] Bosnian Serbs also were victims of atrocities by jihadist units. Schindler chronicles instances from eyewitnesses and videotapes of jihadis killing their captives.[13]

Conflict in Srebrenica, as analyzed after the war, affords a glimpse through the fog of war and competing atrocity stories. The city, in easternmost Bosnia on the Drina River, was largely surrounded by Serb-controlled territory. There was a three-year prelude to the Bosnian Serb attack on the safe haven in July 1995 and the subsequent genocidal massacre of many of its male inhabitants. Srebrenica and its mostly Bosniak population were occupied by Serb forces in April 1992, at the very beginning of the civil war. In a pattern that became operating procedure on both sides, Muslims' homes were ransacked and sometimes burned, their inhabitants arrested, forcibly expelled, and sometimes killed. In May local Bosniak forces, led by Naser Orić, a young and inexperienced militia leader, fought back by attacking Serb villages near Srebrenica and soon drove Serb paramilitary forces from the city. The Serbs then began a siege of the city that lasted for three years.

A decade later Commander Orić was tried by the International Criminal Tribunal for the former Yugoslavia (ICTY) on an indictment that listed six months of deadly attacks he led in 1992–3 against Serb villages near Srebrenica. In an attack that Bosnian Serbs often cited to justify their own actions, Orić's forces attacked Kravica and two neighboring villages on Orthodox Christmas Day, January 7 1993. In Schindler's account 52 civilians died in Kravica, ranging in age from four to eighty-eight. Bosnian Serb records state that 114 Serbs died in the attacks, almost all civilians. The ICTY's investigation, though, concluded that the attacks in and near Kravica killed 43 people of whom 13 were obviously civilians, most others Bosnian Serb troops. Orić was sentenced by the ICTY to two years' imprisonment for his failure during this period to prevent the deaths of Bosnian Serb detainees, on the basis of "superior criminal responsibility," but his conviction was reversed by the ICTY on appeal.[14]

The UN Secretary-General's 2005 report to the General Assembly on the Bosnian Serbs' siege of Srebrenica and the genocidal massacre perpetrated by Ratko Mladic's forces in July 1995 concluded that

> The Serbs repeatedly exaggerated the extent of the raids out of Srebrenica as a pretext for the prosecution of a central war aim: to create a geographically contiguous and ethnically pure territory along the Drina, while freeing their troops to fight in other parts of the country. The extent to which this pretext was accepted at face value by international actors and observers reflected

72 *Militant Islam*

the prism of "moral equivalency" through which the conflict in Bosnia was viewed by too many for too long.[15]

The criminalization of Bosnia: a perfect storm of opportunites for crime–terror alliances

There was massive international engagement in the civil war on all sides. The UN imposed an arms embargo on all of the former Yugoslavia in 1991 that had the unintended effects, as Andreas points out, "to freeze in place the already heavy Bosnian Serb military advantage and make the Sarajevo government dependent on black market arms supplies and covert funding from friendly countries." Saudi Arabia provided money, Iran established an intelligence and security presence, and jihadist networks provided thousands of mujahedeen. Over 20,000 lightly armed UN peacekeepers were eventually deployed to Bosnia, but their rules of engagement sharply limited their capacity to stop fighting or protect civilians. They also faced supply problems, as did the more than 100,000 UN and NGO humanitarian workers in the country.[16] In short, Bosnia at war was a perfect storm that bred all the conditions of unholy alliances: international and local crime networks, official corruption, not least among international personnel, and the proliferation of Islamist influence and jihadists on European ground.

The outgunned SDS government had both sectarian and military reasons to seek assistance from the Islamic world. Closer ties with the Arab world were justified by the supposed indifference of the West and, perhaps more importantly, by the one-sided effects of the UN arms embargo. The process evolved slowly. In the war's initial stages most Islamic governments were officially committed to the arms embargo. Yet leaflets calling for arms to help Bosnian Muslims were distributed by militant Islamic groups in the Gulf and North Africa. The sympathetic portrayal of the Bosniaks' plight by media in the Islamic world, and by imams from their Friday pulpits, also put governments under domestic pressure to support their co-religionists.

Islamic funds for Bosnia

Private individuals in the Arab world gave money to support the Bosnians. King Fahd of Saudi Arabia reportedly contributed $8 million and the emir of Kuwait donated $3 million. Islamic charities and governments contributed much more: the *Muslim World League Journal* reported that by mid-1993 Saudi Arabia had provided $65 million of aid, the United Arab Emirates $5 million, and Pakistan had pledged $30 million.[17]

The Third World Relief Agency (TWRA) was a major though by no means the only conduit for Islamist funding for the Sarajevo government. It was founded in 1987 by Dr Fatih al-Hasayan, a Sudanese national, to promote Islamic causes in Europe. Using funds from private donors and sympathetic governments, TWRA transmitted $2.5 billion to the Bosnian government between 1992 and 1995, according to a post-war Bosnian government investigation. Its main office and bank accounts were in Vienna, from which payments were made by a board consisting of al-Hasayan and four SDS officials. Most weeks during the war al-Hasayan would drive from Vienna in a car with Sudanese diplomatic plates to TWRA's branch in Zagreb and deliver suitcases with $3 million to $5 million, usually in cash, to the SDS officials who ran that branch. From there most reached Sarajevo, but few records were kept of their uses. Some helped pay Bosnian soldiers and mujahedeen, others were used to purchase weapons, supplies, and pay for comfortable accommodations of the officials involved.

Whether or not this flow of funds was licit or not, according to prevailing national and international law, is not relevant to our analysis. The more important issue was the diversion of some of the money. For example, the TWRA raised $100 million for arms for a winter offensive in 1994, but only $60 million was spent on arms and munitions; the remainder was not accounted for. When Austrian authorities raided the TWRA operation in Vienna in 1994 the Bosnian embassy there cleared $60 million from its accounts and disbursed it to senior SDA officials, including the Bosniak foreign minister – and several millions disappeared. This is consistent with the results of post-war investigations of other Islamic charitable operations: some of the money stuck to the hands of those responsible for channeling it to the Sarajevo government.[18]

Weaponry

The military supplies so badly needed by the Bosniaks were obtained from many sources in contravention of the UN embargo. Most were light arms and munitions; badly needed armor and other heavy equipment were much more difficult to obtain. As mentioned above, some munitions were purchased in East Europe including Poland, the former East Germany, and Russia. Arms agreements often were brokered in Austria by the TWRA. Muslim countries were said to have provided about a quarter of the overall weapons flow to Bosnia. Among the most active suppliers were Iran, Turkey, and Malaysia, along with several Gulf countries. Beginning in March 1992 SDS officials arranged with Iran to establish a major arms pipeline that by war's end had brought $200 million worth of weaponry and TNT to Bosnia.

Croatia was both a significant supplier and the main conduit for the flood of military supplies reaching Bosnia from elsewhere.[19] Croatia reportedly provided the Bosnian government army with anti-tank weapons and ammunition for mortars, cannons, and machine guns. A Kuwaiti who sympathized with the Bosnian Muslims was quoted as saying: "People say they want to buy guns for Bosnia. I tell them to go to Croatia."[20] Iranian aircraft made frequent flights to deliver weapons and munitions to Croatia for transshipment to Bosnia with the cooperation of Croat officials, and with the knowledge and tacit approval of the US government. Defense Minister Gojko Susak in particular supported the scheme, allegedly because he received lucrative kickbacks from the trade. By spring 1993 Croat officials were said to take a third to a half of the weapons as a transit tax, and according to Schindler, "Zagreb purchased ex-Soviet helicopters

74   *Militant Islam*

for the Muslim forces, which used them to bring the arms and munitions into Bosnia."[21]

The mujahedeen, and others

Human resources were the other significant Middle East contribution to the Bosnian war. The long-term impact of money, munitions, and manpower was the expansion of the Islamic trans-border identity network and its incorporation into Bosniak society. Major actors in this process were the radical Islamic fighters – the mujahedeen, who first arrived in Bosnia in 1992 and by war's end numbered an estimated 5000–6000 fighters. Many were veterans of other jihadist conflicts, especially in Afghanistan, and some of them went on to fight elsewhere, for example, with the Algerian Islamists (see chapter 5). They reached Bosnia mainly through Zagreb and some carried passports issued by Bosnian embassies, especially in Vienna.[22]

Two mujahedeen factions operated in Bosnia. Abu Abdel Aziz, a charismatic preacher and fighter, headed one of them, Al-Zubair Al-Haili the other. Both were Saudis and veterans of the Afghan war. Abu Abdel Aziz visited Saudi Arabia to get religious sanction for the Bosnian project and met with a number of prominent scholars who gave their backing. According to Pargeter, "the real brains" behind Abu Abdel Aziz's faction was the Egyptian Sheikh Anwar Shaban, a political refugee who had established a mosque in Milan that after 1992 became a major recruitment ground and transit point for immigrant European Muslims who wanted to participate in the Bosnian jihad. Shaban chose to preach and fight with the mujahedeen and was killed by Croats.[23]

The mujahedeens' vanguard unit was the El Mujahid (Holy Warrior) Battalion, founded in August 1993, which served under the Third Corps of the Bosnian Army. It consisted of nearly 3000 Islamic fighters – Algerians, Lebanese Sunni, Moroccans, Afghans, Turks, Pakistani, Sudanese, Saudi, and Syrians. There were also members of Hizbullah and others from Tawhid, the Islamic Unification movement of Lebanon. Most came to fight for the establishment of an Islamist state; some also served as trainers for government forces. "They were very organized," said British peacekeeper Lance-Corporal Mark Waple:

> They come from the Middle East and Africa, are very well armed and act with determination and energy quite alien to the local forces. . . . They were chanting "Allahu Akbar". It was quite deafening if you've got 40 guys doing it.[24]

Another well-known jihadi unit was the 7th Muslim Brigade, organized in November 1992 around a core of Bosnian militants then serving in the el-Mujahid unit. It was funded by the TWRA and recruited local Bosniak fighters throughout the country. Other jihadi units were organized as well but had a mixed record in battle. Non-Islamist Bosnian officers thought the jihadist units were badly led and more interested in propagandizing than winning battles. Yet the el-Mujahid battalion fought ferociously, suffering casualties during the war estimated at 2000 wounded and 500 dead, 400 of them Arabs.[25] And many surviving mujahedeen were granted Bosnian citizenship in recognition of their contribution to Bosnia's survival.

The mujahedeen's impact on the initial stages of the war was limited. Their major objective was to spread militant Islamic ideologies among their co-religionists, including the young Bosnians whom they recruited. By 1994 the mujahedeen had become more aggressive, staging suicide attacks, and harassing and sometimes kidnapping UN humanitarian workers. They also attempted to form a Holy Brigade independent of the Bosnian army. Local Bosnians complained that the mujahedeen were doing more harm than good because they were fighting for Islam, not for Bosnia. Yusuf Abderahman, an *Al Anbaa* journalist and a Yugoslavia observer, in effect agreed when he said that

> The West, after the failure of communism, is looking to Islam as the new enemy. . . . The West was tough about the Iraq-Kuwait conflict. . . . But in Bosnia . . . – nothing. . . . if there is a war and we see a Muslim with a problem we must fight. Yes, it is a jihad.[26]

Another dimension of the Islamist penetration of Bosnia was the presence of personnel from the Iranian Ministry of Intelligence and Security and the Revolutionary Guard. Hundreds of Iranian agents were posted to Sarajevo, and many of them worked closely with the SDS government's security services. They provided SDS officers with training in intelligence work both in Bosnia and Tehran, and their influence reportedly continued long after the civil war ended.[27]

Black markets

The crime–terror networks promoted by Islamists were only one dimension of the process by which Bosnia was criminalized during the civil war. The need to supply civilian needs in besieged areas opened up great opportunities for black marketing. Andreas observes that embargoes, like those imposed on the former Yugoslavia,

> inflate profits and create economic opportunity structures for those best connected in the world of overt commerce. This strengthens the hand of criminal actors, fuels cross-border black market networks, and encourages closer ties between political leaders and organized crime.[28]

The flow of funds and arms into Bosnia provided many opportunities for diversion, as we have shown. The same was true of humanitarian shipments whose convoys were subject to informal taxation at gunpoint and whose remaining contents were often skimmed at their destination. According to Andreas, a quarter of the supplies delivered by air to besieged Sarajevo were handed over to the besieging Serb forces, some of it for sale on the black market. "The 800-meter-long tunnel that was eventually dug under the UN-controlled tarmac became both a lifeline for the city and a major profit centre for moving black market goods." Some UN

76   *Militant Islam*

contingents in Bosnia joined in the process. Ukrainian forces exploited their mobility and access across siege lines to engage in black-market trading in the Sarajevo area and siphoned off fuel from their vehicles for sale to Bosnians.[29]

The Bihać triangle in northwest Bosnia provided a remarkable example of many of these processes at work. Bihać was a mainly Muslim area that adjoined Croat and Serb territory. Fikret Abdic, a prominent local Muslim businessman, headed Agrokomerc, a large food-processing company based in the town of Velika Kladuša. He persuaded French peacekeepers to provide military escorts for shipments of Agrokomerc foodstuffs into the area that reportedly reached 10,000 tons per month, for sale to locals at high prices. After breaking with the Sarajevo government in autumn 1993 he and his paramilitary unit ran the Velika Kladuša region as a private fiefdom. He made lucrative trade agreements with all parties, collecting taxes and transit fees on food and fuel passing through the enclave for Serbs in Krajina, and for Croats and Serbs in Bosnia. "Everybody has accused me of war profiteering," he said, "But who else would have been able to bring these goods into Bihać? Who else would have been able to break the blockade?"[30] In summer 1995 Bosnian forces sent against Abdic's mini-state finally defeated him and his supporters, despite assistance from his Serb allies. Abdic went into exile in Croatia. The next April a police hit team from Sarajevo sought to assassinate him but was thwarted by Croat police.[31] After the war the Croatian government imprisoned him for crimes against both Bosniaks and Croats in the region under his control.

Official corruption

Officials of all Bosnia's wartime entities – Bosnian, Serb, and Croat – were complicit in criminal activity. In part this was an inevitable consequence of their needs for funds, weaponry, and supplies. The pervasive problem was the diversion of some resources and commodities for private and sectarian purposes. Walter Kemp points out, in his analysis of "The Business of Ethnic Conflict," that the communal leaders of de facto states in wartime operate "in an environment in which they can exploit resources, exercise coercion, and accumulate enough wealth and control to keep themselves in power." In our terms armed conflict provided opportunities for theft that selectively benefitted all the warring parties, and in particular their leaders. The diverted resources, examples of which we have cited above, were used to build and sustain patron–client relations between leaders and their co-ethnic and co-religionist followers. In some instances, Kemp argues, the criminal benefits of warfare give the communal contenders incentives to continue war rather than make peace.[32] And even if peace breaks out, the culture and practise of corruption persists – as in Bosnia-Herzegovina after the Dayton Accords, as we show in a later section.

How international Islam and civil war transformed Bosnia

For Islamists and their Saudi backers the Bosnian civil war was an opportunity to establish a conservative Islamic society in the heart of Europe. For mujahedeen, fresh from their victory in Afghanistan, it was another battleground on which to fight under the green banner of Islam against infidels and Crusaders. For the Iranians, where the rule of the Ayatollahs was being consolidated, it was an opportunity to project their political as well as religious influence into the Balkans. The Bosnian Muslims had their own agenda, at the center of which was their collective survival.

Though Bosnian President Izetbegović claimed that the SDS never intended to create an Islamic state in the heart of Europe, despite evidence to the contrary, it is crystal clear that he and the party leadership were prepared to play the Islamic card to gain international support for the Bosniak national movement. This was spurred by reports of ethnic cleansing of Muslims by the Bosnian Serbs (and sometimes Croats). The Umma, the world Muslim community, and many in the West were outraged by these accounts. Dr Muhammad al-Sharhan, Director of the Kuwaiti Red Crescent, said, "In any place where Muslims are being tortured and humiliated jihad should rise to liberate them, whether in Bosnia or in Kashmir."[33] Thus the war that secular Bosniaks and most of their Western supporters saw as nationalist was regarded as a holy war by Muslims elsewhere and by a small but growing cadre of Bosniak Islamists.

Bosnian national identity

The Bosnian Muslim identity cannot be fully understood with reference to Islam alone. It has to be viewed from the perspective of Bosnia's communal heterogeneity. Until the late 1960s the Yugoslav Communist government did not encourage a separate Bosnian identity. In 1971 a national census first offered them the opportunity to declare themselves "Muslim in the national sense."[34] Since then Islam has denoted nationality in Bosnia, but not until the 1990s was it used in a nationalist context. As the country moved toward independence and civil war, the Muslim faith was the sole marker of identity that distinguished the Bosniaks from the ethnonational Serbs and Croats. Moreover there was no strong territorial base to Bosnian Muslim identity: until Bosnia's declaration of independence they were the only Yugoslav people who did not have a distinct national territory that might give mental or physical boundaries to their collective identity. Thereafter they had a national territory (or more accurately, a dispersed set of besieged territories), centered in Sarajevo, but identification with and defense of that territory was a consequence of war, not a cause of it.

Efforts to plant the transnational Islamic network in Bosnia were inspired in part by the global revival of Islam and the spread of Islamic advocacy networks everywhere Muslim communities exist. These processes also were at work elsewhere in the Balkans – in Albania, Kosovo, Macedonia, Greece, and Bulgaria. Throughout the region, Islamic religious institutions, NGOs, and charities flourished during the 1990s, many of them with substantial funding from Saudi foundations. What was unique to Bosnia was the formation of a Bosniak national identity whose core element was Islam. A census held in 1985 indicated that only 17 percent of the Bosniaks considered themselves believers. In 2004 this percentage had increased to 78 percent.

78   *Militant Islam*

How Islam reshaped Bosniaks' identity

Initially there was little reason to believe that the arrival of the preachers and financiers of transnational Islam might change Bosniaks' sense of identity. Regional analysts questioned the capacities of Arab proselytizers and jihadists to convert significant numbers of locals to the fundamentalist way of thinking. Bosniaks were known as secular and closer to the European liberal-democratic tradition rather than that of the Middle East.

However, identity changed as the local Islamic community interacted with transnational Islam. Saudi-funded offices of Islamic charities promoted Wahabist doctrine, values, and lifestyles in large swaths of the Muslim world. Prominent examples are al Haramain Foundation; the Society for the Revival of Islamic Heritage; and the High Saudi Committee. In Bosnia their representatives acted at all social and political levels. The upper levels were taken by the mujahedeen who indoctrinated Bosniak soldiers, and Islamist clerics who proselytized for militant Islam, the lower levels by Islamist relief organizations that funded these efforts.[35] Their local Bosnian counterparts whose activities continued after the war include the Sarajevo-based Active Islamic Youth (AIY), Furqan, the Balkan Center in Zenica, and the Center for the Affirmation of Islamic Science.

Local as well as transnational entities contributed to the identity shift. The SDA's use of religion in support of Bosniaks' national consolidation was facilitated by the Islamic Community (Islamska Zaednica), which comprises the community of indigenous Bosnian Muslims and their respective institutions. Islamska Zaednica established cooperative relations with transnational Islamist networks during and after the war, evolving into a local agency advocating foreign, though not alien interests. Islamic religious institutions – local as well as global – proliferated in the 1990s. There were 250 religious humanitarian organizations in Bosnia in this period, branches or offspring of Middle Eastern or European entities. Attanassoff says the end of the Bosnian war did not slow down the expansion of such institutions, though there was a temporary decline in their activities after 9/11.[36]

The interaction between the Islamic Community and transnational Islamist advocacy networks occurred at various levels, though with tension between moderate and conservative doctrines. Bosnia's indigenous religious institutions practice Sufism. Sufis accommodate easily to local customs and religious practices. The transnational advocacy networks introduced Salafism, a much more conservative and restrictive interpretation of Islam. Many young Bosniaks, raised in the Sufi tradition, were radicalized by the combined effects of Salafist indoctrination and the exigencies of war.

Doctrinal differences aside, the Islamic Community and the transnational Islamist advocacy network readily cooperated on financial and organizational issues. The Islamist network provides funds that are administered through the Islamic Community, for example to finance the surge in construction of new mosques. Islamist institutions also gave opportunities for Bosnian students to receive their education abroad. In the mid-2000s, according to Attanassoff, 100 Bosnian students of Islam were studying in Saudi Arabia; 60 in Syria; 40 in Egypt; 35 in Jordan; 30 in Iran; 10 in Pakistan; 10 in Turkey; and 20 in Malaysia. The Islamic Community for its part employs graduates from Islamic and secular faculties who have received their education at home or abroad. Home educational institutions include the Faculty of Islamic Studies in Sarajevo; three academies for teacher training; six madrassas (Islamic high schools); and 1405 maktabs (Muslim elementary schools). The trans-state Islamist advocacy network also imports a broad spectrum of Islamic literature. And Islamic newspapers are published regularly.[37]

Some of the post-Dayton consequences of Islamicization are widely visible. Men and women of conservative Islamic appearance are often seen, though they are in the minority: men with beards and long robes, women wearing the *hijab*. Saudi-funded organizations contribute to the physical infrastructure of Islam in Sarajevo and elsewhere. One material manifestation of this process is the proliferation of new and reconstructed mosques in Bosniak communities, some new and others replacing those destroyed during the war. The Saudi-financed King Fahd mosque in Sarajevo is said to be the largest in the Balkans. The new mosques, and the cultural and educational institutions associated with them, are not only or mainly an expression of Islamist influence in Bosnia but evidence of the country's new, Islamic-centered identity that emerged from the conflict. Azra Aksamija, a Sarajevo-born student of the symbolic meanings of Islamic architecture, says that

> as built today, these edifices are neither used as purely religious sites, nor are they symbols of a great religious revival. Rather, they are symptoms of the socio-political transformation of Yugoslavia of the 1980s and 1990s, which are increasingly performing as markers of national and trans-national identity construction processes today.[38]

Despite foreign money Bosnia's Islamic Community retains its relative independence from the trans-state Islamist advocacy network. Attanassoff contends that the proliferating advocacy networks have not penetrated Bosnian social networks.[39] The process of Islamization has led to transformation of the Islamic Community's collective identity but not to corresponding modifications in the individual behavior of most of its members.[40] Islamist organizations have been established but there is no widely supported indigenous Islamist social movement. So while the Islamization of national identity has been a substantial process, the converse one – the nationalization of Islam – has not occurred.[41]

Terrorism and ethnic cleansing in Sarajevo

The demographic structure of Bosnia also changed. Post-war Bosnian communities are far more homogenous than in 1991 because of deliberate and informal ethnic cleansing, and the deep reluctance of many of Bosnia's two million displaced people to return to places where they would remain minorities. Sarajevo is symptomatic. In 1991 its metropolitan population area of 527,000 was 49 percent

80   *Militant Islam*

Bosniak and 30 per cent Serb. By 2002 the city's population was 401,000 (boundary changes make the total population figures incomparable) but Bosniaks made up 80 percent and Serbs 7 percent.

Siege warfare explained only some of the decline in the non-Bosniak population. Islamists and security agents aligned with the SDS intimidated and killed enough non-Muslims to lead to many fleeing the city. Musan Topalovic, known as Caco, was a pre-war gangster and rock musician who at the outset of the war organized a special assault unit of his pre-war associates and soon was given command of the Sarajevo-based 10th Mountain Brigade. Caco's unit killed many Serbs in Sarajevo – one post-war estimate is at least 2000. In a dramatic example of local terrorism, on 8 July 1992, six members of a Serb family in the mixed Sarajevo suburb of Gornji Velesici were killed when they gathered for lunch. The gunmen, who used automatic weapons, were wearing uniforms of the SDS Patriotic League and drove away in a Bosnian police car. General Jovan Divjak, a Serbian career officer then serving with the Sarajevo government, said that officials identified the killers within hours but police blocked the investigation – as in many other cases of anti-Serb violence.[42]

Bosnia since Dayton: dismantling unholy alliances

Hosted and pressured by the United States, the warring Bosnian parties agreed in November 1995 to the Dayton Accords. The new political and administrative framework for the country was as flimsy as the flying machine designed by the Wright brothers in Dayton 93 years earlier. The country was nominally governed by a very weak central government, the Federation of Bosnia and Herzegovina (BiH). Effective authority was wielded by two "entities," one of them Serbian and the other a Bosniak and Croat confederation. The latter included ten cantons and four cities, each with their own governments, and was dominated by the Bosniaks. An international High Representative had substantial authority over the BiH and the entities.[43] Like the Wright brothers' first aircraft the new BiH and its amalgam of parts worked – sort of. Fighting ended almost immediately. The new structures provided internationally funded jobs (and side payments) for a great many people who were members or clients of the communal political parties that continued to dominate the political process in all the entities.

A fundamental liability of the new governments was lack of centralization and coordination across key activities, including defense, security, taxation, and so forth. There has been a gradual shift toward centralization, which we examine below. But the diffusion of authority and responsibility remains a major hindrance for efforts to control crime, terror, and corruption. From the beginning many Bosniaks wanted a more centralized state – not surprisingly, since they were the plurality of Bosnia's population. A 1997 survey showed that 91 percent of Bosnia's Serbs and 84 percent of Bosnian Croats opposed a more unitary state while 98 percent of Bosniaks favored it. Haris Silajdzic, a Bosniak politician advocating greater centralization, said that "Bosnia and Herzegovina is now too strong to die, but too weak to function as a self-supporting state."[44]

Bosnia 81

Combating crime, corruption, and terrorism

In the late 1990s the international community, acting through the Office of the High Representative, tried to raise the federal Bosnian government's capacity to deal with crime, terrorism, and official corruption. After September 2001 the legal and institutional efforts intensified. The most important step was to centralize key agencies now responsible for operations on the entire territory of BiH. These included the State Court of Bosnia and Herzegovina and the Prosecutor's Office (established 2003), and the Intelligence and Security Agency of BiH, formed out of civilian intelligence institutions once operating in the Federation of Bosnia and Herzegovina and in the Respublika Srpska. The State Agency for Protection and Investigation (SIPA, established in 2004) is the police unit responsible for cracking down on organized crime and war crimes, terrorism, and human trafficking. SIPA has also a financial intelligence unit (FIU). State-level ministries of Defense and Security were also established. And the State Border Service of BiH was made responsible for establishing control along all Bosnian borders.

Under the Dayton Accords all foreign forces had to be withdrawn from Bosnia. President Izetbegović personally pledged to send the mujahedeen home but he consistently refused to repatriate those who had Bosnian citizenship. In the mid-2000s the BiH Ministry of Security established a Citizenship Review Commission to examine the status of about 1200 naturalized foreign nationals, mostly mujahedeen, who had gained citizenship during and after the war. The Commission withdrew citizenship from 612 of them and 15 officials were accused of illegally granting them citizenship.[45]

The effectiveness of these central institutions is still in doubt. Consider efforts to control fraud and corruption. Kemp says that the mono-ethnic nationalist parties of the entities

> have carved out ethnically dominated enclaves that are characterized by "phoney privatization, hollow reforms, rampant corruption and cronyism, smuggling of goods and people, gangsterism, and ethnic violence." Local government interests, business interests, and the agendas of ethnically based parties overlap to create a situation in which an elite from the titular majority uses public office to maintain so-called "national self-government," diverts public assets and sympathetic businesses (often dubiously privatized) to pay for patronage and support, and plays the ethnic card to legitimize this ethnically biased cartel.[46]

The Office of the High Representative established an anti-fraud unit in December 1997 to deal with this kind of pervasive problem. A specific example that galvanized official US concern came to light in 1999 in the Canton of Tuzla, where US forces were based. Investigators "found vast paint supplies bought for schools with no heat, cars purchased at twice their retail price, loans given to ruling SDA party favorites that were never repaid." The Canton's prime minister stole funds that were supposed to provide gravestones for the Srebrenica massacre victims.[47]

82 Militant Islam

In 1999 David Dlouhy, a US State Department advisor on Bosnia, diagnosed the roots of this kind of corruption in testimony before the US House of Representatives that parallels Kemp's analysis:

> During the war, the nationalist parties took advantage of the breakdown in government structure to gain control of large parts of the Bosnian economy. This economic power enabled, and continues to enable, the large mono-ethnic parties to sustain their party apparatus and exert their influence at all levels of society.[48]

The various Bosnian authorities relied on payment bureaus rather than banks to handle public finance, providing a major channel for fraud and diversion. Dlouhy also pointed out that the judicial sector and the police in the various entities were subject to political pressures that crippled their efforts to investigate and prosecute fraud and corruption. The federal-level agencies were supposed to deal more effectively with economic crimes, corruption, and organized crime. But a 2009 report by Transparency International, reviewing these and other anti-crime and corruption strategies in Bosnia, concluded that "both petty and grand forms of corruption are present in the country, affecting all sectors of society, including the judiciary, tax and custom administration, public utilities, procurement and privitisation schemes as well as all major political processes."[49] The report echoes Kemp's analysis and Dlouhy's testimony a decade earlier: the political parties remain at the heart of the problem. The survey-based 2009 Global Corruption Barometer showed that Bosnian citizens identify political parties as the institutions most affected by corruption, with a score of 4.4 on a 5-point (extremely corrupt) scale. And it cites the *Global Integrity 2007* report to the effect "that the justice system has not indicted any politically connected individuals or major crime figures."[50]

The Council of Ministers of Bosnia also created working groups to address terrorism by legal measures. The Criminal Code of Bosnia and Herzegovina criminalized terrorism and terrorism funding. Bosnia also adopted a law establishing procedures for detecting, preventing, and investigating money laundering and terrorism funding activities. It prescribes measures and identifies responsibilities for international cooperation.

Probably the most important step in instituting effective counter-terrorism policies is the move toward centralization of key state security institutions and agencies, often under international pressure. Thus the establishment of a single Bosnian army has been achieved. The defense reform initiative came from NATO and aims at merging rival ethnic armies into a single Bosnian force under one chain of command and financed from a unified budget. This is a radical departure from the terms of the 1995 Dayton Peace Accord, which gave each ethnic community the right to its own military.[51] A unified Bosnian army also brings Bosnia closer to NATO membership. In a similar vein, a recent EU police reform package aims to reorganize Bosnia's police and its administrative boundaries along non-ethnic lines. The new Bosnian police and army forces are expected to institute more efficient counter-terrorism policies and to impose tighter control over criminal activities.

In general, anti-terrorism and anti-crime measures undertaken so far have strengthened central state institutions. Yet there is still much to do in this respect, especially with regard to implementing laws and activating new institutions. Local analyst Edin Jahic points out that BiH is still a weak state with multiple semi-autonomous centers of power. In such an environment corruption flourishes and opportunities exist for those seeking to launch terrorist activities.[52]

Bosnia: Islamist terrorism's logistical base?[53]

We assess here the extent to which elements of the Islamist crime–terror network are in place in Bosnia and the threat they pose to European security.

The identity network of transnational Islam

Islam has become a central element in Bosniaks' national identity, for reasons analyzed above. Faith itself is not of itself a security threat. Xavier Bougarel concludes, at the end of a comparative assessment, that the emergence of self-consciously Muslim populations in the Balkans is not

> a danger or an anomaly, but a logical consequence of the collapse of the communist regimes and a sign of the integration of Balkan Muslim populations into European political modernity. It would be therefore unjustified and dangerous to present Balkan Islamic identity and its current evolution as a threat to Europe.[54]

The influence of internationally sponsored Islamist institutions in Bosnia is more problematic than Bougarel implies. The global Islamist movement has planted ideological supporters and networks in Bosnia that have been linked to terrorism both domestically and internationally. Of special concern is the Salafi-dominated area of central Bosnia, in the triangle between Zenica, Tuzla, and Sarajevo, where mosques, relief organizations, and other religious agencies provide alternative opportunities for Islamist mobilization. Some former mujahedeen who married local women populate villages in this region and form small societies closed to visitors.[55] Jasmin Merdan, a former Wahabi, who abandoned radical teaching of Islam, told the BBC in 2006 that

> After the war in Bosnia and Herzegovina, authority and leadership have been transferred from the Arabs to the local people and the number of the Wahhabis is growing slowly but surely. Unfortunately the Wahhabis are very active, they have good financial support, extremely strong publishing, and a strong sales network in Bosnia and abroad. On the other hand, the Islamic Community underestimates the Wahhabis and their strength.[56]

84 *Militant Islam*

International Islamists in post-Dayton Bosnia

The fate and potential future influence of the mujahedeen and their international supporters have been the focus of close attention from European and US intelligence agencies and the security services of the new Bosnian governments – that is, those of the Bosnian central government and the Bosnian–Croat federation.[57] A few former mujahedeen, probably no more than 100, have settled in Bosnia. More important are the networks and actions of radicalized Bosniaks who might be mobilized in future conflicts.

In Bosniak towns Islamists have reportedly harassed young people for improper dress and public behavior. A few plots and acts of violence attributable to Islamists have occurred, though less threatening than one might expect from some alarmist writings.[58] For example, in 2008 Bosnian police arrested five terror suspects, Bosnian citizens who had obtained arms to carry out attacks on unspecified targets.[59] In December 2010 a police station in Bogojno was bombed, killing one policeman, and six local men said to be Wahabists were arrested for the attack.[60]

New Islamist organizations continue to be established, for example, the Muslim Brotherhood – an offspring of the Egyptian Muslim Brotherhood – that was set up in 2002 in Sarajevo and targets the families of the Muslim returnees.[61] Kvadrat (Quadrant) is a Saudi-supported organization established in Sarajevo in 1995 to care for war orphans. Its base of operations in the mid-2000s was in rural Bosnia where Iranian intelligence officers reportedly trained its young cadres in militant Islam. One of its members was killed in Chechyna, several others arrested while transiting Turkey, evidence that it is linked to the global jihadist movement.[62]

Anti-terrorist and anti-criminal measures undertaken by Bosnian and international authorities after 9/11 demonstrate both the potential for terror-crime linkages in Bosnia and the capacity of authorities to act against them. On 17 October 2001 the Embassies of the United States and the United Kingdom in Sarajevo were closed down under threat of terrorist attacks. The Supreme Court of BiH issued an arrest warrant for those suspected of planning bomb attacks on the two embassies, and five suspects of North African origin were arrested. Four were Algerians with Bosnian citizenship. One, Bensayah Belcacem, was identified as a high-ranking figure in al-Qaeda and as having personal connections to bin Laden; he also was on the payroll of the Saudi-financed Islamic Balkan Center in Zenica. At the same time the Ministry of Interior revoked the citizenship of the four naturalized Algerians. On 17 January 2002 the Supreme Court released them from custody, a continuation of a long-standing pattern in post-Dayton Bosnia: individuals arrested for alleged participation in Islamist terrorism all too often were released, or simply disappeared. In this instance the detainees were quietly handed over to the NATO Stabilization Force, then transferred to the US military detention facility in Guantanamo Bay. A local Islamist group, the Active Islamic Youth, mounted several demonstrations in Sarajevo against the deportation of the six North Africans.[63] This case is indicative of the extent of radicalization of local Islamic groups and linkages between local Islamic agencies and global terrorist networks.[64]

Bosnia 85

Containing the financial networks of militant Islam

Islamic charities suspected of financing terrorist activities have been shut down. In the 1990s the Saudi-based and -financed al Haramain Islamic Foundation had branches in 55 countries and annual expenditure of $57 million. Its objectives included provision of food and clothing to Muslim refugees and orphans; building of mosques and Islamic centers; training imams; distributing Muslim literature and establishing correct Islamic doctrines. Inevitably some of its funds went to jihadists. Measures against its overseas branches were undertaken by the US and Saudi Arabia, which dissolved the Foundation in June 2004. The Bosnian branch of this organization was reportedly tied to al-Gama'at Islamiya, an Egyptian group that worked closely with al-Qaeda.[65] A Bosnian raid on a local branch of al Haramain Islamic Foundation uncovered tapes calling for attacks on peacekeepers in Bosnia.

Several Bosnia-linked Islamist associations are on the US anti-terrorist black list for allegedly financing terrorist activities. The Bosnian Finance Police and the Bosnian Interior Ministry have been asked by Kuwait to provide information on the Revival of Islamic Heritage Society, a charity with possible links to terrorists. The charity was banned in Pakistan and Afghanistan for having provided financial support for the Taliban regime and al-Qaeda.

The Bosnian police in 2002 also raided the Bosnian offices of the Benevolence International Foundation (BIF), finding weapons, military manuals, a fraudulent passport, and photos of bin Laden.[66] A raid on the Sarajevo office of the Saudi High Commission for Relief netted anti-Semitic and anti-American materials, as well as photos of US military installations.[67] Officials observe that Islamist networks establish new agencies soon after a branch is shut down. Thus Vazir – the al Haramain successor organization – was shut down and the Global Relief Fund was closed down as well.

The raids and arrests carried out by Bosnian authorities in Sarajevo are evidence that the activities and financing of militant Islamists are closely scrutinized. Our own sense is that international funding for Islamist causes in Bosnia has been decoupled from support for jihad and the mujahedeen. Ideological support for jihad can be found in Bosnia but on the margins, and cut off from international funding.

Conclusion

To recapitulate, the Bosnian civil war and the arms embargo imposed on Yugoslavia created conditions for the establishment of alliances of convenience between the political and the criminal. Islamic charities channeled funds to an international cadre of mujahedeen who fought on the side of the Bosnian Muslims, and some of their funds were diverted to private purposes and officials in ways that, in other times and places, would be indictable crimes. Since 1995 branches of the Islamist financial networks have given substantial support to the institutions and proponents of conservative Islam but are barred in law and practise from supporting

86 *Militant Islam*

jihadists. A few militants in Bosnia either host or are linked to al-Qaeda – connected terrorist cells. The planting and funding of militant Islam in a European country is a potentially terrorist enterprise, and there is always a risk that some funds for jihadists might escape the attention of security agencies.

The major factors that condition terrorism-crime interaction were present in Bosnia. First, Bosnia experienced violent armed conflict. Second, opportunities for illicit business activities, including arms trafficking and money transfers to parties in conflict, emerged early in the civil war. Third, a trans-state identity network has taken root among Bosnian Muslims. The Bosnian civil war attracted material support and mujahedeen fighters from the Islamic world, which led to fusion between the transnational Islamist network and the indigenous network, that of the Bosnian Islamic Community. This trans-state network includes well-funded mosques, madrassas, political organizations, and publication programs that advocate Salafist (or Wahabist) doctrines. It also includes a few former mujahedeen fighters and is potentially conducive to trans-state mobilization by jihadist groups. But this could only happen if armed conflict was to recur among Bosnia's communal groups– and as Bosnia moves toward membership in the European Union and NATO, this is ever less likely.

Bosnian Islamist communities and organizations may provide an occasional rest-stop or "gateway" for trans-state militants moving between Europe and the Middle East. The handful of mujahedeen with Bosnian identity documents who have been killed or detained in Islamist wars elsewhere, for example, Algeria and Chechnya, are either veterans of the Bosnian civil war or Bosniak Islamists recruited into the international jihadist network. So the international political-criminal linkage of Bosnian Islamists has been sharply curtailed, and is exclusively ideologically driven. It contrasts with the trans-border Albanian and Kurdish networks that we characterize in chapters 2 and 3 as political-criminal hybrids, and the state-centric Serbian crime–terror network described in chapter 6.

The most problematic legacy of the Bosnian civil war is the practise of graft and corruption by leaders of the communal-based mono-parties that govern each of the Bosnian entities. The practises of favoritism and diversion are not just a normative legacy of the war because the parties, Bosniak, Serb, and Croat, rely on them to maintain their dominant political positions. They are not a regional security threat, but they certainly are a challenge to European efforts to introduce transparency and the rule of law in Bosnia.

5 Greed, grievance, and political Islam in the Algerian revolutionary war of the 1990s[1]

Islam and Islamists played quite a different role in the revolutionary war that began in 1990 between Islamists and the military-dominated government in Algeria than in the Bosnian civil war.[2] In Bosnia money and mujahedeen came from the outset from international Islamist and jihadist networks. In Algeria the Islamist challenge and its financing were indigenous. Only late in the conflict, when the jihadists had been largely defeated, did their survivors form an alliance with the al-Qaeda network. The issues that generated armed conflict in Algeria, the dynamics of crime–terror networks, and the outcomes are analyzed here.

The Algerian revolutionary war has been analyzed from various perspectives. Proponents of the US-led war on terror see it as part of the West's larger contest with militant Islam. Miriam Lowi uses it to evaluate an empirically derived theory of civil war causation that emphasizes economic opportunities and resources.[3] Stathis Kalyvas challenges the assumption that rebel massacres of Algerian civilians were "senseless" and "random butchery," and shows instead, using micro-evidence, that they are best understood as part of a rational strategy to punish and deter villagers in contested areas who did not support them.[4] Two Norwegian researchers examine the Islamists' support network among the Algerian diaspora in France and develop a model of the circumstances in which militants choose to use terror tactics against the "sanctuary" country.[5]

This chapter, following the Unholy Alliances framework, explores factors conducive to the emergence of hybrid terrorist and criminal networks. Identity networks provide a setting for easy collaboration between criminal and terrorist groups. Ongoing armed conflicts create opportunities that such networks can exploit. In Algeria we show how political networks based on Islamic identity provided the rationale and organizational basis for opposition to a corrupt and autocratic state. Islamist doctrines and a mix of economic and political grievances together were the source of justifications and recruits for guerrilla and terrorist action. Both rebels and the regime had ample material motivations and opportunities. The regime aimed to protect the privileges and illicit fortunes acquired by its elite and their clients from their monopoly of oil revenues and control of large sectors of the economy. The rebels participated in widespread criminal activity within Algeria and internationally that for many became an end in itself. The international dimension is complex: the jihadists' support and financial networks

88 *Greed, grievance and political Islam*

in France were disrupted in the 1990s by French security counter-measures, but since 2000 efforts have been made to rebuild their European networks, and the Algerian jihadists have joined a regional network of Islamist militants linked to al-Qaeda. We preface our analysis with a brief overview of the conflict.[6]

Background to Islamist revolution

Algeria gained independence from France in 1962 after a devastating eight-year war fought by the National Liberation Front (FLN) and its military counterpart, the Army of National Liberation (ANL).[7] Veterans of the independence war dominated the single-party state and the military and intelligence services that ruled Algeria through 1989. Others were notables who dominated local politics and enterprise. Oil and gas exports provided 95 per cent of the country's exports and more than half of government revenues. As in other autocratic rentier states, government control of oil revenues, as well as import trade and large public enterprises, fueled corruption and clientelism. Members of the political and military elite and those who benefitted from their patronage – an estimated 600,000 to 800,000 – prospered.[8] For most others unemployment and poverty were pervasive from the 1960s onward. The government's socialist policies ensured that some benefits, including subsidized basic commodities, trickled down to the rapidly growing urban population. In the "black years" of the 1980s, however, oil revenues declined and a creeping retreat from socialism, partly in response to the need to service the country's huge international debt, led to increases in prices of commodities and greater hardship for the poor. In October 1988 major riots in Algiers and elsewhere, initiated by students and unemployed youth, openly and violently challenged the legitimacy of the regime.

The FLN government had been led since 1979 by Colonel, now President Chadli Benjedid. He was a cautious reformer with a power base in the military security apparatus. The riots were suppressed but Benjedid also pursued economic reforms, and opened up the political system by allowing the formation of multiple political parties and scheduling elections for 1990–2 The Islamic Salvation Front (FIS) became the most potent opposition force because its Islamic values and demands for economic reform and local investment of oil revenues appealed to both urban and rural people. Its leaders were Abassi Madani, an older cleric who attracted the support of Islamist notables, entrepreneurs, shopkeepers, and new college graduates; and a charismatic young preacher, Ali Belhadj, who appealed to the unemployed urban youth known as *hittistes* (wall-leaners).

The FIS scored electoral victories in local council elections in 1990 and formed Islamist governments in many communes, especially in the poorer districts of Algiers. FIS candidates also did very well in the first round of parliamentary elections in 1991, and senior generals, fearing an Islamic takeover of the national government, cancelled the second round and established a military-dominated government, the High Committee of the State (HCE). Thousands of FIS members were arrested, including its leaders, and the organization itself was outlawed in 1992. Armed groups proliferated outside the FIS framework. They rejected the reformist approach of the

FIS in favor of a jihadist doctrine that justified war against the government and all who supported it. In 1992 some established an umbrella organization, the Armed Islamic Group (GIA). Cells affiliated with the GIA carried out a loosely coordinated but ever-more-brutal campaign against officials, the army and police, their families, schools and teachers, "anti-Islamist" professionals, civilians, and foreigners. In a challenge to the GIA's total war the FIS established its own armed wing, the Islamic Salvation Army (AIS), which was more selective in its choices of targets but was caught up in a war of reprisals with the more militant GIA.[9]

The government responded to Islamist attacks with massive repression and gross human rights abuses. The campaign was directed by military hard-liners who also were implicated in assassinations of proponents of reform and accommodation with the Islamists – including President Mohammed Boudiaf. He had been the military's choice to head the HCE in 1992 but was too vigorous in investigating elite corruption. By 1993–4 the guerrillas numbered an estimated 27,000.[10] Violence peaked in the mid-1990s in a series of GIA massacres of civilians who were suspected of defecting to the government forces, which were gradually regaining control of suburban and rural areas. Some jihadists defected from the GIA and disbanded in the mid-1990s. The GIA and an affiliated fighting group called a truce and disarmed in 1997. The government, led by elected Presidents General Liamine Zeroul (1994–8) and Abdelaziz Bouteflika (1999–present) encouraged this process, most importantly through Bouteflika's "civil reconciliation" program whose centerpiece was a general amnesty for FIS and GIA members.

By 2000 Islamist terrorists had been reduced by military action and defections to less than 1000. In 2007 Algerian security services reportedly killed, wounded, or captured 1100 jihadists and, in 2008, another 1000.[11] The GIA's brutality and killings of rival Islamists discredited it in the eyes of almost all Algerians, including its former supporters, and prompted international Islamist groups, including al-Qaeda, to withdraw their support. In response to the same conditions a new group, the Salafist Group for Preaching and Combat (GSPC), broke away from the GIA in 1998 and focused its attacks mainly on members of the security forces. Informal cooperation with the al-Qaeda network led to a merger in 2006 that created a rebadged terrorist organization, Al-Qaeda in the Islamic Maghreb (AQIM). During the 2001–10 decade AQIM, formerly GSPC, formerly GIA, carried out a series of deadly attacks in Algeria using improvised explosive devices (IEDs) and, for a brief period in 2007–8, suicide bombings. As of 2011 the AQIM's main bases are in the Sahara where it engages in, and taxes, extensive trans-border smuggling and kidnapping foreigners for ransom. Some AQIM activity may continue in the Atlas Mountains where, in the recent past, it raised significant funds by kidnapping wealthy Algerians and exacting taxes from commercial activity. Attempts to revitalize the jihadists through international connections are described in more detail in the final section of this chapter.

Identity networks and armed conflict

Algerian politics and the conflicts driving armed conflict are based on identity networks that are more complex than a simplistic division between modernists

90 *Greed, grievance and political Islam*

and Islamists. There is a strong secular tendency in Algerian society based on the urban middle class of businessmen, professionals, officials, and army officers. They speak French as well as Arabic, sometimes better, and have long been attuned to French cultural and political life. They are the basis of civil society organizations that emulate those of Western democracies, including associations of journalists, intellectuals, feminists, and human rights activists.[12] Islamist organizations like the FIS also followed the associational model of political action, but were sharply critical of secularists for their lack of close adherence to Islam and their orientation to French culture. To call one's opponent a supporter of the *hizbfrancia* (party of France) was a bitter term of opprobrium in Algerian political dialogue of the war era.

The Umma, the community of believers, is a potent source of social capital in the Islamic world, and in Algeria has been the basis of recurring political opposition to colonial and FLN rule. The faithful, congregating in their mosques and following their preachers, constitute a network of people tied together by common identity, beliefs, and cultural practises that can provide the basis for entrepreneurship, charitable activities, or political movements depending on the time and circumstances. The political uses of Islam are particularly important when Muslim communities confront non-believers. Local resistance to French colonial rule, established in 1830 when the Ottoman governors were forcefully ousted, was always justified by appeals to Islam. Soon after 1830 a 25-year-old man, Emir Abd el-Kadr Al-Jazareiri, proclaimed himself commander of the faithful and called for a jihad against the unbelievers in a resistance that lasted until 1847.[13] The best arable lands were gradually taken over by French and other European settlers – 35,000 by 1839, 430,000 by 1886. In 1871 a local leader, hitherto loyal to French officials, proclaimed a jihad against colonial rule. Though 800,000 answered his call, the rebellion was easily repressed. In its aftermath, "Muslims became sullen and resentful as Algerian society turned in on itself. . . . Algerians found solace in religion as Islam came to be regarded as a bulwark, a safe haven that could not be overcome by colonialism."[14]

Two strands of twentieth-century political opposition to colonial rule emphasized combinations of Islamic and nationalist doctrine. The Association of Algerian Ulema (AAU), founded in 1931, was based on the reassertion of an Islamic and Arab identity in opposition to European power and culture. Its founder was a theologian, Sheik Ben Badis, who famously said "Islam is my religion, Arabic is my language and Algeria is my country."[15] Its doctrine is a direct antecedent of the core beliefs and claims of the FIS. Second was the Etoil Nord-Africaine (ENA), established in the mid-1920s by an Algerian World War I veteran among the hundred thousand-plus immigrant Algerian workers in the Paris region. The ENA seems a polar opposite to the AAU, calling for immediate independence of the Algerian people and radical political reforms, from press freedom to nationalization of industry. Yet ENA also stressed the centrality of Islam and Arabic to Algerian national identity. The successors of the AAU and ENA, including the FIS and the Algerian labor movement, the Union Général des Travailleurs Algériens, have followed the associational model of political action. Both tendencies joined the FLN's war for independence; both were among the groups that contended for seats in local government and the National Assembly in the elections of 1990 and 1991.

Islamic doctrine did not provide a unitary basis for political action in Algeria. The Algerian constitution, formulated by the FLN government after independence, declares Islam to be the state's religion and prohibits government "practices that are contrary to the Islamic ethics." It also bans religious political parties and establishes a High Islamic Council. The government requires the study of Islam in public schools, and from 1971 to the late 1980s the government approved the construction of mosques, appointed imams, and asserted the right to review their sermons.[16] In other words, the FLN government legitimized itself by claiming to be Islamic but at the same time sought to control the expression of Islam. One of Bendjedid's reforms was to relax controls on the mosques, leading to the proliferation of new mosques and the ascendance of imams and sermons that were sharply critical of society and government. Ali Belhadj, later co-founder of the FIS, was one of them: his Friday sermons in a poor district of Algiers called for jihad to re-Islamize Algeria "by ridding it of the intoxicating Western evils of communism, socialism, liberalism and feminism."[17]

Most Islamic activism in independent Algeria was reformist, aimed at resisting the rising secularism of state and society by reaffirming the cultural tenets of Islam. Reformers of the Al Qiyam (values) movement formulated "A Charter for an Islamic State" at Algiers University in 1982. Another strand of reformist demands, led by Mahfoudh Nahnah, "deprecated the leftist proclivities of the regime and the inequities fostered under the banner of socialism."[18] The FIS was established during the brief period of sweeping political liberalization that followed the 1988 riots. It sought to incorporate in one political movement "the totality of Islamist expression: militants and moderates, clergy and laymen, young and old." But it never issued a detailed economic program and its political program was inherently contradictory. Abbas Madani, its older co-founder, emphasized the democratic process, invoking power rotation and pluralism as means to development. His younger partner, Belhaj, stridently rejected democracy and pluralism as Western instruments that undermined the cohesion of the Umma. The radical wing would only concede that elections might be the means by which Islamists could come to power.[19]

Even before the generals cancelled elections and assumed direct power in January 1992 some militant Islamists, within and outside the FIS, believed that only armed struggle would defeat the regime. Several jihadist groups formed in 1991. One was composed mainly of "Afghans," Algerians who had fought in Afghanistan against the Soviets. Between 1986 and 1989 between 2000 and 3000 Algerians, recruited from poor neighborhoods and in mosques, trained and fought in Afghanistan. Their commitment to fight for Islam and experience with guerrilla warfare made them ideal recruits for the jihadist groups. Another group, the Islamic Movement Army (MIA), incorporated survivors of a failed guerrilla campaign led by Mustafa Bouyali in the early 1980s.

At first the jihadists operated mainly in Greater Algiers where they took control of the local councils of large districts dominated by FIS supporters such as

92   *Greed, grievance and political Islam*

the southeast suburbs of Les Eucalyptus, El Harrach, and Baraki. In November 1991 the presence of a growing rural maquis was signaled when an armed Islamist group, led by a veteran of the Afghan war, attacked a police post near the Tunisian border, killing three reservists and capturing an arsenal of weapons. Between late 1992 and mid-1994 most armed groups, including some affiliated with FIS, joined forces in the Armed Islamic Group (GIA). The GIA distinguished itself from the FIS not only by rejecting electoral politics but also by refusing any compromise with moderate Muslims, who it condemned as apostates. The GIA leaders regarded jihad as an Islamist imperative rather than a strategy.

There also is a significant ethnic division in Algerian society between the Arab majority and the Berber minority, an estimated 20 per cent of the population, many of whom live in the mountainous Kabylia region, east and southeast of Algiers. They are the pre-Arab people of North Africa who share a distinct language and culture, which are more central to their identity than Islam. The Kabylia Berbers were favored during French colonial rule and are more likely to be secular than other rural Algerians. They also played a substantial role in the independence war and the FLN governments that held power after 1962. There were major anti-government riots in Kabylia in 1980 and again in 2001. The Berbers' main political concerns are autonomy and promotion of their own culture and Tamazight language, and they have little sympathy for the Islamist emphasis on Arabization, much less the jihadist doctrine of the GIA and its successor, al-Qaeda in the Islamic Maghreb (AQIM).[20]

Greed and grievance: the political economy of the Algerian revolution

The eruption of opposition to the FLN government, signaled by the riots of October 1988 and the explosive growth of the FIS, had economic origins. On the one hand, government elites and their clients prospered. On the other, Algeria had one of the highest birthrates in the world, more than 3 per cent per annum, and its cities were home to hundreds of thousands of unemployed and marginally employed young men. The official unemployment rate was 16 per cent in 1980, 20 per cent in 1990, and 30 per cent in 2000.[21] Many survived by petty crime or worked in the parallel economy; many were susceptible to Islamic appeals to challenge a corrupt regime.

The corruption of privileged Algerians was based on the government's unchecked political authority and its control of revenues from the oil and gas fields in the Sahara. In Joffee's words, "because Algeria depended on oil and gas revenues . . . both to support state service provision and to fund development, the elites were also able to capture control of rent for personal advantage (notably through over-invoicing of imports)."[22] Leading generals who had amassed personal fortunes were identified by an exiled group of Algerian officers in 2000. Among them were Mohammed Mediene, chief of the general staff during the civil war, with $62 million, and Smain Lamari, director of counter-espionage and internal security, with $45 million, both sums being held in Swiss banks.[23]

A lucrative state-aligned private sector also flourished whose firms paid for authorization to engage in consumer production, or obtained goods from the state sector for resale.[24] In the 1980s, when the government of Chadli Bendje did began to liberalize the import trade sector, a parallel economy emerged. Martinez shows in an essay on the wartime economy, "New Ways to Make Big Money," how political insecurity combined with privatization provided risky opportunities for local notables, entrepreneurs, traders, government officials, and jihadist emirs to accumulate wealth.[25] Dillman summarizes the macro-economic effects: "Between 1970 and 1998, the private sector changed from a pariah into an organized force consulted by policymakers and finally into a partner of rent-seeking ruling elites."[26]

The economic reforms also contributed to the pauperization of ordinary Algerians who lost jobs as state enterprises were sold off or closed. Unemployed youth also moved into the parallel economy, gaining criminal skills and connections. According to Joffee,

> As Algerian migrants abroad were able to import goods back into the country and as unemployment grew, parallel trade based on smuggled goods as well as on access to state supplies increased, creating the *trabendo* phenomenon, whereby unemployed youth were drawn into the parallel economy's distribution circuits.[27]

By the 1990s, according to Lowi, the parallel economy accounted for 30 to 70 percent of Algeria's Gross Domestic Product.[28]

Opportunities for crime: financing the Islamist movement

Economic corruption and crime were endemic in Algeria, as shown above. The parallel economy provided social and economic networks that readily evaded state control. It provided the context, the justifications, and the networks in which Islamist reformers and jihadists pursued economic gain to fund their activities and sometimes as an end in itself. From its founding in March 1989 until its suppression in August 1992, the FIS seems to have relied mainly on a voluntary "Islamic tax." In 1990–1 it established "Islamic souks," that is, markets that operated on Islamic principles. As a widely supported grassroots organization, tied closely to the mosques, it depended heavily on the voluntary contributions of congregations and local adherents – the same people who helped finance the spate of new, unofficial mosques built in the late 1980s.

The Muslim diaspora in Europe was and is a potential source of support for political Islamists in Algeria and elsewhere. Throughout the twentieth century emigration to France, and also to other southern Mediterranean countries, was an important safety valve for unemployed Algerians. By 1974, when the Algerian and French governments both officially ended migration, many long-settled Muslims had become assimilated citizens, or *beurs* in French political discourse (*Arabe*, the French word for Arabs, pronounced backwards). By 1991 the Muslim population

94 Greed, grievance and political Islam

of France, which continued to be fed by illegal immigration, was an estimated 4 million. Surveys at the time suggested that only about 15 per cent were observant, and a tenth of these – perhaps 50,000 people – considered themselves supporters of political Islam.[29] At first FIS was not much interested in the Algerian diaspora, on grounds that immigration was temporary. Few Algerians, it was reasoned, would be able to live long "under a non-Islamic regime in 'a reviled and sinful country'." Nonetheless, after winning local elections in Algeria in 1990 the FIS joined with the Algerian Brotherhood in France (FAF), established a few years before by Algerian students, to build support, provide a place of refuge, and collect funds. FAF's weekly news bulletin reported news of struggle from Algeria in ever more strident tones. By 1993, as the civil war entered its most brutal phrase, FAF newsletters began to justify armed operations and executions of civilians, intellectuals, journalists, and foreigners. The French government had by now aligned itself with the embattled Algerian regime and banned all FAF publications.[30]

A French scholar, Gilles Kepel, concluded that FAF had contributed to the radicalization of Muslim youth in France. By extolling jihad in Algeria against the evils of the Algerian regime, secularism, and France, "it passed on to French-Maghrebi youth a far more radical and uncompromising ideology and worldview than the rest of the Islamist movement had embraced in the early 1990s."[31] There is no evidence that the FAF provided any significant financial support to the FIS in Algeria, but it did something more important: it laid the groundwork for the radicalization of some of the diaspora in ways that the GIA and its successors would seek to exploit in the future.

Islamist terrorism: banditry and murder in the name of God

The main jihadist organizations in Algeria in the mid-1990s were the Armed Islamic Group (GIA) and its FIS-supported rival, the Islamic Salvation Army (AIS). In principle the AIS regarded jihad as a means to the establishment of an Islamic state, in other words, a means to a political end. Like the FIS itself, most AIS leaders were prepared to negotiate. The GIA, on the other hand, regarded jihad as an Islamic imperative, an end in itself, as emphasized in the mantra included in its communiqués: "No dialogue, no cease-fire, no reconciliation." In the decade-long conflict between these principles and the state's repressive responses between 100,000 and 200,000 Algerians died, out of a population that numbered about 30 million when the war began. For the tens of thousands of Algerians killed by jihadists between 1992 and 2000 the doctrinal reasons for their deaths scarcely mattered.

GIA and FIS, and other jihadist groups outside their umbrella organizations, had numerous local commands headed by so-called emirs who operated with some autonomy. Despite shifting alliances, leadership rivalries, and doctrinal differences they shared a fundamental commitment to violent jihad against the Algerian regime and those who supported it, directly or indirectly.[32] The ultimate objective was the creation of a sharia state, one governed on Islamist principles, a goal that was widely supported by Muslims elsewhere: "Islamic leaders and opposition parties all over the Muslim world were riveted by the unfolding of the Algerian conflict, with each camp expecting a boost from the success of whichever faction it supported."[33]

The financial basis of the jihadist organizations built on familiar traditions and skills. In 1990–1 local FIS councils and their supporters had been able to control petty crime in the communes they controlled. After the FIS was banned in 1992, however, various jihadist groups – the MIA, GIA, and others – established themselves in the FIS communes. They exploited the parallel economy for financing and recruitment, "linking up with up *trabendo* networks and engaging in smuggling and racketeering."[34] Police largely withdrew from these urban districts, although many informers remained. Petty crime increased substantially after the regime released ordinary criminals from prison in the early 1990s – 6000 of them, according to one of Martinez's sources. Many returned to the poor districts from which they had come, resuming careers of theft and robbery. The jihadist emirs killed some and "persuaded" others to convert to militant Islam, thus gaining recruits with criminal skills.[35]

The jihadists turned these criminal skills to extortion from the local businessmen. They became racketeers "who paraded around in their neighbourhoods, Kalashnikov in hand."[36] Many had *trabendo* experience and either continued smuggling consumer goods to finance the jihadists or extorted funds from the traders. The victims of extortion were mostly the small merchants and petty bourgeoisie who formerly had paid Islamic taxes to the FIS. "The GIA activists began to press these groups for funds. . . . The movement that acclaimed piety and professed to create a virtuous order had turned into a violent street gang."[37] As a consequence the jihadists alienated many of the devout urban middle classes.

Jihadist emirs, especially those in rural and mountainous areas, also relied on raids of military posts and armed robberies of financial and commercial institutions. This was soon supplemented by "extortion and looting of various forms: pillaging commercial traffic, 'taxing' local populations, and seizing property (land, livestock, etc.)."[38] Martinez provides a vivid description of jihadist extortion from a typical target, the owner of a large transport company, whose 50 trucks carried consumer goods and raw materials in the interior of the country.

> When I saw Islamists demanding 500,000 dinars from me, with the threat of destroying one of my vehicles every day, I had to pay up, after the complete destruction of two lorries and the disappearance of a third. I thought I was rid of them, but no, new ones came to demand double that sum, while my drivers passed on to me letters from Islamists in the maquis demanding one third of all goods carried, threatening to seize my vehicles otherwise. It was too much for me, my drivers were afraid. As I no longer knew who to pay, I closed my company temporarily; they came to burn my vehicles and kill two drivers.[39]

Not all entrepreneurs in the interior were put out of business by extortion; some were able to reach accommodations with local emirs and continue their operations.

96   *Greed, grievance and political Islam*

The jihadists also profited from the pervasive smuggling operations that bypassed the officially sanctioned import trade, either by taxing the smugglers or operating them directly. And they taxed legitimate trade: Lowi reports that the transport of building materials between Constantine and Tebessa required a stamped permission slip, obtained by paying a fee to the regional emir of the GSPC, a successor to the GIA.[40] In effect the jihadists took over sectors of the long-established parallel economy and financed their operations much like the Algerian government itself: by a combination of operating and extracting rents from a wide range of economic activity. In Lowi's interpretation, these fundraising activities were so successful that for many militants "the interest in capturing the state gave way to looting it and, eventually, to holding the state at bay so as to focus squarely on gaining and maintaining access to resources."[41]

Yet the trajectory of jihadist terror seems to have been driven more by ideological and strategic differences than a quest for personal enrichment. Initially the jihadists' main targets were the agents of the government that had cancelled elections and banned the FIS. The army and police, numbering about 450,000, were prime targets. A spectacular example was a March 1993 attack by a GIA unit on army barracks at Bourghezoul that killed 41 people, 18 of them soldiers. Government officials were assassinated both in the cities and in rural areas where jihadists secured enclaves that were free from government control. By the summer of 1993, according to Evans and Phillips, "one blue-uniformed police officer was being assassinated every few hours and as many as ten a night."[42]

The jihadists at the outset were led by men most of whom combined Islamic education with military experience in Afghanistan. They provided sophisticated justifications for jihadist strategy. When the GIA was joined by a number of other groups in May 1994, these common principles were agreed upon:

- To abide by the Book, the *sunna*, and the *salafiyya* tradition.
- No dialogue, no cease-fire, no reconciliation, and no security and guarantee with the apostate regime.
- Jihad is an Islamic imperative until judgment day.
- The GIA is the only legitimate organizational framework for jihad in Algeria.
- All holy fighters must join the GIA.[43]

As the first generation of leaders were killed, captured, or defected the GIA's Islamist principles were reinterpreted by new leaders who had little education or knowledge of Islamic doctrine, but had proven their skills as terrorists. In principle they were salafists, committed to the principles of traditional Islam.[44] In practice the GIA relied on the spiritual guidance of a London-based cleric, Abu Qatada al-Filistini, for religious rulings that justified their actions. Abu Qatada was one of a cluster of radical Islamists who took advantage of British tolerance to establish what some called Londonistan, which flourished in the 1990s. The GIA published its newsletter *Al-Ansar* there. The Finsbury Park Mosque, built in 1994, became the center of Islamist preaching and recruitment of jihadists, and a refuge or transit stop for militants throughout the Islamic world. Another militant preacher at Finsbury Mosque, Abu Hamza al-Masri, succeeded Abu Qatada as the GIA's spiritual reference.[45]

The rulings of the militant clerics were used by the GIA to justify killing an ever-expanding circle of military families, journalists, intellectuals, medical doctors, teachers, and foreigners. Intellectuals and journalists were murdered because they were godless secularists. Teachers and schools were attacked because students were taught to support the state and to staff its institutions. Foreigners were targeted as a warning to countries that supported the Algerian government.

The most vicious manifestation of this tendency was the wave of massacres of civilians that began in 1996 and peaked in 1997. They occurred at night when bands of armed men attacked villages and small towns.

> The attackers broke into houses and killed families in their entirety (including babies and the elderly) in a most brutal way, . . . In some cases, corpses were mutilated, houses set on fire, and women abducted to be raped and then killed.[46]

Kalyvas lists 87 such massacres between August 1996 and December 1998 in which more than 2500 reportedly were killed, victims numbering from ten or less to over 200.[47] Journalists rarely were given access to the villages, but an exception was made in the case of Bentalha, 12 miles south of Algiers, which was attacked by 150 or so armed men on 22–23 September. The attackers targeted two neighborhoods and used lists to select households. Soldiers in barracks a half-kilometer away did not intervene, and 400 villagers were murdered.[48] Analysts agree that the GIA carried out most if not all massacres and specifically targeted local opponents, including members of the security forces, the local militias known as "patriots," and informants; supporters of rival political groups, including FIS and AIS; and former supporters who were defecting. Moreover, as Kalyvas points out, most occurred in the "triangle of death" south of Algiers where the GIA was trying to counter the government's increasingly successful efforts to reestablish control.[49]

The massacres were so horrifying to most Algerians, the Western media, and Islamists elsewhere that they raised questions about the complicity of the Algerian government. Insiders described the efforts of the army's security service, the DRS, to infiltrate the jihadist groups. Militants who had been captured, interrogated, and tortured by the DRS sometimes were "turned" and rejoined their groups as informants or agents provocateurs.[50] So for sympathizers of political Islam it was possible to think that the GIA had become an instrument of the Algerian government whose excesses aimed to discredit the Islamists.

Whether or not some massacres were abetted by government agents, by 1997 the GIA had explicitly endorsed the principle of *takfir*, the excommunication of all of Algerian society. The principle justified the massacres and, in fact, the targeting of any individual or group that was not part of the GIA.[51] Among other acts of violence consistent with this doctrine were GIA assassinations of many other jihadists including leaders of the AIS. Already in 1995 GIA attacks on the AIS

98 *Greed, grievance and political Islam*

claimed 60 lives, including – according to FIS – 40 emirs.[52] The GIA's descent into unrestrained violence "gradually cut it off from any possible base within Algerian society, and even within the ranks of the young urban poor from whom its support had originally come."[53] The civilian massacres and the attacks on rival jihadists also prompted leading Islamists outside Algeria to withdraw their support from the GIA. In Kepel's judgment, "by losing the war on the ground, in an orgy of unspeakable atrocities, the GIA drastically weakened Islamism as a whole, not only in Algeria but in the rest of the Muslim world."[54]

International rebirth: Jihad in Algeria since 2000

The conventional wisdom is that by 2000 the Algerian government had won the war against Islamists. Politically, the amnesties that began in the mid-1990s led tens of thousands of fighters to return to civilian life, 8000 of them in January 2000 alone.[55] Many one-time supporters of the FIS participated in electoral politics where their interests were represented by new Islamic parties such as Hamas, whose presidential candidate, Mahfoud Nahnah, with 25 percent of the vote, came in second to President Zeroual in the November 1995 elections. The military and police reestablished effective control over most of the country, and most jihadists who had not defected were killed or captured. Low-level guerrilla war and terrorism continued, but in no way threatened the state. Economic liberalization opened significant entrepreneurial opportunities, as shown above, though it had little effect on the economic status of the urban poor. The principal gain for most people was simply the reestablishment of security and order.

Moreover the government had not won the ideological war. In 1998 the Salafist Group for Preaching and Combat (GSPC) broke away from the GIA, dismayed by the indiscriminate violence that had destroyed its credibility among devout Algerians and Islamists elsewhere. The GSPC was led by veteran jihadists, who established or renewed contacts with the international financial and political support networks of militant Islam. Contacts with al-Qaeda had been initiated in 1993 when Osama bin Laden reportedly provided $40,000 to GIA jihadists who rejected compromise with the regime.[56] In 2003, five years after the GSPC broke from the GIA, the GSPC's new leader, Nabil Sahraoui, sought an alliance with al-Qaeda and aligned itself with the global jihadist agenda.[57] After the US invasion of Iraq the GSPC was instrumental in sending North African insurgents to Iraq. And in September 2006 al-Qaeda's al-Zawahiri announced a formal alliance: "the GSPC has joined Qa'idat al-Jihad, under the blessing and mercy of Allah. We pray to Allah that this event would be a thorn in the neck of the American and French crusaders and their allies, and an arrow in the heart of the French traitors and apostates."[58] A few months later GSPC renamed itself al-Qaeda in the Islamic Maghreb (AQIM). The wave of suicide bombings in 2007 and other terror attacks in 2008 demonstrated that AQIM remained a serious threat.

The larger strategy of the GSPC/AQIM exemplifies what Kepel calls the third phase of militant Islam. Abu Musab al-Suri's *Call to Global Islamic Resistance* (posted online in 2004, in Arabic) criticized the spectacular, media-seeking martyrdom operations that had led to the 9/11 attacks and the loss of jihadist sanctuaries in London mosques and Afghanistan. In his view jihad now was in a phase of weakness:

> it was now necessary to create and train cells whose members – bound by a common global ideology of belief in jihad – could wage war against the West and its apostate Muslim allies through independent harassment operations that they could plan and execute themselves. . . . These cells would have autonomous financial means and operational capacities and would not depend on a weakened central command.[59]

Strategically this characterized the operations of the GSPC/AIQM during the first decade of the twenty-first century. The jihadists have adopted a cellular structure "that is flexible, adaptable, and difficult for counterterrorism forces to penetrate."[60] It developed two main bases of operation in Algeria, one in the Kabylia mountains and the other in the Sahara, encompassing southern Algeria, northern Mali, and Mauritania – an area where jihadists did not operate during the 1990s. The Sahara offers two opportunity factors: few security forces, relative to the vastness of the territory, and proximity to smuggling routes. The Sahara base also makes it easier for the jihadists to network with, recruit, and train militants in Morocco, Tunisia, Mali, Niger, and other countries in the region.

According to Hunt, "the GSPC is one of the few groups to effectively straddle the divide between local and international Islamist terrorism and to give equal priority to attacking both the 'near' and 'far' enemies."[61] The "near" enemies continue to be the Algerian security forces and those who support the government. In the first nine months of 2002, for example, a reported 1070 people were killed by terrorists, including 15 soldiers who were killed in the Kabylia in a GSPC assault. In January 2003 the GSPC ambushed an army convoy, killing 51 soldiers – the army's heaviest loss ever from a single guerrilla attack. Beginning in 2006 they began to use roadside and truck bombs, including suicide truck and car bombings. On 11 December 2007 coordinated suicide bombings in Algiers devastated the Algerian Constitutional Council and the UN's Algerian office, killing some 60 people and wounding 180 others. In August 2008 a suicide car bomber attacked a police academy in Les Issers though only one of the 43 victims was a policeman.[62] By the end of the decade, however, the jihadists had largely abandoned suicide bombings.

The "far" enemies of the Algerian jihadists have included military personnel in neighboring countries, for example, a Mauritanian military base on the border with Algeria, attacked in June 2005; and 12 Mauritanians captured and beheaded in September 2008. Why Mauritanians? Because its government cooperates in joint counter-insurgency operations with Algeria and the US, as described in the last section. Some of the "near" targets were foreign workers whose buses were bombed, for example, in December 2006 in Algiers, and March 2007 near the town of Medea.[63] The GSPC, and later the AQIM, also took over and sought to revitalize jihadist cells in many European countries. In 2000 French police

100 *Greed, grievance and political Islam*

arrested members of a GSPC-affiliated cell before it could carry out the bombing of a market. In the same year a Milan-based cell was broken up by Italian police. Later in the decade suspected terrorists with ties to AQIM were arrested in the United Kingdom, Spain, Germany, Italy, Portugal, and Spain. These cells may have been able to provide some logistical and financial support to the Algerians, despite police surveillance. Probably more important, they were used to recruit Islamists from Europe – as well as the Maghreb –to train and fight in Afghanistan, Iraq, Kashmir and elsewhere.[64]

The GSPC/AQIM has diverse and lucrative sources of financing. The Kabylia-based group funded itself primarily by armed robbery and kidnappings for ransom. Jihadists frequently set up false roadblocks to intercept civilians, and sometimes soldiers, whom they robbed and sometimes murdered. They also robbed post offices and armored cars transporting cash. Hostage-taking seems to have started in 2001 when a senator from the far east of the country was kidnapped and released after his family secretly paid a substantial ransom. In early 2003 a group affiliated with the GSPC kidnapped 31 European tourists in southern Algeria and released them after the German government paid 5 million Euros. In 2007, according to Algerian security officials, 155 people, mostly businessmen and traders, were kidnapped by armed Islamists either from their homes or at checkpoints. The family of a public works contractor in the Kabylia region said they paid the equivalent of $315,000 for his release.[65] The Sahara-based grouping uses kidnapping but to a lesser extent. Under the leadership of Afghan veteran Mokhtara Belmokhtar, who had family connections in the region, the southern cell has profited directly or indirectly from smuggling. It trafficks cigarettes and marijuana as well as government-subsidized household goods for resale in the northern cities. According to Hunt, it also "engages in 'Islamic policing' of traditional trade routes, demanding protection money from smugglers who use the routes and occasionally confiscating and reselling items deemed un-Islamic."[66] The southern group is thought to smuggle weapons to the northern group. And it may have been involved in a narcotic trafficking network in southwest Algeria, where border police carried out a December 2008 sting operation that netted 430 kg of processed marijuana and some weaponry.[67] The Sahara-based AQIM remains viable but Algerian security forces have been relatively successful in counter-terror operations in the Kabylia, and it is questionable whether the GSPC can stay operational in that region.

Some money also reaches the Algerians from the European Islamist cells described above. Hunt offers three examples. In 2005 Spanish police broke up two GSPC-linked cells that obtained funds through robbery and credit card fraud. In 2006 Spanish and Algerian police dismantled a cell that had operated since 2000, selling false travel and residence documents to illegal immigrants to Europe. In the same year Italian police traced $2 million in wire transfers to jihadists in Algeria from a cell in Milan, the proceeds of legal businesses operated by cell members.[68]

The internationalization of Algerian jihad has been paralleled by cooperative international responses. The French have experienced three decades of terror attacks by radical leftists, regional separatist groups, and, since the early 1990s, by jihadists. GIA cells carried out a wave of terror attacks in France in 1994–5 in an attempt to discourage the French government from supporting the Algerian regime – a strategy that backfired badly because it alienated the French public and triggered strong security counter measures.[69] The GIA's attacks prompted a shift in French counter-terrorism policy from suppression to a focus on prevention, by dismantling the logistics and financial networks of armed Algerian groups.[70] The same shift began to occur among police and counter-terrorist authorities elsewhere in Europe and escalated after al-Qaeda's September 11, 2001 attacks in the United States. The raids on Islamist support cells in Europe, described above, are examples of this shift to proactive policies.

Algeria sought international support during the 1990s with indifferent success, its reputation tainted by widely reported and condemned human rights abuses. This changed dramatically after September 2001 when the United States sought allies in its "war against terror." The Algerian government enlisted with enthusiasm, received security assistance, and participates with the US and neighboring states in the Sahel in the Trans-Sahara Counterterrorism Initiative (TSCTI), which replaced an earlier, less ambitious regional program in June 2005.[71] By endorsing and participating in this partnership the Algerian government has relabeled and legitimized its own war on terror and gained political and material support.

The trans-Sahara region from Mauritania to Sudan is now regarded by the US and its allies as a major battleground in the "war against terror" because, as Stephen Emerson points out, it is "one of the most contentious and conflict-ridden areas of the world." It has "[v]ast ungoverned spaces; unsecured frontiers; large uncontrolled population movements; extreme poverty; drought and resulting famine; and persistent political and socioeconomic conflict."[72] The concern of the partner states of the TSCTI is that the region is a potential base area for jihadists. As we have shown, the GSPC/AQIM has exploited precisely these opportunities. On 8 August 2009 a suicide attack was carried out against the French Embassy in Mauritania, reportedly by a Mauritanian trained in an AQIM camp in Mali.[73] In July 2010 a raid by a Mauritanian force with French logistical support killed six AQIM militants. In response the AQIM kidnapped five French nationals and two Africans in northern Niger.[74]

The rebadged Trans-Sahara Counterterrorism Partnership (TSCPI) program's annual budget through 2013 is $100 million, mostly to build up security and counter-terror capacities of governments in the region, especially Mali, Niger, Chad, and more recently Mauritania, in addition to Algeria.[75] This includes joint training exercises in which US forces take part and a parallel effort to secure basing rights for US rapid reaction forces. Some of the TSCPI budget is to be used for development projects in response to the poverty and grievances that provide potential supporters and recruits for the jihadists.[76] The risk of the TSCPI program is that the militarization of the region and the US presence will provide new targets and more compelling justifications for jihadist opposition.[77]

In 2012 a Tuareg rebellion in northern Mali provided a major opportunity for AQIM. A coup in March by junior officers against the corrupt government in Bamako prompted a temporary alliance between the Tuaregs' Movement for the Liberation of Azawad and AQIM, who quickly gained control of northern Mali's vast

102 *Greed, grievance and political Islam*

desert region and its handful of towns. The unlikely allies failed to agree on policies and AQIM fighters forcefully displaced the Tuareg forces from the garrison town of Gao and imposed strict Sharia law on its reluctant inhabitants. A regional response to this strategic AQIM victory had not been formulated as of mid-September.[78]

Conclusion

Our cases of "unholy alliances" are analyzed comparatively in the final chapter. Here we summarize some of the distinctive features of the Algerian case. The jihadist campaign of terror was based on Algeria's Islamist movement, but was mounted by militants within the movement only after the government suspended the electoral process that would have brought the FIS, the Islamist party, to power. During the course of the civil war from 1992 to 2000 the jihadists expanded their targets from officials and security personnel to virtually the entire Algerian population – and the more brutal their attacks, the more support they lost both domestically and internationally. They also became ever more adept at extracting money from an economy that was rife with elite-led corruption. In the 1990s the international dimension of jihadist terrorism was limited to an Islamist support network in Europe, especially in France. An Algerian terrorist campaign in France in the mid-1990s was quickly suppressed. In the first decade of the twenty-first century international linkages have become much more important. Close to military defeat in Algeria itself, some jihadists allied with al-Qaeda in a network that extends across the Maghreb. They have tried to rebuild their support networks in Europe, though France's anti-terrorism judge said in August 2011 that AQIM "has shown no ability to strike in Europe or elsewhere beyond its zone of operations" in the Sahara.[79] And the governments of Algeria and its neighbors in the Sahara have joined with the United States in the regional edition of the "war against terror."

What are the implications for the future of Algerian jihadism? It is entirely possible that for some of the jihadists, especially the militants recruited from the vast reservoir of unemployed city youth, the financial rewards of robbery, kidnapping, and smuggling have become ends in themselves. But the movement as a whole, and its leaders, are avowedly and militantly Islamist, and they continue to carry out attacks on government targets that have no conceivable profit motive. In the early twenty-first century they are linked more closely than ever to the global jihadist movement, which aims to eliminate all apostate (read Western) influence in the Islamic world and unify all Muslims under the rule of a new Caliphate. Given the illusory nature of these goals, banditry and violence are likely to go hand in hand into the foreseeable future, with political and material objectives inextricably linked. But they are not likely to attract many Algerian recruits in the near term. In the American vernacular, "been there, done that," and the results were catastrophic for Algerian society. In 30 years a new generation of impoverished Algerians may be susceptible to Islamist revolutionary rhetoric, especially if there is no further political or economic progress. The most likely scenario, then, is continued jihadist insurgency in the Sahara, never entirely controlled because of political instability in the region, rents from smuggling operations, and financial and ideological support from Islamists elsewhere.

6 Serbia in the 1990s
Militant nationalism and the criminalized state

The Balkan region shows the significance of two agencies that strongly facilitate the interaction and overlap between crime and terrorism. One is *trans-border identity networks* that link divided identity groups. Such a network connects the ethnic Albanian populations surrounding Kosovo with the Albanian diaspora in Western Europe and North America (chapter 2). The Kurdish diaspora in Europe made possible the interaction of crime and politics in the PKK's pursuit of self-determination for Turkish Kurds (chapter 3). And another such network brought Jihadist Muslims into Bosnia to help the Bosnian Muslims fight their war for independence and establish a more enduring presence in the country (chapter 4).

The second agency is the *criminalized state* that tolerates and profits from nodes in conflict or post-conflict areas for illicit trade and other profitable criminal activities. The Balkans provide two examples of states that create conditions for illicit business operations. The criminalized Serbian state, the subject of this chapter, is one. Post-communist Bulgaria is another. It became a criminalized state whose officials and criminal syndicates profited enormously by circumventing the early 1990s international embargo on trade with Yugoslavia as well as by predatory exploitation of privatized state property (chapter 7).

Studying the agencies, or actors, that make trans-border crime–terrorism interactions possible is essential for comparative and policy analysis because the primary subject of this study, that is, the crime–terrorism nexus, is transient in nature and lacks coherent structure. Its trans-border networks are loose and *ad hoc*, and often dissolve into autonomous cells. So the factors that keep networks cohesive should be given special attention in crime–terrorism research. Here we focus on the sources of Serb-based terrorist activities in the 1990s and show how Serb government policies promoted trans-border crime.

Our hypotheses? Serb terrorists gained their inspiration from strong and expansionistic Serb nationalism. Trans-border nationalist terror networks evolved out of traditionally strong relationships between Serbia and cross-border Serb populations. At the beginning of the wars of Yugoslav succession the Serb trans-border terror networks were supported by the Milošević-led government whose extremist nationalist policies inspired and dispatched paramilitary groups to carry out individual and mass terrorist activities in Croatia and Bosnia. Initially they had little or no backing from local Serbs, but elements of those populations soon began to

104 *Militant nationalism and the criminalized state*

cooperate with paramilitary terrorist units backed by the Serb government. Jointly these groups, bound in an alliance based on shared identity, perpetrated acts of genocidal violence and cooperated in very profitable illicit business activities.

Yugoslavia: twenty transitional years

Commenting on Serbia's domestic and international experience in recent decades, Balkan expert Marko Attila Hoare observes:

> There exists a misconception that Serbia is a loser in the "New World Order". This is true only insofar as contemporary Europe is a continent made up of "losers". The developing democratic European order, based on the framework of the EU and NATO, is predicated upon the defeat and frustration of every regional imperialism. The defeat suffered by Serbia, in its attempt at imperial expansion in the 1990s, is broadly equivalent to the defeats suffered by Bulgaria in the 1910s, Greece in the 1920s and Romania in the 1940s; each of these states was, despite enormous effort, military beaten and exhausted and forced to accept more modest borders than its political classes had wanted.[1]

The past twenty years were clearly a period of defeat for Serbia's imperial nationalism. That period contrasted sharply with previous decades when Tito's politically "neutral" and internationally well-accepted Yugoslavia was prospering. The more recent past was full of illusions and frustrated expectations. It was a painful experience; it was the price to be paid by a Serb nation seeking late territorial and political expansion. As Hoare observed, this experience was not unique. All Balkan nations as well as past European powers have gone through it. However, Serbia's uniqueness and its bad fortune were perhaps related to its late timing.

What happened after 1990? Here is a sketch of major episodes in Serbia's official politics motivated by extreme nationalism and checked by regional and international responses. Our focus on Serb nationalism gives us the key to understanding recent Serb terrorism, as well as the Serb elite's politically driven criminal activities. The alliance of crime and terrorism were a consequence of the Serb communist party leader Slobodan Milošević's strategic policy aimed at unifying all ethnic Serbs within a common nation-state. Crime and terrorism found a hospitable environment within rapidly politicizing cross-border identity networks that provided strong bonds of mutual trust, loyalty, and security for clandestine operations.

The Socialist Federal Republic of Yugoslavia – of which Serbia was the central element – began to disintegrate in 1991. In less than twenty years the ex-federation saw four independence wars, fought respectively in Slovenia, Croatia, Bosnia, and Kosovo; the establishment of eight independents states, namely Slovenia, Croatia, Bosnia, Macedonia, the Federal Republic of Yugoslavia, Serbia, Montenegro, and Kosovo; and the establishment and disintegration of an ex-federation, namely the Federal Republic of Yugoslavia composed of Serbia and Montenegro. In all but one of these cases – Macedonia's independence – Serbia intervened actively by some combination of its primary command of the Yugoslav Federal Army (JNA); sending paramilitary terrorist units across borders; and using diplomatic and political strategies. In all but one instance Serbia had a serious stake to defend. The wars in Croatia, Bosnia, and Kosovo were bitter setbacks to Serbia's geostrategic interests, as well as its own territorial integrity. Croatia and Bosnia and, to a lesser extent Kosovo, hosted large Serb populations whose nationalism was even more radical and militant than that of Serbia proper. It inspired cross-border terrorist activities and expanded opportunities for illicit business to prosper in the ungovernable pockets of ethnically contiguous border areas.

Chronologically, Serb nationalism gathered momentum in 1991 with Croatia's declaration of independence. At about the same time the numerous and territorially concentrated ethnic Serbs in Croatia began demanding autonomy and secession. They occupied geostrategic regions bordering respectively on Serbia proper; and on the Bosnian Serbs' territory. Serb nationalism intensified with the declaration of Bosnia's independence. The latter sent a signal to the Bosnian and Croatian Serbs to establish a cross-border paramilitary alliance. Serbia supported its trans-border kindreds' radical claims despite the international embargo imposed on Yugoslavia. And she did so during four years of war. Support was diplomatic and military in nature. But perhaps more importantly for the purposes of this study, Serbia supported its trans-border kindred by sending paramilitary terrorist groups to help its secessionist kindred.

The Dayton Peace Accord of November 1995 brought relative peace to the region, following NATO's intervention in the Bosnian conflict and a successful Croat military campaign against Serb enclaves. But the calm did not endure. Kosovo's Albanians, whose festering resentment against Serb repression was ignored in the Dayton negotiations, began a campaign of guerrilla terrorism for independence that was analyzed in chapter 2. The Kosovo Liberation Army launched its first attacks against the Belgrade regime in 1996. This conflict had still greater consequences for Serbia proper. It not only expanded the cross-border Albanian criminal networks (*fis* or *fares*) that were based mainly on Kosovo clans. It also dragged in NATO, which in March 1999 launched air operations to deter a Serb campaign of ethnic massacres and cleansing. The establishment of Kosovo as an international protectorate in June 1999 gave the ethnic Albanian cross-border terrorist and criminal networks new opportunities to thrive and expand, thereby putting both Macedonia, with a large Albanian minority, and Serbia's Albanian-populated border areas at risk.

In the meantime Serbia for the first time in a decade began to focus on domestic politics. And that, at the turn of the century, was a politics of frustrated nationalism. Loss of territories, human capital, national wealth – and above all – the loss of hopes for the future radicalized Serbs who took to the streets to demand change. The 2000 federal elections saw mass rallies organized by opposition parties that demanded the removal of President Milošević from power. Street protests eventually forced Milošević to concede power to the democratic opposition. Milošević was then extradited to the International Crime Tribunal in The Hague, thereby ending Serbia's international isolation. Madeleine Albright explained this historical moment for Serbia:

106 *Militant nationalism and the criminalized state*

One of the reasons we established the War Crimes Tribunal was to assign individual guilt in order to make clear there is no collective guilt. And so now I think the Serb people under a new leadership will be able to really rejoin the international community and be a part of Europe.[2]

However, the rejoining process was neither quick nor easy. Serbia's acceptance by international institutions was contingent upon the delivery of all indicted war criminals to The Hague. Among them were Radovan Karadžić and Ratko Mladić, leaders of the Bosnian Serbs; Zeljko Ražniatović – Arkan – leader of the Serb paramilitary group called the Tigers who were sent to Croatia and Bosnia to implement Milošević's policy of ethnic cleansing; and Milorad Ulemek – Legija – leader of the Serb state security agency, the Red Berets. So the beginning of the twenty-first century was a time for Serbia to comply with the regulations of international law on war, protection of ethnic diversity, and respect for human rights – and a time also to begin to purge itself of criminality and corruption.

The criminalization of the state was the major domestic problem to be addressed. The criminalization process had begun during the Tito era and gathered momentum in the 1990s. By 2000 the structures of Milošević's post-communist state were closely aligned with the underworld. The assassination of Serb Prime Minister Zoran Djindjić in March 2003 by criminals and state security forces proved that the tasks for the new political agenda were indeed difficult and complex. We show in later sections how criminal groups and state security forces aligned to operate jointly in wartime and into the peace that followed.

Serb nationalism and its ethnoterritorial separatist movement

Modern Serb nationalism originated in the ideas and policies of Ilija Garašanin, interior and foreign minister of autonomous Serbia during the mid-nineteenth century. His *Nacertanije* ("Outline") of 1844 is often cited as a founding document, though in fact it was shared only with like-minded colleagues and not published until 1906. His policies, then, determined the direction of early Serb nationalism: he sought to build a strong state, consisting of Serbs in alliance with other peoples, capable of withstanding pressures from expansionist powers including Austria-Hungary and Russia as well as other Balkan states that, like Serbia, were escaping from Ottoman control.[3] Garašanin's goal of a Serb-dominated state is reminiscent of the multi-national state of twentieth-century Yugoslavia under Tito. But Garašanin also pursued his policy by sponsoring paramilitary action in Serb segments beyond his country's border, a strategy employed in the 1980s in the service of militant and exclusionary nationalism.

Serb nationalism *per se* is not our topic. However, it provides the framework in which alliances formed between trans-border crime and nationalist terrorism. Concretely, Serb *trans-border ethnic identity networks* were one of the two agencies – along with state policies – facilitating the interaction between crime and terrorism. Our unit of analysis is the Serb ethnoterritorial separatist movement (ETSM) that built upon long-established Serb nationalism. ETSMs are trans-border ethnically based social movements, a concept detailed in chapter 3's discussion of the Kurdish ETSM. They are non-state regional actors that evolve from regionally concentrated ethnic groups whose segments populate adjacent areas of neighboring countries. Not all trans-border kindred give birth to ETSMs. Key is that one or several segments persistently seek self-determination and national unification. So ETSMs are political organizations of regionally concentrated groups that build on cultural cohesiveness and political solidarity to contest the ethnic legitimacy of existing state boundaries.[4]

The Balkans in the 1990s were an incubator of radical ethnonationalist movements that occupied geostrategic trans-border locations and established sustainable trans-border networks. Serb, Croat, and Bosniak ETSMs all were active in the Bosnian war. The Albanian ETSM was activated in the early 1990s after Slobodan Milošević's government terminated Kosovo's long status as an autonomous region within Yugoslavia. It played a key role in Kosovo's war for independence and after. However, these movements are not necessarily responsible for terrorist campaigns and international crime. Rather elements within them, and some state actors, use politicized trans-border networks as "freeways" to channel the export of violence and entrepreneurial crime.

Two specific features characterized the Serb ETSM prior to the outbreak of regionalized conflicts in 1991. First, for most of the preceding 150 years Serb nationalism had not developed a mass following. In the early 1990s Serb terrorism was mainly state-sponsored. Trans-border networks were used to send paramilitary units across borders in keeping with militant nationalist doctrine that aimed to unify all Serbs in one state. Second, the Serb ETSM developed a mass following as a consequence of state-sponsored violence. Trans-border Serb communities were radicalized by ongoing conflict, echoing Serbia's official irredentism but often transcending Serbia's official control. In short, the strength of the Serb trans-border identity network and the power of the movement built on it are explained by the reinforcing combination of state-sponsored terrorism and radical trans-border nationalism.

The origins of the Serb ETSM can be traced to the mid-nineteenth century when from 1838 to 1878 Serbia existed as an "autonomous principality" within the Ottoman Empire. Under Garašanin's leadership the principality pursued an ambitious national program aimed not only at the unification of Serbs within a strong and independent state but also to incorporate lands that at some past time had been Serb or Orthodox. These lands included Bosnia-Herzegovina, Vojvodina, and northern Albania as well as Old Serbia – that is, Kosovo, Macedonia, and Montenegro.[5] Garašanin's program was implemented in part through insurrectory networks, a tactic that continued to be used until the late 1930s. The first such network was reportedly created by Garašanin himself in the 1860s in his capacity as the Serb minister of interior.

The establishment of Serbia as a fully independent state in 1878 gave new impetus to the evolution of the Serb trans-border identity networks. Serb statesmen pursued their objectives by establishing and supporting irregular paramilitary groups,

108 *Militant nationalism and the criminalized state*

composed of volunteers, who stirred up uprisings outside Serbia's frontiers. But the Serb national program was pursued by the Serb state alone and excluded mass mobilization of trans-border Serb segments.

Paramilitary units making use of the trans-border identity network's hospitality mushroomed at the beginning of the twentieth century. The irregular military nationalist formation, the Chetnik movement, was said to have been established to take part in World War I. About the same time Serb army officers also founded two societies, Narodna Odbrana (1908) and Unification or Death (1911), whose pan-Serb programs called for the unification of all Serbdom. Both societies made use of the Serb trans-border identity networks that extended to Bosnia. On 28 June 1914 a revolutionary organization called Young Bosnia, which was supervised by Unification or Death, assassinated Archduke Franz-Ferdinand of Austria, the heir to the Austro-Hungarian throne. The political objective of this act was to break away the south-Slav provinces of the Austro-Hungarian Empire and incorporate them into a Greater Serbia. The assassination not only exacerbated tension between Austria-Hungary and Serbia, it led directly to World War I by triggering a chain of ruptures between countries of the Triple Alliance, backing Austria-Hungary, and the Powers of the Triple Entente, backing Serbia.

The establishment of the Kingdom of Serbs, Croats and Slovenes in 1918 and the adoption of its Constitution in 1921 substantially altered the Serb trans-border network. The new Kingdom had a complex and controversial territorial-political organization, incorporating ethnically mixed lands of which the Serb populated areas were part. Nonetheless the Kingdom's Constitution asserted the principle of strict centralization. This principle was strengthened even further with the establishment of the Kingdom of Yugoslavia – a personal dictatorship of King Alexander –and it was also enshrined in the 1931 Constitution. Within these two political entities the ethnoterritorial objectives of the Serb ETSM were attained. All Serbs were integrated in one state, one that also comprised lands that once had been Serb or Orthodox. Therefore the task of the Serb ETSM – embodied in the Yugoslav state – was to maintain the imposed status quo.

But unification itself does not necessarily sustain active identity networks. In Tarrow's words, for a movement to emerge and persist it needs sustained interaction with opponents. In the next two decades the Serb ETSM twice faced external challenges that reinvigorated the Serb identity network. In 1939 the "Cvetković–Maček" Agreement was signed between the Serb authorities and ethnic Croats. It recognized Croat claims to a separate "national unit" and enlarged the Croatian territory within the Kingdom of Yugoslavia to include Dalmatia and parts of Bosnia-Herzegovina.[6] The agreement was deeply frustrating to local Serbs, who demanded a separate unit for themselves within the now territorially differentiated Croatia.[7] The agreement clearly marked a turning point in the evolution of the Serb trans-border identity movement. For the first time ever the movement developed a mass following and showed it was able to pursue political objectives independently from Belgrade.

The Serb ETSM again became active on a mass scale in 1941 following the Axis occupation of Yugoslavia and the establishment of the independent state of

Serbia 109

Croatia under the control of the virulently anti-Serb Ustǎshe. The loss of linkages with Serb ethnic brethren in Croatia and in Bosnia stimulated the resurgence of Serb irredentism. A group of Yugoslav Royal Army officials in western Serbia, the Chetniks, were the major organization to emerge within the Serb ETSM. The Chetniks promoted local uprisings and launched campaigns of terror and destruction against the Croatian Ustǎshe in Bosnia-Herzegovina. Indicatively, these campaigns received popular support from the Serb settlements of Knin and the Lika area in Croatia. However, the Serb ETSM did not attract an enduring *mass following* owing to the emergence of the rival Partisan resistance movement fighting an ideological war against the Axis occupiers.

In the immediate aftermath of World War II there were few activities on behalf of any of the Balkan ETSMs. The new Communist leadership introduced a fundamentally different approach that promised solutions to all national problems. In Yugoslavia the new Constitution, approved in 1946, endorsed the federal arrangement of the country and sanctioned the establishment of ethnic republics. However, the Constitution also specified that the authority of the Yugoslav republics should be largely subordinated to the central Communist Party control of Tito's regime. Trans-republican identity networks seemingly withered and died as the peoples of Yugoslavia focused on the building of socialism. And these conditions did not change significantly until the early 1970s when the Yugoslav communist system first showed signs of decay.

The next period in Yugoslav history is key to understanding the role and significance of the Serb trans-border identity network for the export of violence and crime. In this period the Serb ETSM developed a *sustainable mass following*. In some sense the Serb ETSM is unique in its organizational strength and ideological dedication, one that seemed able to act as one well-coordinated unit, not a composite entity. Serb populations in Croatia and Bosnia were the active segments within the Serb ETSM. Their radical nationalism prompted the establishment of political and military trans-border alliances that had multiple supporters. First, they were incontestably supported by units of the Yugoslav People's Army. Second, they were also aided by weekend warriors of whom we speak later. Third, they were reinforced by extremist paramilitary units arriving from Serbia proper. And, not least, they supported each other. This exceptionally strong identity-based trans-border mechanism was able to carry out terrorist campaigns, ethnic cleansing, mass murder, and genocide. These are the deadly landmarks of this process.

Starting in the early 1970s Yugoslavia underwent an upsurge of mass nationalism. Institutional innovations stimulated this process even further. A new Constitution came into force in 1974, which reorganized the party and state machinery on a more decentralized basis. In Lenard Cohen's words, the Constitution "invested each Yugoslav republic . . . with theoretical statehood and . . . it effectively created a semi-confederative political structure."[8] The Serb ETSM incorporated a large group of ethnic Serbs in Croatia who, according to the 1981 census, numbered 632,000 and constituted 14 per cent of the republic's population; there were another 1,321,000 in eastern and northern Bosnia-Herzegovina who made up 32 per cent of the population. Another 45,000 ethnic Serbs lived in Macedonia,

110 *Militant nationalism and the criminalized state*

42,000 in Slovenia, and 19,000 in Montenegro.[9] In Albanian-dominated Kosovo, an autonomous province within the Serb Republic, 237,000 Serbs and kindred Montenegrins made up less than a fifth of the population.[10]

In the late 1980s and early 1990s, as Yugoslavia's dissolution began, the Serb ETSM's segments rapidly consolidated. The tone was set in Belgrade, where in January 1986 prominent intellectuals sent a petition to the Yugoslav and Serb national assemblies accusing the authorities of condoning national treason and "genocide" against the Serb minority in Kosovo.[11] The Serb Communist Party leader responded by launching a policy of building "a cross-regional alliance of ethnic Serbs" to become the backbone and the driving mechanism for unifying all ethnic Serbs within a common nation-state. And that was the signal that inspired Croatian, Bosnian, and Kosovar Serbs to revive ethnic identities, rebuild trans-border identity networks, and fight for the establishment of Greater Serbia.

The first to respond were the Serbs of Croatia. Headed by Jovan Rašković, they revived their traditional policy of blocking Croatia's ethnonational consolidation. By the fall of 1990 they made clear that they would pursue the establishment of a state unit autonomous from an imminently independent Croatia that would incorporate at the minimum the adjacent Serb communities of Croatia and Bosnia.[12] The Bosnian Serbs for their part were also organizationally quick and strategically clear. In 1990 a branch of Rašković's Serb Democratic Party emerged in Bosnia-Herzegovina headed by Radovan Karadžić, and a Serb National Assembly and a Serb Council were established in Banja Luka. The Bosnian Serbs were resistant to Rašković's proposal to establish a Serb state out of the Serb enclaves in Bosnia and Croatia. Initially they opposed it, and Karadžić suggested instead that the Serb enclaves in Croatia and Bosnia should form a new federation with Serbia, Macedonia, and Montenegro. However, in late 1992 the parliaments of the Bosnian and the Croatian Serbs announced their intention to form a Serb confederation that was to include the self-proclaimed "Serb Republic of Bosnia-Herzegovina" and the "Serb Republic of Krajina" in Croatia. The central idea on which the Croatian and the Bosnian Serbs agreed was not to let Yugoslavia's disintegration fragment the Serb community throughout the former federation.[13]

The close cooperation between the Serbs of Bosnia and Croatia that followed Belgrade's call for the unification of all Serbs in one state helped in the transformation of the Serb ETSM into a mass trans-republican movement. Trans-republican identity networks strengthened and, as we show in the next section, provided the basis for military mobilization and facilitated the criminal activities of paramilitary terrorism units.

Trans-border paramilitary alliances, terrorism, ethnic cleansing, and crime

Serb trans-border paramilitary alliances

Communal identity is a unique cultural code. It is the basis for boundary perceptions that set groups apart. It is salient for the group itself as well as others with whom the group interacts. And it is essential for maintaining and strengthening the cohesion of groups under stress.[14] These principles are illustrated by the communal politics pursued by all active Balkan ETSMs in the 1990s. They were manifested in the most extreme form in the politics of the Serb ETSM. The Balkan experience shows that ethnonational identities have been essential to forging efficient political and military alliances across segments of an ethnopolitical group. Also, based on our Balkan evidence, identity networks provide an ideal setting for collaborations between criminal and political entrepreneurs.

The actors responsible for the export of the regionalized Balkan conflicts of the 1990s, that is, the Croatian and Bosnian wars, were the Serb, Croat, and Muslim ETSMs. The radicalism of the Serb ETSM should be attributed jointly to Slobodan Milošević's uncompromising irredentist politics and the cynicism and provincialism of the trans-border Serbs' nationalism. In the course of the Croatian and Bosnian wars the Serb ETSM established a trilateral political–military alliance binding the Croatian and the Bosnian Serbs, as well as Serbia proper. Here are some major instances of the ETSM in action.

In spring 1991 a violent ethnonational conflict erupted in Croatia between Serbs and Croats. Soon the federal forces of the Yugoslav People's Army (JNA) as well as irregular paramilitary units arrived from Serbia proper to assist the Croatian Serbs. As a result the Serb ETSM established control over one-third of Croatia's territory. It seized East Slavonia and declared independence for the Serb republic of Krajina, which was immediately recognized by Serbia.

In the beginning of 1992 the Bosnian conflict began (see chapter 4). The Bosnian Serbs too were supported by units of the JNA and by extreme ultranationalist paramilitary groups based in Serbia. All engaged in the so-called Drina River campaign against Muslim defenders, aiming to seize land north–south along the Bosnian border with Yugoslavia.

The military trans-boundary mobilization of the Serb ETSM was ratified in the spring of 1994 with the establishment of a military alliance between the Bosnian and Croatian Serbs. The alliance aimed at helping the Serb ETSM fight simultaneously in both breakaway countries. Bosnia's war military records indicate that on a number of occasions Croatian Serbs from the Krajina area fought in support of Bosnian Serbs in the Bihac area. They did so either from bases in Croatia or by crossing the border into Bosnia.

However, the trilateral integration of the Serb ETSM uniting the Croatian and Bosnian Serbs with Serbia proper lasted only until summer 1994 when Serb President Milošević, disappointed with his failure to persuade the Bosnian Serbs to sign the Contact Group Peace Plan for Bosnia, closed his border with Bosnia, thereby disconnecting Serbia's linkages with the Bosnian Serbs.

Terrorism, ethnic cleansing, and trans-border crime

President Milošević designed and established the trans-border identity-based military alliance of Serbia in the service of his national project of uniting all Serbs in one state. One of his principal associates in implementing this plan was Željko

112 *Militant nationalism and the criminalized state*

Ražnatović, known as Arkan, the most feared killer in the Yugoslav wars. Arkan and his paramilitary group, the Tigers, launched unrestrained campaigns of cross-border violence, terrorism, and crime aimed at cleansing ethnically heterogeneous areas in Croatia and in eastern and west-central Bosnia. Experts say this was mainly Arkan's war, with little involvement of the Yugoslav army. The main actors were instead Arkan and his feared militia, along with the Red Berets who are described in a later section. The Tigers may have numbered only 200 hard-core members, with a maximum strength of about one thousand. But they were reinforced by the Red Berets and by the militias of local Serb leaders who pursued the same tasks. Radovan Karadžić, president of the Bosnian Serb's self-styled republic, developed a military strategy of ethnic cleansing, and General Ratko Mladić, military commander of the Bosnian Serbs' irregular troops, fought a deadly three-and-a-half-year campaign to implement it.

Zeljko Ražnatović and his Tigers were state-sponsored terrorists. Support from the Serb state, on the one hand, and from Croat and Bosnian Serb leaders, on the other, increased immensely Arkan's military and political power. One distinguishing characteristic of their terrorist campaigns was its strategy of "ethnic cleansing," not terrorism alone. That is, attacks aimed not just to kill Croat and Muslim villagers but to motivate the survivors and inhabitants of neighboring villages to flee. War correspondent Martin Bell observes:

> We allowed this war to start in which 200,000 people were killed. The war provided an opportunity to Arkan and his people to perfect their ethnic cleansing. Non-Serbs in Bosnia would have two choices, either to flee in terror, or die.[15]

Journalist Misha Glenny was in besieged Sarajevo early in the Bosnian war and observed Muslim villagers packing to flee. They explained, "We've been told that Arkan and the Tigers are on their way." Glenny's comment echoes Bell: "Nothing was more effective in the business of ethnic cleansing than the mere possibility of Arkan's imminent arrival."[16]

We also know that terrorism and crime went hand in hand. Crime for Arkan was not necessary to fund his campaigns. Serb state agencies paid his Tigers and financed his military actions. Rather crime was a profitable activity that became ever more attractive as opportunities provided by cross-border violence increased.

Privileges, protection, and lack of prosecution – this is how the Belgrade regime treated Arkan for some years before the Yugoslav wars began. Arkan established his paramilitary group in his capacity as president of the fan club of the Belgrade Red Star soccer team whose members provided the core of the Tigers. The future fighters were young and outside the structures of the Yugoslav army. Interpol agent Budimir Bobovic said of Arkan that "He was a criminal of high profile: very professional and very rare. He was very strong and smarter than most of his fellows." And he adds for his Tigers: "They were fantastically well trained guys and lots of Muslims and Croats were quite scared when they heard that Arkan and his Tigers are coming."[17]

Arkan's Tigers began their war of "ethnic cleansing" in the city of Vukovar in Croatia. Tigers successfully cleansed the city of its non-Serb population, carrying out executions of Croat prisoners and hospitalized people. While moving house to house they also looted and destroyed property. For those who watched the situation on the ground the Tigers acted as thugs. In Ron Haviv's words, the Tigers' activities in Vukovar were a big robbery disguised as nationalism.[18]

The Tigers later moved to Bosnia to "protect" the ethnic Serbs in this republic. Their strategy was aimed at ethnic cleansing of non-Serbs along the northeastern corridor. They first took Bijelina; then Zvornik, two cities located very close to the Bosnia–Serbia border. Reports of torture, violence, and property crime abounded. Some 20,000 non-Serb civilians were forced out of Bjielina or murdered; 60 per cent of Zvornik's citizens followed suit. Robbery and theft were coterminous. Zvornik citizen Mehmet Hadzic recalls that "It was a common knowledge that he [Arkan] brings in terror with him. He went straight to the main street, he was looking for money, the bank."[19] Establishing control over Zvornik and Bijelina was significant well beyond the initial looting. By gaining control over these two cities Arkan secured new black market trade routes.[20]

As the Tigers moved westward to Banja Luka their strategy of ethnic cleansing assumed more outrageous forms. This area became notorious for its Nazi-like concentration camps. War photographer Paul Madelenat reported:

> We just went to these camps and what we saw were just persons with skin and bones. And rumors persisted that Muslim women were being held in rape camps. Arkan became synonymous with any evil acts being committed.[21]

The Tigers also were among the perpetrators of the Srebrenica genocide of July 1995. They arrived at the UN's so-called safe haven in Srebrenica along with the irregular Bosnian Serb soldiers of General Ratko Mladić. Jointly the two paramilitary units instructed the UN forces to leave, evacuated women and children, and proceeded to liquidate the male population. NATO Supreme Commander George Joulwan comments: "It was systematic ethnic cleansing . . . which was absolutely to me unthinkable."[22]

Arkan was equally successful in his criminal business activities. Smuggling that circumvented the UN sanctions and weapons embargo on Serbia helped him make millions on the black market. Journalist Ojrubadic Bratislav identifies some of the sources of his revenue:

> Arkan was controlling some cigarette markets, parts of the oil market. . . . [And while being] a symbol of those who committed a lot of crimes against Muslims . . . his wife [the famous pop-star Ceca] is one of the best sold singers in Bosnia.[23]

Once the Dayton Accords of November 1995 put an end to the Bosnian and Croat wars the Tigers' strategy of ethnic cleansing was transferred to Kosovo, if

114 *Militant nationalism and the criminalized state*

not by the Tigers then by local Serb paramilitary units who adopted their strategy. A mass grave was found in Kosovo in January 1999. By the late 1990s, however, Arkan was losing state protection because his beneficiary, President Milošević, was given a clear signal that NATO intended to enforce the Dayton Agreement. What ensued thereafter? Milošević made a dramatic change in his state security structures that deprived Arkan of his protection. Arkan also lost shares on the criminal market.[24]

One more characteristic of Arkan's trans-border state-supported terrorism needs comment. It relates to the societal and state support he received in wartime. Arkan, like his associates, strongly believed in the Serb national cause. Neither he nor his partners seemed to have ever questioned what they saw as the uncontestable boundaries of their ethnically uniform world. Neither did they seem to have expected that anyone outside their world could ever enter it. When Arkan established a paramilitary training camp in Erdut, Croatia, he said, "I am protecting the Serb people here from the fascist government of Croatia." His message was that Western democracies should understand that. And he denied any talk of atrocities.[25] He had strong support throughout Greater Serbia, and NATO Supreme Commander George Joulwan observed that "He was hailed as a hero by many Serbs in what was then called Republica Srpska and in Serbia and he moved freely about the country."

One final piece of evidence about Arkan's status. He was simultaneously involved in Serbia's regular politics as well as its trans-border campaigns. In 1992 he was voted into Parliament as an independent from Kosovo. Later he founded the ultra-nationalist Serb Unitary Party and appointed his fellow Tiger Borislav Pelović as chairman.[26] Our next task is to track the process whereby the Serb state integrated into its structures criminals like Arkan who served as the state's extended black hand in conflicts of ideological, ethnic, and strategic significance.

Nationalist terrorism and the criminalization of the Serb state

War, the state, crime, and terrorism

The mechanisms of state-sponsored terrorism in the service of Serb nationalism were established in a long and complicated process – a process that criminalized the entire Serb state during Slobodan Milošević's tenure in office. It is common knowledge that the East European communist states' security apparatus employed criminals to intimidate and murder their political opponents. Few states anywhere, though, can compare with Serbia in the degree to which terrorism, state institutions, and crime networks became symbiotic partners in the 1990s.

The criminalization of the Serb state began in the early 1970s. By that time the employment of criminals to do the regime's dirty work had become common. Arkan's story is telling. He was born Željko Ražnatović in 1952, son of a high-ranking Air Force officer, and was jailed as a teenager for petty crimes. In the 1970s, as Yugoslavia was undergoing an economic crisis, Arkan and others like

Serbia 115

him left the country to pursue criminal opportunities elsewhere.[27] For some years he was a bank robber and killer for hire in Western Europe. Back in Yugoslavia by 1983, Arkan was charged with attempted murder of two Belgrade policemen. He escaped conviction, however, when it was revealed at his trial that he was secretly connected with the Yugoslav state security agency.[28] He was one of some 150 criminals employed by the regime. In effect they had contracts of convenience that provided protection from enforcement of Interpol's arrest warrants in exchange for carrying out illicit services for the regime.

Concretely, Arkan traveled around Europe on "patriotic missions" to silence opponents to the Belgrade regime and was known to have assassinated five political dissidents. In the aftermath of Yugoslavia's disintegration he returned home to be rewarded for his services. As mentioned above, he became president of the Belgrade Red Star soccer team's fan club, from whose members and hangers-on he later formed his private paramilitary unit, the Tigers.[29] Arkan's career was part of a larger process of the criminalization of the state, one that gathered momentum with disintegration of the Yugoslav federation from 1990 onward and the onset of the wars. To sustain those 1990s wars Serbia needed more resources than were available within Serb society and official state structures. Milošević found, for example, that the federal Yugoslav People's Army, the JNA, was not strong enough to pursue the regime's ambitious irredentist objectives. Its morale was low, with nearly half of its reservists failing to report for duty when ordered. So the regime chose to invite in the criminal world. Criminals released from jail were among those sent to Bosnia and Croatia to fight for a Greater Serbia.

Until very recently little was known about the alliances forged between the criminal world and the Serb state. However, testimony before the International War Crimes Tribunal at The Hague has added important details. From them it is abundantly clear that the war in Bosnia was in fact masterminded by Milošević. As president of Serbia, rather than the Yugoslav federation, he had no official responsibility for the Bosnian conflict. However, he reportedly issued orders to Arkan's Tigers and other paramilitaries via the Serb State Security Bureau (RDB). Arkan himself claimed that "without orders from the state security the Tigers never went anywhere".[30]

The RDB is the key institution for our analysis of the state's criminalization before, during, and after the Yugoslav wars. Serb journalist Dejan Anastasievic characterized the RDB during the 1990s as a "typical authoritarian secret service." The agency's major objective was to protect Milošević's regime. In the pursuit of this objective the agency targeted critical journalists and opponents of the regime. It also was directly engaged in establishing and supporting paramilitary formations to be sent to the war areas. Not least, the RDB was responsible for building networks for illicit business activities and money laundering of the profits made by circumventing the UN-imposed embargo on Serbia.[31]

The institution played a key role in the Croatian and the Bosnian wars. It was headed by Jovica Stanisic, one of the best-informed people in Yugoslavia and the most powerful man in the country after Milošević. Stanisic was entrusted with almost all covert operations in Croatia and Bosnia ranging from arms supply to

116 *Militant nationalism and the criminalized state*

drafting plans for military actions. Before the wars' outbreak Stanisic travelled to Serb-populated areas in Bosnia and Croatia to promote the establishment and arming of local paramilitary formations.[32] Stanisic thus was directly or indirectly responsible for many war crimes committed in these countries. Simultaneously, he also played a key role in misrepresenting the Serb-sponsored irredentist conflicts as interethnic wars.[33]

We also know more now about the Red Berets, the RDB's elite paramilitary unit that took part in the Bosnian and Croatian conflicts. Their first commander, Franko Simatović, sent the Red Berets to Croatia and Bosnia where they were involved in the most brutal ethnic cleansing campaigns and also carried out debt collection, assassinations, robberies, and smuggling. Simatović was also directly responsible for planning the activities of Arkan's Tigers. Simatović arranged the Tigers' missions and transportation and was responsible for the payment of Arkan's troops.

The funding of the paramilitary units reveals the further criminalization of the state. Most funds came from the Customs Bureau, which in wartime functioned as a private service to the regime. Taxing licit and illicit trade across Serb state borders emerged as the biggest state enterprise. The then director of the Customs Bureau, Mihalj Kertes, was said to have diverted up to $4 billion in cash to Milošević between 1994 and 2000. According to Milošević's statements before the War Crimes Tribunal, these funds went into the pockets of the Serb paramilitary forces in Croatia and Bosnia. They were not used for his personal enrichment.[34] One witness at The Hague said that Arkan's fighters received up to DM 1500 per month, a large sum in that time and place.[35] Money diverted from customs duties thus financed the paramilitary ethnic cleansing campaigns and also subsidized election campaigns.[36]

Other institutions also were suborned. The Belgrade weekly *Vreme* reported that some 170 most successful state and private enterprises were forced to provide funding for the Red Berets.[37] Paramilitary units – the Red Berets, Tigers, and local militias among irredentist Serbs – needed more than funding. To assure logistical supply the Serb state also criminalized the Yugoslav army, the JNA. Hague witness C-013 speaks of a mission whereby the JNA and state security jointly transported weapons across the Danube River to arm the Croatian Serbs in East Slavonia. This mission was scarcely unique. The JNA, though officially outside President Milošević's direct control, regularly supplied Arkan's Tigers and other paramilitaries with weapons, fuel, and money. More specifically, the KOS – the JNA's Counterintelligence Service – played the decisive role in wartime logistics. Its agents were busy shipping arms across Bosnia and Croatia in 1991 and 1992. The head of the KOS, Aleksandar Vasilijevic, was the first to establish smuggling channels in newly independent Bosnia by concluding an agreement with the Bosnian Defense Minister to assure free passage for weapons, some of which were diverted to the Bosnian Muslim army in the making.[38]

Internationally the state security structures promoted trans-border terrorism-crime networks. Domestically the RDB linked up with organized crime groups to establish and protect grey and black economic networks. Instead of relying on the official budget of the Ministry of Interior, the RDB profited from illicit ventures carried out jointly with the underworld. Criminals formerly employed as paramilitary troops continued to serve as RDB employees upon their return. With trusted partners the interaction between the state security apparatus and numerous smuggling networks and black markets ran smoothly. In 1997 the Serb state security service was placed under Milošević's direct command to the benefit of both the crime networks and the president himself.

The RDB, the Customs Bureau, and the JNA – the activities of these institutions in the 1990s tell us much about the criminalization of the Serb state. This analysis cannot omit one more institution – the police – who in principle should have worked to contain crime and terrorism. Not so. Analyst Marko Nicovic describes the situation in the police as grotesque, a situation where "organized crime had more of its men within the police service, than the police had its agents and informers infiltrated among the criminals."[39] In the early 1990s the police service was centralized under control of the Ministry of Justice and soon gained a reputation as one of the most corrupt institutions in Milošević's regime. Its members carried out protection rackets, cooperated with smugglers and car thieves, and shielded racketeers; profited from contraband traffic in oil, arms, drugs, and stolen vehicles; and were implicated in assassinations and financial manipulations. It was a public secret that high-ranking individuals within the Ministry of Interior masterminded the major contraband schemes.

The wide-ranging criminalization of the Serb state institutions raises the question whether any role was left to be played by the criminal underworld itself. In fact the criminal clans were major actors in Serbia's politics. Enjoying nearly full protection from the state, they operated freely during the 1990s. Criminal groups infiltrated Serbia's politics and economic life, and accumulated large profits by circumventing the embargo. Several underworld clans were known to have interacted closely with customs, the police, and the judiciary. Analysts reported that "[s]tate owned property was plundered; smuggling networks and black markets monopolized; and financial manipulation [was] tolerated."[40]

The Surcin clan was among the best known. By the beginning of the 1990s it had established full control over the car theft business. Its other activities included the smuggling of oil, cigarettes, heroine, and cocaine. Later it was displaced by the Zemun clan. The incorporation of these and other criminal clans in the public economy and politics worked to the state's advantage. Illicit business revenues increased. As a rule they were first laundered, then sent abroad to foreign bank accounts and enterprises. This enabled Serb state companies to survive the embargo regime. Greek and Cypriot companies and banks proved most hospitable to illicitly accumulated Serb state capital. But there were reportedly other havens for dirty money in Switzerland, the South African Republic, Germany, and China.

The end of the Bosnian war in 1995 signaled a turning moment for the state's cooperation with the underworld. The lifting of international sanctions and the end of irredentist campaigns in Croatia and Bosnia put an end to some illicit business operations. More importantly, the symbiotic state–criminal connection had

118 *Militant nationalism and the criminalized state*

to change, not least in view of the low political status of the regime, whose leading politicians were insistently sought by the International War Crimes Tribunal. Initially Serbia was unwilling to comply with arrest warrants from The Hague. In fact, that was not really a matter of willingness but capabilities. Crime and politics were so closely connected that time was needed to divorce the two and decide who had the authority to extradite whom. War criminals were not concerned about The Hague's arrest warrants. The real threat for them was assassinations committed by rival groups.

Arkan's example is telling. While he never publicly denounced Milošević he seemingly switched sides. Belgrade gossips said that Arkan was approached by a representative from The Hague who offered him a secret deal to testify against Milošević.[41] Criminal circles knew quite a lot about the regime's past. And the regime sought to liquidate them. Many criminals implicated in state corruption were murdered by professional killers in the last years of the twentieth century. Arkan himself was assassinated in January 2000 by a former Belgrade policeman, though it was never established at whose direction. And a bloody strike by the underworld was delivered back on the politicians. Serbia entered the twenty-first century as a criminalized state in the process of self-destruction.

The first impetus to fundamental change came from the Serb citizenry who took to the streets of Belgrade in October 2000, demanding Milošević's removal from power. The process of dismantling the criminalized state proved long and difficult, as we show next.

The traumatic divorce between the state and the crime networks

Being asked to denounce or disown her friends "Legija" (Milorad Lukovic) and "Siptar" (Dušan Spasojević, head of the Zemun clan), two of Arkan's associates, pop star Ceca Ražnatović – who married Arkan in 1995 – replied: "I am not a coward. These friendships have lasted for more than ten years. They didn't start yesterday. Do you understand me? They're not recent friendships – where I made a mistake." Ceca had recently met with Legija and Siptar in public, both of them involved in the 2003 assassination of Prime Minister Djindjić.[42]

Ceca's reply could be used as a metaphor for the traumatic divorce between the Serb state and its long-lasting criminal friendships. The separation was difficult because the two structures – those of the state and those of the crime networks –had been interwoven for more than a decade. Was a separation possible at all? Events of the first decade of the twenty-first century show that the goal was attainable but at a very high price.

Milošević's removal from power in October 2000 was not an achievement of the Belgrade citizenry alone. Rather "the coup" was prepared by state structures, helping to guarantee its success. The deal was simple and reasonable. The opposition leaders would be supported in their contest of election results. Once in office, however, the former opposition was expected to prevent extradition of indicted war criminals to The Hague. Thus Jovica Stanišic, head of Serb state security, allegedly played an important role by assuring the police and army's neutrality

Serbia 119

toward popular protest.[43] Stanišic was not alone. Numerous media reports say that Milorad Lukovic – Legija – a high-ranking criminal, a former member of Arkan's Tigers, and a provisional commander of the Red Berets, was asked by Zoran Djindjić to cooperate in the ousting of Milošević. Legija was reportedly promised the consent of the RDB and the Red Berets in exchange for state protection against extraditions of indicted war criminals to The Hague.[44]

How much did the opposition succeed in implementing its plans for reforms of the state structures? The government of Prime Minister Djindjić placed a high priority on the fight against organized crime and corruption. However, the pace of reform was slow and the process was compromised. One reason was that most high-ranking officials in the Ministry of Interior, the RDB, and the Customs Bureau stayed in office and destroyed much of their archives, thereby destroying records of the Milošević regime's criminal and terror activities.

The RDB, for example, was abolished by the Parliament in July 2002. Its place was taken by a new institution, the Information Agency, whose tasks included intelligence and counter-intelligence. It was placed under the government's direct control rather than under the jurisdiction of the Ministry of Interior, former home of the RDB. Critics argue that this agency's reform was a failure because many of its high-ranking employees retained their links with the leading underworld clans.[45]

But most importantly, the government was either unwilling or unable to launch radical reforms because it remained hostage to the crime networks. The government's attempt to comply with The Hague Tribunal war crimes arrest warrants put it in direct opposition to its one-time anti-Milošević underworld allies, to whom the new government owed its rise to power. And when attempts at compliance with The Hague were made nonetheless, key figures in the crime networks responded violently. In 2001 authorities arrested some Red Beret members on charges of war crime. Milorad Legija, who remained the Red Beret's commander, inspired a revolt in which Red Berets blocked main roads in Serbia.

The assassination of Prime Minister Zoran Djindjić in March 2003 was another step in this direction. Known as the "Stop The Hague" conspiracy, its intended victims also included Foreign Affairs Minister Goran Svilanović; Vice Premier Cedomir Jovanović; and the head of the government's Communication Bureau, Vladimir Popović. Djindjić's assassination was masterminded by the 35-year-old Milorad Legija of the Red Berets. His close linkages with the Zemun clan – the most powerful criminal clan at that time – assured him protection and support.

The Serb government's reformers responded to Djindjić's assassination with the first full-scale crackdown on terrorism and crime, Operation Saber. The action was known as the largest of the kind in East Europe and received wide international support. The government imposed a state of emergency to arrest thousands of criminals, politicians, and crime suspects. According to a report by the Sofia-based Center for the Study of Democracy, more than 10,000 people were arrested and over 4500 detained in custody. Police brought in 3919 criminal charges against 3400 persons suspected of committing 5812 criminal offenses. Forty-five persons were charged with involvement in Djindjić's assassination and with terrorist

120   *Militant nationalism and the criminalized state*

activity, 15 of whom were directly charged with murdering the prime minister. Police also confiscated a great many weapons, munitions, and 75 kilos of illicit drugs. Those arrested included many people who had played a key role in Milošević's security structure including Jovica Stanišic, former head of the RDB; Franko Stamatovic, founder of the Red Berets, and Nebojsa Pavkovic, former chief of staff of the Yugoslav army, along with other ranking army officers. The Zemun clan also was targeted.

The government made rapid institutional changes. It disbanded the unresisting Red Berets as well as the Gendarmerie. The key priorities in the reform process were the fight against organized crime, the Army's integration with the international Partnership for Peace program, as well as the country's cooperation with The Hague Tribunal. The Saber action was very radical but also successful in removing many corrupt officials from office and severing ties between state agencies and criminal networks. Saber also triggered a range of institutional and policy reforms to which the international community has provided full support. Next, Serbia's dialogue with NATO was also successful. In 2006 Serbia joined NATO's Partnership for Peace, and in 2008 Serbia was invited to join the intensified dialogue program with NATO. In 2009 it submitted its first Individual Partnership (IPP) for Peace program to NATO, despite limited public support for joining the Alliance.

Serbia's cooperation with The Hague Tribunal has also been efficient, especially during the years 2004–11. In July 2011, Serbia arrested Goran Hadzic, the former leader of Croatia's ethnic Serbs, who was in fact the last indicted fugitive. Hadzic was known to have worked closely with the criminal gangs, involved in the smuggling of cars, cigarettes, and gasoline. He was also one of those who cooperated with Arkan's Tigers and who bore responsibility for the destruction of the Croatian city of Vukovar in 1991. Serbia's cooperation with The Hague Tribunal has been received positively by the international community. London-based Balkan analyst Tim Judah said Hadzic's arrest should end any kind of lingering doubts about Serbia's sincerity within the EU. And a recent joint statement by EU President Herman Van Rompuy, European Commission chief Jose Manuel Barroso and foreign policy chief Catherine Ashton says, "This is a further important step for Serbia in realizing its European perspective and equally crucial for international justice."[46]

As of 2012 Serbia's nine-year fight against crime and terrorism is impressive. A recent report from the EU says that the Anti-Corruption Agency provides the legal and institutional framework for remedial action, though the Agency needs to be strengthened and "Law enforcement authorities need to adopt a more proactive approach in investigating and prosecuting corruption." The same report praises Serbia for establishing "a good framework for police cooperation and the fight against organized crime," including cooperative arrangements with Interpol and eighteen other European states.[47] The extent of progress is amazing given Serbia's exceptionally low departure point. The Serb case shows one way by which a criminalized state can be brought back to "normality" by a combination of domestic political reform and international support. The biggest challenges in the future will be to continue the coordinated effort to control crime and corruption, and to provide guarantees of the rule of law. The country's official admission to EU candidacy in 2012 should strongly reinforce the Serbian reformist strategies. The principal obstacle is the government's refusal, thus far, to recognize Kosovo's independence.

Conclusions

The close connection between international terror and crime networks in post-communist Serbia was the direct result of state policy, specifically of Milošević's campaign to incorporate the Serb communities of Bosnia and Croatia in a Greater Serbia. The networks and policies of his regime had significant precedents, as we have shown. Paramilitary forces have occasionally been used to promote irredentism outside the borders of the Serb state since the late nineteenth century. The Communist Yugoslav regime had for a decade or more employed criminals-turned-agents of the Serb security service to target opponents in Western Europe. But the degree to which the Serb state promoted and funded terrorism and ethnic cleansing in Croatia and Bosnia in the early 1990s had no precedents either in Serb history or elsewhere in post-Communist Eastern Europe. And the Serb state itself was criminalized by these policies to an extreme degree. In none of the other cases in the Unholy Alliances project have we seen as close and deep a "triple alliance" among terrorists, criminals, and state agencies as in Serbia.

Many features of the Serb case merit comparative analysis, some of which is provided in chapter 9. It is important to observe, here, that this extraordinary complex of militant nationalism, trans-border terrorism, and deep-rooted domestic and international criminality has been largely dismantled. In part this was due to international military and political action in the 1990s that obliged Milošević to disengage and demobilize. Domestic networks and agencies were much more difficult to dismantle. Forces in civil society took the lead in ousting Milošević from office in 2000, but internecine political violence followed among criminals, paramilitary leaders, and corrupt state officials. Only after Prime Minister Djindjić was assassinated in 2003 did reformist leaders mount a sweeping crackdown and institutional reforms. Trans-boundary terrorism in the service of Serb nationalism has been effectively ended. Can the 1990s alliance between criminal networks and corrupt officials reemerge from its remnants? The more closely Serbia is linked to the European Community, the less likely this will be.

7 The state and crime syndicates in post-communist Bulgaria[1]

British journalist Misha Glenny begins his recent book, *McMafia: A Journey through the Global Criminal Underworld*[2] with a case study of Bulgaria. Why does he place Bulgaria at the start of his journey into global criminal networks? Bulgarian crime syndicates seem less threatening than their counterparts in Russia, Mexico, or even neighboring Serbia and Albania. They are also more or less nation-centric, and their trans-border connections seem to be fewer and weaker compared to other transnational criminal structures. Glenny's selection of Bulgaria as his leading case study of trans-border crime is significant in another respect because it exemplifies the emergence of a partially criminalized state in contemporary Europe. It is the end result of a decade-long attempt to establish a market economy in the country, and has led many Bulgarians to wrongly perceive the processes of criminalization as part of the transition to democratic governance. It was especially common during the first transitional decade, that is, the 1990s,[3] although evidence of criminalization can be found well after that time.

This chapter provides a structured and focused discussion of the criminalization of a state in transition. It shows that where malign domestic and international conditions combine, an "unholy alliance" of domestic actors can embark upon predation of state property, the corrosion of state institutions, and even the beginning of what David Jordan has diagnosed as *narcostatization*.[4]

Obviously this is not a country-specific policy analysis. Bulgaria (and Serbia, in chapter 6) is a case study of a general phenomenon, common to all post-communist transitions in South-Eastern Europe. Analysts argue that in Bulgaria there is a proven linkage between organized crime and some former state agencies, as well as the official security apparatus. The nexus between state functionaries and active members of organized crime networks is common throughout the Balkans and by no means coincidental. This is the result of a process aimed at the systemic conquest of the state.[5] We have no methodology for measuring the degree of state criminalization. What we aim to do here is to conceptualize and trace the origins of *state criminalization* within the regional context of our comparative study of trans-border violence and crime networks on the European periphery.

In analytical terms, we show how a criminalized state emerges and identify its preconditions; and also how it interacts with predatory trans-border networks. We identify the actors who lay down its foundations, and who assist its consolidation. As we track down these processes we demonstrate that the core indicators of a state's criminalization include (1) institutional disarray and the erosion of state authority, followed by *the institutionalization of private violence*; (2) the emergence and flourishing of *structural corruption*; as well as (3) the onset of *narco-criminalization*. The immediate economic conditions of criminalization in Bulgaria lay in the crisis of the late socialist economy and the malaise of the transitional years, when opportunities for profit-seeking in the black economy soared.

The economic crisis of Bulgarian socialism

Background factors explaining the collapse of East European socialist economies are well known. Recurring mistakes in strategic economic planning from the 1950s onward, in combination with the inefficiencies of central planning, gradually exhausted the capacities of national economics. In Bulgaria the overly ambitious development of heavy industry and the electronic technology industry, as well as the development of a big export-dependent military-industrial complex, demanded huge long-term investments. However, international economic, commercial and financial partners were few, the most important among them being the Soviet Union and the Soviet-oriented countries of the Council for Mutual Economic Assistance (COMECON). Privileges stemming from Bulgaria's traditionally good bilateral relationship with the Soviet Union helped compensate for the structural problems of the country's socialist economy for quite some time. Recurring Soviet donations helped the development of significant structural branches of the national economy, agriculture being one of them. A 1967 agreement gave Bulgaria most favorable conditions for the supply of fuel and raw materials from the Soviet Union. However, in the long run Bulgaria's socialist economy became a giant standing on clay feet. And once strategic, economic and commercial partners withdrew, the collapse of the country's economy was inevitable.[6]

In the early 1980s the Bulgarian economy faced a deep crisis because of unfavorable shifts in its relationship with the Soviet Union. Prices of essential raw material imports increased, and export earnings of electronic products declined. In 1984 Bulgaria's Communist Party leader Todor Zhivkov asked for Soviet leader Chernenko's help but he could not provide much other than a 1986 loan. When, pressed by increasing foreign debt, in 1989 Zhivkov sought another loan from Moscow, Mikhail Gorbachev recommended that the Bulgarian communists deal with the problem on their own – but they lacked the means to do so.[7]

A related problem was the belated quest of the Party leadership to reform the socialist economy along market lines. Bulgaria's foreign debt in early 1989 was $10 billion, most of it accumulated in the last five-year plan of 1986–9.[8] The explanation is simple. A major principle under socialism was that upward economic development should be registered each year, a policy pursued committedly until the regime's last days. The reluctance of the Party elite to adopt a more flexible economic approach after 1986, which could have led to looser expectations and more realistic planning, was motivated by the quest to prevent socialism from overall collapse.[9] In the face of decreasing investment resources from COMECON, the

124   *State and crime syndicates*

Soviet Union and Western banks, sustained growth on traditional lines could only be achieved by further increases in foreign debt.[10] So a policy aimed at reforming and strengthening the socialist system eventually had the opposite effect.

At the start of the market transition Bulgaria's economy was also burdened by $1.5 billion in debts accumulated by foreign states toward Bulgaria. This debt was mostly the result of a complex economic program that Bulgaria developed with 29 Third World countries beginning in the early 1970s. The program was designed to provide technical and infrastructural loans to friendly regimes in Africa, Asia, and Latin America. Symptomatically, Bulgaria was one of the most generous credit providers among the socialist states.[11] The parallel arms trade was expected to increase the country's revenues in foreign currency but it was financed with loans provided by the Bulgarian state. After 1986, however, Bulgaria incurred significant losses because the country's strategic commercial partners – oil-producing countries among them – had difficulty in repaying their loans, partly because of declining oil revenues in the Middle East.

The post-communist transition

In 1989 when Bulgaria began its post-communist transition it had high foreign debt totaling $10 billion;[12] the country's economy was relatively closed to world trade and the emerging global economy; its GDP was declining; and there was a demographic crisis as emigration increased and birthrates declined. The country had an authoritarian political system in which power was monopolized by a single party, and security was challenged by ethnic conflict and terrorism.

By the start of the transition the Bulgarian economy had declined to one of the poorest in Europe. Indicators for the first transitional decade show that economic problems worsened. Per capita GDP varied wildly, from EU 1200 in 1990 to EU 500 in the next two years, and did not return to the 1990 level until 1998.[13] For comparison, Slovenia's per capita income during the same period was close to ten times greater.[14] Official unemployment rates in Bulgaria varied between 10.8 per cent, when they were first reported in 1995, and 18 per cent in 2000.[15] There was hyperinflation, which peaked at over 1000 per cent in 1997.[16] The international embargo of warring Yugoslav states (1991–5) worsened Bulgaria's economic plight at a strategically significant moment. The government accepted UN Resolution 754 that imposed economic and commercial sanctions, but no compensating mechanisms were arranged. So at the onset of transition the country's commercial transportation networks with West Europe were closed down. Bulgaria's monthly losses from the embargo amounted by mid-1993 to $234 million, while the country's overall losses exceeded $4 billion.[17]

The last two decades have seen uneven progress toward democratization and belated establishment of an opposition movement; political instability; inefficient state institutions; high levels of government corruption; and sporadic urban gangster war. The Transparency International ratings of perceptions of corruption in Bulgaria at the end of the 1990s were low, varying between 2.9 and 3.9.[18] Pervasive poverty and high unemployment rates are also typical. And the emerging small business sector has experienced continuous frustration because of its dependence on local protection services as well as with its decreasing role in global markets. On the other hand, large-scale predation of state property brought public funds into private hands that could in principle be used for capital investment. And protracted ethnic conflicts in neighboring Yugoslavia opened opportunities for extensive and profitable contraband activities. Transborder criminal networks – and in particular drug-related ones – have made their way through Bulgaria and the Balkans more broadly. And the globalization of finances and the global financial crisis provided local gangsters and Bulgarian oligarchs with favorable opportunities for illicit transnational financial transactions. In sum, many global, regional, and local conditions for the emergence of a criminalized state have been present in Bulgaria over the past two decades. So its establishment was not accidental. It was the systemic capture of the state by security and some party officials, as well as by some social groups with predatory aims, and accomplished under most favorable circumstances.

The criminalization of the state developed in three different though partially overlapping modalities. One was the emergence of the *market of violence*. The term "market of violence" was introduced in the 1990s by ethnologist Georg Elwert to denote economically driven conflicts including civil wars motivated by profit-seeking and predatory warlord systems. Actors in the market of violence can include warlords, private military and security agencies, and multinational corporations. These actors use calculated and premeditated violence to enrich themselves by trade in weapons, drugs, fuel, human trafficking, extortion, and illegal or semi-legal exploitation of resources.[19]

The Sofia-based Center for the Study of Democracy uses the term in its report on *Organized Crime in Bulgaria* in the sense intended by Elwert, though without a specific definition. The *market of violence* or the *market for the provision of violence and defense* in Bulgaria initially denoted a system of predation in which actors used violence to enrich themselves by illicit business activities in an economic and political structure that was supportive of black market activities and tolerant of widespread gangster violence to establish and protect economic turf. The term also has a more narrow meaning. As in other East European countries, the *market of violence* also denotes the provision of private protection and security services.[20] This justifies the discussion of the Bulgarian *market of violence* within the context of the security governance framework that has developed since the 9/11 attacks. Increasing security challenges globally have led to multiplication of societal and corporate security agencies that have privatized security functions.[21]

The second modality was the establishment of *structural corruption*. Violence here was structural rather than physical: economic crime has reached immense proportions, causing irreparable corrosion of the institutions of the state. Newly established oligarchs, many of whom have recently accumulated wealth of criminal origin, have aligned with state and political officials to engage in intense money laundering, most often investing dirty money in the privatization process.

The third direction was the emergence of *narco-criminalization*. In an atmosphere of expanding structural corruption narco-bosses came to seek long-term protec-

126 *State and crime syndicates*

tion from state institutions, as well as commitments of institutional assistance for drug-related business activities.

The market of violence: security and market at twilight

> *While celebrating euphorically the defeat of communism nobody came to inquire what the reality in the former dictatorships was. The Western elite indiscriminately implanted the ideology of the seemingly self-regulating market thereby completely undermining the need for the establishment of lawful standards in the countries of transition.[22]*

State criminalization commenced in Bulgaria in the early 1990s. An immediate reason was the speedy but inefficient institutional reformation launched at the beginning of the democratic transition. The transformation of the Committee for State Security (CSS) was a primary and pressing task on the agenda of post-communist institutional change. Its six Main Directories had collected and systematized important personal and institutional information about various domestic and international activities in politics, economics, and the military. The abolition of the political police – the "watchdog" of the communist system – was the first step in transforming the CSS. Further decentralization of the security forces was to follow. The institutions responsible for the overall reform process included the State Council and the Council of Ministers. And those undertaking responsibility for national security thereafter were the Ministry of Interior and the Ministry of Defense, as well as the Presidency. Large as it was, the process affected structures as well as personalities. Eventually it brought about a near total institutional collapse. So inter-institutional coordination decreased, public order broke down, and the routine enforcement functions of the state were nearly paralyzed. And there were also financial reasons for the increasing disarray in the security sector. It was reported that owing to budget constraints the Ministry of Interior pulled out from guarding industrial facilities. Institutional inconsistency and power vacuums were not confined to the security sector. The judicial system too showed growing evidence of incompetence and inefficiency. So with the security and the justice sector paralyzed, the state came to abdicate some of its key responsibilities. The road to the market of violence was clear.[23]

However, the establishment of the market of violence was not a fully spontaneous process. It was facilitated by other domestic political circumstances. Concretely, the Ministry of Interior explicitly endorsed the establishment of private protection services in order to secure employment for experienced former security officials, and to provide protection for state-owned enterprises and emerging private businesses alike.[24] But the new institutions suffered from a basic disadvantage: they also opened the door of the new security services to organized criminal groups. And the latter found them a secure shelter, promising long-term protection for their criminal (business) activities.[25]

The accompanying Figure 7.1 traces the phases and the structural elements in the criminalization of the state, and illustrates how the state interacts with the global illegal economy. Although the specifics relate to the Bulgarian experience,

Bulgaria 127

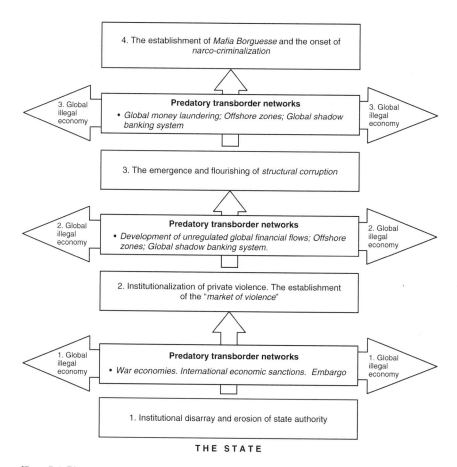

Figure 7.1 Phases, structural elements, and international factors in state criminalization

the process is a more general one. The figure identifies the three branches of the global illegal economy discussed in chapter 1. It also shows how the interaction of the global illegal economy with a state in the process of criminalization assists the establishment and functioning of predatory trans-border networks.

So within a power vacuum but with a blessing from the state, former security officials and criminal groups came to establish the Bulgarian market of violence. In the absence of state institutions, "the market of violence" could not be an economic structure alone. In some sense it was the newly emerging "state" itself, rising from the bottom up to replace or to provide a temporary substitute for the dysfunctional post-socialist institutions.

The market of violence was initially confined to typical black market services. They included racketeering, private protection services, collection of bad debts and provision of insurance; car theft and trans-border commerce in stolen vehicles; trafficking of arms and drugs; human trafficking; and contraband of com-

128 *State and crime syndicates*

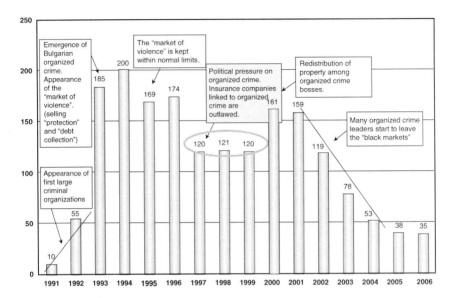

Figure 7.2 Bombings in Bulgaria by year, 1991–2006

modities – the latter of primary significance at time of the Yugoslav embargo. The market of violence subsequently expanded and evolved.

The accompanying Figure 7.2 shows different periods in the development of organized crime in Bulgaria.[26] The "violence market" dominated Bulgaria's politics from 1991 through 1997. After 1997 the state undertook active measures to counter organized crime. That period only lasted for two years or so, though with some positive effects. Criminal violence increased in 2000, when mafia bosses redistributed property, but has declined since 2001. In that year bosses started moving out of the criminal sector and into the legal business sector.

As implied above, two different social groups were especially active in the establishment of the market of violence. One consisted of former state security officials who had been dismissed for ideological reasons in the early 1990s. More than 50 per cent of Communist-era state security officials reportedly were dismissed by 1991. The second group consisted of the so-called "fighters," that is, former martial arts athletes who enjoyed special financial and social privileges under communism but lost them with the change of regime. The nexus between these two groups prompted the establishment of wrestlers/security hybrids that became the major actors of the market of violence.[27]

There were two other groups, from different ends of the socioeconomic continuum, whose involvement was less central but crucial. Former party officials and managers of ex-state socialist enterprises were active, especially when their blessing was needed as a prerequisite for the success of any serious criminal enterprise. Not least, a fourth rather marginal group consisted of some 4000 criminals who

Bulgaria   129

were amnestied from prisons in the early 1990s and who readily joined the market of violence.

Two wrestlers/security hybrids emerged in the early 1990s to become the most famous, or notorious, actors in the Bulgarian market of violence. One of them was the *VIS*, an acronym for trust, investments, security, founded by Vassil Iliev. The other, named *SIC*, was founded by Milcho Bonev aka Baie Mille, Mladen Mihalev, aka Madzho, and the brothers Margini. Both *grupirovki* established themselves in the capital city of Sofia and engaged in the same kinds of black market business activities. Simultaneously local groups emerged in other big cities to contest the status of *VIS* and *SIC* as nation-wide security services. The Club 777 was established in Plovdiv; Marc 93 appeared in Varna; and the first private militia emerged in Bourgas.

Securing control or a monopoly over territories is a major objective pursued by criminal groups. So a gangster turf war broke out in 1993 between elements of the *VIS* and *SIC*. Other groups occasionally joined in. The war was especially violent in the first few years. Bomb attacks were most common. Figure 7.2, published by the local Center for the Study of Democracy (CSD), shows that in 1994 there were 200 bomb attacks altogether.[28]

The Bulgarian market of violence emerged in the 1990s as a homegrown venture. However, it could not have been sustained exclusively as a domestic enterprise. Illegal business activities are largely commercial, and so cross-border trafficking of goods and services is key for their survival. So if racketeering, protection and security services, as well as debt collection, can thrive locally, then commercial activities, and especially those related to illegal goods, demand cross-border operations. From this perspective the contraband trade was the linkage that connected the domestic market of violence to regional networks and markets, thereby sustaining and expanding it in the years to come.

Over time contraband became a chief source of income for the market of violence. With the opening of the national economy analysts estimate that "up to 80 per cent of the country's GDP has passed through state borders."[29] A Bulgarian journalist has investigated an overseas Bulgarian–Georgian project that connected the Black sea ports of Varna and Poti. A public undertaking launched in the early 1990s, the project aimed at the establishment of a *ro-ro* line[30] for transferring commercial goods between Bulgaria and the Caucasus. Though officially administered, the project built on a private partnership established previously between Bulgarian and Georgian counterparts working for a firm of Varna's *SIC* leader, Dancho Markov.[31] By opening a commercial connection between the two Black Sea countries the project simultaneously opened a gateway for intense contraband activities. Later the line was also reportedly used for drug trafficking.

So contraband became a major source of income for the violent syndicates. However, the real catalyst for the development of the Bulgarian market of violence was the 1992–6 embargo imposed on Yugoslavia.[32] This multiplied contraband opportunities for the Bulgarian syndicates and expanded the market of violence to unprecedented proportions. The syndicates became involved in new kinds of high-liquidity businesses, including smuggling of fuel and arms and illicit commerce in

130   *State and crime syndicates*

excise goods, like cigarettes, as well as foodstuffs such as sugar and beverages. The amount of dirty money earned from illegal cross-border business increased proportionately and later was available for reinvestment in the process of privatization of socialist state-owned enterprises.

The Yugo-embargo has also had wider implications. It gave "a forward thrust to the mutually beneficial relationship between the security sector and criminal and quasi-criminal trafficking and smuggling groups."[33] Moreover, it expanded the wrestlers/security alliances, the groups we call violent syndicates, to incorporate some oligarchs, among them former enterprise managers, representatives of the political elite, and customs officials. Especially telling was the organization of smuggling fuel into Yugoslavia by tankers and rail. The chief organizer of the venture was said to be an oligarchic entity called *Multigroup*,[34] discussed below. The division of labor among different agencies was impressive. The enterprise managers allocated fuel and strategic raw materials; former policemen and agents secured contacts with the customs and border administration; wrestlers guarded the embargoed goods and later became key players in the process.[35] It also should be mentioned that the National Security Agency, which controlled the borders, was the successor of the Second Main Directory of State Security, which before 1989 was said to have tolerated the trans-border smuggling of arms and drugs.[36] In short, the Yugo-embargo gave rise to a quadruple alliance between criminals, ex-policemen, the economic elite, and the state. And so it provided a proto-model of structural corruption that not surprisingly flourished in the years thereafter.

Structural corruption: oligarchs, privatization, banking, and international partners

> *The dominating culture of powerful economic actors, whose unlimited arbitrariness, profound corruption and structured rackets was a long tradition, as was the case with the countries of the former Soviet Union, easily blended with the economic culture of democratic states. Some call this process globalization.[37]*

The *VIS* and *SIC* syndicates were established by ex-security officers and the wrestlers and, as shown above, were especially active in the establishment of the market of violence. However, as their size and wealth increased they began looking for alternative and more profitable business activities. Potential partners for new undertakings were the newly established and more influential oligarchs, a diverse group of influentials – including some sportsmen and state security officials – who had secured the protection and help of the highest-ranking Communist Party officials. The linkage binding the oligarchs with some party and state officials was the core mechanism of emerging structural corruption. During the Yugo-embargo such linkages were established *ad hoc*. After the wars next door ended, the emerging partnership between the oligarchs and some state and party officials had to be tested in transitional politics at home. This partnership proved strategically significant, efficient, and durable. Sadly, it diverted the direction of the Bulgarian transition from the establishment of a liberal market economy to the establishment of what Giulio Tremonti has termed *marketism*, a totalitarian-like ideology that replaced Marxism-Leninism and was wrongly perceived as liberalism.[38]

The highest-ranking state security officials and party *nomenklatura* had established themselves as oligarchs after 1987 when the Bulgarian Communist Party, under pressure from the Soviet Union, adopted Decree 56, which allowed for the establishment of private enterprises. In the first year after the Decree members of the Bulgarian State Security agencies founded 90 per cent of the new joint stock companies.[39] A well-known international partner in these ventures was Robert Maxwell, a British media magnate. The working connection between Maxwell and the Bulgarian Communist mafia exemplify what we called in chapter 1 a predatory trans-border network.[40] These networks, similar to those established in other transitional Communist states, aimed at the speedy asset-stripping of the new democracies. "Together with Prime Minister Loukanov, Maxwell arranged the transfer of $2 billion from Bulgaria to Western tax havens."[41] Bulgarian politician Dimiter Popov claimed that $2 billion left the country in just a few months of 1990 during Loukanov's premiership alone. Altogether the money stripped from the state's assets was an estimated $9 billion, which approximated Bulgaria's pre-1990 foreign debt.[42]

So the Bulgarian economy and society came to be dominated by a financial and economic elite rooted in the mafia Communist *nomenklatura*. It is evident after the fact that this elite never really meant to establish a market economy. Instead, it aimed to monopolize the country's economic life and suppress market competition. It also had the effect of marginalizing international businessmen and helped destroy the country's middle class.[43] The concrete strategy employed in pursuit of the above tasks was complex. It included the predation of state property, export of state assets and their subsequent reinvestment in Bulgaria under oligarchic control, and of course the money laundering that was essential to the process. It needed partners as much in state and party institutions as in the market. And it also needed international partners. The conclusion of German journalist Roth is clear and precise: "Organized crime *is* a function of political corruption in Bulgaria."[44] We are inclined to update Proudhon's classic dictum that "Property is theft": in contemporary Bulgaria, "Capital is theft." *Multigroup* was one of the first established oligarchic companies and soon became the face of capitalist Bulgaria. Initially established as an art business for the import and export of antiques and high art, it later expanded enormously into a multi-agency international holding company with branches in Bulgaria, Russia, Switzerland, Lichtenstein, the US, and Paraguay. Its president, Ilya Pavlov, himself a former sportsman, is said to have owed his company's successful start to his close relationship with two key individuals. One was Andrei Loukanov, Bulgaria's leading reform Communist; the other was Dimiter Ivanov, boss of the political police under the old regime. Misha Glenny says this triple alliance was quite efficient: "Loukanov controlled the political machine; Dimiter Ivanov mobilized the security services networks; Ilya and his wrestlers provided the muscle."[45] Chronologically, this alliance became a prototype of emerging structural corruption.

Multigroup was in effect a union of the representatives of Bulgaria's foreign commercial enterprises under state socialism. By 1992 Ilya Pavlov was an established

132 *State and crime syndicates*

multimillionaire, and by 2002 5500 people were working for *Multigroup* in Bulgaria.[46] Advertising his company, President Pavlov observed that *Multigroup* was an investment fund or bank that invested in certain enterprises. Some of them should be sold out; others should be kept as basic businesses.[47]

Various schemes have guided predation of state property and have contributed to the institutionalization of structural corruption. Export of state-owned funds and their subsequent reinvestment in Bulgaria was particularly well suited for *Multigroup*'s organizational capacities: trans-border financial transactions were easily accomplished because they used the trans-border channels that had been established by its member enterprises when they served as foreign commercial agencies for the socialist state. With good reason *Multigroup* was considered to be the largest money laundering institution of the former Communist Party.[48]

The oligarchs' privatization schemes were just as ingenious and provide another good example of emergent structural corruption. The main strategy at the initial stages of privatization was called the *Spider Trap*. This allowed the new companies to privatize the profitable activities of state enterprises without incurring "unreasonable" expenditures.[49] So *Multigroup* would position itself at the entrance, as well as at the exit, of the production process of large enterprises, forcefully monopolizing the supply of raw materials as well as the sale of their products. In the meantime, Loukanov's and later governments provided subsidies to keep the enterprise alive. Bulgarian banker Emil Kyulev describes the process metaphorically: "You hang a goat on a hook and cut it at its foot and it will expire very slowly as the blood leaves the body drop by drop – it agonizes over the years."[50] And when eventually the enterprise announces bankruptcy the oligarchs are there to buy it up at a low and nearly symbolic price. And the oligarchs' self-serving privatization strategies proliferated as the privatization process went on.

Later in the 1990s and after 2000 the oligarchs also took an active part in new policies aimed at redistribution of the national wealth. Structural corruption schemes again underlay the officially launched processes. Two privatization strategies were especially common in that period of transition. One was mass privatization, also known as voucher privatization. This distributes shares of ownership to all citizens either for free or at a very low price, and it also establishes privatization funds, where vouchers accumulate. The ultimate goal is to establish a liquidity capital market. Structural corruption was in place when oligarchs' participation in the privatization funds enabled them to establish control over the smaller fund investments of ordinary citizens and also launder money previously earned by illegal means.[51] The second privatization strategy was cash privatization, also known as asset sale privatization, whereby the entire organization or a part of it is sold out to a strategic investor. The oligarchs purchased large enterprises at minimal prices, while the privatization process was preceded by siphoning of the enterprise's funds through the oligarchs' offshore companies.[52] Cases of hidden privatization were also reported. For example, the famous Black Sea resort, the Golden Sands, was privatized by *SIC* related groups and individuals allied with corrupt politicians from nearly the entire spectrum of the main political parties, including the Union of Democratic Forces, the Movement for Rights and Freedoms, and the

Bulgaria 133

Bulgarian Socialist Party. The resort's infrastructure was also privatized, thereby turning the whole resort area into a near-feudal possession of the *SIC* syndicate and corrupt politicians.[53]

As we move along the list of privatization structures and enterprises we encounter the state-owned Bulgarian Merchant Fleet, whose privatization provides another instance of structural corruption at work. A Bulgarian journalist reports that millions of BGL from the Fleet's accounts were channeled into offshore private sea firms.[54] The Fleet's funds were also said to have subsidized electoral campaigns of the National Movement, "Simeon II."[55] An Italian Mafioso reportedly was selected and initially "employed" as the representative of the Bulgarian Black Sea Fleet in London, a strategy that facilitated the Fleet's subsequent privatization. The Fleet's office in London was known as an "island of treasures," and reportedly it has held 50 to 100 per cent of the capital of a handful of other Europe based but non-Bulgarian companies.[56]

Structural corruption is also documented in the banking sector. In 1996–7 the country experienced a huge financial crisis that threatened the entire Bulgarian financial system. The bank crisis led to the closure of nearly 90 per cent of all private banks from which the loss of national wealth was estimated at approximately $10 billion.[57] The immediate cause of this financial crisis was the "bad-loans" policy attributed to the oligarchs and the security groups. Easy loans were provided by state-owned banks to private banks, including the Bulgarian National Bank, on terms that envisaged low interest rates, delayed payment, etc. The tacit expectation was that most of the credits were provided to establish the private banks and that some of these loans were never meant to be repaid. A report drawn up by the Anti-Mafia Committee at the 38th National Assembly reveals that "in the period of proliferation of private banks (1991–1994), there were no regulations setting the requirement for the proof of the capital's origin before the bank was granted a license. The prohibition for founding banks with borrowed capital was only issued in 1994."[58] The Law on Information about Nonperformance Loans later showed that nearly 3000 private individuals and companies profited from the "bad loans" policy. They were given the emblematic sobriquet "the credit millionaires." The loss incurred by the state financial system amounted to BGL 2.746 billion of which only a fifth, BGL 547 billion, was said to have been later repaid.[59] The high inflation rates that followed the crisis led to devaluation of the lev in 1996, and thereby also devaluated the millionaires' huge debts to the banking system.

Local policy analysts might say this review of instances of structural corruption is incomplete. Our purpose, however, has been accomplished: we have diagnosed the essence and extent of structural corruption, explicated the various schemes by which it was carried out, and identified some of its principal actors. Only one important detail needs to be added. Starting in the mid-1990s the structures of illicit and oligarchic markets began to conflate. Criminal businesses began moving into the legal business sector in response to political change. In an effort to crack down on the market of violence Ivan Kostov's Government of Democratic Forces, which came to power in 1997, contracted with the wrestler/security syndicates to legalize their gray business activities on the condition that they would

134 *State and crime syndicates*

end violence. And so, with the black market being outlawed altogether, the divide between the syndicates on the one hand and the oligarchs on the other hand have become inconsequential. Ilya Pavlov, *Multigroup*'s president, described this process using the metaphor "the lizard cuts off its tail."

The emerging symbiotic market that binds the syndicates with the oligarchs is the prototype of what Jürgen Roth has termed the new multidimensional economy. It has blended legal with illegal elements in an all-encompassing structure of organized quasi-criminal activity and facilitates the transfer of money and resources from one actor to the other. It was known for its independent network of individuals owning dozens of legal companies that mushroomed where resources from corruption provided nourishment, and then closed down upon their exhaustion in a particular sector.[60] The multidimensional economy also is characterized by its close linkages to politicians, MPs, and magistrates as well as national and local administrative officers. Evidence suggests that in the 39th (2001–5) and 40th National Assemblies (2005–9) about twenty MPs on average have actively advocated legislation in the interest of economic structures related to organized crime. They sought to influence a number of draft laws and amendments to existing laws on gambling, insurance, electronic media, spirit production, etc.[61] Obviously, the multidimensional economy was a further step in the development in what we have called the *criminalized state*. What we examine next is how the criminalized state promoted drug production, drug trafficking and drug distribution, that is, how it contributed to narco-criminalization.

Mafia Borguesse: is the state at risk of narco-criminalization?

> *Three interrelated phenomena work synergistically to produce the narcostate: organized crime, government policy, and transnational capitalism. The narcostate may develop in existing democratic regimes, in authoritarian regimes, or in regimes that are in transition to or from democracy. Narcostatization undermines weak democracies and transforms consolidated and transitional democratic regimes into pseudo democracies, or anocracies. In the anocratizing process both consolidated and transitional democracies are in fact corrupted, and the political or ruling class maintains itself in power despite the apparent existence of contested elections and full public participation.[62]*

There are a handful of narco-economies in the world today. Afghanistan, Myanmar, and Laos are the leading producers of the poppy flower of which heroin is made. Other heroin-producing and trafficking countries include Mexico, Egypt, China, and Pakistan. The main coca leaf producers are the three Latin American countries of Colombia, Peru, and Bolivia. Morocco is known as a key producer of Indian hemp, the raw material in the manufacture of cannabis. Other countries in this drug production business include Brazil, Paraguay, Turkey, India, Bangladesh, and Indonesia, as well as several African states. So though narco-economies are few the number of potential narco-states increases. These are states whose politics and practices facilitate the international illegal drug trade. David Jordan identifies two specific state policies that contribute to the global increase in number of the narco-states. The growing dependence of states on drug profits to service

Bulgaria 135

debts is one condition; the expanding dependence of a worldwide population on addictive drugs is the second.[63]

Bulgaria is not a narco-economy. It is neither a major drug producer nor is its drug market large. Drug market indicators are tracked since the late 1990s in reports by the United Nations Office on Drugs and Crime (UNODC). These indicators help in evaluating the relative size of drug markets and in tracking development trends. Drug seizures per year is one of them, a strong though indirect indicator of drug markets' size and development. Other indicators include the size of the area cultivating drug crops; seizures of illicit laboratories; the annual prevalence of drug abuse as percentage of the population aged 15–64; and retail and wholesale drug prices.[64] Not least, drug market evaluations also draw on a base of national expert perceptions. The data suggest that the Bulgarian drug market does not differ much from the rest of the East European drug markets while its values rank in the middle to bottom of the overall regional European drug market. This said, however, the Bulgarian state is yet at risk of narco-criminalization. That risk cannot be judged from the indicators alone, rather it is captured in national expert perceptions as well as from public and expert investigations of emerging alliances between narco bosses and some state institutions and public individuals.

"*Criminalized states*" are those in which governments collaborate with organized crime, that is, where structural corruption is in place. East European states in transition are especially vulnerable to criminalization due to the mutually irresistible attraction between governments on the one hand and organized economic crime on the other. *Criminalized state*, however, also has a narrow meaning, referring specifically to long-term arrangements established between officials and/or state institutions and black marketeers. In theory, states in transition should interact easily with black markets. Their security sectors were engaged in the market of violence; and structural corruption gathered momentum as privatization progressed and penetrated state institutions at all levels. So narco-criminalization can be seen as a virus that finds a hospitable environment within the networks of structural corruption and easily infects the body of the vulnerable state.

In the 1980s Bulgaria was a producer of amphetamine, also known as captagon. The amphetamine production was based on the well-developed socialist pharmacology and was managed by security sector officers. However, during the Communist era domestic consumption of amphetamines was almost entirely unknown.[65] The country exported this synthetic drug to the Middle East; the West European markets were supplied by the higher-quality Polish amphetamines.[66] National experts further suggest that drug markets emerged in Bulgaria in the mid-1990s. This occurred as the trans-border trafficking of drugs was making its way through the country.

The risk of narco-criminalization for Bulgaria ensues from the development of a national drug market. The Bulgarian crime networks and syndicates were faced with the challenge of integrating trans-border drug trafficking into their homegrown black market activities. In the process some government agencies and public individuals have been involved in the establishment of domestic narco-networks and drug markets. A large-scale business as it is, trafficking and drug

136 *State and crime syndicates*

market establishment needed institutional protection as well as strategic political support. It gained them through the pattern of drug-related structural corruption known as *Mafia Borguesse*.[67] This metaphor is here used exclusively to refer to the nexus between government officials and drug bosses.

The process of narco-criminalization began in Bulgaria as drug distribution networks came to seek protection against criminal investigation and penal measures. A tight scheme of reporting evolved in the country, connecting upper-level drug distributors to corrupt law enforcement officers, criminal investigators, and some judges. Narco-criminalization ensued also from money laundering of drug-related profits and payoffs to law enforcement, judiciary, and government officials.[68] Drug market profits were reportedly distributed in a strictly stratified manner, most often through the intermediary of the so-called "black lawyers," discussed below.[69]

Four separate domestic drug markets have been established. The heroin market was structurally most significant and durable as of 2007. It has been run by Turkish, Albanian, Serb, and Kurdish networks[70] that import drugs across the borders, through the Black Sea ports as well as through Sofia's international airport. Konstantin Dimitrov, aka Samokovetza, was known as the Bulgarian narco-boss of this business until he was assassinated in the Netherlands in 2003 by an international criminal organization. Cannabis and amphetamines are local products. The amphetamine synthetic drug production is run by two alternative structures. One is run by Serb criminal syndicates; the other is controlled by local Bulgarians.[71] Relatively little is known about the cocaine market, which was taken over by *VIS* in 2007 after the assassination of key narco-bosses like Samokovetza and Poli Pantev, as well as after the arrest of Mitio Ochite, the narco-boss of the Black Sea area.[72]

Each of the four drug markets is well established. The growth and consolidation of the heroin market illustrates well what in essence is the *Mafia Borguesse*. Since the mid-1990s regional heroin markets have developed in different Bulgarian cities to meet the drug addiction needs of some 15,000 to 30,000 heroin users.[73] The drug-consuming urban areas were initially supplied by hierarchical networks. The *Mafia Borguesse* emerged as the narco networks made durable connections with the police. The initially hierarchical organization of the heroin market, with its strict division and control of territories, made police a strategic partner. Drug markets analysts observe that organized crime in Sofia has laid out the city's heroin market districts following the boundaries of its main police districts. So the city had been divided in nine regional markets with organized crime structures negotiating which group controls what region. Narco-dealers acknowledge that "The overlap of police territorial organization and the drug distribution regions is a natural solution, made in view of the experience and taking into consideration the key role played by the police in the redistribution of territories."[74] In Varna, a city at the Black Sea coast about 400 km from Sofia, the nexus between police and drug bosses has assumed a different outlook. The partnership between police officers and narco-bosses was aimed not only at institutional protection of the evolving local drug markets; it was also directed against the invasion of Russian criminal groups interested in the Bulgarian drug market.[75] In other cities similar kinds of symbiotic partnerships empowered local mafiosi to take the lead in nominating individuals for appointment as local police director.[76]

The *Mafia Borguesse* also extended its tentacles to include a circle of lawyers. These are the so-called "black lawyers," that is, professionals who provide judicial services to narco-criminals in particular. They are more often than not former law enforcement officers or investigative magistrates. Some are former public prosecutors and occasionally former judges. The strategies that "black lawyers" use in defense of their clients show how much the *Mafia Borguesse* can penetrate and damage the administration of justice. They use clientelistic privileges or corrupt practises at various system levels. Since they work in networks, not as individuals, they take a case over depending on their "influence" in various districts or parts of the judiciary. Their role is to make deals on behalf of their client, which can include cash payments, leakage of information in the media, and private arrangements with the police. Police officers, police investigators, investigating magistrates, public prosecutors, and judges all have been approached with an aim to secure a "breakthrough" at every step of the pre-trial phase and the proceedings.[77]

Overall, narco-criminalization is a narrow sector within a wider system of structural corruption. However, it is most problematic, especially now that the transition to a market economy has been officially completed. Drug-related structural corruption is the essence of the criminalized state. And countering it effectively presents a problem both to newly emerging democracies and established ones. So our task in the next section is to discuss briefly the relative strength or weakness of states vis-à-vis controlling trans-border drug networks that cross their territories.

The criminalized state and predatory trans-border networks

The interaction between the criminalized state and trans-border crime networks can best be understood in terms of the chicken-and-egg dilemma. We cannot say which came first but have to recognize the interaction as a cyclical repetition. Some analysts observe that during the socialist era state agencies established trans-border organized crime channels. They argue that this was accomplished by involving security staff in the economy, specifically by assigning security staff tasks going beyond the conventional intelligence and counter-intelligence. These tasks included gathering scientific and technological information by circumventing international restrictions and regulations.[78] Additional tasks included establishing control over the contraband channels for arms, excise goods, and prohibited medications.[79] When the transition to market economy commenced the material assets of the former technological intelligence service remained in the hands of a few individuals who by no means represented legitimate economic entities.[80] So by 1989 a sizeable group of security officers had established legal businesses whose activities could be said to be trans-border criminal activities.[81]

This argument is accurate but incomplete. The state should not be viewed as a unitary agency. It is instead a web of multiple actors, agencies, and networks. In socialist times some state agencies outweighed the others by means of expanding

138   *State and crime syndicates*

their territorial outreach; by establishing monopolies over technological and scientific information; and by increasing their number of international commercial contacts, as well as by controlling the state's legitimate means of coercion. These state agencies set up the pre-1989 trans-border predatory networks. The post-1989 trans-border trafficking, however, proliferated at a time when the state lost its legitimate monopoly of violence and security was nearly completely privatized. From this perspective the post 1989 trans-border crime networks could be seen as trans-border extensions of the market of violence.

Some Balkan contraband channels were initially established with the help of state agencies in the early 1990s to assist neighboring states at war; they were mostly used for trafficking of arms and oil. But soon thereafter they turned into cross-border "highways" trafficking drugs, excise goods, humans, and cars in all directions. As the state weakened, trans-border criminal networks were rapidly privatized as were their pre-1989 prototypes. Revenues flowed to private actors. Thus the hypothetical unidirectional connection from the "state" to trans-border crime networks has rotated in the opposite direction and now promotes further state criminalization.

What are the major trans-border illicit and criminal networks and how did state actors facilitate their establishment? And how have illicit trans-border networks contributed in turn to the state's further criminalization? We turn to some evidence. Seven trans-border criminal networks are identified below, some established to break embargos, others related to contraband, still others exclusively drug-related. Their cross-border channels partly overlap. More importantly their actors, who represent various state institutions and some societal segments, also reappear in different trans-border networks.

We begin with the state-protected channels run by oligarchs. Trade in oil and contraband to Yugoslavia was one of a kind. It was a state-protected channel run, however, by the oligarchic *Multigroup*.[82] Complex, yet non-violent, it involved many partners and also active associates including key partners in the state. The security syndicates also lent support, drawn into business by *Multigroup*. Thus, for instance, *SIC* leader Milcho Bonev, aka Baie Mille, is said to have facilitated shipment of contraband oil to Yugoslavia by state institutions, including the Ministry of Interior and the Finance Ministry.[83] Another *SIC* leader, Mladen Mihalev, aka Madzho, is said to have arranged independent contraband trade in oil with *Multigroup*'s president Ilya Pavlov.[84]

Smuggling of arms to Yugoslavia was another state-protected trans-border channel. Researchers point to the "Albanian" arms deal, whereby Bulgarian criminal structures in 1993 provided arms to Serbia by sending a shipment valued at $670,000 to Macedonia, claiming it was destined for Albania.[85] Jürgen Roth mentions that *Kintex* supplied Bosnia and Herzegovina and Croatia with Russian arms in the fall of 1992.[86] *Kintex* was a state-owned firm established during the socialist era to run foreign commercial and currency operations. It was Bulgaria's exclusive weapons export company.[87] One strategy for carrying out trans-border arms transactions was partnering with international arms and drugs dealers. Syrian citizen Monser al Kasar is mentioned as one of the *Kintex*'s traditional clients.[88]

Transnational drug networks are a joint collaborative business by local Bulgarian structures and international partnering groups. Locally the two wrestlers/ security groups – the *VIS* and *SIC* – were especially active. The division of the national drug markets between the *VIS* and the *SIC* seems conditional, but overall *SIC* appears in journalist and expert publications as more closely connected to the heroin market,[89] and *VIS* to the cocaine market.[90] Linkages are documented between the *SIC* leader Baie Mille and his Serb counterpart, Sreten Josic.[91] Less is known about the cocaine markets. Reportedly some Bulgarian nationals were involved in transnational cocaine trafficking, some of them connected to the Bulgarian market and others not.[92]

Synthetic drug production too has established trans-border networks. Several Serb nationals have reportedly been involved in the local production of amphetamines, including Budimir Kuiovic and Dragomir Raikovic.[93] Local observers say Serbian drug-producing facilities have been in use in Bulgaria for some time. One interpretation is that Serb organized crime has participated in synthetic drug production in Bulgaria since the early days of the Yugoslav wars; another is that they were moved to Bulgaria for safety reasons in 2003 in response to the sweeping anti-crime, anti-corruption reforms of the Saber Operation in Serbia.[94] It also has been said that for risk reduction purposes the Serb laboratories were moved after 2005 to Turkey and the Middle East.[95]

The contraband channels followed the previously established embargo-breaking channels. They were shared by some political actors as well as by former security sector officials. Two political parties – the Bulgarian Socialist Party (BSP) and the Movement for Rights and Freedom (MRF) – are known to have established networks of firms that worked mainly in the gray economy. The contraband channels that dealt with alcohol and cigarettes were reportedly controlled mostly by BSP.[96] The contraband trade in cigarettes was said to be a heritage of the state security services,[97] one that has become the most lucrative revenue source for the governing elites since 1989. Its channels are said to have been politically protected, and customs and the police actively collaborate in the trade. The money earned from contraband trafficking has been widely used, reportedly including the subsidizing of political parties and elections.[98] Ivan Todorov, aka Doctora, who was killed in February 2006, was known as the main person involved in contraband tobacco trade from Moscow to London.

Car theft and the international trade in stolen vehicles is another specialty of the Bulgarian crime networks. The distribution network for stolen cars in Bulgaria is known to have been run by the wrestlers, working in cooperation with amnestied criminals. This contributed in a major way to the establishment of the *VIS* and *SIC* as powerful groups. The cross-border nature of the stolen car trade ensured that the emerging Bulgarian syndicates established links with similar groups in other Balkan and East European countries. The stolen car contraband route originated in West Europe but passed through Central Europe to the Balkans and beyond to the Middle East and the former Soviet Republics. It was a complex chain of a half-dozen links involving expert auto thieves as well as corrupt police and border officers from various states. In the 1993 and 1994, according to official statistics,

140　*State and crime syndicates*

the number of imported stolen vehicles in Bulgaria reached 20–25 per cent of all imported vehicles, both new and used ones.[99]

This discussion should end where it began. The chicken-and-egg dilemma has provided a sensible interpretation of the interaction between trans-border crime and the criminalized state. It poses challenges, however, when a reform program aimed at state decriminalization is to be developed. Where should reforms begin? How efficient could it be if trans-border predatory networks recurrently revive the state's criminal structures and threaten to reproduce them in the long run?

Two major tasks should occupy the agenda of democratizing Bulgarian politics. One is related to the development of efficient anti-corruption policy; the other to the implementation of a comprehensive anti-drug policy. Structural corruption is a pressing problem in Bulgaria's current politics. Now that privatization has been nearly accomplished, the factor that continues to sustain it is the trans-border contraband networks. Countering contraband activities is a challenging task for a number of reasons. As suggested above, contraband is an especially valuable gateway, a "switch" equalizing the standards between the domestic and international criminal markets. Contraband operates on the demand-and-supply principle and is the basis for trans-border criminally exploitable ties, a term introduced in chapter 1 to denote shared criminal dispositions that align illicit commercial partners. Substantively, contraband is a strong compensating mechanism that helps "war economies" and global "peripheral economies" to make ends meet. However, contraband has one more valuable trait. It reinforces local cultures of corruption, where "corruption behavior is . . . . not only driven by greed and structural forces, but also by informal codes of conduct associated with reciprocity ties within particularistic and communitarian social networks."[100] To the extent that contraband provides a regular supply of fresh resources it also keeps corruption alive and so contributes to the continuous reproduction of a basic pattern of social conduct where reciprocity in law-breaking is a public norm that secures the stability of the criminalized state.

In the second place, narco-criminalization has also been identified as a potential threat. In comparative perspective Bulgaria-related trans-border drug trafficking networks do not appear as key players. However, international drug markets develop over time, they expand and contract, and factors that determine their evolution are regional and global. So, hypothetically what can be placed under control are only the domestic factors shaping drug markets' development. The process demands substantial changes in some state institutions, but it should also affect political factions suspected of having protected drug business activities. Destroying the *Mafia Borguesse* is a major step and a key precondition toward the decriminalization of the state.

Conclusion: explaining predatory networks

This book is focused on the economics of trans-border violence networks. Case studies deal with alliances established between trans-border criminal networks on the one hand, and political militants on the other. Terrorism in post-Communist

Bulgaria has assumed a different outlook. It was an instrument of rivalries among criminal/security syndicates competing over markets. Ironically, they did not aim to capture the state yet large sectors of it were criminalized as some officials and some politicians became complicit in the predation of public property and the operation of international contraband networks, while others protect the growing domestic drug market. These are our general findings:

- First, predatory trans-border networks are strong and persistent where the *criminalized state* assists their establishment. In Bulgaria some predatory networks were established by state security officials under the totalitarian control of the communist state.
- Second, the state can succumb to *criminalization* where two conditions are in place. The widespread practice of political corruption is the necessary condition; the privatization of the security sector is the sufficient condition.
- Third, the criminalized state forges explicitly economic-driven alliances among various groups domestically that thereafter easily extend across borders.
- Fourth, once established, a criminalized state becomes a hospitable shelter for trans-border drug networks and domestic drug-related activities.

These are the structural factors prompting the establishment of predatory networks and the criminalized state. We showed above that the underlying causes in Bulgaria were economic: the collapse of the socialist economy and the malaise that persisted during the first transitional decade. One of Bulgaria's oligarchs, Ivo Kamenov of the *TIM* group, recently offered this positive assessment of what has been accomplished in the second decade of the transition:

> We pride ourselves on our accomplishments. Ninety-nine per cent of our businesses – the air company, the banks – would have bankrupted without us. . . . 22,000 people work for our companies. . . . We have not collaborated with SIC and VIS . . . because we are soldiers, and they were criminals. They are no more.
>
> I can tell you one thing. . . . Every society [i.e. at the stage of its primitive accumulation] begins with speculations. . . . The biggest problem of Bulgaria is drug trafficking. I know one thing. The drugs whether they come from Afghanistan, or Turkey or Bulgaria, they go to Kosovo. I am sure. Part of them remains here for local consumption. . . .
>
> If you would analyze the structure of assassinations in Bulgaria, you won't discover economically driven assassinations. Ninety-nine per cent of them are either family driven, or are drug related. . . .
>
> The business behavior of our rivals was anarchical. Do you know what distinguishes us from the others? . . . [T]he discipline. Because we are soldiers. . . . And please you never call a warrior a mafiozo. This is a big insult! . . . And one more difference between you and us, between moral and immoral – the world for us is always black and white.[101]

142   *State and crime syndicates*

Ivo Kamenov is one of the three managers of the *TIM* group. *TIM* is the largest, the most powerful, and the sole "transitional" survivor of the Bulgarian oligarchic and wrestlers/security groups. Based in Varna, *TIM* was established by former Fleet intelligence officers. Exceptionally disciplined and non-transparent, the group has achieved unquestionable economic success. For an outside observer Kamenov's words are optimistic. Indeed, what else could a post-transition society wish for itself? The transition has been completed; illicit businesses have been replaced by legal ones; the drug market has been isolated and denounced; and moral values are reaffirmed. For many Bulgarians, however, the optimism is premature. State decriminalization and countering contraband channels and trans-border drug networks are still pending projects. Perhaps now they are even more challenging precisely because the market transition has been supposedly completed. The country's EU membership now sheds a revealing light on the heap of the country's unresolved problems, but it does not resolve them.

8 Militants and money

The political economy of communal rebels in post-communist Europe and the Middle East

Step outside the box of conventional thinking and labeling about terrorism. "Terrorists" are militants who use acts or threats of violence to create fear and compliant behavior in a target audience as a strategy, seldom their only one, in pursuit of their political objectives. The militant groups most durable and likely to succeed are those that have committed supporters, ample resources, and a secure base, preferably a territorial one. In Mao's words "[t]he guerrilla must move amongst the people as a fish swims in the sea." They begin with a nucleus of activists who try to take advantage of local and international opportunities that give them space in which to operate. Most are defeated or fade away, some persist and a few succeed. Grabosky and Stohl point out that "those that have shown the greatest resilience have been . . . ethno-nationalist movements," and, we would add, those whose social ties and commitments come from a shared religious identity.[1] Politically they may gain enough support to negotiate or force their way into power. Economically they may develop sources of income and markets through which they and their followers prosper.

This chapter looks specifically at the role of money in the growth and decline of trans-state terrorist organizations, or in other words the linkage between political militancy and economic crime.[2] We focus on organizations that represent ethnic and religious identity groups, that is, imagined communities that potentially support militants' political aims. Our evidence comes partly from surveys of identity groups in the Middle East and the post-Communist states from the 1980s to the mid-2000s. But we rely mainly on case study evidence from the chapters in this book.

Three issues are of particular concern here. One is whether and how militants can gain enough funding to survive. If they engage in criminal activities, either on their own or in alliance with international criminal syndicates, then they should comply with the informal rules of the domestic and international gangster economy.[3] Some kinds of fund-raising are better than others. Contributions from ethnic kindred, for example, are a more reliable and less risky source of funds than, say, armed robbery. Trafficking in drugs and women for European and North American markets is more lucrative than ransom kidnappings. Some militant organizations have gone into businesses that have generated profits enough to provide an economic base outside the underworlds of terrorism and crime. The

144   *Militants and money*

Palestine Liberation Organization was spectacularly successful in both criminal and business activities long before implementation of the 1993 Oslo Accords gave it a territorial home. In 1976, during the Lebanese civil war, the PLO carried out a hugely profitable robbery of the British Bank of the Middle East. By the mid-1980s its commercial activities generated annual income of $600 million of which $500 million came from investments.[4] The factual question is, which means are most often employed, by which groups, and with what success?

The second issue is whether and how militants' economic successes either subvert or facilitate their political objectives. There are competing arguments on this issue. James Adams, in the conclusion to his classic 1986 study of *The Financing of Terror*, points out that

> . . . to survive terrorist groups need to cross an economic divide that separates those who live a hand-to-mouth existence from those who can actually plan ahead. All those groups which have come and gone in the last twenty years have failed to cross that divide. . . . The few who remain have cooler heads and have been able to see that good financial planning means having enough cash to buy and keep support, to pay for arms and to build a propaganda base among the people that the organisation claims to represent.[5]

One possibility is that militants who develop reliable sources of income may experience an agenda shift in which profit-seeking becomes more important than power-seeking. Jeremy Weinstein argues, in his recent comparative study *Inside Rebellion*, that the kinds of resources available to militants shape their strategies and success – but in quite different ways than Adams would have it. Weinstein's case studies of insurgencies in Africa and Latin America show that movements based mainly on appeals to identity and ideology – "social endowments" is his term – are more resilient and have less need of coercion to secure support. Groups with ample economic endowments, on the other hand,

> lend themselves to recruitment on the basis of short-term material interests, generating a flood of opportunistic joiners. . . . [M]is behavior and indiscipline plague opportunistic organizations, as individual members take advantage of their positions of authority over civilians for personal gain.[6]

Even if militants' money and political strategies lead to a political outcome that is successful in the short run, as they did for the PLO, their leaders inherit a legacy of self-serving profit-taking that fosters corruption and may discredit them for followers. A disillusioned jihadist interviewed by Jessica Stern said,

> Initially I was of the view [the leaders] were doing jihad, but now I believe that it is a business and people are earning wealth through it. I thought [the leaders] were true Muslims, but now I believe that they are a fraud, they are selling Islam as a product. . . . First I was there for jihad, now I am there for my financial reasons.[7]

The 2010 *Globalization of Crime* report from the UN Office on Drugs and Crime provides a recent example of militants' agenda shift from politics to profit-seeking:

> Modern piracy off the coast of Somalia is said to have arisen from efforts of local fishermen who formed vigilante groups to protect their territorial waters. Today, in a situation similar to what has happened in the Niger Delta, the political aims of the pirates are all but forgotten. While the rhetoric remains, the true end of these attacks is the enrichment of the pirates. . . . At present, most of the piracy appears to be conducted by a small number of dedicated groups, with limited ties to militants and insurgents on the mainland.[8]

The report goes on to point out that because the pirates have had such success, they are a lucrative target for takeover by insurgent groups on the mainland, in particular the al-Qaeda-linked force known as al-Shabaab whose campaign to establish an Islamist state in Somalia has thus far been thwarted by military intervention from the African Union, Kenya, and Ethiopia.

A third issue is how the financial basis of militant organizations counters efforts at conflict management by governments and regional organizations. It is obvious that economically successful militant organizations are likely more resilient in the face of counter-insurgency. Conflict management is much more complex when they develop symbiotic relations with compliant governments, or in fact capture or create governments. In such circumstances officials as well as prospering militants have a vested interest in perpetuating conflict. Our case studies of Kosovo, Serbia, Bosnia, and Bulgaria all provide evidence of the different kinds of bonds that can develop among corrupt officials, crime networks, and terrorist organizations. Kemp provides ample European evidence in support of his thesis that "corruption and organized crime, while threats in themselves, become significantly more destabilizing when they are linked with ethnic issues (and vice versa)."[9] In the conclusion to this chapter we mention strategies that may help break up the nexus among crime, corruption, and communal extremism – political strategies that are rather different from familiar international approaches to counter-insurgency, crime control, and conflict management.

A typology of militant fund-raising strategies

Terrorists and other insurgents have many potential sources of money, some easier and some more risky than others. So we begin with a general discussion of four modalities by which militants can get the money needed to secure arms, pay rank-and-file members, carry out operations, propagandize their cause, buy the cooperation of officials, and provide welfare services for their supporters. We call them *Sponsorship, Donation, Predation,* and *Entrepreneurship.*[10]

Sponsorship is the provision of funds (and sometimes armaments and personnel) by foreign states and organizations allied with them. States may provide substantial support to militants in pursuit of their own foreign policy objectives. In chapter 3 we report evidence that the Kurdish Workers Party (PKK) for nearly twenty

146   *Militants and money*

years received support from Syria, Iran, Iraq, the USSR, and possibly Greece in an undeclared war against Turkey. But states are perhaps the least desirable external source of support because they often impose constraints on what the militants can and cannot do, and they may pull the plug if it suits them. In the 1960s the Kurdish Democratic Party of Iraq, fighting for an autonomous Kurdish state in northern Iraq, received support from the governments of the US, Israel, and the Shah of Iran as a way of bringing pressure on the Saddam Hussein regime. The support ended in 1975 because of a shift in international alignments and interests, and the KDP rebellion collapsed.[11]

In the 1970s the USSR was widely thought to head an international conspiracy to overthrow Western democracies by funding terrorist movements. Adams concludes this was largely a myth. PLO supporters he interviewed, for example, "talked in the most insulting terms about their alleged ally. Not only have the Soviets never contributed financially to the PLO cause, but they make the Palestinians pay in hard-earned foreign exchange for all arms delivered." The PLO's Arab allies were more generous but "the PLO has been used more as a tool by its state sponsors. . . . Every Arab country contributes to its own favoured group within the PLO, and the money that is given is invariably expected to bring with it loyalty to the donor nation."[12]

After the Cold War ended major powers were ever less likely to support terrorist movements as an instrument of foreign policy. Analysts have suggested that terrorist movements turned to other kinds of crime out of necessity; we suspect they did so because the globalizing post-Communist world provided many new and expanded opportunities for making and moving illicit money. In any case, terrorist movements and the crime networks with which they often intersect, interact, and share common business strategies are now widely recognized as threats that require concerted international action.[13]

Sponsorship remains significant outside the post-Communist sphere, where regional powers continue to support insurgencies in neighboring states. The Pakistani government, for example, aided the Taliban during and after its 1990s campaign to take power in Afghanistan, and some elements of the Pakistani military and intelligence service (ISI) support the Taliban in its resistance to the US-led military coalition. Support for insurgent and terrorist movements is also widespread in Africa south of the Sahara. The Khartoum government, in another example, for a long time supported and provided sanctuary for the Lord's Resistance Army (LRA) of Uganda, not because Khartoum supported the LRA's inchoate, religiously justified campaign of murderous violence against civilians but to counter the Ugandan government's policy of assisting Sudanese groups that oppose the Khartoum regime. Africa, however, is outside the scope of this survey.[14]

Donation is the provision of funds (and sometimes volunteers and materiel) from non-state sympathizers external to the movement. Potential sources include charitable organizations, diasporas, and members of civil society elsewhere who identify with the militants and their cause. One advantage of donations is that they require relatively little effort by the militants and usually carry few constraints. In the past they have not usually been illegal in the countries of origin, but international efforts to restrict them have increased substantially since 2000. A disadvantage they share with sponsorship is that militants have little control over them. Some illustrations follow.

For a decade beginning in the early 1970s the Irish Republican Army received contributions from NORAID, a network of Irish-American supporters. It provided only a small portion of the IRA's income and dried up because of a decline in diaspora sympathy, and US investigation and prosecution of IRA sympathizers for arms procurement.[15]

The Tamil Tigers fought an insurgency against the Sri Lankan government from 1976 to 2009 that relied heavily on terror attacks and pioneered the contemporary use of suicide bombings. They depended on substantial financial and material support from the Tamil diaspora in North America and Western Europe. In the aftermath of the September 11, 2001 al-Qaeda attacks the US, Canadian, and European governments began to restrict remittances to terrorist groups everywhere. Reportedly the decline in diaspora funding was one consideration that led the Tigers to announce a ceasefire in late 2000 and to begin peace negotiations with the government.

Since 2000 international support for jihadist terrorism is commonly attributed to the states, institutions, and individuals that control Arab oil wealth. There is ample evidence that Saudi-based religious and charitable foundations and prominent banking and business families sponsor Islamic institutions abroad – madrassas, mosques, social services, publications, scholarships for study at Islamic universities, and so forth. Some of these funds reach militant organizations like al-Qaeda and the local jihadist organizations inspired by it throughout the Islamic world – either by design or diversion. Ehrenfeld, citing unnamed intelligence sources, says that in 2000 "Saudi citizens' contributions to various Islamist groups amounted to $500 million."[16] Other sources say that over two recent decades the Saudis have spent $87 billion propagating Wahabism abroad. Some of this flood of resources directly or indirectly supports al-Qaeda and similar groups, but exactly how much is usually unknowable.

We document more specific examples in the preceding case studies. During the Bosnian independence war in the early 1990s, Saudi religious foundations were among the Islamic supporters of embattled Muslims fighting Serb and Croat forces. After the war they provided funding for Islamist schools and activist organizations. During the late 1990s the armed forces of the Republic of Kosovo in exile – later absorbed by the Kosovo Liberation Army – were supported mainly by a 3 per cent tax paid by the Albanian diaspora.[17]

Predation is perhaps the most widely publicized funding strategy used by militant organizations. Extortion, especially in the form of "revolutionary taxes" exacted from compliant populations and businessmen in the militants' home countries and among its diaspora, is widely practiced. Robbery is another tactic, the targets including businesses, banks, armored cars, and travelers. Kidnappings for ransom are another. Theft of weaponry from armories and police stations provides armaments for militants and an exchangeable commodity. These tactics differ from donation in that all involve the direct use or threat of force. A particularly

148   *Militants and money*

grisly form of predation was practiced by some Kosovar networks after the Serbian withdrawal in mid-1999 and before the international Kosovo Stabilization Force was in place: Serbians captured by the KLA were taken to rural locations in Albania proper, killed, and their organs clinically removed and sold abroad for transplantation.[18]

Militants also have become adept at diverting funds from financial institutions and individuals, including ATM theft and the creative use of the Internet for credit card and other kinds of fraud. The advantage of predation is that, unlike sponsorship and donation, it is under the direct control of the militants. The main disadvantage is that such actions are almost invariably crimes that attract countermeasures by security forces and lead to hardening of the targets and, frequently, the arrest, prosecution, and imprisonment of the perpetrators.

Depending on the targets and the extent of violence done to them, predation also can undermine militants' legitimacy among their supporters and the wider public.[19] For example, during the Algerian civil war Islamists at first relied on contributions from the faithful. Soon, however, jihadist cells turned to armed robbery (the victims often were murdered) and kidnappings, along with extortion from truckers and other businessmen. In 2007 alone 155 people, mostly businessmen and traders, were reportedly kidnapped by armed Islamists either from their homes or at checkpoints. Our case study of Algeria provides more detail and shows that predation, combined with killings of Muslims who did not support the Algerian jihadists, contributed directly to the movement's transformation from the Islamic Front's popular movement to politically and geographically isolated gangs of bandits.

Entrepreneurship. Profit-making businesses are a more reliable long-term source of income for militant organizations than sponsorship and donation (because of donor fatigue) or predation (tightened security measures and loss of support). The single most profitable business for militants in the Middle East and post-Communist world is drug trafficking. The estimated 4.1 million cocaine users in Europe provided a $34 billion market in 2008, according to UN estimates. This market is supplied almost entirely by Latin American criminal networks, though many groups including political militants are involved in its distribution within Europe. An estimated 340 tons of Afghan heroin supplies a global market worth about $55 billion, of which about 21 percent goes to Russian consumers and 20 percent to the rest of Europe (where the UK, Italy, and France are the major consumers). Middle Eastern groups, both criminals and militants, smuggle heroin via Tajikistan to Russia and via Iran and through the "Balkan route" to West Europe. Our case studies show that Kosovar nationalists and the Kurdish PKK have had a profitable role in both smuggling and distribution in European markets. Well more than half the money generated by the trade in both drugs goes to the wholesalers and retailers, with the traffickers themselves netting perhaps a quarter. The producers get a very small share.[20] The value of the trade, sustained as it is by stable demand in Western Europe and growing demand in the Soviet successor states, is enormously attractive to both criminal and militant networks. Local and international anti-drug actions increase both the risks and profits for traffickers.

Militants and money 149

The smuggling of consumer goods generates far less income overall but can be quite lucrative in local situations. Its profitability depends mostly on differential tax rates across countries. During the Balkan wars a Serbian businessman-smuggler, Vanja Bokan, set up a very lucrative trade in smuggled cigarettes via the Serbian republic of Montenegro. Cigarettes are heavily taxed in Western Europe but are available tax-free from free trade zones in Europe and the Middle East. Bokan's Ilyushin cargo planes, filled with tax-free cigarettes supposedly en route to destinations like Malta, would have "technical landings" in Montenegro with the complicity of local authorities. The cigarettes were off-loaded and soon on board fleets of speedboats operating between Montenegrin ports and southern Italy. The speedboats could just as easily carry drugs and high-value human cargo. In Italy the cigarettes were sold by organized crime groups, with the profits shared back along the chain.[21]

Most consumer goods smuggling is less complex, though just as profitable, as goods move across borders by truck, car, and pack animal. The IRA easily took advantage of a differential in the VAT tax on luxury goods, 35 per cent in Northern Ireland and 15 per cent in the Republic. Officials estimated that 24,000 color TVs were smuggled into the Republic in 1983, at very little risk to IRA businessmen who could make use of 240 unauthorized border crossing points that were virtually impossible to control.[22] Elsewhere, especially in the Balkans and the Middle East, payoffs to border guards and customs officials eat into the profits of smugglers and traffickers but help make it a low-risk business.

Human trafficking also is a significant source of income for both militants and criminal networks. In Europe an estimated 70,000 people were smuggled in each year in the early 2000s, most of them women from Russia and the Balkans who were recruited by deception for a sex trade whose gross receipts the UN estimates at $3 billion per year.[23] The illegal arms trade is of considerable importance for militants, though not necessarily for the profits it generates. They need arms for their own use and often are in a position to acquire weaponry by theft, which in turn can be traded across borders. This is small business, though. A recent UN study points out that most large-scale arms trafficking takes place under a "veneer of legality. . . . Most transactions involve a combination of officials and international arms brokers. These brokers sell their connections, their access to fraudulent paper work, and their transportation services to both insurgent groups and embargoed states."[24]

Almost every kind of international crime can be and has been used by communal militants to generate income. Grabosky and Stohl mention the sale of pornographic materials by militant groups and intellectual property piracy as other examples.[25] Militants as entrepreneurs often find themselves in competition with criminal networks for access to the same markets and may lack the requisite contacts and expertise. On the other hand they have special advantages. One is that shared identity is the connective tissue of their networks – this means that trust is more easily established and criminal actions carried out based on more than narrow self-interest. There may be "no honor among thieves" but there is usually mutual obligation among coethnics and other communal militants. Moreover

150   *Militants and money*

terrorists, which some of them are, have considerable capacity to use violence to enforce contracts or kill rivals. Sometimes militants have become involved in violent turf wars with criminal networks, as happened with some Kosovar drug traffickers in Italy (the Albanians won). More likely they enter into "unholy alliances" of mutual advantage with crime networks, in which case profits must be shared.

The most important challenge for many terrorist and militant entrepreneurs is crossing the divide from illicit to licit business. Legal status protects them from local and international law enforcement and helps ensure the long-term profitability of their activities. Like alliances with criminal networks, legality also increases the likelihood that militants will become more interested in profits than political objectives – an agenda shift that from both security and enforcement perspectives is arguably a good thing.[26] The PLO's success in establishing legitimate businesses during the 1970s and 1980s was summarized above. Its manufacturing, agricultural, and service businesses in Lebanon before the Israel invasion of 1982 were staffed largely by Palestinian refugees and generated about $45 million a year for PLO coffers – though some of it went directly into the private bank accounts of PLO officials. The PLO also was linked to Middle Eastern banks, more or less legally, while its factions simultaneously exacted taxes or bribes on goods passing through Lebanese ports and participated in very lucrative robberies.[27]

Money laundering is key to the transition from illicit to licit enterprise by militants and criminals alike. In discussions of terrorism the term often is used to refer to any illicit transfers of money to or from militant organizations. It has this more precise meaning: "Money laundering involves disguising assets so they can be used without the detection of the illegal activity that produced them."[28] The term originated in a simple kind of transaction that developed in the United States in the 1920s: to conceal the origins of bootlegging and other illicit proceeds: criminals invested in high-cash-flow businesses like laundromats whose coin-based income was "clean." Money laundering now is a diverse and complex activity in which money can be cleaned through almost any high-cash-flow business, the international banking system, investments in real estate, etc.[29] A recent study by Belli and associates has examined about a hundred financial schemes used by Islamist extremists in the United States between 1990 and 2010, based on criminal prosecutions. These schemes were both domestic and international and often involved "money-dirtying," that is, "using money raised legitimately (e.g., through donations or legitimate investments) for illicit purposes (e.g., terrorism financing)." The extremists used "traditional money transfer mechanisms both domestically and internationally (wire transfers, cash deposits, checks)" as well as "simpler methods that do not leave paper trails, like conducting transactions in cash and physically transporting money across borders." The study also points out that non-extremist accomplices often helped carry out the transactions.[30] There are compelling reasons to think, based on our comparative evidence, that the same kinds of schemes are universally used by militant and criminal networks.

The uses of cleaned money by militant organizations are seldom known in detail. Some proceeds pay salaries and living expenses for terrorists, others merely support comfortable living. The May 2011 raid on bin Laden's compound in the

Militants and money 151

Pakistani town of Abbottabad showed that he was living in relative comfort, not in a cave. The higher an individual is in a group's hierarchy, the greater the payouts. Adams quotes a critic of Yasser Arafat who told him in the mid-1980s that "The members of the financial council of Fatah – numbering between nine and eleven –have almost to a man become millionaires."[31] Criminal investigation of the Italian Red Brigade terrorist organization revealed rare details of how the group disbursed $1 million in proceeds from a 1981 kidnapping (the money was not laundered, but its uses are suggestive about how militants use illicit gains). It was divided equally among three different cells and then to members who used it for such purposes as major dental work, a holiday on Capri, purchase of a modest flat, and an elaborate wedding celebration. Within a year almost all the money was dissipated.[32] A 1999 Dutch study showed that criminal – not militant – income was spent in more conservative ways: 57 percent of the total was invested in real estate and securities; another 23 percent was directly invested in coffee houses, shops, hotels, and brothels. Some of the remainder was spent on luxury goods, and some was reinvested in the criminal enterprises that generated the income.[33]

Like the Dutch criminals, more far-sighted militants will invest some of the proceeds of predation and illicit entrepreneurship in licit businesses. Two contemporary examples come from the case studies of the Unholy Alliances project. In Kosovo some war-generated criminal profits reportedly have been invested in hotels and brothels, construction firms, gasoline stations, and vacation properties. In Bulgaria, after the end of the 1990s Balkan wars, many crime syndicates that had profited from war-spawned smuggling and the plundering of state enterprises reportedly shifted assets into legitimate commercial enterprises, sometimes after laundering them abroad. And violent competition among crime syndicates over access to markets and resources subsequently declined.

Insofar as militants are successful in establishing licit businesses a new set of possibilities arises. One is that, individually or collectively, their interests shift away from the political agenda that motivated them at the outset to the pursuit of economic gain. Or they may use their new resources to pursue their political objectives in the conventional political arena – which is precisely the direction in which Gerry Adams led the IRA in the early 1980s. Much of the resources earned by the IRA from illegal smuggling, construction fraud, and licit businesses were invested in the electoral campaigns of its Sinn Fein political arm. The political ascendency of Sinn Fein ultimately led to the negotiations and agreements by which the party became an accepted player in Northern Irish politics and agreed to the disarmament of the IRA. Militant Protestant organizations that had fought the IRA followed a similar trajectory. They emulated some of the IRA's fundraising strategies but, as the conflict moved into the political sphere, also suspended their violent tactics and eventually disarmed. However, long after the Good Friday Agreement of 1998, some one hundred weapons used for political killings by the Provisional IRA were also found to have been used in purely criminal operations or personal vendettas.[34]

152 *Militants and money*

Regional surveys: the Middle East and the post-communist states

Thus far we have relied on examples from case studies. Here we report some survey data on the nature of ethnic and religious militants' criminal fund-raising. Note that we survey all organizations that purport to represent the interests of minorities, not only those that use militant strategies. The Minorities at Risk Organizational Behavior (MAROB) project has surveyed the political and criminal activities of organizations that acted in the name of ethnic and religious minorities in the Middle East and in the post-Communist states between 1980 and 2006.

The Middle East

There were 29 communal minorities in the larger Middle East region (including North Africa, Cyprus, Pakistan, and Afghanistan) identified in the second author's Minorities at Risk project. The MAROB survey identified 112 organizations that represented one or another of these groups sometime between 1980 and 2004.[35] The Kurds, Palestinians, Shi'a, and Berbers all had multiple political organizations while others like the Alawi of Syria, the Druze of Lebanon, and the Saharawi had only one each. Annual codes of each organization's traits and activities include a profile of their involvement in crimes such as smuggling, arms trafficking, and the drug trade.[36]

A total of 21 communally based organizations out of the total of 112 both used violence as a strategy and operated across state borders: these are the entities that meet our broad criteria of trans-border militant (or terrorist) networks. Of these 21 organizations, eight also engaged in criminal activities (according to the coded information) at least once in the 25-year period studied. Four of them were simultaneously involved in crime and trans-border political violence in the same year(s): Amal, the Fatah Revolutionary Council, Hamas, and the Partiya Karkan Kurdistan (PKK). The MAROB study, on which we rely here, did not attempt to identify or code evidence about sponsorship or donation, though examples above suggest that these are widely used sources for militant groups in the Middle East.

Table 8.1 shows the country-years of different kinds of criminal activities in which these 21 groups engaged. Entrepreneurial activities were far more common than predatory ones. Almost all the entrepreneurial ones involve transit of interstate boundaries: smuggling consumer goods, drug trafficking, arms smuggling, and money laundering (sometimes local, sometimes international). The predatory crimes of robbery and ransom kidnappings are mostly but not necessarily intrastate. Totals add to more than 84 because some organizations engaged in more than one type of criminal activity in a given year.

The MAROB survey data show that the Palestinian Hamas organization, for example, was engaged in money laundering and robbery from the early 1990s through 2004. The Turkish Hizbullah, a militant Kurdish organization, engaged throughout the 1990s in money laundering, arms smuggling, human trafficking, and was held responsible by the Turkish Interior Minister for "997 kidnappings,

Militants and money 153

Table 8.1 Criminal activities by communally based organizations in the Middle East, 1980–2004

Any criminal activities	84 country-years
Predation:	
Robbery	16
Kidnappings for ransom	1
Entrepreneurial:	
Smuggling of consumer goods	36
Drug production or trafficking	20
Money transfers or laundering	20
Arms trafficking	17

murders and blackmail."[37] The longest and most diverse criminal record was racked up by Hizb-i Islami Afghanistan, the Pashtun organization headed by warlord Gulbuddin Hekmatyar. From the 1990s to 2002 (and no doubt thereafter) this organization systematically engaged in money laundering, counterfeiting, robbery, resource expropriation, kidnapping, and – in cooperation with Pashtun heroin syndicates in Pakistan – drug smuggling.[38]

Beginning in the mid-2000s the Taliban built its political renaissance in Afghanistan partly on money from the opium poppy (heroin) trade, the country's most lucrative export and the source of more than 90 percent of the world's supply.[39] In July 2000, when in power, the Taliban banned poppy production and their militia virtually eliminated it. After the US and British invasion of October 2001, the Taliban – now a loose alliance of insurgents – has reportedly encouraged villagers in the south and east of the country to plant poppies, protects villagers against the government's eradication program, taxes the harvest, and protects – and engages in – the transport of the processed drug to the Pakistani border. The proceeds are used to recruit followers, to pay off local and regional officials, and to buy arms. Counter-narcotic eradication programs sponsored by the US and carried out by Allied and Afghan forces have not slowed the trade. Instead, Vanda Felhab-Brown points out, eradication programs in Afghanistan and elsewhere neither end the drug trade nor weaken militant groups that rely on it for financing. The Taliban, she says, has gained legitimacy and popular support from locals in significant part because it protects the producers from eradication efforts.[40]

The post-communist world

The MAR project identifies 60 communal groups in the Soviet and Yugoslav successor states that were represented by 271 organizations. The coded MAROB data for this region cover the years from 1980 to 2006, but the vast majority of communally based organizations were established after 1989. A total of 2615 organizational years were coded.

Of the 271 organizations a small minority of eight were reported to have engaged in political violence in at least one year, a finding that highlights the non-violent

154 *Militants and money*

political strategies of the great majority of communally based organizations in the region. Criminal activity was more common: 16 organizations were coded for crime in at least one year, with a total of 79 organization-years of reported crime. Five of these groups engaged in both crime and political violence: the Albanian National Army and the Democratic Party of Kosovo; Respublika (the national movement of Bosnian Serbs); and two Chechen groups, General Dudaev's Army and the Riyadus-Salikhin Reconnaissance and Sabotage Battalion.

The most frequent criminal activity recorded for militant ethnically based organizations in the post-Communist world was drug trafficking; arms trafficking and robbery were distant seconds. Table 8.2 summarizes the coded data.

Expropriation was most likely to happen during wartime. In Chechnya, headed by a secessionist regime after 1991, the government profited enormously "by pirating oil directly from pipelines, siphoning off for sale high-grade oil and replacing it with lower-grade oil, and exporting oil or oil products under license." Complicit Russian officials and military officers also profited from a trade that was variously estimated to generate between $100 million and $900 million annually.[41] In a one-off example, during the Bosnian war of independence, a senior official of the Serbian Democratic Party – which ran the Republika Srpska (RS) within Bosnia – reportedly masterminded the theft of thousands of Golf Volkswagens from an assembly factory located in an area under its control for the use of the RS government.[42]

The territorial bases of unholy alliances

It seems from the coded data that "unholy alliances" between violent communal militants and crime networks have been rare in the post-Communist world, or more likely, are not fully reported in open sources. In fact almost all the coded data reflect the activities of six ethnonational groups out of the 60 surveyed: Chechens in Russia, Slavs in Moldova (Transdniestria), Adzhars in Georgia, Serb and Croat minorities in Bosnia, and the Kosovar Albanians. As our case studies of Kosovo

Table 8.2 Criminal activities by communally based organizations in post-communist states, 1980–2006

Any criminal activities	79 country-years
Predation:	
Robbery	22
Kidnappings for ransom	10
Resource expropriation	12
Entrepreneurial:	
Drug production or trafficking	43
Arms trafficking	22
Smuggling of consumer goods	18
Human trafficking	7
Money transfers or laundering	7

and Serbia have demonstrated, during the Balkan wars ethnonational movements were the principal actors in crime networks, terrorism, and conflict spillovers. In all six of the instances cited above militant ethnonationalists gained effective control of territory from which they carried out substantial profit-making activities. Whether their activities were licit or illicit by international standards is irrelevant; most were done by and for the benefit of the militant organizations and their supporters. They parallel the PLO's earlier economic achievements when based in Lebanon before the Israeli invasion of 1982, summarized above.

Chechnya, a republic with 1.5 million people, is in the north Caucasus. Two-thirds of its population are Muslim Chechens, with a diaspora of about half a million in neighboring republics, including 300,000 in Russia alone. The republic declared its independence in the aftermath of the breakup of the USSR and, unlike other Soviet successor states, resisted any compromise with Moscow.

From 1991 until 2000 the republic was nominally governed by the All-National Congress of the Chechen People and allied organizations. It facilitated a wide range of criminal activities, some of them run by and for the government, some by mafias for profit. Oil pipelines that transited the republic were tapped, as documented above. Chechens bought and trafficked in weapons from the Russian military, especially during the First Chechen War of 1994–6, which briefly established the country's independence from Russia. In the same decade the Chechen capital of Grozny was a hub for the illicit transshipment of Western goods into Russia and also for drugs in transit from Afghanistan and Tajikistan.[43]

From 1996 onward an enormously profitable criminal enterprise was run by Arbi Basayev. During and after the 1994–6 war Basayev commanded an irregular Special Purpose Islamic Regiment that carried out a multimillion dollar kidnapping and "people for sale" business. More than 70 foreigners as well as some prosperous Chechens were abducted, and most of them were successfully ransomed, among them journalists, businessmen, NGO workers, and Russian soldiers, and in November 1998 the Russian special envoy to Chechnya. The latter was released for $3 million in ransom, the others for lesser but usually substantial sums.[44] The Islamic Regiment successfully fought a Chechen government attempt to disarm it in 1997. The following year Basayev videotaped the decapitation of four hostage mobile-phone workers. He reportedly told another hostage that bin Laden had paid him $30 million to carry out the executions, but it is much more likely, as others reported, that he was in league with and on the take from Russian intelligence, probably because his Regiment was a counterweight to the rebel Chechen authorities.

The Chechens' independence during the 1990s and the Republic's strategic location, coupled with a network of Chechens living in the Middle East and in Russia, provided spectacular opportunities for crime and terrorism in the name of nationalism. Equally spectacular was the unwillingness or inability of Chechnya's nominal authorities to control crime. Symbolic support for Islamic causes by Basayev and others contributed to the external perception that the Chechens had joined the global jihadist movement. His video taped executions and a terrorist bombing in Moscow provided a pretext for the Russian invasion of 2000 that began the Second Chechen War and gradually crushed almost all Chechen

156 *Militants and money*

resistance. In fact Basayev, whatever his political ambitions, was a murderous bandit who justified his actions under the color of Chechen nationalism and militant Islam. He was killed in a 2001 raid by Russian Special Forces.

Transdniestria and Adjaria are other autonomist ethnonational regions in the post-Communist world that provide sanctuaries for criminal enterprise. These mini-states are not sources of significant terrorist violence because their ethnonational leaders have no external ambitions and face no serious challenges to their control. Moreover their existence is not seen as a security threat by outside powers, however much they are an irritating challenge to the sovereignty claims and revenues of the governments of Moldova and Georgia, respectively.

Transdniestria, known to its 700,000 mostly Slavic citizens as the Pridnestrovian Moldavian Republic (PMR), is a de facto independent region on the eastern boundary of Moldova, a country whose people are otherwise close kindred of the Romanians to their west. It is another instance of what Kemp calls ethno-kleptocratic societies. Transdniestrian nationalists in 1992 fought a mini-war with the Moldovan government that established their effective independence. In that year locals seized large quantities of munitions from a Russian Army division stationed in the region – apparently with no military resistance. Since then trade in illicit arms is very frequently cited, with the PMR government as well as crime groups – and rogue elements of the Russian military – said to profit from them. Most of the arms apparently come from Soviet-era arms factories that continue to operate in the PMR and have been trafficked to other Caucasian states including Chechnya. The Moldovan and Romanian governments regard this trade as criminal, but from the perspective of a state that claims to be sovereign – even though unrecognized – they are arguably a legitimate business.[45]

In the early years of the PMR's existence some higher-level government officials reportedly ran a protection racket, jailing businessmen and bankers who refused to pay bribes. In the early 2000s, according to Kemp, its politics and economy were both dominated by the Sheriff group.

> This financial-industrial group, run by former policemen and closely linked to "President" Smirnov's family, controls key sectors of the economy, including petrol stations, telecommunications, media outlets, and a supermarket chain. It also recently built a European-standard football ground. . . . This economic empire keeps the regime afloat and strengthens the sense of "Transdniestrian" identity.[46]

Interpol said in 2005 that the PMR derived almost all its foreign income from illicit trade including oil, metals, cigarettes, weapons, narcotics, and human trafficking, according to a German press report. High-level Romanian and Moldovan officials labeled the PMR a "black hole of trans-border organized crime."[47] Specifics were hard to come by, though. In response to such concerns in December 2005 a European Union monitoring mission was placed on the Transdniestrian segment of the Moldovan–Ukrainian border. Initial reports from the monitoring unit said that no evidence of arms smuggling had been found.[48]

The PMR's neighbors have understandable reasons for over-the-top criticism of criminal activities in the PMR. Undoubtedly it occurs but it is impossible to judge its extent from the external evidence. The core problem, from its neighbors' perspective, may have been the PMR government's complicity in smuggling schemes designed to evade Moldovan and Ukrainian import duties. As Kemp points out, because such de facto states "exercise internal sovereignty without external legitimation, it stands to reason that their form of government will be considered illegitimate and their sources of revenue illegal."[49] One thing is reasonably clear: the PMR government and the region's criminal elements have not, since the early 1990s, supported any actions that might be labeled terrorism.

Adjara, on Georgia's Black Sea coast, has about 375,000 Muslim inhabitants in an otherwise Christian state. It asserted its autonomy from Georgian control in the early 1990s, a move that was not contested by a central government that was fighting violent separatist conflicts in South Ossetia and Abkhazia. Until 2004 Adjara's government and economy were tightly controlled by Aslan Abashidze and his family. Evidently the regional government and the Abashidze clan engaged in, or profited from, drug production and trafficking, car smuggling (the region's capital is the Black Sea port of Batumi), side payments from shipments of oil from the Batumi terminal, and also some trafficking in nuclear and radiological material that originated in Russia.[50]

Adjara posed no serious threat to regional or international security except for a few instances of nuclear/radiological trafficking. Its leaders did not resort to armed conflict, terrorism, or Islamist posturing. Rather they ran a tight, profitable fiefdom free from Georgian or international control. In 2004 Georgian authorities engineered the ouster of Abashidze and redefined the region's status, but the evidence is that members of his internal circle continue to profit, directly or indirectly, from the privatization of public entities in Adjara and from crime networks that extend across Georgia, Russia, and Kazakhstan.

Conclusions

No more than a tenth of the 300 organizations that represented ethnic and religious minorities in the Middle East and the post-Communist states reportedly have engaged in economic crime either within their home territories or across bordersin the survey period from the 1980 to the mid-2000s. Most were nonviolent and noncriminal. Among those coded for criminal activity, some activities were entrepreneurial, some were part of strategies of militant fund-raising. In times of war and regional instability the two converged, sometimes with spectacular consequences. By far the greatest concentrations of reported crime emanated from contested areas where local militants, warlords, and their networks of supporters could operate freely. These were the main foci and actors of communally based criminal/political alliances of the last three decades.

- In the Middle East: areas controlled by the Palestinian Hamas; the Turkish–Iraq borderlands where the PKK is based; and the Pashtun areas of

158 *Militants and money*

Afghanistan, home to Hizb-i Islami Afghanistan, headed by warlord Gulbuddin Hekmatyar, and more recently the Taliban.

- In the post-Communist region: the Yugoslav successor states of Serbia, Croatia, Bosnia, and Kosovo; and in the former Soviet sphere Chechnya, Transdniestria, and Adjaria.

Criminal networks – so-called mafias – were responsible for some kinds of economic crime. So were some political leaders. Often there was collusion among them, so much so that conventional labels do not apply – hence our use of the term "unholy alliances." Motives were as mixed as lines of responsibility. Criminals sought economic gain, so did the militants' political leaders. The Serbian government of Milošević actively supported the criminal activities of Arkan and his Tigers as a weapon against Bosnian Muslims and Croats, and a source of funds that corrupted and enriched many Serbian officials. Kosovar clan leaders organized a nationalist terror movement, ran international trafficking and smuggling networks, and some of them ultimately became political leaders of an autonomous state. Leaders of Chechnya, during its decade of independence, funded their state with the proceeds of criminal expropriation and tolerated, and may have profited from, the ransom kidnappings and robberies committed by criminal militias such as Basayev's Special Purpose Islamic Regiment.

Militant communal groups and the criminal networks aligned with them in these two regions have used just about every conceivable domestic and international licit and illicit strategy for raising money. Our regional survey data show that predatory tactics like robbery and kidnapping are less common than entrepreneurial activity, especially trans-border trafficking and smuggling. As the American criminal Willie Sutton said, when asked why he robbed banks, "That's where the money is." So it is with militants: trafficking in drugs and people and smuggling consumer goods is where the money is to be earned. As for donation, a substantial amount of Arab and especially Saudi oil money is distributed to Islamists throughout the world, and some of it is diverted to jihadists. The global Islamist movement, though, is neither centrally directed nor centrally funded. Rather it is animated by a shared ideology.

At the outset of this chapter we identified two contending arguments about money and militancy. James Adams' argument that money is essential for the survival of terrorist groups was contrasted with Jeremy Weinstein's contention that militants who rely more on social endowments than economic endowments are more resilient and less likely to rely on strategies of coercion to secure support. We have plentiful case study evidence on this issue. Adams is correct that some funding is necessary for groups to survive. Yet social endowments, including strong identity networks, are just as important as money for survival. A more interesting question concerns shifts in militants' agendas and strategies, a subject addressed in the final section of the next chapter.

9 Conclusions

Responding to ethnonational and Islamist crime–terror networks

Trans-border ethnonational and religious identity groups provide the basis for militant organizations that use insurgency and terrorism for political objectives. To gain funds and weapons militant networks may establish criminal enterprises or align with existing trans-border criminal networks. These hybrid trans-border networks that we call "unholy alliances" command economic and political resources; and suborn officials wherever their communal networks extend. In some instances states, or corrupt agencies within states, play a major role in sponsoring and facilitating these networks and in turn profit from them.

This chapter begins with a comparative overview of the six case studies of chapters 2 through 7. They include four from the Balkans in the aftermath of the break up of the Yugoslav Federation and two from Islamic states whose militants – Kurdish nationalists of the PKK and Algerian Islamists – have carried out terror campaigns and criminal activities domestically and in Western Europe. The case studies are organized around theoretical arguments about the conditions under which hybrid trans-border crime–terror networks are established, adapt, and persist. The second section of the chapter discusses the intrinsic advantages of identity-based crime–terror networks vis-à-vis governments and regional authorities.

There are three meta-strategies to reduce the security challenges posed by regional crime and terror networks that we call Control, Reconstruction, and Transitions. The third section of this chapter examines in detail the imperfectly coordinated efforts of European states and supra-national institutions to formulate policies aimed at controlling cross-border crime and terrorism. The second meta-strategy, examined in the fourth section, is to devise policies of conflict management and post-conflict development and reconstruction in the regions that have given birth to unholy alliances. One dimension of this strategy is to rebuild institutions of public order so that local authorities can deal with crime–terror threats. The European experience in Bosnia and Kosovo shows how difficult this can be. The fifth and last section of the chapter takes a broader view. It discusses transitions, or agenda-shifts, by which militant and criminal energies may be diverted into conventional politics and the licit economy. Public policies may contribute to these transitions but as often they follow from processes of political and economic change within crime–terror alliances and in their operating environment.

160   *Conclusions*

I. Unholy alliances: an overview of six cases

The Balkan wars that accompanied the break up of the Yugoslavian Federation provided great incentives and opportunities for the establishment of hybrid networks in which militant nationalists pursued their political objectives and at the same time profited from economic crime. The existence of diasporas among most of the national peoples of the region provided congenial settings. Separatist conflicts weakened state structures, opening up spaces for networks to function with impunity. The collapse of state socialism left many state functionaries and intelligence agents unemployed and simultaneously made state resources available for looting. International sanctions on warring successor states created demands for fuels, arms, and goods that could only be satisfied by smuggling. The West European markets for drugs and sex trade workers provided another lucrative set of opportunities for diaspora-based crime networks.

The Balkan wars have ended and criminal justice systems are being rebuilt by the actions of states in the region and by policies and missions of the European Union, as we show. Elements of the networks continue to function, though with less political and economic impact. Political corruption in the states that hosted and sponsored them may be their most enduring legacy. The specific circumstances of our two Middle Eastern cases are quite different from one another, and from the Balkans, but nevertheless demonstrate how wars provide opportunities for hybrid criminal-militant networks, and pose serious regional security challenges.

- *Kosovo*. Kosovar clans took advantage of the wars of Yugoslav succession to establish their hegemony over Albanian crime networks that took over the trans-Balkan smuggling trade in drugs and women to Western Europe. The same clan leaders formed and led the Kosovo Liberation Army terror campaign against Serbian authorities, to which the Serbs responded with genocidal violence. NATO intervention compelled the Serb withdrawal and led to the establishment of a UN protectorate. Many KLA members and most of its command structure were incorporated in the internationally sanctioned Kosovo Protection Corps. Senior KLA and clan leaders also formed political parties and through them became elected leaders of the autonomous Kosovar government. They brought with them the clan and criminal ties that allowed them to exploit both government and economy for their own purposes. Since Kosovo's independence in 2008 Albanian nationalist terrorism has ended and the clans' international crime networks have lost some of their market share, but government corruption remains a major problem.
- *The Kurdistan Workers Party (PKK)*. The PKK is one segment of the Kurdish ethnoterritorial separatist movement (ETSM). Its four segments, the Kurds of Syria, Iran, Iraq, and Turkey, provide the context in which the PKK emerged and has pursued a hybrid political-criminal agenda. The PKK for 30 years has used terror strategies aimed at establishing an independent Kurdistan in southeast Turkey. In the 1990s it was able to extract about $50 million annually in "taxes" and contributions from the Kurdish diaspora in Europe, and earned a

similar amount from smuggling drugs from the Middle East and dealing them in European cities. After the 2003 US invasion of Iraq the PKK expanded its base areas in northern Iraq, intensified attacks on Turkish targets, and thus became a source of serious conflict between the Iraqi Kurdish Regional Government and Turkey. Our analysis of the regional Kurdish movement, and the interaction of constraints and opportunities that have shaped the PKK's political and economic strategies, leads to conclusions about how the PKK's political and criminal strategies may change in response to shifts in Turkish domestic politics and the policies of the Iraqi Kurdish Regional Government. Also relevant will be the shifting power balance in the Arab world and the tightening of EU anti-terrorism and anti-trafficking policies.

- *Bosnia.* The new Bosnian state declared in 1991 almost immediately came under devastating attack from Serb paramilitary groups. In response activists from the Islamic world provided a flow of internationally banned arms, aid, and volunteers. This illustrates the potential for contemporary ethnonational movements in predominantly Muslim countries to collaborate with radical trans-state Islamic movements. Nationalist movements may host terrorist cells within their networks, provide sanctuary to individual jihadists, and provide recruits for trans-state terrorist activities. But we also speculate, based on the Bosnian Muslim example, that ethnonational movements tend not to compromise their initial nationalist objectives or to replace them with religious ones. After the Dayton Accords ended the civil war, the Bosnian government sought to deport Mujahadeen and establish state control over terrorist and criminal networks. Jihadists nonetheless established and maintain a significant presence in Bosnia that is active in spreading Wahabist doctrine locally and providing support for jihadists in transit to Western Europe.

- *Islamists in Algeria.* The dynamics of the Algerian case grew out of its domestic political economy, not regional war or instability. After the French withdrawal in 1962 the army, especially its security service, became the basis and source of political power. Senior officers and those who benefitted from their patronage extracted a great deal of personal wealth through their direct or indirect control of the economy during socialist (1960s and 1970s) and quasi-capitalist (1980s to present) phases. This included rents from the exploitation of vast oil reserves in the Sahara. The corrupt and self-serving nature of rule by Algeria's post-revolutionary elite was the main grievance that fueled the Islamist resistance that began during the brief period of democratic contestation in 1991–2. When the army abruptly terminated the electoral process in January 1992, in which Islamic parties were poised to take power, the country descended into a prolonged and bloody civil war in which the armed Islamists, especially the Armed Islamic Group (GIA) and its successors, were defeated. We show how they too extracted money from the Algerian economy as well as from the diaspora of Algerians. The French and other European governments checked this source of funds and the remnant jihadists survive by banditry in the Sahara, in cooperation with al-Qaeda-aligned groups elsewhere in North Africa.

162 *Conclusions*

- *Serbia.* The close connection between trans-border terror and crime networks centered in post-1990 Serbia was the direct result of state policy, specifically of Slobodan Milošević's campaign to incorporate the Serb communities of Bosnia and Croatia in a Greater Serbia. The Communist Yugoslav regime had for a decade or more employed criminals-turned-agents of the state security service to target opponents in Western Europe. But the degree to which the Serb state promoted and funded terrorism and ethnic cleansing in Croatia and Bosnia in the early 1990s had no precedents in Serb history or elsewhere in post-Communist Eastern Europe. And the Serb state itself was criminalized by these policies to an extreme degree. In none of the other cases in the Unholy Alliances study have we seen as close and deep a "triple alliance" among terrorists, criminals, and state agencies as in Serbia. After 2005, however, this extraordinary complex of militant nationalism, trans-border terrorism, and deep-rooted domestic and international criminality began to be dismantled by Serbian reformers.
- *Bulgaria.* We analyze Bulgaria as a contrast case. The key actor was not a trans-border identity group but rather criminal networks that worked in consort with state agencies and state-linked oligarchs. The socialist state had posted out-of-state networks of intelligence, diplomatic, and trade officials. When the socialist state collapsed its newly unemployed security agents and state-sponsored athletes formed criminal syndicates that became instruments for personal gain both domestically and across borders. The post-communist state security sector had a threefold role in establishing the "market of violence." One was privatization of national capital; second was to assure state protection for illicit business at home; third was to provide state protection for illicit trans-border trade. All these activities were carried out during the 1990s in an atmosphere of extensive terror and gangster war across the country that challenges the widespread understanding of the East European democratic transitions as "velvet revolutions." The activities of the post-communist state security sector contributed to the establishment of corrupt practices throughout the public sector, as they did in Serbia.
- The Bulgarian crime syndicates had no overt political agenda other than taking advantage of the enormous opportunities to smuggle goods across highly permeable boundaries into UN-embargoed Yugoslavia. They were interest-driven rather than identity-driven. The syndicates' smuggling networks continued to function after the end of the Yugoslav wars, and they have been instrumental in promoting and profiting from the domestic narcotics trade. The Bulgarian case also helps clarify concepts like "mafia," "underworld" and "organized crime." Their traditional meanings are irrelevant to contemporary analyses. "Organized crime" – as suggested by analysts – is nowadays a globally spread and uncontrollable kind of entrepreneurial activity that is not necessarily confined to structurally weak societies.[1]

A schematic comparison of the cases on our main conceptual variables is provided in the accompanying table.

Table 9.1 Unholy alliances comparisons: the impact of conflict, identity, and opportunities on criminal/political linkages

Group	Conflict factors	Basis of identity	Opportunity factors
Serbian nationalists	Secessionist wars in Bosnia and Croatia	State-sponsored trans-border ethnonationalism	Need to circumvent UN embargo on Serbia Militant paramilitary units and criminals closely tied to state security agencies
Bosnian Islamists	Bosnian civil war 1992–95	Common Islamic identity, weakened by Bosnian Muslim moderate (Sufi) and secular tendencies	Wartime needs of Bosnian government for arms, munitions, fighters; postwar pressures to reduce jihadist influence
Bulgarian crime syndicates	Dissolution of Communist rule after 1990; no armed conflict	Mainly interest-based	Strategic location on smuggling routes to other Balkan states and West Europe Active cooperation with state security agencies Alliances of interest-based convenience with other Balkan crime networks
Albanian nationalists in Kosovo and Macedonia	KLA and Presovo rebellions 1998–2001	Strong trans-border ethnonationalism	Conflict-driven market for arms Demand for consumer goods throughout the region Albanian diaspora situated in proximity to West European drug markets
Turkish Kurdish nationalists (PKK)	Iraq war 2003–2011	Strong trans-border ethnonationalism	Safe havens in Iraqi Kurdistan Situated on drug transit routes from Middle East Kurdish diaspora well-organized to supply European drug markets, transmit funds to PKK
Algerian Islamists	Algerian civil war 1992–c. 2005	Commitment to Salafist (jihadist) doctrine	Widespread popular support; weak state control of rural areas; growing sympathy from diaspora and jihadists elsewhere; new trans-Sahara bases

II. Advantages of identity-based networks

Trans-state networks based on identity groups have a number of intrinsic advantages vis-à-vis the states and regional authorities that in principle are expected to control their activities. First, they mobilize support from kin groups and co-religionists in conflict zones. All the militant-criminal networks in this study flourished in regions characterized by political instability and armed conflict. Since civil administration and policing are weak and sometimes nonexistent in conflict zones, identity-based networks can exploit both political and criminal market opportunities. Cockayne and Lupel observe that in ineffective states "alternative forms of organization" emerge and "often coexist with, and even penetrate, states, splicing together transnational networks and traditional, local authority structures."[2] In countries where state structures are being reformed and loyalties are divided, in the post-Communist states of the Balkans, for example, state officials often are susceptible to corruption. Appeals of kin groups and the prospect of gain may outweigh any sense of obligation officials may have to the state's claim of authority. In some instances, illustrated by the Bulgarian case, political-criminal syndicates may be entwined within state institutions and share the capital and profits of joint ventures.[3] Bulgaria has no co-religionists or kin groups to mobilize in conflict areas. But trans-border illicit business networks, established by the Communist regime, greatly facilitated trans-border criminal activity in the post-communist era.

Criminal justice systems work imperfectly in weak post-conflict states like those of the Balkans. In Bosnia the division of the country into ethnically based cantons by the Dayton Accords "contributed to a climate of impunity for criminals, who were generally tried in their home venues, where they could exert pressure on the judiciary."[4] In Kosovo under the administration of the UN Mission in Kosovo, the Kosovo judiciary was composed almost entirely of Kosovo Albanians and consistently released kinsman accused of criminal and political offenses while treating the Kosovo Serb minority differently. It was and remains very difficult to get witnesses to testify in such cases – witness protection programs have been too weak to prevent prosecution witnesses from being murdered.[5]

Second, recent macroeconomic shifts have played into the hands of militant and criminal networks operating at times of conflict. The emergence of an illiberal economy in what was once Yugoslavia is especially telling. The country's formal economy collapsed in the late 1980s because the state was unable to adapt to the rules of global neoliberalism. The 1980s domestic conditions in Yugoslavia and especially the Federation's decentralization blocked the centralized implementation of externally inspired neoliberal structural adjustment programs and shock therapy. And at the onset of the 1990s Yugoslav wars, the emerging political economy of war and sanctions explicitly contributed to the emergence of illiberal economies. Symptomatically, illiberal economies are driven by populist ideology; rest upon informal/traditional ties; are managed by new economic and klepto-cratic elites; cause corrosion and criminalization of the state; and create an opportunity structure for illicit trans-border business activities.[6]

Paradoxically, post-conflict development aid in South-East Europe also has contributed to strengthening trans-border political-criminal networks. The post-Cold War reconstruction and development projects have focused primarily on building "civil societies" rather than nation-states. The Stability Pact for South Eastern Europe, launched by the EU in 1999, for instance, targeted NGOs, societies and populations as partners within the emerging complexes of global governance. It aimed at integrating donors, international organizations, security units, and private agencies. But in the absence of the nation-state as a primary local recipient of donor aid, the most likely outcome is the emergence of criminalized economies. The post-conflict international reconstruction efforts in Kosovo, for instance (1999–2007) collapsed largely due to the province's unresolved status, that is, the missing Kosovo state.[7]

A third advantage of identity-based networks is that trans-state alliances operate locally in multiple states, making it easier for them to evade surveillance and control by moving among jurisdictions. The identity-based networks surveyed in this book have diasporas in most Western European cities – Serbs, Albanians, Turkish Kurds, North African Muslims. These communal groups have many legitimate institutions – civil and ethnic associations, small businesses, mosques – that can provide cover, recruiting grounds, and fund-raising for militants. Close monitoring by authorities is difficult and militants, when facing crackdowns, can find havens among kinsmen elsewhere.

Another advantage of most trans-state movements is the network form of organization in which there is no readily identifiable leadership structure. This makes it difficult for intelligence services to penetrate them and difficult for prosecutors and courts to establish responsibility. The centralized leadership of the Turkish Kurds' PKK is something of an exception, but even in this case the political objectives and the fund-raising activities of Kurdish nationalists are pursued mostly by networks of autonomous local organizations.

Last, militant-criminal networks have the same technological advantages as other international crime networks. In the twenty-first century electronic communication and money transfer systems are global, border controls are easily avoided, documents are readily falsified, and ever-more-creative ways are devised to smuggle goods. These advantages are a given, as are the efforts of criminal justice agencies of Western countries to play technological catch-up.[8]

III. Controling unholy alliances: the European Union

States and regional authorities are typically external parties to hybrid militant-criminal networks. In theory it is the obligation of state agencies – the institutions of state security and criminal justice – to police and sanction illegal political and criminal activity. It is worth reviewing in some detail the recent history of the European Union's efforts to establish trans-European policies and institutions for controlling crime and terrorism.[9] The following review shows that the establishment of efficient trans-border counter-terrorism and crime mechanisms has been imperfect. There are three general issues. One is that the Europeans have never

166   *Conclusions*

established central operating institutions to deal with these issues. Instead successive EU entities have formulated common policies whose implementation depends upon individual states. Second is that the diffusion of responsibility for dealing with trans-boundary crime and terrorism across multiple agencies within countries and across the Union means that responses tend to be slow, inefficient, and hamstrung by interagency rivalries. The third is that efforts to coordinate counter-terrorism policies have been driven by specific crises, like al-Qaeda's September 2001 attacks in the US and the train bombings in Madrid in March 2004. They have been reactive rather than preemptive.[10]

The European Union, a relatively new international organization, based on a three-pillar system, was created in the 1992 with the signing of the Treaty of Maastricht. Since its establishment the Union has acted as both a supra-national and an intergovernmental organization. In the areas of defense, security, and criminal justice the Union has operated exclusively as an intergovernmental organization concerned with formulating and coordinating the policies of member states.

The EU's second pillar dealt with the EU Common Foreign and Security Policy (CFSP). From 1998 through 2001 there evolved the European Security and Defense Policy (ESDP). Born out of the WEU–NATO partnership, the ESDP emerged as the military wing of CFSP. The emphasis of the EU's foreign and security policy was and still is on *soft politics* in which common strategic foreign policy and security objectives are pursued multilaterally. Indicatively, the mandate of the EU peacekeeping operations is limited to the "Petersberg tasks," that is, to issues of crisis management, humanitarian and rescue operations, and provision of expertise and assistance in capacity building in military, security, and "the rule of law" areas.[11] As defined in the 2010 "A Strategy for EU Foreign Policy," the key objective of the EU's common security and defense policy is to prevent conflict and rebuild societies emerging from war.[12] The second pillar's major agencies included the Political and Security Committee, the EU Military Committee, and the High Representative for the Common Foreign and Security Policy.

The third pillar, the EU Police and Judicial Cooperation in Criminal Matters (PJC/ PJCC), was given responsibility for coordinating responses to a wide range of international security challenges. It promoted judicial, customs, and police cooperation in preventing terrorism and controlling the drug trade; dealing with asylum and immigration issues; fighting international fraud; and judicial cooperation in civil and penal matters. The pillar's larger objective was to create an area of freedom, security, and justice for all Europeans, mainly by promoting cooperation in criminal and justice fields among member states that otherwise retained their sovereignty. An important agency within this pillar was the Justice and Home Affairs Council. It promoted the third pillar's objectives using instruments such as Framework decisions, which were binding on the member states but had to be implemented by incorporation into national laws. The third pillar's other main agencies include Europol, Eurojust, and the European Police College. Europol is the criminal intelligence agency of the European Union, in operation since July 1999. Its aim is to increase cooperation among the competent authorities of nation-states to combat serious international organized crime. Europol has had no

Conclusions 167

executive power, however. It only gives support services for the law enforcement agencies of EU member states.

After the founding Maastricht Treaty the EU pillar structure underwent continuous transformations as new treaties came into effect. An important milestone in the institutional development of the EU was the 1997 Treaty of Amsterdam, which established the institution of the High Representative of the EU Common Foreign and Security Policy[13] whose primary tasks included strategic planning and early warning. The institution of the High Representative has given significant impetus to the development of the EU second pillar by placing the development of the CFSP in the hands of the most active intergovernmental agency in the EU decision making and legislative process. The Treaty of Amsterdam also transferred some of the third pillar's areas of responsibility to the integrated first pillar – the European Communities. These areas included policies concerning illegal immigration, visas, asylum, and judicial cooperation in civil matters. But the activities of the third pillar's key agencies, that is, those of Europol and Eurojust, remained confined to increasing police and judicial cooperation among member states.

To sum up, the major responsibilities for initiating anti-terrorism policy *strategies* are dispersed across the intergovernmental European Council; the Council of the EU with its rotating presidency; and the Secretary General/High Representative for CFSP. The major responsibilities for launching counter-terrorism and crime *legislation* rest with member states and the Commission. The *enforcement process* is a primary obligation of member states, not supra-national institutions. It is important to emphasize that, although the EU's counter-terrorism and crime strategy has been developed in view of the EU member states' security and protection, this strategy goes well beyond the EU borders. It applies also to the EU accession countries and the EU neighborhood as well as to other EU partners. The actions of French and Italian authorities to interdict Islamist fund-raising for Algerian jihadists, documented in our case study of Algeria (chapter 5), illustrate this strategy in action.

The out-of-the-Union anti-crime and terrorism activities are inter-pillar ventures. They are either launched as external action in the fields of justice, freedom, and security; or they emerge as tasks of the EU crisis management and peace operations agenda. They therefore fall under different areas of competence of the Community, either the CFSP or police and judicial cooperation. And they demand close coordination between the Council, the Commission, and the Secretary General/High Representative for the CFSP, at some cost to the efficiency and speed of crisis response.

The Treaty of Lisbon, in force since December 2009, aims to simplify the EU structure by abolishing its three pillars and transforming the EU into a consolidated legal personality. The Treaty of Lisbon replaced the CFSP pillar with the institution of the High Representative of the Union for Foreign Affairs and Security Policy to ensure greater consistency in EU foreign policy. The institution merged the High Representative for the Common Foreign and Security Policy with the European Commissioner for External Relations and European Neighbourhood Policy. Likewise, the pillar status of Police and Judicial Cooperation in Criminal

168 *Conclusions*

Matters also was ended. This function was integrated within the EU's consolidated structure as the Area of Freedom, Security and Justice. The hope was that this would increase the efficient implementation of the Union's counter-terrorism and anti-crime policies.

What was the EU counter-terrorism/crime basic legislation before the 2009 Treaty of Lisbon went into effect? The terrorist attacks of September 11, 2001 in the US, followed by the March 2004 bombings of Madrid commuter trains, prompted the EU to confront regionally the threat of terrorism and terrorism-related crime. There are three forms in which the relevant EU legislation appears. First are *Framework Decisions*, which approximate the law and regulations of the member states. They are binding on the member states, although the methods for implementing them are to be decided by national authorities. Second are the *Regulations*, which become law in all member states at the moment when they come into force and automatically override conflicting domestic provisions. Third are the *Directives*, which require member states to achieve certain results, leaving national authorities to decide on the means. However, the EU counter-terrorism and crime legislation is just one "slice" of a broader political strategy that also includes political decisions, general guidelines, programs, and communications that in turn are potential sources of new legislation.

These are the pre-Lisbon milestones of EU counter-terrorism policy, presented in a chronological order. They continue to shape Union responses. The main legal instrument for dealing with terrorist offenses was the *Framework Decision on Combating Terrorism* (2002). This defined terrorist offenses and aligned the level of anti-terrorist sanctions among member states.[14] It also incorporated the *European Arrest Warrant*, a procedure aimed at increasing the speed and ease of extradition throughout EU countries by removing political and administrative obstacles, and integrating the process entirely within the judiciary system.

In 2003 the *European Security Strategy* emerged as the second pillar's contribution to the fight against crime and terrorism. It was elaborated under the authority of Javier Solana, EU High Representative for the CFSP; and adopted by the European Council. The *Strategy* identifies global challenges and key security threats for the Union, which the document specifies as (1) terrorism; (2) proliferation of weapons of mass destruction; (3) regional conflicts; (4) state failure; and (5) organized crime. The strategic objectives were to respond to these threats; to build security in the EU neighborhood; and to promote an international order based on effective multilateralism.[15] The *Strategy* also asked the Presidency of the Council and Secretary- General/High Representative Solana, in coordination with the Commission, to present concrete proposals including recommendations for combating terrorism and dealing with its root causes.[16] One strategic objective was to draft a *Revised EU Plan of Action to Combat Terrorism*, another was to establish a Counter-Terrorism Coordinator. But most importantly for our purposes, the *Strategy* called for developing policies that integrated the fight against terrorism and crime within the major activities of the European Security and Defense Policy (ESDP).

In 2004, the *Declaration on Combating Terrorism* was adopted by the European Concil. Following the terrorist bombings in Madrid, the *Declaration* proposed a

Solidarity clause, endorsing the political commitment of the member and acceding states to act jointly against terrorist acts "in the spirit of the Solidarity Clause contained in Article 42 of the draft Constitution for Europe."[17] It thus went a step further in setting the counter-terrorism and crime agenda.

The *Conceptual Framework on the ESDP Dimension of the Fight Against Terrorism* draws on the above two documents. It says that the ESDP's main areas of action are prevention, protection, response/consequence management, and support to third countries. Dealing with terrorism requires a comprehensive approach integrating measures in the fields of intelligence, police, judiciary, and the military. The *Framework* also highlights *solidarity* and *cross-pillar coordination* in the fight against terrorism amid its basic principles. It acknowledges that the ESDP contribution must be complementary, that is, it should respect member states' responsibilities as well as take account of the principles of appropriateness and effectiveness. The *Framework* identifies the EU Counter-Terrorism Coordinator as the responsible agent to ensure synchronization between the ESDP anti-terrorism efforts, on the one hand, and the overall EU framework on the other.[18]

In 2004 *The Hague Program* was adopted by the European Council and set out ten priorities to strengthen the area of freedom, security and justice. It included ambitious measures aimed at developing a comprehensive response to terrorism, including exchange of information, protection of vulnerable infrastructure, and the fight against terrorism financing. It also envisaged measures on border control, security and travel documents; and aimed at establishing a common asylum procedure, and enhancing police and judicial cooperation.[19]

Of special interest for this study are measures aimed at countering terrorist financing. The main legislative instrument dealing with this issue is the *Directive on Money Laundering* adopted by the Council in September 2005, which built on the recommendations of the international Financial Action Task Force on Money Laundering. The measures adopted included compelling banks to provide personal details of anyone sending money into and out of the EU; confiscation of the proceeds of crime; orders freezing property or evidence; controlling the transfer of cash across the EU external borders; introducing a code of conduct preventing misuse of charities by terrorists; and tightening up the financial transparency and accountability practises of not-for-profit organizations through a code of conduct.[20]

Another important step in the development of EU counter-terrorism and crime policy was the 2005 *EU Counter-Terrorism Strategy.* This was developed by the European Union and the United Nations "to contribute to global security and build a safer world."[21] It introduced four pillars around which policy strategies and legislation should evolve, pillars named "prevent," "protect," "pursue," and "respond." It is worth mentioning some of the policies developing thereafter around these pillars. The "protect" pillar, for instance, instigated improvements of border security, "including the development of a second generation Schengen Information System (SISII) and the Visa Information System (VIS)."[22] The "pursue" pillar endorsed measures stepping up cross-border cooperation and exchange of information especially on the financing of terrorism; as well as the European Evidence Warrant.

170   *Conclusions*

The following years saw reinforcement of the justice, freedom, and security aspects of the EU's external relations. The European Council has ruled that a *strategy* had to be elaborated and adopted on these issues. The principles guiding policy toward non-EU countries included among all else (1) establishing geographical priorities and objectives; (2) "inter-pillar coordination in external action"; and (3) partnership with non-EU countries in enlargement, external relations, and development policies. The instruments for implementing this *strategy* included bilateral agreements, the enlargement process, the EU neighborhood policy, the external aid programs, and regional cooperation, among others.

The most recent EU counter-terrorism initiative to date is the *Stockholm Program*, adopted in 2010, which sets out priorities for the EU's newly integrated area of Justice, Freedom and Security for 2010–14. Building on the EU basic principles of respect for human rights and guarantees for human security, this program recommends the development of an internal security strategy for the EU "with a view to improving the protection of citizens and the fight against organized crime and terrorism."[23] It also focuses on the fight against cross-border crime and on reinforcement of the system of external border control.

In 1992 the British scholar Alan Milward made a contrarian argument that the European institutions founded after World War II were not aimed to supercede the nation-state, rather their purpose was to rescue and restore legitimacy to the nation-states that survived the war.[24] Our review of EU counter-terrorism and crime policies is consistent with his interpretation. It shows that the Union has laid the foundations of an efficient *supra-national* network that promises a more vigorous and coordinated fight against trans-border crime and terrorism within as well as beyond the EU external borders, but it has not established supra-national institutions to carry out such a fight. It remains the responsibility of individual states to defend their security, in cooperation with other states. The major institutional achievements of the Union include four legal instruments and a specialized EU-wide crime–terror information system. The legal instruments include *The Council Framework Decision*; *The European Arrest Warrant*; *The European Evidence Warrant*; and *The Money Laundering Directive*. The information system is Europol-centered. It is accessible by national specialized authorities, and is designed to enhance cooperation among them. Parallel to the EU programs to promote intergovernmental action against terrorism and crime we should point out that member states on their own initiative have developed more efficient anti-terrorism and crime policies. Now that the Lisbon Treaty is in force it remains to be seen if and how the Area of Justice, Freedom and Security will lead toward more uniform EU-wide anti-terrorism and crime policies. The most likely parameters of the latter include issues such as human rights, external border control, and EU internal security. Other parameters might include the security of the EU accession countries, as well as the security of the EU neighborhood.

From the perspective of the Unholy Alliances project, we suggest three guidelines for EU policies aimed at controlling trans-border violence and crime.

- When responding to hybrid cross-border crime–terror networks, emphasis should be placed on local and regional conflict management and resolution.

Conclusions 171

- Where actors are trans-border militant identity networks, the emphasis should be on developing coordinated policies of conflict prevention, border control, and anti-crime and anti-terrorism, in both the EU neighborhood and in accession areas.
- Where the primary actors are states, the emphasis should be on long-term economic strategies, control of corruption, the EU accession process and border control.

IV. Controlling unholy alliances: conflict management and post-conflict reconstruction

Strategies of conflict management

International capacities for preventing and containing armed conflicts have improved markedly since the end of the Cold War, and nowhere have they been employed more widely than in East Central Europe. In Macedonia a full-court diplomatic and political press by European and international actors reversed escalation to civil war in the mid-1990s and again in 2011 (see below). Overt intervention by peacekeeping forces and setting up international protectorates, as in Bosnia and Kosovo, are contingent strategies sometimes called "coercive diplomacy," to be kept in reserve if needed to back up political strategies. The whole package of preventive strategies can be employed in future to contain armed conflict, and hence eliminate settings in which militant-criminal networks can set up shop.[25] This holds for the larger European space – the 56 states encompassed by the OSCE. It is less applicable for regions beyond Europe and in particular the Middle East and the Islamic world. Networks based there can only be dealt directly in their home states, not by European institutions.

The Organization for Security and Cooperation in Europe (OSCE)

The work of the OSCE has been directly relevant for containing unholy alliances because, since its origins late in the Cold War, one of its primary aims has been crisis management and conflict prevention in the larger European space. It has taken a hands-on observer and diplomatic approach to a number of ethnopolitical conflicts since 1993, when the OSCE established the office of High Commissioner on National Minorities with a small staff. During the 1990s the first High Commissioner, Dutch diplomat Max Van der Stoel, monitored and carried out missions in 20 post-Communist states in the Baltics, the Balkans, the Caucasus, and Central Asia aimed at defusing conflicts over the status of national and other minorities. In some instances, for example in Georgia, his work complemented country-specific OSCE missions that also aimed to mitigate identity-based conflicts. His activities, in parallel with other OSCE missions, and sometimes EU and UN diplomacy, helped mitigate a number of conflicts that might otherwise have fueled trans-border crime–terror alliances.[26]

172   *Conclusions*

The Commissioner's focus on Albanian national issues is illustrative. From the beginning of his term in 1993 Van der Stoel was concerned with Kosovo. The conflict potential was clear but he was caught on the horns of a dilemma between contradictory political expectations. The Milošević government welcomed him in his role as High Commissioner for National Minorities, but the then-shadow Kosovo government of Ibrahim Rugova would not meet publicly with him because of their basic principle that the Kosovar Albanians were a nation, not a national minority in Serbia. He was able to promote agreements about some specific contentious issues such as bilingual education. But in a 1999 interview Van der Stoel said that

> western policies were based on two illusions. The first was that Rugova, with his great prestige, would be able to keep the internal situation in Kosovo under his control. . . . The second illusion was that the Kosovo problem could be solved by concentrating on partial solutions, regarding education, the health services, the judiciary and so on. . . . What was overlooked was that it was virtually impossible to make progress regarding partial solutions without touching the central question . . . with Milošević refusing to restore the autonomy the Albanians enjoyed until 1989, and the Albanians insisting on independence.[27]

The underlying problem persists in 2012, with the issue of autonomy versus sovereignty still not fully resolved. Not all OSCE members accept Kosovo's independence, and the current High Commissioner continues to be closely involved in efforts to keep contentious issues from escalating into renewed violence between Albanians and Serbs.[28]

Preventive diplomacy was much more effective in neighboring Macedonia. In the mid-1990s and again in 2001 the country was on the verge of civil war initiated by its Albanian minority, in part promoted by arms, activists, and encouragement from neighboring Kosovo (see chapter 2). The Commissioner made more than 50 visits to Macedonia in the 1990s, part of an intensive diplomatic campaign backed by UN-authorized peacekeepers that eventually convinced the Macedonian government to compromise with Albanian demands for political and cultural rights. If not for the success of these efforts, the spill over effects of the Kosovo conflict would have been much greater.[29]

Reconstruction in the Balkans

EU policy toward the Balkans has had an ambitious agenda. After the end of the 1999 Kosovo war the EU initiated the *Stability Pact for South Eastern Europe*. This initiative pursued multiple objectives. On the one hand it set out a common position in EU foreign and security policy. On the other hand it endorsed the principle of donor coordination. Substantively the initiative has addressed three sets of issues: democracy and human rights; economic reconstruction and development; and security. This broad agenda, which also integrated the fight against crime and corruption, could only be pursued by means of regional cooperation. So Balkan

Conclusions 173

countries were encouraged to actively join this initiative alongside major donor governments and international organizations.[30]

The EU refined its regional approach in the 2000 *Stabilization and Association Process* (SAP). This aimed to encourage regional cooperation and to promote democratic standards and liberal economies. Concretely, relations with the Union were conditional on the rule of law, compliance with the International Crimes Tribunal for Yugoslavia, economic stability, and minority protection. The EU support then was channeled through CARDS programs. The European Agency for Reconstruction was also created to operate in Kosovo, Serbia, Montenegro, and Macedonia in order to promote good governance and transitions to a market economy.[31]

The integrated EU approach to the Balkans also included security initiatives. Countering active trans-border criminal and violent networks was one of the objectives of three EU peace missions that have been launched in the region under the EU's common security and defense policy. These included the EUFOR-ALTHEA mission (2004) in Bosnia; EUPM (2003) in Bosnia; and EULEX (2008) in Kosovo. What did they achieve?

EUFOR-ALTHEA was launched in Bosnia in 2004 to oversee the military implementation of the Dayton Peace Accords. It assumed all responsibilities from its NATO predecessors, SFOR and IFOR. One notable exception was the hunt for war crimes suspects. EUFOR has police duties aimed at controlling organized crime, working with the Bosnian Police. EUFOR also cooperates with the European Union Police Mission in Bosnia (EUPM), successor to the UN International Police Task Force. The EU Police Mission, in turn, is a part of an international effort to address issues of the rule of law. Its achievements include developing multiple police arrangements under Bosnian ownership, among them a number of large-scale anti-organized crime operations, some with cross-border operations included.

The European Union Rule of Law Mission in Kosovo (EULEX) is the largest civilian mission launched under the European Security and Defense Policy. Its mandate includes assisting and supporting Kosovo in its quest to reestablish the rule of law, in particular in the areas of police, judiciary, and customs. The EULEX has only limited executive powers, however. It is an assistance and technical mission consisting of police officers, prosecutors, and judges. The military and civilian forces of UNMIK remain in Kosovo to monitor and provide assistance.

The EU's post-conflict policies in the Balkans have had complex effects on security issues. As noted in the 2010 *A Strategy for EU Foreign Policy*, the emphasis "has moved from an agenda dominated by security issues . . . to an agenda focused on the Western Balkans' EU accession prospects." The EU thus has moved from crisis management to establishing Europeanized protectorates and then overseeing the transition of Bosnia and Kosovo from protectorates to EU candidate states. For the first time in its history the Union has become involved in the process of creating future member states, including Serbia as well as Bosnia and Kosovo.[32]

And the problems of protectorates persist. Protectorates, as noted in the 2010 *A Strategy for EU Foreign Policy*, ensured stability but reinforced dysfunctionality. Indeed, nearly two decades after the Dayton Accords of 1995, Bosnia remains a

174   *Conclusions*

country with a constitution that enshrines divisions along ethnic lines. And while this helps ensure peace it nonetheless prevents the emergence of integrated policy. Moreover it creates conditions that are protective of identity-based trans-border criminal networks. The country has no Supreme Court nor an independent judiciary. It operates under three legal systems and four penal codes.[33] The situation in Kosovo is not very much different. It is still unclear there which laws apply and to what spheres of activity. There are at least three competing legislations: the international regulations adopted under UNMIK in the past decade; the new laws passed by the democratically elected Kosovo parliament; and the Serbian/ex-Yugoslav laws applied in the Serb-dominated enclave around Mitrovica.[34]

Contributors to the 2007 handbook *Combating Serious Crimes in Postconflict Societies* deal with the security issues in detail. They note that in both Bosnia and Kosovo police capacity – from training recruits to establishing intelligence units to purchasing communications equipment – has had to be rebuilt, sometimes from the bottom up. Establishing effective border security units is equally challenging. Judicial systems with well-trained and impartial judges and prosecutors are essential. Prison systems must be rebuilt, witness protection programs established, and so on. In post-conflict Kosovo and Bosnia it was almost always necessary to bring in international experts to help design and operate these institutions, at considerable economic and political cost. Successes were partial at best. Building internationally assisted local institutions was a key objective, but local conditions – including the characteristics of identity-based criminal networks we analyze here – presented formidable obstacles that have not yet been overcome.[35]

Observers of the EU reconstruction programs have criticized them for working in a "political vacuum." They have bypassed the state as a primary local partner, emphasizing instead the establishment of a free market and promoting the establishment of small to medium-sized enterprises. The peace missions on the other hand have been criticized for being overly technical and explicitly "neutral."

The European Union is a union of independent states, not a federal entity. Given this fundamental constraint on common security policy, the first and in some instances the last and only line of defense against trans-border militant-criminal networks consists of the security and criminal justice agencies of individual states. Improving their capacities to intercept, apprehend, prosecute, and thus deter militants is an ongoing Europe-wide process, as detailed above. We cannot tell specialists how best to do this, but can point out that if the objective is controlling trans-border networks, they can do their jobs best if (1) criminal justice strategies are part of broader economic and political strategies aimed at the bases of the networks, and (2) strategies for public order encompass all of Europe. The networks are trans-state, and effective counter-strategies must be the same.

V. Transitions and agenda shifts: why unholy alliances come apart

European policies aimed at controlling trans-border crime and terrorism, and post-conflict reconstruction, rely mainly on criminal justice and police systems

Conclusions 175

to deter militants and criminals. We have become increasingly convinced, during the course of our comparative research, that diversion of criminal energies and resources into quasi-legitimate activities is an important complement to strategies aimed at strengthening criminal justice policies. This means, for example, devising situation-specific policies that wean away opportunistic supporters of terrorist movements with material inducements. Criminal entrepreneurs can be encouraged to move their activities and capital into the licit economy, though side-payments may corrupt officials and political parties. Politically it may mean negotiating arrangements that offer opportunities like power-sharing or regional autonomy for communal leaders who are prepared to compromise. Entrepreneurship gets a firmer base when the militants, or their politically legitimate successors, secure internationally recognized territory. If and when that does happen, what we call donation (in chapter 8) becomes foreign aid and predation gives way to taxation.

In terms of our theoretical model, policies that prompt transitions should help limit the spillover effects of armed conflict; provide non-violent and non-criminal opportunity structures for identity groups; and reduce market opportunities for criminal activities. At the same time increasing political and juridical constraints, locally and regionally, increase the risks and costs of criminal/political actions. Here we review some evidence about the conditions under which transitions have happened, drawing on our case studies and other examples.

One policy approach is to reduce the ethnic and communal grievances that provide the social capital for unholy alliances. European states, often with the prompting of the OSCE, have implemented many policies aimed at reducing discrimination against immigrant and other minorities – Turks in Germany, Muslims throughout Western Europe – but these are not uniformly effective, and in any case could not be wholly effective without political changes in immigrants' home countries. The appeal of violent militancy for the Turkish Kurd minority would be much reduced, at home and abroad, if the Kurdish minority had real opportunities to pursue collective interests within conventional Turkish politics.[36] Not likely, not now.

In Algeria, the criminal terrorism of Islamists began in reaction to their exclusion from conventional politics in 1991. Amnesties from 1995 to 2000 allowed many armed Islamists to return to civilian life. Many one-time supporters of the Islamic Front (FIS) participated in electoral politics where their interests are represented by new Islamic parties such as Hamas and the Islamic Renaissance Movement.[37] But hard core members of the movement and its network of West European allies are unlikely to be dissuaded by any political reforms at home. The Armed Islamic Group (GIA) and the Salafist Group for Preaching and Combat continue their violent campaigns to undermine the secular government. In 2004–5 they rejected a presidential offer of negotiations toward a peace settlement and also rejected an offer of amnesty to all Islamic insurgents who would lay down their guns. The failure of belated efforts at political incorporation of the Islamists has meant that the Algerian government must continue to use harsh security measures that have prompted accusations of serious human rights abuses. They also have pushed the surviving jihadists into the ungoverned spaces of the Sahara and beyond into Mauritania and Mali.

176   *Conclusions*

Many recruits to the militant–criminal networks in the European space are attracted more by the opportunities for material gain than solidarity with kindred. Some of the networks' resources are gained from robbery and hostage-taking, as was the case for Islamists in Algeria. Some also come as contributions from diasporas in West Europe, as they do for Kurdish nationalists. But the networks' principal sources of income are smuggling and selling arms, drugs, consumer goods, and people – women for prostitution, fee-paying illegal immigrants. Government-sponsored economic opportunity programs designed for immigrants may have a long-term diversionary effect but are fraught with problems both economic (lack of sufficient funds) and political (public opposition to reverse discrimination). Reducing the economic opportunities for trans-border crime should provide more immediate leverage. Ending armed conflict dries up most of the lucrative trade in smuggled arms. Drug smuggling, though, remains enduringly profitable for those who produce, traffic, and distribute heroin, cocaine, marijuana, and designer drugs. The European market will not diminish, and European strategies aimed at controlling trans-border crime and money laundering are not likely to eliminate the trade but rather to increase the networks' costs of doing business. The only larger strategy that might drastically reduce this source of criminal income is comprehensive legalization and regulation of drug production and marketing – very unlikely in the near term.[38]

There is also a larger theoretical point to be made about the relationships between public authorities and militant-criminal alliances. The distinction between them is permeable and not inevitably antagonistic. The experience of UN peacekeepers in Bosnia in 1992–5 suggests that international authorities have in some circumstances cooperated with trans-state political-criminal networks to mutual advantage. Andreas identifies numerous ways in which peace operations in Bosnia facilitated illicit business activities, while simultaneously "in some respects illicit business also contributed to a number of peace operation goals – including helping to sustain the civilian population and even bringing an end to the conflict."[39] In some circumstances these connections contributed to corruption. But in post-war Bosnia and Croatia they led some criminal militants into the licit economy (see chapter 4).

Other examples of transitions come from our review of militants' funding strategies, in chapter 8. Some communal militants have used monetary resources and support networks to attain their political objectives – control of internationally recognized states or autonomies. The Palestine Liberation Organization and its constituent entities began as an international terrorist movement in the 1970s, gained a substantial resource base and international following in the 1980s, and negotiated autonomy just short of independence in the 1990s. The Irish Republican Army made a similar transition from terrorism to political action and then power-sharing in Northern Ireland between the early 1970s and the late 1990s. The Kosovar nationalists accomplished a similar transition from coercive Serbian control in 1981–97 to autonomous status under European tutelage in 2008. The political transformation of these ethnopolitical groups was paralleled by a shift in economic activity. Predation gave way to entrepreneurial funding strategies and eventually to mostly licit and self-sustaining economic activities. Granted, Kosovo's independence is heavily subsidized from outside, the result of a sort of political entrepreneurship.

Other communal militants failed to accomplish either an economic or political transition. We have cited the Algerian jihadists and the Chechen nationalists as examples. In each instance they continued to rely on predation, their acts of terror undermined their political support (mostly domestic in the Algerian case, Russian tolerance in the Chechen case), and they were suppressed by military action. The verdict is out on others. The Taliban and its allies – a Pashtun-based political movement – are thriving on money and political support gained mainly from taxing opium/heroin production and trafficking. They may eventually coerce and buy their way into partnership with the Karzai or a successor government in Kabul. In Transdniestria and Adzharia, which we reviewed briefly in chapter 8, political leaders have developed a mix of licit and illicit funding resources that enable them to survive both economically and politically. If they posed security threats to their neighbors, or were nodes of major international crime networks, they likely would be eliminated. So long as they serve mainly the economic interests of their leaders, they are likely to be tolerated – subject to increasing international control, perhaps, but not put out of business.

Just as militant movements may join forces with international criminal networks, we have seen how militant predators may become assimilated to states. Many Kosovar nationalists – a group linked to regional crime and terrorism during the 1990s – have become members of the government of now-independent Kosovo. An indeterminate number of fighters of the Kosovo Liberation Army were incorporated into the Kosovo Protection Corps (subsequently replaced by the Kosovo Security Force) and the Kosovo Police Service. The point is that, as political circumstances change, militants can become politicians and security personnel – it is in fact a deliberate strategy in post-conflict situations to provide precisely these kinds of employment to former insurgents to reduce their incentives to resume fighting.

VI. Concluding observations

In conclusion, opportunities and constraints are as important as communal identities and ideology in determining the origins and viability of unholy alliances. As political and economic circumstances change, so does the survivability of militant-criminal networks. Their agendas may shift between the political and the economic, and between licit and illegal kinds of activities. Their political appeals are muted when their homelands become self-governing, as in Kosovo, or when they gain political representation, as in Algeria. The complex and changing programs of the European Union have established control over the political spaces in the Balkans in which networks once flourished. At the same time regional policies aim at restricting their economic opportunities by shutting down criminalized markets, hardening border controls, and interdicting their financial transactions. The routine work of security, police, and criminal justice agencies is an essential complement to these larger strategies. Some offenses against public order cannot

178 *Conclusions*

go unpunished, some militants and criminals will not be deterred except by apprehension, prosecution, and imprisonment. But in the larger scheme of things, local and regional policies that aim at deterrence and diversion are as important in the long run as punishment of offenders is in the short run.

Our evidence has some general implications for international counter-terror and crime control. As crime and political terror have gone international, so have the responses. A great many UN and European Union conventions have been passed aimed at controlling these international bads, and cooperation among national security and criminal justice agencies has grown accordingly. But conventions and cooperation are effective mainly in the advanced industrial societies and have little effect elsewhere in the world.

Moreover terrorists and criminals are more adaptable than the bureaucracy-bound international community, afflicted as it is by interstate and interagency rivalries. Criminals and militants quickly move into new areas of international economic crime while responders are playing catch-up. International crime control efforts have their successes, but only enough to keep pressure on and, paradoxically, to push the perpetrators into more creative strategies of evasion.

A hard core of true believers will not be susceptible to such strategies. Jihadist leaders, for example, are unlikely to accept buy-outs or power-sharing arrangements. Counter-intelligence and counter-insurgency remain the best, perhaps only means for dealing with hard-core criminals and ideologues. It is widely recognized by those who design counter-insurgency strategies that it is much easier to detect and defeat the hard-core activists after many of their supporters have defected and locals feel safe to provide information.

The legacy of official corruption may be the most difficult to deal with. The practise is widespread not only in new, fragile, and unrecognized states but throughout the post-Communist world – and indeed wherever officials have been implicated in international trafficking, diversion of public funds, and illicit international financial transactions. Corrupt and self-serving officials have strong incentives to resist efforts by international organizations and domestic civil society to give up lucrative sources of income, especially when those derive from and help reinforce their influence with kindred ethnic and communal groups. How to deal with this set of issues is beyond the scope of our Unholy Alliances project.

Notes

Preface and acknowledgments

1 The prime minister first earned his nickname because of his ability to evade the Serbian police during his leadership of the KLA; see http://www.balkaninsight.com/en/article/hashim-thaci-from-snake-to-prime-minister [accessed 15 March 2012]. Terrorists-turned-national leaders are not unknown; what is remarkable about Hashim Thaqi is the close connection he is said to maintain with the Drenica group's international trafficking network; see a 2010 Council of Europe report at http://assembly.coe.int/ASP/APFeaturesManager/defaultArtSiteView.asp?ID=964.

2 On the criminal exploitation of women, see Sarah E. Mendelson, *Barracks and Brothels: Peacekeepers and Human Trafficking in the Balkans* (Washington,DC: Center for Strategic and International Studies Press, 2005); and chapter 7 in Louise Shelley, *Human Trafficking: A Global Perspective* (Cambridge: Cambridge University Press, 2010). The UN Office on Drugs and Crime estimates that 70,000 women each year are trafficked to Europe for sexual exploitation, in *The Globalization of Crime: A Transnational Organized Threat Assessment* (New York and Vienna: UN Office on Drugs and Crime, UN publication sales no. E.10.IV.6), pp. 16–40. Trafficking of women is common; what is unusual in Kosovo is that traffickers-turned-businessmen are extracting profits from an illegal trade that caters in part to international personnel whose mission is to maintain peace and help build civil society in Kosovo. In neighboring Bosnia 30 percent of those visiting brothels were UN or NATO personnel or aid workers, according to a 2004 report of the UN High Commissioner for Human Rights cited by Victoria K. Holt and Alix J. Boucher, "Framing the Issue: UN Responses to Corruption and Criminal Networks in Post-Conflict Settings," *International Peacekeeping*, vol. 16 (February 2009), p. 25 and note 27.

3 Two recent examples are Christine Jojarth, *Crime, War, and Global Trafficking: Designing International Cooperation* (Cambridge: Cambridge University Press, 2009), and Peter Lilley, *Dirty Dealing: The Untold Truth about Global Money Laundering, International Crime and Terrorism*, 3rd edition (London and Philadelphia: Kogan Page, 2006). The United Nations Office on Drugs and Crime (UNODC) issues excellent analytic accounts of international crime, including its recent global survey, *The Globalization of Crime.*

4 UNODC estimates that in 2009 Afghan drug traffickers earned $1.9 billion from the trade in opiates. The Taliban extracted at least $121 million from this trade by taxing cultivation, production, and trafficking; *The Globalization of Crime*, pp. 246–9. The illegal commodities trade in Southeast Asia is analyzed in the same report, in chapters 8 and 9 *passim* and pp. 257–60.

5 See Ted Robert Gurr, "Economic Factors," in Louise Richardson, ed., *The Roots of Terrorism* (New York and London: Routledge, 2006), pp. 85–101.

6 Early versions of our ISA papers on Kosovo and Bosnia have been published elsewhere: Lyubov Mincheva and Ted Robert Gurr, "Unholy Alliances? How Trans-state Terrorism and International Crime Make Common Cause," in Rafael Reuveny and

180 *Notes*

William R. Thompson, eds, *Coping with Contemporary Terrorism: Origins, Escalation, Counter Strategies, and Responses* (Albany, NY: State University of New York Press, 2010), pp. 169–89; and Mincheva and Gurr, "Unholy Alliances: Evidence on Linkages between Trans-State Terrorism and Crime Networks. The Case of Bosnia," in Wolfgang Benedek et al., eds, *Transnational Terrorism, Organized Crime, and Peace-Building: The State of the Art in Human Security in the Western Balkans* (London: Palgrave Macmillan, 2010), pp. 190–206.

1 Unholy alliances

1 Petrus Van Duyne, "Medieval Thinking and Organized Crime Economy," in Emilio C. Viano, José Magallanes, and Laurent Bridel, eds, *Transnational Organized Crime: Myth, Power, and Profit* (Durham, NC: Carolina Academic Press, 2003), pp. 23–44.

2 See citations in Bartosz Stanislawski and Margaret Hermann, "Transnational Organized Crime, Terrorism, and WMD," discussion paper prepared for the Conference on Non-State Actors, Terrorism, and Weapons of Mass Destruction, Center for International Development and Conflict Management, University of Maryland, 15 October 2004. Equally relevant is Rem Korteweg and David Ehrhardt, "Terrorist Black Holes: A Study into Terrorist Sanctuaries and Governmental Weakness," The Hague: Clingendael Center for Strategic Studies, November 2005.

3 John Martin and Anne Romano, *Multinational Crime: Terrorism, Espionage, Drugs and Arms Trafficking* (Newbury Park, CA: Sage Publications, 1992), pp. 14–15.

4 Paul Collier, Anke Hoeffler, and Nicholas Sambanis, "The Collier–Hoeffler Model of Civil War Onset and the Case Study Project Research Design," in Paul Collier and Nicholas Sambanis, eds, *Understanding Civil War: Evidence and Analysis*, Volume 2: *Europe, Central Asia, and Other Regimes* (Washington, DC: World Bank, 2005), p. 3.

5 Glenn Curtis and Tara Karacan, "The Nexus among Terrorists, Narcotics Traffickers, Weapons Proliferators, and Organized Crime Networks in Western Europe" (Washington, DC: Library of Congress, 2002), p. 5, URL http://www.loc.gov/rr/frd/.

6 Ibid., p. 2.

7 See José Magallanes, "The Uses of Social Myth: Drug Traffickers and Terrorism in Peru," in Viano, Magallanes, and Bridel, *Transnational Organized Crime*, pp. 73–90.

8 See, for example, Jennifer S. Holmes, Sheila Amin Gutiérrez de Piñeres, and Kevin M. Curtin, "A Subnational Study of Insurgency: FARC Violence in the 1990s," c. 2004, URL http://usregsec.sdsu.edu/docs/holmes3. See also Douglas, "Terrorist–Criminal Pipelines and Criminalized States. Emerging Alliances," URL http://www.ndu.edu/press/emerging-alliances.html [accessed November 2011].

9 Klaus Von Lampe, "Criminally Exploitable Ties: A Network Approach to Organized Crime," in Viano, Magallanes, and Bridel, *Transnational Organized Crime*, pp. 9–22.

10 Curtis and Karacin, "The Nexus among Terrorists," p. 4.

11 Ibid., pp. 21–3.

12 M. Bozinovich, "The New Islamic Mafia,"10 September 2004. URL www.serbianna.com/columns/mb/028.shtml [accessed November 2005].

13 Curtis and Karacan, "The Nexus among Terrorists," pp. 18–21.

14 Hayri Burler, "PKK as an International Organized Crime Outfit," *Turkish Daily News*. 2 July 1996.

15 Curtis and Karacan, "The Nexus among Terrorists," p. 19.

16 E.J. Hobsbawm, *Social Bandits and Primitive Rebels: Studies of Archaic Forms of Social Movement in the 19th and 20th Centuries* (New York: The Free Press, 1959).

17 Misha Glenny, *McMafia: A Journey Through the Global Criminal Underworld* (New York: Alfred A. Knopf, 2008), pp. 9–10. A more general analysis is Jürgen Roth, *Gangsterwirtschaft [Gangster Economics]: Wie uns die organisierte Kriminalität aufkauft* (Berlin: Eichborn, 2010).

18 See Tihomir Bezlov, Emil Tzenkov, Marina Tzetkova, Filip Gounev, and Georgi

Petrunov, *Organized Crime in Bulgaria: Markets and Trends,* in Bulgarian (Sofia: Center for the Study of Democracy, 2007), and other sources cited in chapter 7.

19 Monty G. Marshall, *Third World War: System, Process, and Conflict Dynamics* (London and Boulder, CO: Rowman & Littlefield, 1999), especially chapters 4 and 5.

20 The dynamics of these crises are specified in Lyubov Grigorova Mincheva, "Spillover Crises and Regionalization of Ethnic Conflict by Transnational Kindred Groups," chapter 2 in "Ethnoterritorial Separatist Movements and Spillover Crises: The Balkans in the 1990s," PhD dissertation, Department of Government and Politics, University of Maryland, 2000.

21 Sidney Tarrow, *Power in Movement: Social Movements, Collective Action and Politics* (New York: Cambridge University Press, 1994), p. 96.

22 Lyubov Mincheva, "The Albanian Ethnoterritorial Separatist Movement: Local Conflict, Regional Crisis," *Nationalism and Ethnic Politics,* vol. 15, no. 2 (April–June 2009), pp. 211–36.

23 Our tabulation from information in Deepa Khosla, "Self-Determination Movements and Their Outcomes," in Monty G. Marshall and Ted Robert Gurr, *Peace and Conflict 2005* (College Park, MD: Center of International Development and Conflict Management, University of Maryland, 2005), pp. 21–7 and 84–90. Different segments of cross-border groups such as Kurds and Croats are counted separately in this tabulation for each country in which they fought for self-determination.

24 Our tabulation from the "Appendix – Major Armed Conflicts," in J. Joseph Hewitt, Jonathan Wilkenfeld, and Ted Robert Gurr, eds, *Peace and Conflict 2010* (Boulder, CO: Paradigm Publishers, 2010), pp. 123–42.

25 These tabulations and examples, and those that follow on Islamic identity groups, are from the latest update of the Minorities at Risk dataset and were compiled by Amy Pate, then the MAR project research director. The MAR dataset includes only politically significant groups; a sample of other minorities has been identified and is being coded. The MAR project website lists all data on the 281 groups and provides group descriptions; see http://www.cidcm.umd.edu.mar/.

26 Derek S. Reveron and Jeffrey Stevenson Murer, eds, *Flashpoints in the War on Terrorism* (New York and London: Routledge, 2006).

27 As shown in a comparative analysis by Mariya Y. Omelicheva, "Ethnic Dimension of Religious Extremism and Terrorism in Central Asia," paper presented to the Annual Meeting of the International Studies Association, Chicago, March 2007.

28 *The Globalization of Crime: A Transnational Organized Crime Threat Assessment* (Vienna: United Nations Office on Drugs and Crime, 2010), pp. 16–17. Most of the $130 billion is the estimated market value of drugs; it also includes the proceeds of human trafficking and the market values of illegally trafficked natural resources and counterfeit consumer goods.

29 Martin and Romano, *Multinational Crime,* p. 14.

30 Peter Klerks, "The Network Paradigm Applied to Criminal Organizations: Theoretical Nitpicking or a Relevant Doctrine for Investigators? Recent Developments in the Netherlands," in Adam Edwards and Peter Gil, eds, *Transnational Organized Crime: Perspectives on Global Security* (London and New York: Routledge, 2003), pp. 100–1.

31 Ibid., p. 12.

32 Ibid., p. 101.

33 See Paul Ekblom, "Organized Crime and the Conjunction of Criminal Opportunity Framework," in Edwards and Gil, *Transnational Organized Crime* and Klerks, "The Network Paradigm."

34 Von Lampe, "Criminally Exploitable Ties," p. 14.

35 R.T. Naylor, "Predators, Parasites, or Free-Market Pioneers: Reflections on the Nature and Analysis of Profit-Driven Crime," in Margaret E. Beare, *Critical Reflections on Transitional Organized Crime, Money Laundering and Corruption* (University of Toronto Press, 2003) p. 36.

36 Ibid., p. 52.

182 Notes

37 Raymond Baker, "Money Laundering and Flight Capital: The Impact on Private Banking," US Senate Committee on Governmental Affairs, Permanent Subcommittee on Investigations, 10 November 1999, http://www.brook.edu, and subsequent discussions with Baker summarized in Loretta Napoleoni, *Terror Incorporated: Tracing the Dollars Behind the Terror Networks* (New York: Seven Stories Press, 2005), pp. 205–6.

38 See Loretta Napoleoni, *The New Economy of Terror: An Excerpt from Modern Jihad. Tracing the Dollars behind the Terror Networks*, URL http://coldtype.net/Assets.04/Essays.04/ModernJihad.pdf [accessed 14 November 2011].

39 David C. Jordan, *Drug Politics: Dirty Money and Democracies* (Norman, OK: University of Oklahoma Press, 1999), p. 104.

40 This discussion is drawn from Jordan's analysis of "The Criminalization of the International Finance System," pp. 99–119.

41 Roth, *Gangsterwirtschaft*, p. 210.

42 Ibid.

43 Ibid., p. 8; Jordan, *Drug Politics, passim.*

44 Napoleoni, *The New Economy of Terror*, p. 11.

45 Ibid., p. 12.

46 Napoleoni, in chapters 13–18 of *Terror Incorporated*, provides ample evidence that Islamist and other terror networks have effectively exploited these opportunities.

47 See, for example, Mancur Olson, *Power and Prosperity: Outgrowing Communist and Capitalist Dictatorships* (New York and London: Oxford University Press, 2000).

48 Susan E. Rice and Stewart Patrick, *Index of State Weakness in the Developing World* (Washington, DC: The Brookings Institution, 2011). Also see Robert Rotberg, ed., *When States Fail: Causes and Consequences* (Princeton, NJ: Princeton University Press, 2003).

49 Barbara Harff uses the concept of national (i.e. political) upheaval to refer to "an abrupt change in the political community, caused, for example, by the formation of states through violent conflict, when national boundaries are reformed, or after a war is lost." The concept also includes internal wars and violent replacement of political elites. Harff, "The Etiology of Genocide," in Isidor Walliman and Michael N. Dobkowski, eds, *Genocide and the Modern Age: Etiology and Case Studies of Mass Death* (New York: Greenwood Press, 1987), pp. 42–9, quote 43. The US government's Political Instability (formerly State Failure) Task Force uses a similar but more narrow, empirically defined concept that includes internal wars, abrupt regime transitions, and genocides and politicides. See Jack A. Goldstone, Robert H. Bates, David L. Epstein, Ted Robert Gurr, Michael B. Lustik, Monty G. Marshall, Jay Ulfelder, and Mark Woodward, "A Global Model for Forecasting Political Instability," *American Journal of Political Science*, vol. 54 (January 2010), pp. 190–208.

50 Stanislawski and Hermann, "Transnational Organized Crime."

51 Korteweg and Ehrhardt, "Terrorist Black Holes: A Study into Terrorist Sanctuaries and Governmental Weakness," cited in Douglas Farah, "Terrorist-Criminal Pipelines and Criminalized States," FEATURES. PRISM 2, no. 3, p. 20. URL http://www.ndu.edu/press/emerging - alliances.html [accessed 26 October 2011].

52 Tamara Makarenko, "The Crime–Terror Continuum: Tracing the Interplay between Transnational Organized Crime and Terrorism," *Global Crime*, vol.6, no.1 (February 2004), p. 138. URL http://www.silkroadstudies.org/new/docs/publications/Makarenko-GlobalCrime.pdf [accessed 14 November 2011].

53 Louise I. Shelley and John T. Picarelli, "Methods and Motives: Exploring Links between Transnational Organized Crime and International Terrorism," *Trends in Organized Crime*, vol. 9, no.2 (Winter 2005), p. 62. URL http://www.scribd.com/doc/7156253/Shelley-e-Picarelli-Organized . . . [accessed 14 November 2011].

54 An in-depth study of cases mainly from Africa and Latin America would show that these "alternatively governed areas" vary in the means by which administrative/political control is established and exercised. Douglas Farah offers a conceptual and case study discussion of this issue in "Terrorist–Criminal Pipelines and Criminalized States," p. 19.

Notes 183

55 Ibid.

56 Jones, *Drug Politics*, especially chapter 3, "The Corruption of Elites."

57 Giulio Tremonti, *La paura e la speranza – Europa: la crisi globale che si avvicina e la via per superarla* ("Fear and hope – Europe: The approaching global crisis and how to overcome it," 2008). Bulgarian edition, trans. Jordan Vassilev, Lyubov Mincheva, and Simona Vassileva (Sofia: Ciela, 2010), pp. 63–4.

58 Jordan, *Drug Politics*, pp. 8, 10, 46.

59 The term *Mafia Borguesse* denotes the policy of the aristocratic Borgia family in fourteenth- and fifteenth-century Rome. By using bribery, among other means, they managed to secure strong positions in the Vatican, including a Papal title and large political influence. See Roth, *Gangsterwirtschatft*, p. 41.

60 Tremonti, *La paura e la speranza – Europa*, p. 44.

61 Center for the Study of Democracy, *Organized Crime in Bulgaria: Markets and Trends* (Sofia: author, 2007), p. 5.

62 See Jens Stilhoff Sørensen, *State Collapse and Reconstruction in the Periphery: Political Economy, Ethnicity and Development in Yugoslavia, Serbia and Kosovo* (New York: Berghahn Books, 2009).

63 Jordan, *Drug Politics*, p. 9. His case studies include Mexico, post-communist Russia, and Colombia.

64 UN Office on Drugs and Crime, *The Globalization of Crime*, our calculations from estimates on pp. 16–17. Heroin and cocaine are valued "at destination."

65 Jordan, *Drug Politics*, pp. 44–5.

66 Two analyses we have found useful are Jordan, *Drug Politics*, chapter 8, and George Grayson, "Mexico and the Drug Cartels," *Foreign Policy Research Institute*, E-Note, August 2007. URL http://www.fpri.org/enotes/200708.grayson.mexicodrugcartels. html [accessed 9 November 2011].

67 Javier Argomaniz, *The EU and Counter-Terrorism: Politics, Polity, and Policies after 9/11* (London and New York: Routledge, 2011), is highly critical of the lack of consistency and coherence in policies in this area and reviews studies that have reached similar conclusions about other areas of EU responsibility.

68 J. Joseph Hewitt, "The Peace and Conflict Instability Ledger: Ranking States on Future Risks," chapter 2 in Hewitt, Wilkenfeld, and Gurr, *Peace and Conflict 2010* and in *Peace and Conflict 2012* (Boulder, CO: Paradigm Publishers, 2010 and 2012 respectively).

2 Crime, political violence, and governance in Kosovo

1 This chapter incorporates some materials from Lyubov Mincheva and Ted Robert Gurr, "Unholy Alliances? How Trans-state Terrorism and International Crime Make Common Cause," paper presented at the Annual Meeting of the International Studies Association, San Diego, 24 March 2006 and published in Rafael Reuveny and William R. Thompson, eds, *Coping with Contemporary Terrorism: Origins, Escalation, Counter Strategies, and Responses* (Albany, NY: State University of New York Press, 2010), pp. 169–89. Majid Shirali, a doctoral student in the Department of Political Science, University of Nevada, Las Vegas, provided high-value research assistance for this revision. Thanks also to Želimir Kešetović of the University of Belgrade for his comments.

2 Michael Pugh, "Crime and Capitalism in Kosovo's Transformation," paper presented at the International Studies Association Annual Meeting, Honolulu, Hawaii, 2005.

3 An estimated quarter million Serbs fled Kosovo when Serbian forces withdrew at the end of the NATO intervention. Those who remain are an embattled minority subject to discrimination and harassment by Kosovar Albanians. International policies aim at easing, or at least managing, interethnic tensions.

4 See Jens Sørensen, *State Collapse and Reconstruction on the Periphery: Political Economy, Ethnicity, and Development in Yugoslavia, Serbia and Kosovo* (New York and Oxford: Berghahn Books, 2009).

184 *Notes*

5 Albanian population estimates vary. All these are calculated from 2009 data in the Wikipedia entry for Albanians, which provides country-specific numbers and sources. The numbers for the diaspora do not necessarily include undocumented Albanians.

6 On the origins and persistence of the clan basis of Albanian society, see Noel Malcolm, *Kosovo: A Short History* (London: Pan Macmillan, 1998), pp. 15–17 and 114–15. A note on terminology: some sources refer to the clan families as *fis*, others use the term *fares*. Sørensen, *State Collapse and Reconstruction*, and some other analysts call them mafias. In this chapter we use either the Albanian *fis* or the neutral term clan networks.

7 Emil Giatzidis, "The Challenge of Organized Crime in the Balkans and the Political and Economic Implications," *Journal of Communist Studies and Transition Politics*, vol. 23, no. 3 (September 2007), p. 330. Other scholars who elaborate on this connection include Pugh, "Crime and Capitalism," and Francesco Strazzari, "L'Oeuvre au Noir: The Shadow Economy of Kosovo's Independence," *International Peacekeeping*, vol. 15, no. 2 (April 2008), pp. 155–70.

8 Jana Arovska and Philippe Verduyn, "Globalization, Conduct Norms, and 'Culture Conflict': Perceptions of Violence and Crime in an Ethnic Albanian Context," *British Journal of Criminology*, vol. 48, no. 2 (March 2008), pp. 226–46.

9 Quote from Gordon Bardos, "Containing Kosovo," *Mediterranean Quarterly*, vol. 16, no. 3 (Summer 2005), p. 22. Also see the references in note 7. Especially useful for details on Kosovo clans, their leadership and political/criminal activities, is the Serbian Security Information Agency's (BIA) report *Albanian Terrorism and Organized Crime in Kosovo and Metohija* (Belgrade: BIA, September 2003). The bias in this report is evident in the labeling of any Kosovar political activity as "terrorist." But the factual information is very detailed and consistent with other sources.

10 Sørensen, *State Collapse and Reconstruction*, pp. 197–8.

11 Ibid.

12 On Serbian repression and Albanian responses, see Malcolm, *Kosovo: A Short History*, pp. 334–45.

13 On the FARK and the financing arrangements, see Sørensen, *State Collapse and Reconstruction*, p. 203.

14 A balanced and detailed analysis is Peter Russell, "The Exclusion of Kosovo from the Dayton Negotiations," *Journal of Genocide Research*, vol. 11, no. 4 (December 2009), pp. 487–511.

15 Susan Fink Yoshihara, "Greater Albania," in Derek S. Reveron and Jeffrey Stevenson Murer, eds, *Flashpoints in the War on Terrorism* (New York and London: Routledge, 2006), pp. 67–8. Radio Free Europe/Radio Liberty referred to it as the All Albanian Army, vol. 3, no. 4 (28 January 1994). By whatever name, it and the KLA were both manifestations of the larger Albanian ethnoterritorial separatist movement.

16 BIA, *Albanian Terrorism and Organized Crime*, p. 8.

17 Yoshiara, "Greater Albania," p. 68.

18 BIA, *Albanian Terrorism and Organized Crime*, p. 8.

19 Eske Wright, "A Balkan Version of the IRA," *New Statesman*, 9 April 1999.

20 Chris Hedges, "Kosovo's Next Masters?," *Foreign Affairs*, May–June 1999, p. 28.

21 Anthony Cordesman, *Kosovo: Unpleasant Questions, Unpleasant Answers* (Washington, DC: Center for Strategic and International Studies, 1999), p. 6.

22 On the collapse of the Republic of Albania's economy under the weight of post-Communist neoliberal policies, and those who exploited them, see Michael Chossudovsky, "The Criminalization of Albania," in Tariq Ali, ed., *Masters of the Universe? NATO's Balkan Crusade* (London and New York: Verso, 2000), pp. 285–317. A detailed analysis of crime networks in the Republic of Albania and how they penetrated both the public sector and the legitimate economy, by an Albanian scholar, is Vasilika Hysi, "Organized Crime in Albania: The Ugly Side of Capitalism and Democracy," in Letizia Paolil and Cyrille Fijnaut, eds, *Organized Crime in Europe: Concepts, Patterns, and Control Policies in the European Union and Beyond* (New York and Heidelberg: Springer, 2004).

Notes 185

23 See Chossudovsky, *The Criminalization of Albania*, pp. 299–304, and James Pettifer, "The Kosovo Liberation Army – The Myth of Origin," in Kyril Drezov, Bulent Gokay, and Denica Kostovicova, eds, *Kosovo: Myths, Conflict, and War* (Staffordshire, UK: Keele European Research Center, 1999), p. 26.

24 Barbara Harff, "Assessing Risks of Genocide and Politicide," in Monty G. Marshall and Ted Robert Gurr, eds, *Peace and Conflict 2005: A Global Survey of Armed Conflicts, Self-Determination Movements, and Democracy* (College Park, MD: Center for International Development and Conflict Management, University of Maryland, 2004), p. 58.

25 BBC World, "Europe UN gives figure for Kosovo dead," URL http://news.bbc.co.uk/2/hi/europe/514828.stm.

26 Yoshihara, "Greater Albania," p. 68, citing Derek S. Reveron, "Coalition Warfare: The Commander's Role," *Defense & Security Analysis*, June 2002. Derek Reveron was a US Navy officer attached to NATO during the Kosovo war.

27 *Los Angeles Times*, 19 April 2001; *Washington Post*, 12 April 2005.

28 On the NUF, see *BBC*, 8 September 2005. A detailed account of Albanian separatist terrorism during this period is LyubovMincheva, "Spillover Crisis: Major Challenge to the Regional Stabilization Processes in the Western Balkans," in *Macedonia and the Region towards EU and NATO: Needs, Experiences and Lessons, Regional Conference, Skopje, November 5th, 2005* (Skopje, Macedonia: Frederich Ebert Stiftung, 2006), pp. 59–66.

29 *Financial Times*, 21 December 2000; *Daily Telegraph*, 28 February 2001; *Daily Telegraph*, 6 March 2001.

30 *Financial Times*, 2 March 2001; *Washington Post*, 10 March 2001.

31 *BBC Worldwide Monitoring*, 2 November 2005. Serbian intelligence says the ANA was founded in late 1999; BIA, *Albanian Terrorism and Organized Crime*, p. 5.

32 *BBC*, "Macedonian Government Confirms Ethnic Albanians Buying Arms from Drug Funds,"19 February 2002. The Ministry said its analysis was based on Western police records and information from the UN Vienna office.

33 A comprehensive analysis is LyubovMincheva, "The Albanian Ethnoterritorial Separatist Movement: Local Conflict, Regional Crisis," *Nationalism and Ethnic Politics*, vol. 15, no. 2 (April 2009), pp. 211–36.

34 Seth Jones, Andrew Rathmell, Jack Riley, and Jeremy Wilson, *Establishing Law and Order after Conflict* (Santa Monica, CA: RAND Corporation, 2005), p. 53.

35 BIA, *Albanian Terrorism and Organized Crime*, p. 18. A more detailed account is Tzvetomira Kaltcheva, "Kosovo's Post-Independence Inter-Clan Conflict," www.allacademic.com, p. 7.

36 "Islamic Community Head says Kosovo 'At Risk from Terrorism,'" *BBC Monitoring Europe – Political*, 4 September 2009, excerpt from a panel discussion that aired on Kosovo public radio-television on 3 September.

37 Leigh Phillips, "Violent Protests against EU Mission in Kosovo," *EU Observer*, http://euroobserver.com/13/28583 (26 August 2009).

38 A detailed assessment by Kosovar analysts is Bejtush Gashi and Sedat Burrniku, "Crisis Management in Kosovo: Challenges and Perspectives," in IztokPrezelj, ed., *The Fight Against Terrorism and Crisis Management in the Western Balkans* (Amsterdam: IOS Press for the NATO Science for Peace and Security Series, 2008), pp. 195–210. An international analysis and proposal for damping the conflict is International Crisis Group, *Serb Integration in Kosovo: Taking the Plunge*, 12 May 2009, at http://www.crisisgroup.org.

39 Strazzari, "L'Oeuvre au Noir," p. 156. A detailed analysis that includes maps of the transit routes for various kinds of smuggled commodities is Marko Haidinjak, *The Contraband Channels in South East Europe: The Conflicts in Yugoslavia and the Emergence of the Regional Criminal Networks* (Sofia: Center for the Study of Democracy, 2002).

40 Strazzari, "L'Oeuvre au Noir," analyzes the political and economic circumstances and official complicity that allowed this trade to flourish, pp. 199–202. A vivid journalistic description of the trade and crime networks that ran it is Misha Glenny, *McMafia: A Journey Through the Global Criminal Underworld* (New York: Knopf, 2008), pp. 21–45.

186 *Notes*

41 "Drugs Money Linked to the Kosovo Rebels," *The Times* (London), 24 March 1999; Jerry Seper, "KLA Finances Fight with Heroin Sales," *Washington Times*, 3 May 1999.
42 Steve Boggan and Kim Sengupta, "KLA Weapons on Sale in Britain," *The Independent*, 16 August 1999.
43 John R. Schindler, *Unholy Terror: Bosnia, Al-Qaida, and the Rise of Global Jihad* (St Paul, MN: Zenith Press, 2007), p. 267. On crime–terror linkages in the Bosnian civil war, see chapter 4 in this book.
44 A very detailed draft report by the Council of Europe's Committee on Legal Affairs and Human Rights was circulated in December 2010: *Inhuman Treatment of People and Illicit Trafficking in Human Organs in Kosovo*, URL http://assembly.coe.int/ASP/APFeaturesManager/defaultArtSiteView.asp?ID=964/. The rapporteur, Dick Marty, makes it clear that the Albanian perpetrators are very unlikely to be formally accused and tried because no one will testify against them due to very strong bonds of clan loyalty.
45 CARPO project, *Update of the 2006 Situation Report on Organised and Economic Crime in South-eastern Europe* (Strasbourg: Council of Europe and European Commission, June 2007), p. 106.
46 *Europol Annual Report (2003/04)*, p. 2, http//www.europol.eu.int/.
47 Bureau for International Narcotics and Law Enforcement Affairs, *2009 International Narcotics Control Strategy Report – Volume I. Drug and Chemical Control* (Washington, DC: US Department of State, February 2009), p. 379.
48 Strazzari, "L'Oeuvre au Noir," p. 158 and sources cited there. Also see his comparative analysis, "The *Decade Horribilis*: Organized Violence and Organized Crime along the Balkan Peripheries, 1991–2001," *Mediterranean Politics*, vol. 12, no. 2 (July 2007), pp. 185–209.
49 Quoted in *Free Republic*, 17 February 2002.
50 Giatzidis, "The Challenge of Organized Crime," p. 338. Like most other discussions of this period, this source does not distinguish between Kosovar-based crime networks and those in the Republic of Albania. Other sources indicate that some of the Kosovar clans had kindred in Albania proper. They also say that during the late 1990s the Kosovar clans came to dominate those in Albania, but incorporated or collaborated closely with them and other mafia groups as they expanded internationally.
51 UN Office on Drugs and Crime, *Crime and its Impact on the Balkans and Affected Countries*, March 2008, http://www.unodc.org/documents/data-and-analysis/Balkan_study.pdf, p. 14.
52 Cited in M. Bozinovich, "The New Islamic Mafia," www.serbianna.com/columns/mb/028.shtml, 10 September 2004. News and articles on this website are distinctly pro-Serbian and usually sharply critical of developments in Kosovo.
53 Ibid.
54 BIA, *Albanian Terrorism and Organized Crime*, pp. 16–17. The other clans described in this source also have territorial bases and specialize in specific kinds of goods, usually in alliance with one of the three major clans. Our summary is consistent with and draws on other accounts, for example, Strazzari, "L'Oeuvre au Noir"; Emil Giatzidis, "The Challenge of Organized Crime in the Balkans and the Political and Economic Implications," *Journal of Communist Studies and Transition Politics*, vol. 23, no. 3 (September 2007), pp. 327–51; and Gordon Bardos, "Containing Kosovo," *Mediterranean Quarterly*, vol. 16, no. 3 (Summer 2005), pp. 17–43.
55 BIA, *Albanian Terrorism and Organized Crime*, p. 18.
56 Bardos, "Containing Kosovo," p. 22.
57 Quote from Ioannis Michaletos, "Organized Crime Concerns in the Balkans," *World Security Network*, 22 June 2009.
58 See John Rosenthal, "Corruption and Organized Crime in Kosovo: An Interview with Avni Zogiani," *World Politics Review*, www.worldpoliticsreview.com, 2 February 2008.
59 See Sarah E. Mendelson, *Barracks and Brothels: Peacekeepers and Human Trafficking in the*

Balkans (Washington, DC: Center for Strategic and International Studies Press, 2005). KFOR had 16,000 military personnel in Kosovo, UNMIK civilian administration many thousands more. KFOR personnel remain under EULEX along with 2000 civilian officials.

60 Ilir Gjonir, "Organized Crime and National Security: The Albanian Case," unpublished MA thesis, Monterey, CA: Naval Postgraduate School, 2004, p. 33. Other sources that comment on the corrupting influences of criminal network capital are Giatzidis, "The Challenge of Organized Crime," especially pp. 344–7; Pugh, "Crime and Capitalism in Kosovo's Transformation"; and Strazzari, "L'Oeuvre au Noir."

61 Bardos, "Containing Kosovo," pp. 27–30.

62 BIA, *Albanian Terrorism and Organized Crime*, pp. 26–9.

63 Yoshihara, "Greater Albania," pp. 71–3, quotation on 71.

64 Schindler, *Unholy Terror*, p. 267.

65 Bardos, "Containing Kosovo," p. 29; Yoshihara, "Greater Albania," p. 72.

66 Quoted by Yoshihara, "Greater Albania," p. 72.

67 Frank Cilluffo and George Salmoiraghi, "And the Winner is…the Albanian Mafia," *The Washington Quarterly* (Autumn 1999), p. 24.

68 See Hysi, "Organized Crime in Albania," on these phenomena in the Republic of Albania. A three-part article by Matt McAllester in the *Global Post*, 27 March 2011, documents the persistence of crime–terror–governance linkages in contemporary Kosovo: Part I: Kosovo's Mafia: How the US and allies ignore allegations of organized crime at the highest levels of a new democracy – Prime Minister Thaqi, friend of world leaders and suspect in crime, http://www.globalpost.com/dispatch/news/regions/europe/110321/kosovo-hashim-thaci-organized-crime.
Part II: Kosovo's Mafia: Assassinations and intimidation – Investigating an intelligence service in the shadows. http://www.globalpost.com/dispatch/news/regions/europe/110321/kosovo-intelligence-services.
Part III: Kosovo's Mafia: A hotbed of human trafficking – Allegations of sexual slavery reach the highest levels of the Kosovo government. http://www.globalpost.com/dispatch/news/regions/europe/110322/kosovo-human-trafficking.

69 Jones, Rathmell, Riley, and Wilson, *Establishing Law and Order after Conflict*, p. 30.

70 A good overview of the institutional design approach is chapter 3, "Kosovo," in Jones, Rathmell, Riley, and Wilson, *Establishing Law and Order after Conflict*. Many examples of the operational challenges and limited successes in Kosovo are incorporated in the comparative analyses in Colette Rausch, ed., *Combating Serious Crimes in Postconflict Societies: A Handbook for Policymakers and Practitioners* (Washington, DC: United States Institute of Peace Press, 2006). Data on KPC positions (and KLA applicants for them) are from BIA, *Albanian Terrorism and Organized Crime*, p. 9, note 12.

71 Strazzari, "L'Oeuvre au Noir," p. 162.

72 Rosenthal, "An Interview with Avni Zogiani".

73 Commission of the European Communities, *Kosovo: 2008 Progress Report* (Brussels: author, May 2008).

74 Michaletos, "Organized Crime Concerns in the Balkans."

75 *Kosovo Criminal Justice Score Card* (New York: Human Rights Watch, March 2008), p. 2. This report provides ample and critical documentation for the conclusions of the Commission of the European Communities report, cited above. These and other reports also contain numerous recommendations for dealing with the problems.

76 Jones et al., *Establishing Law and Order after Conflict*, describe the training and growth of the Kosovo Police Service, pp. 35–7. Pond, "The EU's Test in Kosovo," assesses the effectiveness and public acceptance of the KPS as of 2008, p. 106.

77 Rosenthal, "An Interview with Avni Zogiani."

78 A detailed economic analysis is outside the scope of this study. See Pugh, "Crime and Capitalism in Kosovo's Transformation," which is the source of the official 2002 GDP data, p. 1. For a more general account of the illiberal or shadow economies of post-war

188 *Notes*

Kosovo and Serbia, see Sørensen, *State Reconstruction on the Periphery*, pp. 277 ff. The two billion Euro figure is cited in a number of sources including Pond, "The EU's Test in Kosovo," p. 104, without specifying whether it is an annual or cumulative sum. The UNMIK estimate is cited by Rosenthal, "An Interview with Avni Zogiani."

79 Quotation from Pond, "The EU's Test in Kosovo," p. 106. She gives a detailed and balanced analysis of EULEX objectives and challenges to their achievement. A more general, and more pessimistic assessment is Sladana Durić, Vladimir Cvetković, and Želimir Kešetović, "Kosovo – Between a Prosperous Future and Present Security/Safety Challenges," pre-publication paper, Faculty of Security Studies, University of Belgrade, no date [2011].

80 Strazzari, "L'Oeuvre au Noir," p. 162.

81 *Kosovo: 2008 Progress Report*, p. 19.

82 Rosenthal, "An Interview with Avni Zogiani."

83 Pond, "The EU's Test in Kosovo," pp. 108–9.

84 A critical view of NATO's campaigns in the Balkans is Diana Johnstone, *Fool's Crusade: Yugoslavia, NATO and Western Delusions* (New York: Monthly Review Press, 2002).

85 Ilir Gjoni, "Organized Crime and National Security: The Albanian Case," pp. 10–11.

86 See the reports on its activities, posted at www.iks.org in Albanian and English. IKS was founded in 2004 with international funding. Reports by IKS analysts have focused on "issues of governance, economic development, urban planning, corruption in post-war reconstruction, education, Kosovo's image problem and environmental issues." Each of its reports includes specific policy recommendations.

3 Kurdish nationalists and criminal networks

1 We are very grateful to Major Sean Cosden and Captain Daniel Rueth, US Air Force, both Olmsted Fellows at the Department of Political Science at the University of Sofia, for having prepared pilot studies of the PKK and its terrorist-criminal activities. We are also obliged to Mohamed Khalaf, an Iraqi journalist in Bulgaria, for his comments, feedback, and expert opinions. Special thanks go to Prof. Gunay Goksu Ozdogan of the Department of Political Science and International Relations at Marmara University, Istanbul, Turkey for providing thorough feedback and research suggestions on a draft of this chapter.

2 Aliza Marcus, *Blood and Belief: The PKK and the Kurdish Fight for Independence* (New York and London: New York University Press, 2007), p. 1.

3 Aliza Marcus, "Turkey's PKK: Rise, Fall, Rise Again?," *World Policy Journal*, vol. 24, no. 1 (22 March 2007), pp. 75–84.

4 "Kurdish Rebels Kill Turkey Troops," *BBC News*, 8 April 2007, at http://news.bbc.co.uk/2/hi/europe/6537751.stm [accessed 18 September 2007].

5 *EU Terrorism Situation and Trend Report*, TE-SAT, 2011.

6 See chapter 1.

7 Minorities at Risk project (MAR), URL http://www.cidcm.umd.edu/mar/. The *Minorities at Risk* (MAR) project monitors and analyzes the status and conflicts of 283 politicallyactive communal groups globally. *MAR* focuses specifically on ethnopolitical groups, non-state communal groups that collectively suffer, or benefit from, systematic discriminatory treatment vis-à-vis other groups in a society, and which have thecapacity for political mobilization and collective action in defense or promotion of their self-defined interests.

8 For analyses of the status of Kurds in Turkey and the political context of government policies, see Henri J. Barkey and Graham E. Fuller, *Turkey's Kurdish Question* (Lanham, MD: Rowman & Littlefield, 1998), for the Carnegie Commission on Preventing Deadly Conflict; and Michael M. Gunter, *The Kurds in Turkey: A Political Dilemma* (Boulder, CO: Westview Press, 1999). More recent references are provided in later sections of this chapter.

Notes 189

9 This concept has been introduced by Edward Azar. The main characteristics of protracted conflicts include protracted hostility and insecurity characterized by periods of armed violence and crises; fluctuation in the intensity and frequency in interactions; absence of a distinct termination point; and conflict spillover in terms of actors and issues, so that the conflict is no longer intrastate or one-dimensional but regional and multicausal. For more on protracted conflicts, see Edward Azar, "Protracted Social Conflicts and Second Track Diplomacy," in John Davies and Edward Kaufman, eds, *Second Track/ Citizens' Diplomacy. Concepts and Techniques for Conflict Transformation* (Lanham, MD: Rowman and Littlefield, 2002), pp. 15–30.

10 Barbara Harff and Ted Robert Gurr, *Ethnic Conflict in World Politics*, 2nd edn (Boulder, CO: Westview Press, 2004), p. 40. Turkish Kurds make up about half the total Kurdish population in these four states. There is much conjecture and dispute about the size of the Kurdish population in all four countries for lack of censuses that ask questions about Kurdish identity.

11 Gerard Chailand, ed., *People Without a Country: The Kurds and Kurdistan* (London: Zed Press, 1980).

12 For an extended discussion of ETSMs, see Lyubov Mincheva, "The Albanian Ethnoterritorial Separatist Movement: Local Conflict, Regional Crisis," *Nationalism and Ethnic Politics*, vol. 15, no. 2 (April–June 2009), pp. 211–36.

13 Sidney Tarrow, *Power in Movement: Social Movements, Collective Action and Politics* (New York: Cambridge University Press, 1994).

14 See Ted Robert Gurr, *Minorities at Risk: A Global View of Ethnopolitical Conflict* (Washington, DC: United States Institute of Peace, 1993), p. 133; and George Tsebelis, *Nested Games: Rational Choice in Comparative Politics* (Berkeley: University of California Press, 1990).

15 Tarrow, *Power in Movement*, p. 96.

16 For more on the national liberation movements of this era, see Rupert Emerson, *From Empire to Nation* (Cambridge, MA: Harvard University Press, 1960).

17 Harff and Gurr, *Ethnic Conflict in World Politics*, p. 39.

18 For the conception of modern nationalism, see Ernest Gellner, *Nations and Nationalism* (Oxford: Blackwell Publishers, 1983).

19 This situation has changed only recently, when the Kurdish elite diversified as a result of multiple factors and as Kurdish society changed it's profile. Intense migration has led to urbanization; and interaction with the Kurdish European diaspora has transformed Kurdish society into a socially complex and de-territorialized group. For an extended discussion on the formation of Kurdish national identity see *European Journal of Turkish Studies*, no. 10, 2009, URL http://ejts.revues.org/.

20 Kurds in Syria, Wikipedia, URL http://en.wikipedia.org/wiki/Kurds_in_Syria [accessed 30 April 2012]; and Riccardo Dugulin, "The Kurds' place in the 'Arab Spring'," *Open Democracy*, 10 December 2011. URL http://www.opendemocracy.net/riccardo-dugulin/kurds%E2%80%99-place-in-%E2%80%98arab-spring%E2%80%99 [accessed 29 April 2012].

21 Mincheva, "The Albanian Ethnoterritorial Separatist Movement: Local Conflict, Regional Crisis," pp. 217–18.

22 Andrei Sherikhov, "Kurds, Syria and the Chessboard," *International Affairs*, 25 April 2012. URL http://en.rian.ru/international_affairs/20120425/173044108.html [accessed 30 April 2012].

23 The latter includes, among others, the acknowledgment of the leading role of the Arab actors in the SNC, as well as the number of seats to be allocated to the ethnic Kurds within it. See Riccardo Dugulin, "The Kurds' Place in the 'Arab Spring'."

24 Ibid.

25 For a more detailed analysis of the factors impacting on the Syrian Kurds' selection of a policy strategy in the aftermath of the Arab Spring, see Sherikhov, " Kurds, Syria and the Chessboard."

26 Tsebelis, *Nested Games*, p. 7.

190 *Notes*

27 This is the opinion of Iraqi Kurdistan's director of security and intelligence, Masrour Barzani. He has suggested that "being a part of the Middle East, the Kurds should be prepared for a worst-case scenario and receptive to whatever opportunities – if changes create greater stability, everybody will enjoy the enhanced security, but otherwise security will deteriorate and preparations have to be made accordingly." Quoted in Sherikhov, "Kurds, Syria and the Chessboard."

28 *See* Dugulin, "The Kurds' Place in the 'Arab Spring'."

29 Amnesty International, Wikipedia. URL http://en.wikipedia.org/wiki/Iranian_Kurdistan [accessed 2 May 2012].

30 The head of the PJAK, Abdul Rahman Haci Ahmedi, has worked with the PKK in the past; the PJAK's coordination committee head, Ihsan Varya, once commanded a PKK regional unit.

31 Party of Free Life of Kurdistan, *Wikipedia*. URL http://en.wikipedia.org/wiki/PJAK [accessed 2 May 2012].

32 Soner Cagaptay and Zeynep Eroglu, "The PKK, PJAK, and Iran: Implications for US–Turkish Relations," The Washington Institute for Near East Policy, *Policy Watch*, #1244, 13 January 2007. URL http://www.washingtoninstitute.org/templateC05.php?CID=2617 [accessed 6 October 2007].

33 The Qasim government was overthrown in a coup in 1963 by Colonel Abdul Salam Arif.

34 The government of Abdul Rahman Arif was overthrown in 1968 by the Arab Socialist Ba'ath Party.

35 In 1980 Saddam Hussein declared war on Iran, claiming the change of regime in Iran after the Islamic Revolution of Ayatollah Khomeini threatened the stability of the Iraqi government.

36 In 1990 Iraq invaded Kuwait, claiming Kuwait misused to Iraqi's disadvantage the drilling of its oil wells; and also manipulated to Kuwait's advantage the oil revenues. The UN imposed economic sanctions on Iraq and demanded immediate withdrawal. Iraq declined to comply. And the UNSC unanimously voted for military action against Iraq.

37 The 2003 war on Iraq was launched by a US-led coalition because of Iraq's alleged failure to comply with UN restrictions on its nuclear and chemical weapons development program. A Coalition Provisional Authority was thereafter established, followed by an interim government and then by a permanently elected government.

38 The conflict between the KDP and PUK of the mid-1990s became a civil war that claimed the life of 3000 to 5000 fighters and civilians. In 1998 the leaders of the KDP and PUK, Barzani and Talabani, signed a US-brokered power-sharing agreement that put an end to the warfare.

39 Dugulin, "The Kurds' Place in the 'Arab Spring'."

40 Marcus, *Blood and Belief*, p. 11.

41 Ibid., p. 11.

42 Soner Cagaptay and H. Akin Unver, "Iraqi Kurds and the Turkish–Iraqi Memorandum Against the PKK," The Washington Institute for Near East Policy, *PolicyWatch* #1275, 21 August 2007. URL http://www.washingtoninstitute.org/templateC05.php?CID=2651 [accessed 6 October 2007].

43 "Kemalist Ideology," *Wikipedia*. URL http://en.wikipedia.org/wiki/Kemalist_ideology [accessed 15 October 2007].

44 "Kurds in Turkey," *Wikipedia*. URL http://en.wikipedia.org/wiki/Kurds_in_Turkey [accessed 25 October 2012].

45 "Kurds in Turkey," *Wikipedia*. URL http://en.wikipedia.org/wiki/Kurds_in_Turkey [accessed 4 May 2012].

46 For more on the recent development of Kurdish identity, society and politics, see Busra Ersanli and Gunay Goksu Ozdogan, "Obstacles and opportunities: recent Kurdish

struggles for political representation and participation in Turkey," *Southeastern Europe*, vol. 35, no. 1, 2011, pp. 62–94.

47 Cagaptay and Uslu, "Is the PKK Still a Threat to the United States and Turkey?"

48 Marcus, *Blood and Belief*, p. 41. The PKK's territorial objectives have gone even further. The PKK is the only Kurdish organization in the region that has ever pronounced the idea of the establishment of a Greater Kurdistan. This ambition was unrealistic and short-lived. Yet the PKK has managed to establish itself as a leading political organization in the region and to set the tone of overall Kurdish regional politics.

49 Marcus, "Turkey's PKK: Rise, Fall, Rise Again?"

50 "Turkish–Kurdish conflict," *Wikipedia*. URL http://en.wikipedia.org/wiki/Turkey_%E2%80%93_Kurdistan_Workers%27_Party_conflict [accessed 20 May 2012].

51 Marcus, *Blood and Belief*, p. 41.

52 Thus the Revolutionary Unity of the People, the Liberation of the People, as well as the Revolutionary East Cultural Association are known to have been decimated at the hands of the PKK.

53 The village guard system was introduced in 1985 by Prime Minister Turgut Özal.

54 Francois Haut, "Kurdish Extremism and Organized Crime: The Kurdistan Workers Party," Pan European Turkish Organized Crime Conference, "The Way Forward," London, 3–5 March 1998. URL http://www.drmcc.org/sommaire_en.php?tp=6&id=141 [accessed 5 October 2007].

55 Soner Cagaptay and S. Fikret Cem S., "Europe's Terror Problem: PKK Fronts Inside the EU," The Washington Institute for Near East Policy, *PolicyWatch* #1057, 2 December2005. URL http://www.washingtoninstitute.org/templateC05.php?CID=2413 [accessed 5 October 2007].

56 "Child Soldiers: 1379 Report," *Coalition to Stop the Use of Child Soldiers*, November 2002, p. 50. URL http://www.child-soldiers.org/document_get.php?id=740 [accessed 20 September 2007].

57 The Turkish government came under attacks about the same time for reasons related to its alleged linkages to the world of organized crime. A big scandal, known as the Susurluk scandal, revealed the intentions of government institutions to compete with the PKK's drug business instead of cracking down on it. See "Susurluk scandal," *Wikipedia*. URL http://en.wikipedia.org/wiki/Susurluk_scandal [accessed 22 May 2012].

58 Ocalan was convicted to death but his sentence was commuted to life imprisonment, and he was sent to Imrali Island in the Marmara Sea. Turkey had to abolish the death penalty to meet one of the Copenhagen criteria for EU membership. He remains in prison as of this writing.

59 Ocalan even urged the PKK's leaders to turn themselves in to Turkish authorities. Sixteen did and all were arrested and tried. See Marcus, "Turkey's PKK."

60 Links to all three groups can be found at "Related groups – Terrorist Organizations: Kurdistan Workers' Party," *MIPT Terrorism Knowledge Base*. URL http://www.tkb.org/MoreRelatedGroups.jsp?groupID=63 [accessed 17 October 2007].

61 See Gareth Jenkins, "The PKK Insurgency Enters a New Era," *The Central Asia Caucus Institute Silk Road Studies Program*, vol. 3, no.12 (21 June 2010). URL http://www.silkroadstudies.org/new/inside/turkey/2010/100621A.html [accessed March 2012].

62 *Federation of American Scientists*, accessed at http://www.fac.org

63 Some analysts think that TAK is a PKK faction. See"Kurdistan Freedom Hawks," *MIPT Terrorism Knowledge Base*, 10 September 2007. URL http://www.tkb.org/Group.jsp?groupID=4381 [accessed 8 October 2007]..

64 "Turkish Resort Blast Kills Five," *BBC News*, 16 July 2005. URL http://news.bbc.co.uk/2/hi/europe/4688575.stm [accessed 16 October 2007].

65 Damage to the Turkish tourist industry has a significant impact on Turkey's economy in general. In 2005 21 million tourists visited Turkey, generating estimated revenue of $28 billion. See "Kurdish Group Claims PKK Bombing," *International Herald Tribune*,

192 *Notes*

29 August 2006. URL http://www.iht.com/articles/ap/2006/08/29/europe/EU_GEN_Turkey_Explosions_Claim.php [accessed 16 October 2007].

66 Ben Lando, "Analysis: PKK's Oil Attack Requires New Turkish Strategy," *UPI*, 25 November 2008. URL http://www.upi.com/Business_News/Energy-Resources/2008/11/25/Analysys-PKKs-oil-attack-requires-new-Turkish-strategy/UPI-16631227648974#ixzz1nZjjsNPa.

67 See Anthony H. Cordesman, "International Cooperation in Counterterrorism: Redefining the Threat and the Requirement," Center for Strategic and International Studies, 13 January 2010. URL http://csis.org/files/publication/100125_IntCoopinfightterror.pdf.

68 See Carol Migdalovitz, "2010 Congressional Brief Turkey: Selected Foreign Policy Issues and US Views," 28 November 2010 URL www.crs.gov [accessed March 2012].

69 The Turkish parliament passed a motion authorizing cross-border military operations against PKK targets in northern Iraq, following weeks of violence in late 2007, during which PKK attacks claimed scores of killed or wounded Turkish soldiers and citizens. See Cordesman, "International Cooperation in Counterterrorism."

70 Ibid.

71 The PKK's insurgency temporarily subsided at the start of 2009 following the announcement of the government's Kurdish Democratic Initiative. It envisaged various steps aimed at improving the status of the ethnic Kurds. Plans included renaming Kurdish villages; expanding the freedom of expression; restoring Turkish citizenship to Kurdish refugees; strengthening local government; and partial provision of amnesty for the PKK fighters. The initiative, however, failed as the Turkish Constitutional Court at the end of the year banned the official Kurdish party, the DTP, arrested its leaders and subsequently tried them for terrorism. Clashes between Kurdish demonstrators and Turkish security forces resulted in injuries and fatalities.

72 Jenkins, "The PKK Insurgency Enters a New Era."

73 *BBC News*,"Turkey Steps Up Offensive in Iraq after Kurdish Raids," 20 October 2011. URL http://www.bbc.co.uk/news/world-europe-15390006 [accessed March 2012].

74 James Adams, *The Financing of Terror* (New York: Simon and Schuster, 1986), p. 251.

75 PKK terrorists were often issued Palestinian or Iraqi ID cards. See Marcus, *Blood and Belief*, pp. 59–60.

76 Alan Makovsky and Michael Eisenstadt, "Turkish–Syrian Relations: A Crisis Delayed?," The Washington Institute for Near East Policy, *Policy Watch*, #345, 17 October 1998. URL http://www.washingtoninstitute.or/templateC05.php?CID=1223 [accessed 7 October 2007].

77 F. Stephen Larrabee, "Turkish Foreign and Security Policy: New Dimensions and New Challenges," *The RAND Corporation*. URL http://www.washingtoninstitute.org/templateC05.php?CID=1282 [accessed 9 October 2007].

78 Marcus, *Blood and Belief*, pp. 120–1.

79 F. Stephen Larrabee, "Turkey Rediscovers the Middle East," *Foreign Affairs*, vol. 86, no. 4 (July–August 2007), pp. 103–14.

80 Cagaptay and Eroglu, "The PKK, PJAK, and Iran."

81 Marcus, *Blood and Belief*, p. 122.

82 The organization operates under the name "Kurdistan Democratic Solution Party" and has enjoyed Iraqi hospitality thanks to the central government's preoccupation with the country's overall instability. See Cagaptay and Eroglu, "The PKK, PJAK, and Iran." Also see Soner Cagaptay and H. Akin Unver, "Iraqi Kurds and the Turkish–Iraqi Memorandum Against the PKK," The Washington Institute for Near East Policy, *Policy Watch*, #1275, 21 August 2007. URL http://www.washingtoninstitute.org/templateC05.php?CID=2651 [accessed 6 October 2007].

83 While Turkey claimed the right to cross the border in hot pursuit operations, Iraq

insisted on receiving notice each time before cross-border security operations. See Evren Mesci, "Turkey, Iraq SignTerrorism Deal Amid Border Row," *Washington Post*, 28 September 2007. URL http://www.washingtonpost.com/wp-dyn/content/article/2007/09/28/AR2007092800261.html [accessed 8 October 2007].

84 Suzan Frazer, "Turkish Parliament Approves Iraq Mission," *Yahoo! News*, 17 October2007. URL http://news.yahoo.com/s/ap/20071017/ap_on_re_mi_ea/turkey;_ylt=Ahyehh0GPxbj6aGMZJzTGSms0NUE [accessed 17 October 2007]

85 Larrabee,"Turkish Foreign and Security Policy."

86 Nur Bilge Criss, "Development in Managing Terrorism in Turkey," *Perceptions: Journal of International Affairs*, vol. 1, no. 4 (December 1996–February 1997). URL http://www.sam.gov.tr/perceptions/Volume1/Dec1996-Feb1997/DEVELOPMENTINMANAGINGTERRORISMINTURKEY.pdf [accessed 19 September 2007].

87 Ian O. Lessor, "Countering the New Terrorism: Implications for Strategy," *The RAND Corporation*, 1999. URL http://www.rand.org/pubs/monograph_reports/MR989/MR989.chap4.pdf [accessed 9 October 2007]

88 Criss, "Development in Managing Terrorism in Turkey."

89 *Federation of American Scientists.*

90 F. Stephen Larrabee and Ian O. Lessor, "Turkish Foreign Policy in an Age of Uncertainty," *The RAND Corporation*, 2003. URL http://www.rand.org/pubs/monograph_reports?MR1612/MR1612.ch4.pdf [accessed 9 October 2007].

91 *CNN.com*, 22 February 1999.

92 "Ocalan Reportedly Implicates Greeks in Supporting PKK," *CNN.com*, 22 February 1999. URL http://www.cnn.com/WORLD/europe/9902/22/kurds.02/index.html [accessed 18 September 2007]..

93 Soner Cagaptay and S. Fikret Cem, "Europe's Terror Problem: PKK Fronts Inside the EU," The Washington Institute for Near East Policy, *PolicyWatch*, #1057, 2 December 2005. URL http://www.washingtoninstitute.org/templateC05.php?CID=2413 [accessed 5 October 2007].

94 Marcus, *Blood and Belief*, p. 229.

95 *Federation of American Scientists.*

96 Marcus, *Blood and Belief*, p. 57.

97 "Armenian Secret Army for the Liberation of Armenia (ASALA) and Kurdistan Workers Party (PKK) Attacked Diplomatic Target (Nov. 10, 1980, France)," *MIPT Terrorism Knowledge Base*, 3 April2001. URL http://www.tkb.org/Incident.jsp?incID=2735 [accessed 18 September 2007].

98 Note that no linkage existed between Turkish Hezbollah (KH) and the PKK except for some short- lived joint training in the early 1980s. KH is an Islamist group formed in 1980 that has been at odds with the anti-Islamist, Marxist-Leninist PKK. The two organizations even fought each other in the 1980s. See Soner Cagaptay and Emrullah Uslu, "Hizbullah in Turkey Revives – Al-Qaeda's Bridge between Europe and Iraq?," The Washington Institute for Near East Policy, *PolicyWatch*,# 946, 25 January 2005. URL http://www.ict.org.il/index.php?sid=119&lang=en&act=page&id=5224&str =PKK [accessed 7 October 2007].

99 Mark Burgess, "In the Spotlight: PKK (A.k.a KADEK) Kurdish Worker's Party (A.k.a. Kurdish Freedom and Democracy Congress)," Center for Defense Information Terrorism Project, 21 May 2002. URL http://www.cdi.org/terrorism/pkk-pr.cfm [accessed 17 September 2007].

100 Francois Haut, "Kurdish Extremism and Organized Crime: The Kurdistan Workers Party," Pan European Turkish Organized Crime Conference, "The Way Forward," London, 3–5 March 1998. URL http://www.drmcc.org/sommaire_en.php?tp=6&id=141 [accessed 5 October 2007].

101 Cagaptay, "Can the PKK Renounce Violence?"

102 Cagaptay mentions a case when, on 16 November 2005, Prime Minister Erdogan walked out of a joint press conference with his Danish counterpart, Andres Fogh

194 *Notes*

Rasmussen, when the Danish side refused to remove ROJ TV reporters from the room. See Cagaptay and Fikret, "Europe's Terror Problem."

103 Yigal Schleifer, "Denmark Again? Now It's Under Fire for Hosting Kurdish TV Station," *The Christian Science Monitor*, 21 April 2006. URL http://www.csmonitor.com/2006/0421/p01s01-woeu.html [accessed 18 September 2007].

104 Bruce Hoffman et al., "The Radicalization of Diasporas and Terrorism," *The RAND Corporation*, Zurich, 2007. URL http://www.rand.org/pubs/conf_proceedings/2007/RAND_CF229.pdf [accessed 9 October 2007]..

105 Marcus, *Blood and Belief*, pp. 230–1.

106 TE-SAT.EU Terrorism Situation and Trend Report, *EUROPOL*, p. 21.

107 Marcus, *Blood and Belief*, p. 232.

108 "Mafia Threatens UK Turks and Kurds, " *BBC News*, 14 November2002. URL http://news.bbc.co.uk/2/hi/uk_news/2284780.stm [accessed 8 October 2007].

109 Haut, "Kurdish Extremism and Organized Crime."

110 See Lyubov Mincheva and Ted Robert Gurr, "Unholy Alliances: How International Terrorists and Crime Make Common Cause," in Rafael Reuveny and William R. Thompson, eds, *Coping with Contemporary Terrorism: Origins, Escalation, Counter Strategies, and Response* (Albany, NY: State University of New York Press, 2010).

111 United Nations Office of Drugs and Crime, *The Globalization of Crime: A Transnational Organized Crime Assessment* (Vienna: author, 2010), p. 122. From 2000 to 2008 27 per cent of heroin traffickers arrested were of Turkish nationality (far more numerous than any other nationality except Bulgarian), while in Germany it was 19 per cent, far outnumbering any non-Germans; ibid., pp. 123–4.

112 "FAQs: Arguments used PKK/KONGRA-GEL against Turkey," *Republic of Turkey Ministry of Foreign Affairs*, 16 September 2005. URL http://www.mfa.gov.tr/MFA/ForeignPolicy/MainIssues/Terrorism/FAQs.htm [accessed 20 September 2007].

113 Frank J. Cilluffo, "The Threat Posed from the Convergence of Organized Crime, Drug Trafficking, and Terrorism," Testimony before the US House Committee on the Judiciary Subcommittee on Crime, 13 December 2000. URL http://www.gwu.edu/`dhs/congress/dec13_00.html [accessed 17 September 2007].

114 Ibid.

115 *BBC News*, 14 November 2002.

116 "Reports of Foreign Police and Foreign Officials," *Republic of Turkey Ministry of Foreign Affairs*.

117 Capagtay, "Can the PKK Renounce Violence?"

118 According to Germany's chief prosecutor, 80 per cent of drugs seized in Europe are connected to the PKK. *Federation of American Scientists*.

119 "Reports of Foreign Police and Foreign Officials," *Republic of Turkey Ministry of Foreign Affairs*.

120 Steven W. Casteel, "Narco-Terrorism: International Drug Trafficking and Terrorism – a Dangerous Mix," Statement before the US Senate Committee on the Judiciary, 20 May 2003. URL http://www.usdoj.gov/dea/pubs/cngrtest/ct052003.html [accessed 9 October 2007].

121 Cagaptay, "Can the PKK Renounce Violence?" This is probably an estimate of the street value, only a fraction of which goes to the networks of distributors and dealers.

122 Glenn Curtis and Tara Karacan, "The Nexus Among Terrorists, Narcotic Traffickers, Weapons Proliferators and Organized Crime Networks in Western Europe," US Library of Congress, 2002. URL http://www.loc.gov/rr/frd/pdf-files/WestEurope_NEXUS.pdf [accessed 22 February 2008].

123 Ibid.

124 "Turkey's Efforts Against the Drug Problem," *Republic of Turkey Ministry of Foreign Affairs*, 14 August 2007. URL http://www.mfa.go2-v.tr/MFA/ForeignPolicy/MainIssues/CombatingDrugs/ [accessed 21 September 2007].

Notes 195

125 Hayri Birler, "PKK as an International Organized Crime Outfit," *Turkish Daily News*, 2 July 1996. Some of these networks may even extend to Latin America. In November 1993 a PKK courier was arrested with drugs in Caracas, Venezuela, showing a possible link between the PKK and the Latin American drug cartels.

126 Bejamin Freedman and Matthew Levitt, "Contending with the PKK's Narco-Terrorism," The Washington Institute for Near East Policy, *Policy Watch, # 1611*, 8 December 2009. URL http://www.washingtoninstitute.org/templateC05.php?CID=3151 [accessed March 2012].

127 Turkish security expert Ali Koknar observes that the PKK's cooperation with Kurdish criminal clans is similar to the cooperation among Sicilian mafia families. See Curtis and Karacan, "The Nexus Among Terrorists, Narcotic Traffickers, Weapons Proliferators and Organized Crime Networks in Western Europe."

128 US Department of Treasury, "Treasury Designates Three Leaders of the Kongra-Gel as Significant Foreign Narcotic Traffickers," 14 October 2009. URL http://www.treasury.gov/press-center/press-releases/Pages/tg318.aspx.

129 "What is the PKK?," *Republic of Turkey Ministry of Foreign Affairs*, 16 September 2005. URL http://www.mfa.gov.tr/MFA/ForeignPolicy/MainIssues/Terrorism/What+PKK.htm [accessed 20 September 2007].

130 Curtis and Karacan, "The Nexus Among Terrorists, Narcotic Traffickers, Weapons Proliferators and Organized Crime Networks in Western Europe."

131 Cagaptay, "Can the PKK Renounce Violence?" Cagaptay also mentions the possibility of PKK-organized prostitution rings.

132 Michael Roth and Murat Sever, "The Kurdish Workers Party (PKK) as Criminal Syndicate: Funding Terrorism through Organized Crime, A Case Study," *Studies in Conflict and Terrorism*, vol. 30 (2007), pp. 901–20.

133 Curtis and Karacan, "The Nexus Among Terrorists, Narcotic Traffickers, Weapons Proliferators and Organized Crime Networks in Western Europe."

134 Haut, "Kurdish Extremism and Organized Crime," claims that Operation Sputnik clearly showed the link between the "political" and the "criminal" sides of the PKK.

135 Curtis and Karacan, "The Nexus Among Terrorists, Nacotic Traffickers, Weapons Proliferators and Organized Crime Networks"; Haut, "Kurdish Extremism and Organized Crime."

136 See Figure 3.1, p. 43.

137 See Figure 3.1, p. 43

138 See pp. 46–47.

139 See p. 59.

140 In 1991 the PKK established bases in northern Iraq, taking advantage of the no-fly zones and safe havens established by the international community to protect the Kurdish population from attacks by the Saddam Hussein air force. The no-fly zone allowed the three Kurdish organizations, the PKK, the KDP and the PUK, to act without interference from Baghdad. Fighting, however, ensued between the PKK on the one hand; and the PUK and KDP on the other. Moreover intra-group fighting broke out between the Iraqi KDP and PUK, a conflict known as the Iraqi Kurdish Civil War. It played into the hands of the PKK, which remained in the country to strengthen its presence in northern Iraq. However, when in 2000 the PKK evacuated Turkey for Iraq, large-scale battles broke out between the PKK and the PUK.

141 Since the 2003 US-led invasion, the KDP and the PUK have essentially let the PKK live and train unimpeded in northern Iraq. The Kurdish Regional Government sends mixed signals to the PKK and Turkey. While it sides with Turkey in viewing it as the major economic investor in Iraqi Kurdistan, it nonetheless tends sometimes to turn a blind eye to the insurgence activities of the PKK in north Iraq, directed against Turkey. The KRG indicated that it will not support Turkey or at least look the other way, when it comes to battling the PKK and honoring the Memorandum of Understanding, signed between the two countries in 2007. See Soner Cagaptay and

196 *Notes*

H. Akin Unver, "Iraqi Kurds and the Turkish–Iraqi Memorandum Against the PKK," The Washington Institute for Near East Policy, *PolicyWatch* #1275, 21 August 2007. URL http://www.washingtoninstitute.org/templateC05.php?CID=2651 [accessed 6 October 2007].

142 The Party of Free Life of Kurdistan (PJAK) is considered to be a splinter group of the PKK. Its recent insurgency against Tehran is fought out of PJAK bases in northern Iraq.

4 Militant Islam and Bosnia's civil war 1991–1995

1 This is a substantially revised and updated version of Lyubov G. Mincheva and Ted Robert Gurr, "Unholy Alliances: Evidence on Linkages Between Trans-State Terrorism and Crime Networks: The Case of Bosnia," in Wolfgang Benedek, Christopher Daase, and Vojin Dimitrijević with Petrus van Duyne, eds, *Transnational Terrorism, Organized Crime and Peace-Building: Human Security in the Western Balkans* (London and New York: Palgrave Macmillan, 2010), pp. 190–206.

2 Most accounts from the 1990s represent the dominant narrative, for example, Robert J. Donia and John V.A. Fine, Jr, *Bosnia and Hercegovina: A Tradition Betrayed* (New York: Columbia University Press, 1994), and Norman Cigar, *Genocide in Bosnia: The Policy of "Ethnic Cleansing"* (College Station, TX: Texas A&M Press, 1995). John R. Schindler, a former intelligence officer, assembles the evidence for the alternative post-9/11 perspective in *Unholy Terror: Bosnia, Al-Qaida, and the Rise of Global Jihad* (St Paul, MN: Zenith Press, 2007). Unfortunately, he is as uncritical about anti-Muslim evidence, often relying on biased Croat and Serb sources, as were the observers he criticizes who uncritically accepted the pro-Muslim narrative. For a broader perspective, see Noel Malcolm, *Bosnia: A Short History*, revised edition (New York: New York University Press, 1996). An excellent analysis of Yugoslav's breakup is Susan L. Woodward, *Balkan Tragedy: Chaos and Dissolution after the Cold War* (Washington, DC: Brookings Institution, 1995). A Pulitzer Prize-winning account of the genocidal massacres is Roy Gutman, *A Witness to Genocide* (New York: Macmillan, 1993).

3 There is a third narrative that blames Muslim Bosnians for attacks and atrocities against the Serb and Croat minorities and justifies Serbian actions as self-defense. This interpretation, whose political purpose is to justify or rehabilitate Serbian nationalists, is widely discredited – see, for example, the UN Secretary General's 2005 Report, cited in note 15 below.

4 *A note on terminology*: Citizens of Bosnia of all nationalities and religions are Bosnians (Bosnian Serbs, Bosnian Croats), while those who identify themselves as Muslims are Bosniaks. In this chapter, as elsewhere, we distinguish between Islamic and Islamist objectives and activists. Islamic refers to observant Muslims in general, Islamist to those who seek to establish societies governed by sharia law and custom. Salafism (from the Arab word for ancestors) refers to reformist movements that advocate a return to the pure principles and practices of traditional Islam. Wahabism is the Saudi-supported stream of salafism. Jihadists are Islamists who support armed struggle; mujahedeen are the armed warriors of jihad. Jihadist strategies and rationales are diverse and often inspired by, but not necessarily linked to, the al-Qaeda network. Alison Pargeter, *The New Frontiers of Jihad: Radical Islam in Europe* (Philadelphia: University of Pennsylvania Press, 2008), is a useful guide to the evolving movements and doctrines of political Islam.

5 Another 5.5 percent, slightly fewer than a quarter-million, said they were Yugoslavs or without nationality – mostly secularists who did not identify with any of the three groups that were on the verge of civil war. Cited in Schindler, *Unholy Terror*, p. 53. Comparison with Bosnian census data for 1981, in Ted Robert Gurr, *Minorities at Risk: A Global View of Ethnopolitical Conflict* (Washington, DC: United States Institute of Peace Press, 1993), pp. 215–16, shows a four percent increase in Muslim identifiers and a corresponding decline in those who reported no identity.

Notes 197

6 Translated in Schindler, *Unholy Terror*, p. 52.
7 The above summary is mainly from Schindler, *Unholy Terror*, chapter 2. Also see Laura Silber and Allan Little, *Yugoslavia: Death of a Nation* (New York: Penguin, 1997).
8 Ibid.
9 For example, in *Balkan Battlegrounds: A Military History of the Yugoslav Conflict, 1990–1995*, two volumes (Washington, DC: Central Intelligence Agency, 2002, 2005).
10 See Peter Andreas, "Symbiosis between Peace Operations and Illicit Business in Bosnia," *International Peacekeeping*, vol. 16, no. 1 (February 2009), pp. 36–40; and also by Andreas, *Blue Helmets and Black Markets: The Business of Survival in the Siege of Sarajevo* (Ithaca, NY: Cornell University Press, 2008).
11 The International Criminal Tribunal in den Haag estimated that 102,000 Bosnians lost their lives in the war: 60,000 Muslims, 31,000 Serbs, and 12,000 Croat; cited in Schindler, *Unholy Terror*, pp. 85–6. A multiethnic Bosnian research team independently arrived at similar numbers: out of a documented 97,890 people killed in Bosnia, 64,767 or two-thirds were persons of "Bosniak" nationality. Serbs made up 26 per cent and Croats 8 percent. Research and Documentation Center, Sarajevo, available online at http://www.idc.org.ba[checked January 2007] and summarized in Edin Jahic, "Development of Events in Bosnia and Herzegovina Following the 11th September 2001," paper presented at the First Conference on Human Security, Terrorism and Organized Crime, Ljubljana, November 2006, and available online at http://www.humsec./eu/cms/fileadmin./user_upload/humsec/Working_Paper_Series/Working_Paper_Jahic.pdf.
12 Schindler, *Unholy Terror*, pp. 98–9. Accounts of these and many other atrocities blamed on jihadists would be more convincing if they came from independent sources. Schindler's sources for these 1993 killings are mostly Bosnian Croat publications from 1997 onward, and thus suspect.
13 Ibid., p. 166.
14 Schindler, *Unholy Terror*, p. 106. The Wikipedia entry for Naser Orić provides a balanced account of the ICTY's indictment and investigation of his war crimes; conflicting assessments of Serb casualties are evaluated in the Wikipedia entry "Srebrenica," section on "Disputes regarding Serb casualties around Srebrenica" [accessed July 2011].
15 UN General Assembly, 2005: "Fifty-fourth session, Agenda item 42: The Fall of Srebrenica—Role of Bosniak Forces on the Ground," para. 475–9.
16 Andreas, "Symbiosis," p. 34.
17 *Muslim World League Journal*, vol. 21, nos 2–3 (August–September 1993), summarized in Pargeter, *The New Frontiers of Jihad*, p. 40.
18 Schindler, *Unholy Terror*, pp. 147–56.
19 *The New York Times*, 5 November 1994.
20 *Christian Science Monitor*, 28 January 1993.
21 Schindler, *Unholy Terror*, pp. 138–9.
22 Osama bin Laden was one of the jihadists who reportedly were issued a Bosnian passport by the Vienna Embassy for a low-profile visit to Bosnia in November 1994. Several non-Bosnians, journalists included, reported seeing him in Sarajevo. According to Schindler, Bosnian embassy officials also sold passports to criminals for $500 and up, ibid., pp. 160–1. According to Pargeter, bin Laden sent an al-Qaeda emissary to Bosnia in the early 1990s to meet with leading mujahedeen but was never enthusiastic about supporting jihad there "because it was surrounded by *kufar* states and its geographical situation was extremely difficult." Pargeter, *The New Frontiers of Jihad*, p. 45, citing sources close to bin Laden.
23 Pargeter provides biographical details about these and a number of other mujahedeen who fought in Bosnia, including analysis of the ideological and political circumstances that led them to participate, *The New Frontiers of Jihad*, pp. 33–46.
24 *The Independent*, 14 July 1993.
25 Schindler, *Unholy Terror*, pp. 164–70.

198 *Notes*

26 *Christian Science Monitor*, 28 January 1993.
27 Schindler, *Unholy Terror*, pp. 137–42.
28 Andreas, "Symbiosis," p. 35.
29 Ibid., pp. 35–6.
30 Quoted in Andreas, "Symbiosis," p. 38. Andreas and Schindler, *Unholy Terror*, pp. 187–90, both provide numerous other examples of collaboration among traders, officials, and peacekeepers that involved all the warring parties. In besieged Srebrenica, for example, Naser Orić and his associates also ran a lucrative black marketing operation that included trading with Serbs.
31 Schindler, *Unholy Terror*, pp. 217–21. In chapter 5 Schindler provides a number of other examples from the mid-1990s of operations in which the so-called Larks and other Bosniak security service operatives carried out attacks on opponents of the SDA leadership and on Serbs living in Sarajevo.
32 Walter A. Kemp, "The Business of Ethnic Conflict," *Security Dialogue*, vol. 35, no. 1 (March 2004), pp. 43–59; quote from 45.
33 *Christian Science Monitor*, 28 January 1993.
34 Mitja Velikonja, *Religious Separation and Political Intolerance in Bosnia and Herzegovina* (College Station, TX: Texas A&M University Press, 2003), pp. 19–20.
35 Velko Attanassoff, "Bosnia and Herzegovina – Islamic Revival, International Advocacy Networks and Islamic Terrorism," *Strategic Insight*, vol. 4, no. 5 (May 2005).
36 Ibid.
37 Ibid.
38 Azra Aksamiji, "(Re)Constructing History: Post-Socialist Mosque Architecture in Bosnia and Herzegovina," in *Divided God And Intercultural Dialog*, edited by Tomislav Žigmanov (Ljubljana: Dijaški Dom Ivana Cankara (DIC) and KUD Pozitiv, 2008), pp. 106–33. URL http://www.pozitiv.si/dividedgod/index.php?option=com_conten t&task=view&id=212&Itemid=68, quotation from p. 9 in the web version [accessed August 2011].
39 Attanassoff, "Bosnia and Herzegovina – Islamic Revival." Also see Xavier Bougarel, "Islam and Politics in the Post-Communist Balkans," URL www.hks.harvard.edu/ kolzkalis/GSW/GSW1/13%20Bougarel.pdf [accessed August 2011]
41 Attanassoff, "Bosnia and Herzegovina – Islamic Revival."
42 Schindler, *Unholy Terror*, p. 104. He provides many other examples, pp. 103–6. General Divjac was second in command of the Bosnian army throughout the civil war. In May 1993 he gave President Izetbegović a five-page letter summarizing crimes and attacks by uniformed gangs, and in October special army and police units shut down Caco's brigade. Caco himself died "under unclear circumstances," ibid., p. 105.
43 The US delegation, led by Secretary of State Warren Christopher and Ambassador Richard Holbrooke, was the driving force behind the Dayton talks and the principal architect of the agreement. See Richard Holbrooke, *To End a War* (New York: Random House, 1999).
44 Sumantra Bose, *Bosnia after Dayton: Nationalist Partition and International Intervention* (Oxford: Oxford University Press, 2002), pp. 1, 26, cited in Aida Lepara, *Political Situation in Bosnia and Herzegovina after Dayton Agreement – Disintegration or Transition into Democracy?* (Saarbrucken: Lambert Academic Publishing, 2000), pp. 37–8.
45 US Department of State, "2007 Country Reports on Terrorism: Bosnia and Herzegovina," http://sarajevo.usembassy.gov/terrorism-2007.html [accessed August 2011]. Our sources do not say whether the illegals were denied residency or whether the officials were in fact punished; probably not, because in post-Dayton Bosnia the symbolism of government actions usually trumps substance.
46 Kemp, "The Business of Ethnic Conflict," p. 48; interior quote from International Crisis Group, *Bosnia's Precarious Economy: Still Not Open for Business*, ICG Balkans Report no. 115 (Brussels: author), p. 8.
47 Statement by Chairman Benjamin Gilman to the US Congress House of Representatives

Committee on International Relations, *Balkans Oversight I: Corruption in Bosnia*, Hearing on September 15, 1999 (Washington, DC: US Government Printing Office, 2000, Serial No. 106–65), p. 2.

48 David B. Dlouhy, "On Corruption in Bosnia-Herzegovina," Testimony to the House International Relations Committee, 15 September 1999, *Bosnia Report*, new series no. 11–12 (August–November 1999).

49 U4 Expert Answer (by Marie Chene), "Corruption and Anti-Corruption in Bosnia and Herzegovina (BiH)," *Transparency International*, November 2009, p. 1 [accessed at www.U4.no, August 2011].

50 Ibid., pp. 3, 4.

51 "NATO Aims to Merge Rival Armies into a Single Bosnian Force," in *Radio Free Europe/Radio Liberty Balkan Report*, vol.9, no. 24, 26 August 2005.

52 Jahic, "Development of Events in Bosnia and Herzegovina."

53 "Bosnia: Terrorism's Logistical Base" is the title of an article in *Defense & Foreign Affairs Strategic Policy*, October 2004, accessed at http://www.slobodan- milošević.org/dfasc1004.htm[August 2011]. As we suggest below, the evidence does not support the alarmist conclusion implied by the title.

54 Bougarel, "Islam and Politics in the Post-Communist Balkans," p. 13. Also see Pargeter, *The New Frontiers of Jihad*, for a nuanced discussion of the diversity of Islamist beliefs in Europe, *passim*.

55 Jahic, "Development of Events in Bosnia and Herzegovina," p. 10.

56 *BBC*, 22 August 2006.

57 James W. Patterson surveys NATO's involvement in Bosnia after 1995 but offers no substantive information on terrorist threats or intelligence operations, in chapter 6 of *NATO and Terrorism: Organizational Expansion and Mission Transformation* (New York and London: Continuum International Publishing, 2011).

58 Yossef Bodansky, director of a US Congress Task Force on Terrorism, alleged in 2006 that there was a terrorist network in Bosnia composed of several well-trained groups directly responsible to bin Laden. The cells used Bosnia as training ground and a gateway to send militants to West European countries or to shelter them on their way east. The cells reportedly operated secretly in remote mountainous areas in the Zenica region. *Agence France Press*, 16 February 2006, Lexus/Nexis Academic University electronic subscription.

59 "Bosnia Police Arrest Five Terror Suspects," *New York Times*, 21 March 2008.

60 *Associated Press*, 17 December 2010.

61 Jahic, "Development of Events in Bosnia and Herzegovina." The Muslim Brotherhood has a deserved reputation for radical Islamist politics but has evolved over time, including the development of what Pargeter calls reformist discourse. See Alison Pargeter, *The Muslim Brotherhood: The Burden of Tradition* (London, San Francisco, Beirut: Saqi Books, 2010).

62 "Bosnia: Terrorism's Logistical Base."

63 Jahic, "Development of Events in Bosnia and Herzegovina." Schindler, *Unholy Terror*, pp. 283ff, summarizes other terror plots by Islamists in Bosnia.

64 One piece of evidence is the arrest of Bensayah Belcacem. The arrested Algerians likely were networked with the Algerian terrorist network in Europe, the Salafist Group for Preaching and Combat (GSPC). While GSPC continues to engage in terrorism operations in Algeria, the group also emphasizes "out of Algeria" operations through its European network of cells. It is known as the largest, most cohesive, and dangerous terrorist organization in the al-Qaeda orbit. Other evidence is the Bosnian connection to the Groupe Islamique Combattant Morocain, which carried out car bombings in Morocco on 16 May 2003, and the organizers of the commuter train bombing in Madrid on 11 March 2004. Leaders of both groups had served in the Bosnian Army. See Schindler, *Unholy Terror*, pp. 296–98.

65 US officials have tracked al Haramain's connections to other Balkan countries. The

200 *Notes*

CIA has worked in Albania with local security officials to track and arrest Egyptian al Haramain leaders wanted on criminal charges.

66 BIF leader Enaam Arnaout was charged in US courts with concealing his relationship to al-Qaeda. He received an 11-year sentence albeit not for terrorism charges, but for fraud.

67 Steven Woehrel, "Islamic Terrorism and the Balkans," URL http://www.history.navy. mil/library/online/islamic_terrorism.htm

5 Greed, grievance, and political Islam

1 Research assistance for this chapter was provided by Majid Shirali, a doctoral student in the Department of Political Science at the University of Nevada, Las Vegas. We also thank Alison Pargeter of the University of Cambridge for her detailed comments on a draft of the chapter.

2 Consistent with usage in conflict analysis, the war in Algeria was revolutionary because the Islamists fought to take control of the central state. Bosnia was a civil war because the contenders fought to establish and consolidate their own states within Bosnia.

3 Miriam R. Lowi, "Algeria, 1992–2002: Anatomy of a Civil War," in Paul Collier and Nicholas Sambanis, eds, *Understanding Civil War: Evidence and Analysis*, Volume 1: *Africa* (Washington, DC: World Bank, 2005), pp. 221–46. The empirically derived model that provides Lowi's framework is summarized in "The Collier–Hoeffler Model of Civil War Onset and the Case Study Project Research Design" by Paul Collier, Anke Hoeffler, and Nicholas Sambanis, in Collier and Sambanis, *Understanding Civil War*, I, pp. 1–34. The Algeria case has features that differ significantly from the Collier–Hoeffler model.

4 Stathis N. Kalyvas, "Wanton and Senseless? The Logic of Massacres in Algeria," *Rationality and Society*, vol. 11 (August 1999), pp. 243–85. Other analysts report evidence that supports Kalyvas's interpretation, for example, pp. 584–6 in Mohammed M. Hafez, "Armed Islamist Movements and Political Violence in Algeria," *Middle East Journal*, vol. 54 (Autumn 2000), pp. 572–91; and pp. 68–70 in Quintan Wiktorowicz, "Centrifugal Tendencies in the Algerian Civil War," *Arab Studies Quarterly*, vol. 23 (Summer 2001), pp. 65–81. To maximize the effects of deterrence rebels ordinarily killed entire families of militiamen, informants, supporters of rival groups, and suspected defectors.

5 Brynjar Lia and Ashild Kjok, *Islamic Insurgencies, Diasporic Support Networks, and Their Host States: The Case of the Algerian GIA in Europe 1993–2000* (Kjeller: Norwegian Defence Research Establishment, FFI/RAPPORT-20001/03789, 2001).

6 The principal sources used for this summary are Martin Evans and John Phillips, *Algeria: Anger of the Dispossessed* (New Haven: Yale University Press, 2007); Lowi, "Algeria, 1992–2002"; Gilles Kepel, "The Logic of Massacre in the Second Algerian War," chapter 11 in *Jihad: The Trail of Political Islam*, trans. Anthony F. Roberts (Cambridge, MA: Harvard University Press, 2002); and Luis Martinez, *The Algerian Civil War 1990–1998*, trans. Jonathan Derrick (New York: Columbia University Press, 2000). All are balanced and nuanced accounts. Evans and Phillips provide a contemporary history of the war and its social and political context. Lowi emphasizes its political economy. Kepel examines the shifting doctrinal and political bases of Algerian jihadism. Martinez, the pseudonym of a young French–Algerian scholar, relies on interviews and observation to provide exceptionally detailed accounts of the relationships at the local level among government agents, Islamists, criminals, and businessmen, and interprets them as part of the larger conflict for control of power and resources. An excellent analysis of the networks developed by Algerian militants in France and their activities – including terror campaigns – is Alison Pargeter, *The New Frontiers of Jihad: Radical Islam in Europe* (Philadelphia: University of Pennsylvania Press, 2008), chapter 6. Another useful source that came to our attention after the chapter was drafted is James D. LeSueur, *Between Terror and Democracy: Algeria since 1989* (London and New York: Zed Books, 2010).

Notes 201

7 Most political groups and organizations in Algeria have both French and Arabic names and usually are referred to by the initials of their names in French. Here we give their names in English translation and subsequently refer to them by their French initials. LeSueur provides a detailed chronology of modern Algerian history and a useful list of government, political, and insurgent organizations with their French names and initials, *Between Terror and Democracy*, pp. vii–xxvi.

8 Two detailed accounts of the Algerian elite's exploitation of the economy for their own and their clients' benefit are George Joffee, "The Role of Violence Within the Algerian Economy," *Journal of North African Studies*, vol. 7 (Spring 2002), pp. 29–52; and Bradford Dillman, *State and Private Sector in Algeria: The Politics of Rent-seeking and Failed Development* (Boulder, CO: Westview, 2000).

9 The details of the formation of armed groups, their divisions, and sometimes-violent rivalries are discussed in Hafez, "Armed Islamist Movements"; Wiktorowicz, "Centrifugal Tendencies in the Algerian Civil War"; Pargeter, *The New Frontiers of Jihad*; and Kepel, *Beyond Terror and Martyrdom*. Pargeter and Kepel both analyze the shifting currents of Islamic doctrine, within Algeria and in the larger Islamic world, that were used to justify changing jihadist strategies and deadly rivalries among competing organizations.

10 Lowi, "Algeria, 1992–2002," p. 232.

11 Office of the Coordinator for Counterterrorism, US Department of State, *Country Reports on Terrorism – 2008*, issue date 30 April 2009, p. 113.

12 See John P. Entelis, "Civil Society and the Authoritarian Temptation in Algerian Politics: Islamic Democracy vs. the Centralized State," in Augustus Richard Norton, ed., *Civil Society in the Middle East*, Vol. II (London: Brill, 1996), pp. 45–86.

13 One of his grandsons, a graduate of the elite French military academy Saint-Cyr, founded the Young Algerian movement in 1912. The movement was neither Islamist nor nationalist but rather reformist and assimilationist, asking for expanded Muslim citizenship rights and representation in the National Assembly in Paris.

14 Evans and Philips, *Algeria*, pp. 28–40, quotations on 40.

15 Quoted in ibid., p. 44.

16 Jonathan Fox, *A World Survey of Religion and the State* (New York: Cambridge University Press, 2008), p. 236.

17 Evans and Phillips, *Algeria*, p. 132.

18 Ray Takeyh, "Islamism in Algeria: A Struggle Between Hope and Agony," *Middle East Policy*, vol. 10 (Summer 2003), p. 65.

19 Ibid., pp. 66–8, quotation from 66.

20 The AQIM is discussed below. On the Berbers, see Evans and Phillips, *Algeria*, pp. 12–21, 35–6, and 122–5; and Graham Fuller, *Algeria: The Next Fundamentalist State?* (Santa Monica, CA: RAND Corporation, 1996), pp. 13–16. AQIM established cells in Kabylia, however, which raises the possibility that AQIM may cooperate with some of the most militant Berber nationalists; see "Algerian Islamists' Financing Tactics," *Jane's Islamic Affairs Analyst*, March 10, 2009, http://jiaa.janes.com/subscribe/jiaa/doc (available only by subscription).

21 Cited by Miriam R. Lowi, "Oil Rents and Political Breakdown: The Case of Algeria," *Journal of North African Studies*, vol. 9, no. 3 (2004), p. 97.

22 Joffee, "The Role of Violence Within the Algerian Economy," p. 30.

23 Evans and Phillips, *Algeria*, p. 269.

24 Dillman, *State and Private Sector in Algeria*, describes in detail the developmental policies followed by the state and their dysfunctional consequences.

25 Martinez, *The Algerian Civil War 1990–1998*, pp. 119–46.

26 Dillman, *State and Private Sector in Algeria*, p. 59.

27 Joffee, "The Role of Violence within the Algerian Economy," p. 42. The word *trabendo* derives from the French word for smuggling, *contrabande*.

28 Lowi, "Algeria, 1992–2000," p. 225.

29 From surveys cited by Lia and Kjok, *Islamic Insurgencies*, p. 13.

202 Notes

30 Ibid., pp. 19–21, quote from 20. Pargeter provides a detailed account, *The New Frontiers of Jihad*, pp. 78–83.
31 Gilles Kepel, *Allah in the West: Islamic Movements in America and Europe* (Oxford: Polity Press, 1997), summarized in Lia and Kjok, *Islamic Insurgencies*, p. 20.
32 The Islamic Salvation Army (AIS) differed from the other groups in tactics, focusing on military and official targets but not civilians.
33 Kepel, *Jihad*, pp. 255–6.
34 Joffee, "The Role of Violence within the Algerian Economy," pp. 43–4; quote from Lowi, "Algeria, 1990–2002," p. 225.
35 Martinez, *The Algerian Civil War 1990–1998*, pp. 73–6.
36 Evans and Phillips, *Algeria*, p. 190.
37 Ray Takeyh, "Islamism in Algeria: A Struggle between Hope and Agony," *Middle East Policy*, vol. 10 (Summer 2003), p. 70.
38 Lowi, "Algeria: 1990–2002," p. 232, citing Djillali Hadjadj, *Corruption etdemocratie en Algerie* (Paris: La Dispute/Snedit, 1999), pp. 240–54.
39 Martinez, *The Algerian Civil War 1990–1998*, pp. 131–2. The owner sold his remaining trucks in 1994 and fled to France.
40 Lowi, "Algeria, 1990–2002," p. 233.
41 Ibid., p. 233.
42 Evans and Phillips, *Algeria*, pp. 186–7.
43 Translated by Hafez, "Armed Islamist Movements," p. 577.
44 In writings on the Algerian revolution the term salafist often is used as a synonym for jihadism, likely because the GIA claimed its adherence to salafist doctrine, and one of its successor organizations, the Groupe Salafiste pour la Prédication et le Combat, made titular use of the word. But there is no necessary connection between faith in traditional Islam and violent jihad. Alison Pargeter points out (personal communication, 27 April 2010) that the Algerian government is promoting a form of salafism (*salafiaalamia*) as a counter to more militant ideologies. One might say – this is our interpretation – that it is politically correct for contemporary Islamists to say they are salafist (or Wahabist, one stream of salafist doctrine), whatever means they advocate or practise to achieve it.
45 From Kepel, *Beyond Terror and Martyrdom*, pp. 183–97. Pargeter provides a detailed account of the origins and evolution of political Islam in Britain, *The New Frontiers of Jihad*, chapter 9. British authorities cracked down on militant Islamists in London and the mosque's leadership, after they were linked to terrorism in Britain that included the suicide bombings in London on 7 July 2005.
46 Kalyvas, "Wanton and Senseless?," p. 247.
47 Ibid., pp. 249–50.
48 As reported in grisly detail by Evans and Phillips, *Algeria*, pp. 238–44. One of them was among the journalists on the scene on 23 September. The official death toll was 98. This massacre is not included in Kalyvas's list.
49 See references in note 2.
50 Evidence and suspicions about security forces' involvement in atrocities are reviewed by Evans and Phillips, *Algeria*, pp. 223–5. LeSueur summarizes later evidence that French security forces orchestrated the GIA's 1996 kidnapping of seven Trappist monks from their monastery in the Atlas, though not their subsequent murder, *Between Terror and Democracy*, pp. 132–5. Also see Kalyvas, "Wanton and Senseless?," *passim*.
51 Hafez, "Armed Islamist Movements," and Kepel, *Beyond Terror and Martyrdom*, provide detailed accounts of the formation of jihadist organizations, their different ideological justifications, and the operations and rivalries that followed from their disputes over doctrine and tactics.
52 Hafez, "Armed Islamist Movements," p. 584.
53 Kepel, *Jihad*, pp. 273–4.
54 Ibid., p. 256.

Notes 203

55 Wiktorowicz, "Centrifugal Tendencies in the Algerian Civil War," p. 78. The 8000 were members of the AIS.

56 Lawrence Wright, *The Looming Tower: Al-Qaeda and the Road to 9/11* (New York: Knopf, 2006).

57 Blake Mobley and Eric Rosenbach, *GSPC Dossier* (New York: The Manhattan Institute's Center for Policing Terrorism, June 1, 2005), pp. 7–8. Alison Pargeter says (personal correspondence) that Sahraoui and his associates approached al-Qaeda through Abu Musab al-Zarqawi, al-Qaeda's leader in Iraq, and did so mainly to gain credibility for the GSPC. Not all the GSPC supporters accepted the alliance, some continued to fight under the GSPC banner.

58 Translated in Emily Hunt, "Islamist Terrorism in Northwestern Africa: A 'Thorn in the Neck' of the United States?," Washington Institute for Near East Policy, *Policy Focus #65* (February 2007), p. 10.

59 Gilles Kepel, *Beyond Terror and Martyrdom: The Future of the Middle East*, trans. Pascale Ghazalem (Cambridge, MA: Harvard University Press, 2008), chapter 3, quotation 118. Kepel describes al-Suri's thinking in some detail and cites a partial translation by the US CIA's Office of Terrorism Analysis and English-language commentaries on al-Suri's life and thinking.

60 Hunt, "Islamist Terrorism in Northwestern Africa," p. 3.

61 Ibid., p. 5.

62 These examples are from a chronology prepared by Marzena Orlowska, a graduate student at Sofia University's Department of Political Science. LeSueur provides more details on the AQIM's terror campaign, *Between Terror and Democracy*, pp. 160–7.

63 Examples from ibid. At no time during 20 years of terrorist violence did Algeria's oil and gas producing facilities or pipelines suffer serious damage. Cement plants, hotels, a power plant, the Algiers airport yes, the oil and gas industry no. LeSueur points out that the oil companies were very effective in providing security for oil and gas facilities, and that very little publicity was given to the occasional attack that did disrupt the pipelines, so as not to alarm European investors; *Between Terror and Democracy*, pp. 111–14.

64 Andrew Hansen and Lauren Vriens, *Backgrounder: Al-Qaeda in the Islamic Maghreb (AQIM)* (New York: Council on Foreign Relations), last updated 21 July 21 2009 [retrieved from *cfr.org* on 19 August 2009]; Hunt, "Islamist Terrorism in Northwestern Africa," pp. 8–9; and Blake and Rosenbach, *GSPC Dossier, passim*.

65 "Algerian Islamists' Financing Tactics."

66 Hunt, "Islamist Terrorism in Northwestern Africa," p. 6.

67 "Algerian Islamists' Financing Tactics."

68 Hunt, "Islamist Terrorism in Northwestern Africa," p. 9.

69 John R. Schindler, *Unholy Terror: Bosnia, Al-Qaida, and the Rise of Global Jihad* (St Paul, MN: Zenith Press, 2007), pp. 193–4, 207–9, describes the GIA cells in France and details their bombings, plots, and a dramatic hijacking of an Air France Airbus on Christmas Eve, 1994. Algerian mujahedeen returning form the war in Bosnia played a major part in the GIA terror campaign in France. Pargeter, *The New Frontiers of Jihad*, chapter 6, provides a detailed analysis of the objectives and consequences of GIA and GSPC activities in France, which included recruiting amateurish would-be terrorists from the local Muslim population.

70 See Jeremy Shapiro and Benedicte Suzan, "The French Experience of Counter-Terrorism," *Survival*, vol. 45 (Spring 2003), pp. 67–98.

71 In 2005 the project was renamed the Trans-Sahara Counterterrorism Partnership and was directed by the US Department of Defense's European Command. Later it became an Initiative and responsibility was transferred to the new African Command.

72 Stephen A. Emerson, "The Trans-Saharan Arc," in Derek S. Reveron and Jeffrey Stevenson Murer, eds, *Flashpoints in the War on Terrorism* (New York and London: Routledge, 2006), p. 249.

204 *Notes*

73 *UPI*, "Algeria plans regional terrorist effort," URL http://upi.com/Top_News/Special/2009/08/13/Algeria-plans-regional-terrorist-effort/
74 "French Police Brace for Attack After Threat by al-Qaida Group," *Associated Press*, 23 September 2010.
75 Morocco has a separate counterterrorism alliance with the US.
76 For an official summary of its objectives and elements, see US Department of State, *Country Reports on Terrorism – 2008*, pp. 14–15.
77 Emerson provides a good analysis of the risks of relying too heavily on short-term security gains, "The Trans-Saharan Arc," pp. 258–63. Hunt raises similar questions including the consequences of an overly visible US military presence, ibid., pp. 14–21, *passim*.
78 Bruce Whitehouse, "What went wrong in Mali?" *London Review of Books*, vol. 34, no. 16 (30 August 2012), pp. 17–18; *BBC*, "Mali Islamists seize Gao from Tuareg rebels," URL www.bbc.co.uk/news/world/africa_18610618, 27 June 2012.
79 James Keaten, Associated Press, "Al-Qaida Group Lacks Ability to Hit Europe, Judge Says," *Las Vegas Review Journal*, 6 August 2011, p. 8A.

6 Serbia in the 1990s

1 Marko Attila Hoare, "The Serbia–Kosovo Dispute as a Factor of Instability in the Balkans," paper presented at the Third Annual Conference on Human Security, Terrorism and Organized Crime in the Western Balkan Region, organized by the HUMSEC project in Belgrade, 2–4 October 2008. Paper available at http://www.humsec.eu/cms/fileadmin/user_upload/humsec/Workin_Paper_Series/WP_Hoare.pdf [accessed 23 January 2010]. For an extended discussion on Balkan nationalisms see Lyubov Grigorova-Mincheva, ed., *Comparative Balkan Parlamentarism* (Sofia: International Center for Minority Studies and Intercultural Relations, 1995).
2 "Karadzic's Arrest Sparks Clashes," 23 July 2008, *Al Jazeera English*. URL http://www.youtube.com/watch?v=vgUrnFvdqgg [accessed 25 January2010].
3 See Edislav Manetovic, "Ilija Garašanin: Nacertanije and Nationalism," *The Historical Review/La Revue Historique*, vol. 3 (2006), pp. 137–73.
4 The concept is developed more fully and applied to Albanians in Lyubov Mincheva, "The Albanian Ethnoterritorial Separatist Movement: Local Conflict, Regional Crisis," *Nationalism and Ethnic Politics*, vol. 15, no. 2 (April 2009), pp. 211–36. We refer to the segments of such groups as *trans-border kindred* or *segments* and reserve the word *diaspora* for migrants from a group's core region who have established residence and networks elsewhere, for example, in Western Europe and North America.
5 Barbara Jelavich, *History of the Balkans. Eighteenth and Nineteenth Centuries*, 2 vols (New York: Cambridge University Press, 1983).
6 Lenard Cohen, *Broken Bonds. Yugoslavia's Disintegration and Balkan Politics and Transformation* (Boulder, CO: Westview Press, 1995), pp. 17–18.
7 Robert Hislope, "Nationalism, Ethnic Politics and Democratic Consolidation. A Comparative Study of Croatia, Serbia and Bosnia-Herzegovina," PhD Thesis, Ohio: The Ohio State University, 1995, p. 114.
8 Cohen, *Broken Bonds*, p. 33.
9 From the 1981 Yugoslav census, summarized by Monty G. Marshall in "States at Risk: Ethnopolitics in the Multinational States of Eastern Europe," chapter 7 in Ted Robert Gurr, ed., *Minorities at Risk: A Global View of Ethnopolitical Conflict* (Washington, DC: United States Institute of Peace Press, 1993), pp. 215–16.
10 From Noel Malcolm, *Kosovo: A Short History* (London: Pan Macmillan, 2002), pp. 329–32. The Serb share of Kosovo's population steadily declined from the 1960s to the 1990s, leading to Serb nationalist claims of genocide, or at least ethnic cleansing, by the majority Albanians. Some Kosovo Serbs did in fact emigrate, but their declining population share was mainly due to exceptionally high Albanian birthrates.

Notes 205

11 Hugh Poulton, *The Balkans: Minorities and States in Conflict* (London: Minority Rights Publications, 1991), p. 19.
12 Cohen, *Broken Bonds*, pp. 132, 142.
13 Ibid., p. 142.
14 See Ted Robert Gurr, *Peoples Versus States: Minorities at Risk in the New Century* (Washington, DC: United States Institute of Peace Press), pp. 3–7, 65–9.
15 Arkan War Criminal 2/5.http://www.youtube.com/watch?v=Hli-0cJQoSg&feature= related History Channel.
16 Misha Glenny, *McMafia: A Journal Through the Global Criminal Underworld* (New York: Knopf, 2008), p. 39.
17 Arkan War Criminal 1/5.http://www.youtube.com/watch?v=Hli-0cJQoSg&feature= related History Channel.
18 Arkan War Criminal 2/5.http://www.youtube.com/watch?v=Hli-0cJQoSg&feature= related History Channel.
19 Arkan War Criminal 3/5.http://www.youtube.com/watch?v=L1576qHHtXs&feature =related History Channel.
20 Ibid.
21 Ibid.
22 Arkan War Criminal 4/5.http://www.youtube.com/watch?v=L1576qHHtXs&featur e=related History Channel.
23 Ibid.
24 Ibid.
25 Arkan War Criminal 2/5.http://www.youtube.com/watch?v=Hli-0cJQoSg&feature= related History Channel.
26 Arkan War Criminal 3/5.http://www.youtube.com/watch?v=L1576qHHtXs&featur e=related History Channel.
27 Misha Glenny quotes an interview with General Boyko Borissov, director of the Bulgarian Ministry of Interior, who said that Bulgarian criminals in the early 1990s had a big shock when they came in contact with their Yugoslav counterparts. "Our guys were just playing at being gangsters – the Yugoslavs had been thieving and killing in Europe for real over decades. They were seriously tough, and to this day, if you want to kill somebody in Bulgaria and you want the job done reliably and cheaply, then you hire a Serb. They are the best assassins." Glenny, *McMafia*, pp. 41–2.
28 Ibid., pp. 38–40.
29 Arkan War Criminal 1/5.http://www.youtube.com/watch?v=Hli-0cJQoSg&feature= related History Channel.
30 Chris Stephen in The Hague (TU 309),"Courtside: Serbia's Dirty War, 14–18 April, 2003." ICTY – Tribunal Update, Institute for War and Peace Reporting. URL http://www.iwpr.net/?p=tri&s=o=165870&apc_state=henitri2003.
31 *Partners in Crime* (Sofia: Center for the Study of Democracy, 2004), p. 43.
32 Ibid., p. 44.
33 Ibid., pp. 44–5.
34 Ibid., p. 54.
35 Chris Stephen in The Hague (TU 309), "Courtside: Serbia's Dirty War, 14–18 April, 2003. ICTY – Tribunal Update, Institute for War and Peace Reporting. URL http://www.iwpr.net/?p=tri&s=o=165870&apc_state=henitri2003.
36 *Partners in Crime*, p. 54.
37 Ibid., p. 45.
38 Ibid., p. 47.
39 Ibid., p. 49.
40 Ibid., p. 56.
41 Arkan War Criminal 1/5.http://www.youtube.com/watch?v=Hli-0cJQoSg&feature= related History Channel.
42 Adam Higginbotham, "Beauty and the Beast: She was the biggest pop star in the Balkans,

206　*Notes*

he was a bank robber, gangster, politician, paramilitary leader and war criminal. 'Ceca' Raznatovic tells Adam Higginbotham about living with Arkan," *The Observer*, 4 January 2004.

43 *Partners in Crime*, p. 45.

44 Ibid., p. 63.

45 Ibid., pp. 45–6.

46 *Huff Post World*, The Internet Newspaper: News Blogs Video Community. URL http://www.huffingtonpost.com/2011/07/20/goran-hadzic-last-balkan-war-crimes-fugitive-arrested-serbia-_n_904290.html.

47 "Communication from the Commission to the European Parliament and the Council: Commission Opinion on Serbia's Application for Membership of the European Union" {COM(2011) 668}, http://ec.europa.eu/enlargement/pdf/key_documents/2011/package/sr analytical_rapport_2011_en.pdf. For a chronology of reformist political developments, policies, investigations, and indictments, see "Serbia Timeline 2011," *Global Integrity Report*, http://www.globalintegrity.org/report/Serbia/2011/timeline.

7 The state and crime syndicates in post-communist Bulgaria

1 We are endebted to Tihomor Bezlov, Prof. Anton Parvanov, Ivan Krastev, Hristo Hristov, Vesselina Tomova, Iordan Vassilev, Maria Pirgova, Maria Dermendzhieva, Stoycho Stoychev, Anton Andonov and Boris Kostov for their comments and guidance on this chapter.

2 Misha Glenny, *McMafia: A Journey through the Global Criminal Underworld* (New York: Knopf, 2008), pp. 3–21 ff.

3 On 30 June 1999 the democratic government of the Union of Democratic Forces announced that the Bulgarian transition to a market economy had been accomplished. Prime Minister Ivan Kostov pointed to the completion of structural reform as evidence, specifically the privatization of economically inefficient state enterprises. Analysts, however, argue that this could only be an element of overall structural reform, which also demands the development of a strategic national platform for the establishment of an efficient market economy. See Evgenia Kalinova and Iskra Baeva, *The Bulgarian Transitions 1939–2005* (Sofia: Paradigma, 2006), p. 314.

4 David C. Jordan, *Drug Politics: Dirty Money and Democracy* (Norman, OK: University of Oklahoma Press, 1999). Aside from a brief discussion of Russia he focuses on Latin America. The processes he describes in Latin America parallel concurrent and subsequent developments in South-Eastern Europe.

5 See Jürgen Roth, *Die Neuen Daemonen. Das Bulgarische Mafianetzwerk*, in Bulgarian (Sofia: Slance, 2009), p. 24, and his more general analysis in *Gangsterwirtschaft: Wie uns die organisierte Kriminalität aufkauft* (Berlin: Eichborn, 2010).

6 For more on the economics of communism, see Hristo Hristov, *The Secret Bankruptcies of Communism*, in Bulgarian (Sofia: Ciela, 2007).

7 Ibid., pp. 298, 321.

8 Kalinova and Baeva, *The Bulgarian Transitions*, p. 240.

9 Comment by Ognyan Doinov, Communist Party official, cited in ibid., p. 240.

10 Comment by Vassil Kolarov, Executive Director of the Bulgarian National Bank, cited by Hristov, *The Secret Bankruptcies of Communism*, p. 301.

11 COMECOM Secretariat Archives show that in 1986 Bulgaria was first in the amount of state- provided credits to Third World countries, with 270 currency rubles per capita. In comparison, the Soviet Union provided 68 currency rubles per capita in the same year, while the German Democratic Republic gave 58. See Hristov, *The Secret Bankruptcies of Communism*, p. 211.

12 Kalinova and Baeva, *The Bulgarian Transitions*, p. 239.

13 Bulgaria: Eurostat GDP per capita. URL http://epp.eurostat.ec.europa.eu/portal/page/portal/national_accounts/data/database [accessed 10 February 2012].

Notes 207

14 Slovenia: Eurostat GDP per capita. URL http://epp.eurostat.ec.europa.eu/portal/page/portal/national_accounts/data/database [accessed 10 February 2012].

15 National Employment Agency, Bulgaria. URL http://www.az.government.bg/ [accessed 10 February 2012].

16 National Statistical Institute, Bulgaria. URL, http://www.nsi.bg/index.php [accessed 10 February 2012].

17 See Bisser Banchev, "The Yugo-embargo and the Transportation Blockade of Bulgaria," *Geopolitics*, no. 5 (2008) (in Bulgarian). URL http://seesbg.com/?b=art&art=240 [accessed February 2012].

18 The *CPI Score* relates to perceptions of the degree of corruption, and ranges between 10 (highly clean) and 0 (highly corrupt). Transparency International: Bulgaria. URL http://www.transparency.bg/ [accessed 10 February 2012].

19 *Markets of Violence and Perpetrators of Violence*. Gunda Werner Institute of Feminism and Gender Democracy. URL http://www.gwi-boell.de/web/violence-conflict-markets-violence-perpetrators-1966.html.

20 For an extended discussion on the establishment and the essence of the market of violence, see Tihomir Bezlov, Emil Tzenkov, Marina Tzetkova, Filip Gounev, and Georgi Petrunov, *Organized Crime in Bulgaria: Markets and Trends*, in Bulgarian (Sofia: Center for the Study of Democracy, 2007), *passim*. URL http://www.csd.bg/artShow.php?id=9120 [accessed 4 February 2012].

21 See Alan Bryden and Marina Caparini, eds, *Private Actors and Security Governance* (Geneva Centre for the Democratic Control of Armed Forces, 2006). See also Philip Gounev, "Bulgaria's Private Security Industry," in Bryden and Caparini, pp. 109–29.

22 Jürgen Roth, *Gangsterwirtschaft*, in Bulgarian (Sofia: Slance, 2010), p. 31. First published as *Gangsterwirtschaft: Wie uns die organisierte Kriminalität aufkauft* (Berlin: Eichborn, 2010).

23 *Partners in Crime: The Risks of Symbiosis between the Security Sector and Organized Crime in South East Europe*, in Bulgarian (Sofia: Center for the Study of Democracy, 2004), pp. 13–14. URL http://www.csd.bg/artShow.php?id=9626 [accessed 4 February 2012].

24 Bezlov et al., *Organized Crime in Bulgaria*, p. 15.

25 Ibid., p. 16.

26 Ibid., p. 36.

27 Ibid., p. 14.

28 Ibid., p. 36.

29 *Partners in Crime*, p. 25.

30 The line connects railroads at both ends of the Black Sea. It provides for switching the railroad engine standard from Russian to European and back.

31 Vesselina Tomova, *The Gangster Varna*, in Bulgarian (Sofia: Slance, 2009), p. 94.

32 The UN Security Council imposed economic sanctions on Serbia and Montenegro with Resolution 754, adopted on 30 May 1992.

33 *Partners in Crime*, p. 25.

34 Iovo Nikolov, "The Genesis of Organized Crime," *The Capital* newspaper, 20 October 2009. URL http://grigorsimov.blog.bg/politica/2009/10/28/genezisyt-na-organiziranata-prestypnost.424462 [accessed 14 January 2012].

35 *Partners in Crime*, pp. 25–6.

36 Nikolov, "The Genesis of Organized Crime."

37 Roth, *Gangsterwirtschaft*, p. 15.

38 See p. 20.

39 Stanimir Vangelov, cited in Glenny, *McMafia*, p. 8.

40 See pp. 7–8.

41 Glenny, *McMafia*, p. 12.

42 Roth, *Die Neuen Daemonen*, p. 247.

43 Alexander Andreev, *Deutsche Welle*, cited by Roth, *Die Neuen Daemonen*, p. 247.

44 Roth, *Die Neuen Daemenon*, p. 124.

45 Glenny, *McMafia*, pp. 8–9.

208   *Notes*

46 Multigroup: Wikipedia. URL http://bg.wikipedia.org/wiki/Multigroup [accessed 15 January 2012]. According to the official census, as of 2001 the country's population was 7,932,984. URL http://en.wikipedia.org/wiki/Demographics_of_Bulgaria.
47 Multigroup: Wikipedia. URL http://bg.wikipedia.org/wiki/Multigroup [accessed 15 January 2012.
48 Roth, *Die Neuen Daemonen*, p. 251.
49 Bezlov et al., *Organized Crime in Bulgaria*, p. 25.
50 Glenny, *McMafia*, pp. 9–10.
51 Bezlov et al., *Organized Crime in Bulgaria*, p. 26.
52 Ibid., pp. 25–6.
53 Tomova, *The Gangster Varna*, pp. 199–203.
54 Ibid., p. 226.
55 Ibid., p. 227.
56 Ibid., p. 233.
57 Bezlov et al., *Organized Crime in Bulgaria*, p. 25.
58 Petya Shopova and Yordan Tsonev, "Report on the Causes of the Collapse of the Banking System," *Parliamentary Committee for Combating Crime and Corruption, Bankers*, no. 21 (30 May 1999), cited in *Partners in Crime*, p. 24.
59 Law on Information about Nonperformance Loans, SG 95/1997, cited in *Partners in Crime*, p. 24.
60 Bezlov et al., *Organized Crime in Bulgaria*, pp. 31–2.
61 Ibid., p. 36.
62 Jordan, *Drug Politics*, p. 9.
63 Ibid., p. 7.
64 *See* the chapter on Methodology, *World Drug Report, Volume 2: Statistics* (United Nations Office on Drugs and Crime, 2004), pp. 409–27. URL: http://www.unodc.org/pdf/WDR_2004/volume_2.pdf [accessed 6 February 2012].
65 Bezlov et al., *Organized Crime in Bulgaria*, p. 39.
66 *1997 International Narcotics Control Strategy Report, March 1998* (US Department of State, Bureau for International Narcotics and Law Enforcement Affairs, Europe and Central Asia, Poland). URL: http://www.hri.org/docs/USSD-INCSR/97/Europe/Poland.html.
67 *Mafia Borguesse* refers to the policies of the Borgia family, which by means of bribes and corruption secured immense political influence in Rome and the Vatican in the fifteenth and sixteenth centuries. The concept has gained currency among politicians, experts, and public individuals working on global organized crime and drug trafficking. Antonio Maria Costa, Executive Director of the United Nations Office on Drugs and Crime, defines this concept as a network of bankers, notaries, lawyers, corrupt politicians, and other public individuals cooperating with organized crime, and in particular with the black market criminal structures. See Roth, *Gangsterwirtschaft*, p. 41.
68 Bezlov et al., *Organized Crime in Bulgaria*, p. 41.
69 Ibid., p. 41.
70 Ibid., p. 43.
71 See Roth, *Die Neuen Daemonen*, pp. 127–42.
72 Bezlov et al., *Organized Crime in Bulgaria*, pp. 85–7.
73 Ibid., p. 47. The estimate of the number of heroin users is based on 2002–3 research by the Center for the Study of Democracy, as well as on 2004–5 data provided by the National Center on Drugs.
74 Bezlov et al., *Organized Crime in Bulgaria*, p. 61.
75 Tomova, *Gangster Varna*, pp. 113–14.
76 Roth, *Die Neuen Daemonen*, p. 122.
77 Bezlov et al., *Organized Crime in Bulgaria*, p. 57.
78 *Partners in Crime*, p. 8.

Notes 209

79 Ibid., p. 17.
80 Ibid., p. 19.
81 Ibid., p. 17.
82 Iovo Nikolov, 2009, "The Genesis of Organized Crime." URL http://grigorsimov. blog.bg/politika/2009/10/28/genezisyt-na-organiziranata-prestypnost.424462 [accessed 14 January 2012].
83 Testimony of Ivan Kostov, leader of the Union of Democratic Forces, before the court on the occasion of the assassination of Milcho Bonev, cited by Roth, *Die Neuen Daemonon*, p. 53.
84 Nikolov, "The Genesis of Organized Crime."
85 *Partners in Crime*, p. 26.
86 Roth, *Die Neuen Daemonen*, p. 242.
87 *Partners in Crime*, p. 17.
88 Mohamed Khalaf, Bulgarian and Iraqi journalist, reports that Kasar was arrested in Spain in 2010. *See also* Roth, *Die Neuen Daemonon*, p. 242.
89 Bezlov et al., *Organized Crime in Bulgaria*, p. 60.
90 Ibid.
91 Tomova, *Gangster Varna*, p. 135.
92 Bezlov et al., *Organized Crime in Bulgaria*, p. 87.
93 Roth, *Die Neuen Daemonen*, pp. 129, 132, 139.
94 Bezlov et al., *Organized Crime in Bulgaria*, p. 74.
95 Ibid.
96 Anonymous police officer cited by Roth, *Die Neuen Daemonen*, p. 233.
97 Vesselina Tomova, interview.
98 Ibid.
99 Bezlov et al., *Organized Crime in Bulgaria*, p. 164.
100 P. Chabal and J.-P. Daloz, *Africa Works: Disorder as Political Instrument* (Oxford: James Currey, 1999), cited by Philippe Le Billon, "Buying Peace or Fuelling War: The Role of Corruption in Armed Conflicts," *Journal of International Development*, vol. 15 (2003), p. 415. URL www.interscience.wiley.com DOI:10.1002/jid.993 [accessed 26 January 2012].
101 Roth, *Die Neuen Daemonen*, pp. 196–217. Author's text in brackets.

8 Militants and money

1 Peter Grabosky and Michael Stohl, *Crime and Terrorism* (London: Sage, 2010), p. 113. Our working definition of terrorism is adapted from the same source, p. 4.
2 Recent studies on this issue include Grabosky and Stohl, *Crime and Terrorism*; C. Dishman, "The Leaderless Nexus: When Crime and Terror Converge," *Studies in Conflict and Terrorism*, vol. 28 (2005), pp. 237–52; S. Hutchinson and P. O'Malley, "A Crime–Terror Nexus? Thinking on Some of the Links between Terrorism and Criminality," *Studies in Conflict and Terrorism*, vol. 30 (2007), pp. 1095–1107; Walter A. Kemp, "The Business of Ethnic Conflict," *Security Dialogue*, vol. 35, no. 1 (2004), pp. 43–59; T. Makarenko, "The Crime–Terror Continuum: Tracing the Interplay between Transnational Crime and Terrorism," *Global Crime*, vol. 6, no. 1 (2004), pp. 129–45; and John Rosenthal, "For-profit Terrorism: The Rise of Armed Entrepreneurs," *Studies in Conflict and Terrorism*, vol. 31, no. 6 (2008), pp. 481–98.
3 Two studies by journalist Jürgen Roth examine the operating principles of crime networks in Bulgaria, and in Europe more generally: *Die Neuen Daemonen. Das Bulgarische Mafianetzwerk* (Sofia: Slance, 2009), in Bulgarian (no German edition exists) and *Gangsterwirtschaft: Wie uns die organisierte Kriminalität aufkauft* (Berlin: Eichborn, 2000). An accessible English-language study is Misha Glenny, *McMafia: A Journey Through the Global Criminal Underworld* (New York: Knopf, 2008).
4 James Adams, *The Financing of Terror: How the Groups that are Terrorizing the World Get the Money to Do It* (New York: Simon & Schuster, 1986) documents the PLO's economic

210   *Notes*

successes in chapters 4 and 5. Donations from Arab states made up the remainder of its mid-1980s income. Rachel Ehrenfeld gives an overview of PLO and Palestinian Authority financing c. 2000–1 in chapter 3 of *Funding Evil: How Terrorism is Financed and How to Stop It* (Chicago: Bonus Books, 2003, 2005). Her factual information appears more solid than her assumption that all PLO and PA funding supports terrorism.

5 Adams, *The Financing of Terror*, pp. 237–8.

6 Jeremy M. Weinstein, *Inside Rebellion: The Politics of Insurgent Violence* (New York and Cambridge: Cambridge University Press, 2007), p. 300.

7 Jessica Stern, *Terror in the Name of God: Why Religious Militants Kill* (New York: Harper Collins, 2003), pp. 213–17.

8 UN Office on Drugs and Crime, *The Globalization of Crime: A Transnational Organized Crime Threat Assessment* (Vienna: United Nations, June 2010), p. 11 and chapter 9. Somali piracy is a high-profit, low-risk form of crime because most shippers and their insurers prefer to pay large ransoms rather than risk destruction of ships and cargoes. According to RAND researcher Peter Chalk, attacks off the Somali coast in 2010 netted the pirates $238 million in ransom ("2011 is Turning into a Boom Year for Piracy," *Providence Journal*, 4 March 2011). And see Martin N. Murphy, *Somalia: The New Barbary? Piracy and Islam in the Horn of Africa* (New York: Columbia University Press, 2010). Four examples of Asian and Latin American organizations that have shifted from terrorism to crime, or vice versa, are identified in Grabosky and Stohl, *Crime and Terrorism*, pp. 76–7.

9 Kemp, "The Business of Ethnic Conflict," quote on 44. James Cockayne and Adam Lupel discuss these complex connections in the context of peacekeeping operations in "Introduction: Rethinking the Relationship Between Peace Operations and Organized Crime," *International Peacekeeping*, vol. 16, no. 1 (February 2009), pp. 4–19.

10 This is our set of categories. There is a comparative literature on insurgent financing but most of it focuses on specific modalities such as state sponsorship, trafficking or money laundering, and we are not familiar with any attempt to propose and use general categories. Rohan Gunaratna lists but does not analyze the principal sources of terrorist financing in "The Lifeblood of Terrorist Organizations: Evolving Terrorist Financing Strategies," in Alex P. Schmid, ed., *Countering Terrorism through International Cooperation* (Milan: ISPAC, 2001), pp. 182–5. More detailed recent studies are Ehrenfeld, *Funding Evil*; Christine Jojarth, *Crime, War, and Global Trafficking* (New York and Cambridge: Cambridge University Press, 2009); Peter Lilley, *Dirty Dealing: The Untold Truth about Global Money Laundering, International Crime and Terrorism*, 3rd edn (London and Philadelphia: Kogan Page, 2006); and Loretta Napoleoni, *Terror Incorporated: Tracing the Dollars Behind the Terror Networks* (New York: Seven Stories Press, 2005). The best comparative study of how specific groups raised funds and what they did with them remains Adams' 1986 book *The Financing of Terror*. A useful general discussion of how the modalities of terrorist fundraising are related to group strategies is Dipak K. Gupta's analysis of "Terrorism and Organized Crime," chapter 7 in *Understanding Terrorism and Political Violence: The Life Cycle of Birth, Growth, Transformation, and Demise* (London and New York: Routledge, 2008).

11 From Barbara Harff and Ted Robert Gurr, *Ethnic Conflict in World Politics*, 2nd edn (Boulder, CO: Westview Press, 2004), p. 149.

12 Adams, *The Financing of Terror*, pp. 239, 243.

13 International containment of terrorist and criminal threats is the primary focus of most works cited above, including Ehrenfeld, *Funding Evil*; Lilly, *Dirty Dealing*; Jojarth, *Crime, War, and Global Trafficking*; and Napoleoni, *Terror Incorporated*. UNOCD's *The Globalization of Crime* focuses on international crime but with some reference to the uses of its proceeds by militant organizations. Peter Andreas and Ethan Nadelmann take a broader and more critical view in *Policing the Globe: Criminalization and Crime Control in International Relations* (New York: Oxford University Press, 2006). Their central argument, summarized in their preface, p. vii, is that "the internationalization of crime control is primarily the outcome of ambitious efforts by generations of Western powers

to export their domestically derived definitions of crime." They add that "Today's global counterterrorism campaign very much builds on and extends policing capacities and initiatives originally developed to suppress drug trafficking and related money laundering."

14 For other examples, see Ted Robert Gurr, "How Africa's Internal Wars Ended: Lessons for Prevention?," in Yehuda Bauer, Andrea Bartoli, and Ted Robert Gurr, eds, in *Prevention and Mitigation of Genocide and Mass Atrocities: Focus on East and Central Africa and the Islamic World* (Arlington, VA: George Mason University, School for Conflict Analysis and Resolution, for the Genocide Prevention Advisory Network [also posted at GPAnet.org], 2010), pp. 29–33.

15 Adams, *The Financing of Terror*, chapter 6.

16 Ehrenfeld, *Funding Evil*, p. 24.

17 See Jens Sørensen, *State Collapse and Reconstruction on the Periphery: Political Economy, Ethnicity and Development in Yugoslavia, Serbia and Kosovo* (New York: Berghahn Books, 2009), pp. 197–8.

18 A very detailed draft report by the Council of Europe's Committee on Legal Affairs and Human Rights was circulated in December 2010: *Inhuman Treatment of People and Illicit Trafficking in Human Organs in Kosovo*. URL http://assembly.coe.int/ASP/APFeaturesManager/defaultArtSiteView.asp?ID=964/. The rapporteur, Dick Marty, makes it clear that the Albanian perpetrators are very unlikely to be formally accused and tried because no one will testify against them because of very strong bonds of clan loyalty – and fear of retribution.

19 Gupta, *Understanding Terrorism and Political Violence*, discusses this possibility in theoretical perspective on pp. 147ff. Jeffrey Ian Ross and Ted Robert Gurr show how predation and murder led to the decline in public tolerance of several radical movements in Canada and the United States during the 1970s and 1980s, in "Why Terrorism Subsides: A Comparative Study of Terrorism in Canada and the United States," *Comparative Politics*, vol. 21 (July 1989), pp. 405–26.

20 UNODC, *The Globalization of Crime*, p. 16 and chapter 4. A more recent UNODC report estimates that the gross wholesale plus retail profits of the cocaine trade in 2009 were $84 billion, compared with about $1 billion earned by the Andean farmers who produced it. United Nations Office on Drugs and Crime, *Estimating Illicit Financial Flows Resulting from Drug Trafficking and Other Transnational Organized Crimes: Research Report* (Vienna: author, 2011), pp. 9 ff.

21 Glenny, *McMafia*, pp. 34–7.

22 Adams, *The Financing of Terror*, p. 160.

23 UNODC, *The Globalization of Crime*, pp. 43–52. Also see Louise Shelley, *Human Trafficking: A Global Perspective* (New York and Cambridge: Cambridge University Press, 2010).

24 UNODC, *The Globalization of Crime*, p. 144.

25 Ibid., pp. 48–9.

26 A recent UNODC report cautions, however, that "investment of 'dirty money' into licit economies can create problems ranging from distortions of resource allocation to the 'crowding out' of licit sectors," *Estimating Illicit Financial Flows*, pp. 99–120, quotation from 9.

27 Adams, *The Financing of Terror*, chapter 4.

28 US Department of the Treasury, cited by Peter Lilley, *Dirty Dealing*, p. viii.

29 Ibid., especially chapter 4. Bulgaria's crime syndicates and oligarchs were very adept at international laundering of funds gained illicitly from the 1990s privatization of state enterprises, as we document in chapter 7.

30 "Research Brief: Financial Crime and Political Extremism in the U.S." (College Park, MD: National Consortium for the Study of Terrorism and Responses to Terrorism, January 2011), pp. 1–2; personal correspondence with Roberta Belli.

31 Adams, *The Financing of Terror*, p. 103.

32 Ibid., pp. 188–90.

212   *Notes*

33 Summarized in UNODC, *Estimating Illicit Financial Flows*, pp. 110–11.

34 Ibid., pp. 162–7; Alex Schmid, personal correspondence.

35 The MAROB study is a project of the National Consortium for the Study of Terrorism and Responses to Terrorism [START] at the University of Maryland. A preliminary report is Victor Asal, Carter Johnson, and Jonathan Wilkenfeld, "Ethnopolitical Violence and Terrorism in the Middle East," in J. Joseph Hewitt, Jonathan Wilkenfeld, and Ted Robert Gurr, eds, *Peace and Conflict 2008* (Boulder, CO: Paradigm Publishers, 2008), pp. 55–66.

36 The coding categories used were developed by the co-authors of this chapter. The coded data summarized here were prepared by the MAR project's research director, Amy Pate, and updated by Victor Asal in March 2011. Data are based on published information and no doubt understate the extent to which militant communal groups are engaged in economic crime.

37 *Xinhua*, Chinese Press Agency, 20 February 2000.

38 MAROB coding sources; also Barnett R. Rubin, *The Search for Peace in Afghanistan: From Buffer State to Failed State* (New Haven CT: Yale University Press, 1995).

39 The Taliban is not among the groups included in the MAROB survey because it is a broad-based political movement that does not claim to represent any one communal group – though the substantial majority of its supporters are Pashtuns.

40 See Vanda Felhab-Brown, "Drugs and Instability in Afghanistan: The Taliban's New Mobilization," paper presented at the annual meeting of the International Studies Association, San Francisco, March 2008. Her skepticism about the political effects of international eradication campaigns is based on her comparative study, *Shooting Up: Counterinsurgency and the War on Drugs* (Washington, DC: Brookings Institution, 2009).

41 From Robert Seely, *Russo-Chechen Conflict 1800–2000: A Deadly Balance* (London: Frank Cass, 2001), pp. 197–202. Also see James Hughes, *Chechnya: From Nationalism to Jihad* (Philadelphia: University of Pennsylvania Press, 2007), pp. 27 and 63–5.

42 Associated Press Worldstream, 14 April 1995, "Karadzik, Mladic Well-Known: Stanisic Obscure Figure in War with Yugoslavia."

43 In addition to Seely, *Russo-Chechen Conflict*, and Hughes, *Chechnya*, cited above, crime in Chechnya is documented by John B. Dunlop, *Russia Confronts Chechnya: Roots of a Separatist Conflict* (New York and Cambridge: Cambridge University Press, 1998), pp. 125–34, and a number of reports and news accounts accessed by MAROB coders. For a detailed description of where and how drugs were transported through the region, see Yossef Bodansky, *Chechen Jihad: Al Qaeda's Training Ground and the Next Wave of Terror* (New York: HarperCollins, 2007), pp. 29 ff.

44 Paul Murphy, *The Wolves of Islam: Russia and the Faces of Chechen Terror* (Dulles, VA: Brassey's, 2004).

45 From news and other reports accessed by MAROB coders. More general analyses are Pal Kolsto, *Nationalities Papers: The Transnistrian Republic: A Case of Politicized Regionalism*, vol. 6, no. 1 (1998); Oleh Protsyk, "Moldova's Dilemmas in Democratizing and Reintegrating Transnistria," *Problems of Post-Communism*, vol. 53, no. 4 (July/August 2006), pp. 29–41; and Graeme P Herd, "Moldova and the Dniestr Region: Contested Past, Frozen Present, Speculative Futures?" Conflict Studies Research Center, 2009, at http://74.125.155.132/search?q=cache:4mDMvf2N_44J:www.da.mod.uk/colleges/arag/document-listings/cee/05(07)-.

46 Kemp, "The Business of Ethnic Conflict," p. 47.

47 Deutsche Presse-Agentur, 8 June 2005, "Moldova asks for E.U. observers in disputed Trans-Dniestr province."

48 "Weapons Smuggling Not Found by OSCE," BBC Monitoring, Kiev Unit, 3 June 2006.

49 Kemp, "The Business of Ethnic Conflict," p. 46.

50 Alexander Kupatadze, "Radiological Smuggling and Uncontrolled Territories: The Case of Georgia," *Global Crime*, vol. 8, no. 1 (February 2007), pp. 52–5.

9 Conclusions

1 Jürgen Roth, *Die Neuen Daemonen: Das Bulgarische Mafianetzwerk*, Bulgarian translation (Sofia: Slance, 2009), p. 17. See our discussion of the expanding scope of international crime in chapter 1, pp. 12–15.

2 James Cockayne and Adam Lupel, "Introduction: Rethinking the Relationship between Peace Operations and Organized Crime," *International Peacekeeping*, vol. 16, no. 1 (February 2009), p. 6.

3 Ibid., pp. 7–11.

4 Colette Rausch, ed., *Combating Serious Crimes in Postconflict Societies: A Handbook for Policymakers and Practitioners* (Washington, DC: United States Institute of Peace Press, 2006), p. 83.

5 Ibid., pp. 86–7.

6 Jens Soerensen, *State Collapse and Reconstruction in the Periphery: Political Economy, Ethnicity and Development in Yugoslavia, Serbia and Kosovo* (New York: Berghahn Books, 2006), pp. 136–9.

7 Ibid., pp. 30–6 and 243–54.

8 Misha Glenny, *McMafia: A Journey Through the Global Criminal Underworld* (New York: Alfred Knopf, 2008), is a semi-popular account of how global crime networks function.

9 For an overview of international efforts to deal with crime, see Peter Andreas and Ethan Nadelmann, *Policing the Globe: Criminalization and Crime Control in International Relations* (New York: Oxford University Press, 2006), especially chapters 4–6.

10 Javier Argomaniz, *The EU and Counter-Terrorism: Politics, Policy, and Policies* (London and New York: Routledge, 2011) provides a critical analysis of the inconsistencies of EU policies toward terrorism.

11 Thus the EU responsibilities in multilateral peacekeeping operations usually concern the provision of resources while NATO is expected to take care of the military operations. The UN is relied on to provide overall political guidance and organizational coordination among participating organizations.

12 *A Strategy for EU Foreign Policy*, Report N7 (European Union Institute for Security Studies, 2010), p. 22.

13 Other key CSDP agencies within the pre-Lisbon Treaty EU were the Political and Security Committee; the European Union Military Committee; and the European Union Military Staff.

14 *EU Anti-terrorism Policy*. URL http://www.euractiv.com/en/security/anti-terrorism-policy/article-136674 [accessed February 2008].

15 *European Security Strategy*. URL http://europa.eu/legislation_summaries/justice_freedom_security/fight_against_terrorism [accessed February 2011].

16 The European Council, *Declaration on Combating Terrorism*, March 2004.

17 Ibid.

18 *Conceptual Framework on the ESDP Dimension of the Fight against Terrorism*.

19 The Hague Program acknowledged that "Initiatives in the field of justice, freedom and security are relatively recent, compared to other actions taken at the EU-level." It also acknowledged that ". . . insufficient progress was made . . . on the prevention of and fight against organized crime, police and customs cooperation, and judicial cooperation in criminal matters." The good news concerned the fight against terrorism. See http://europa.eu/legislation_summaries/justice _freedom_security/fight_against_terrorism.

20 Ibid.

21 Ibid.

22 Ibid.

23 The Stockholm Program, http://europa.eu/legislation_summaries/justice_freedom_security/fight_against_terrorism.

24 Alan S. Milward, *The European Rescue of the Nation-State* (London: Routledge, 1992, 2000).

214 *Notes*

25 Good examples of the voluminous literature on this topic include Bruce W. Jentleson, ed., *Opportunities Missed, Opportunities Seized: Preventive Diplomacy in the Post-Cold War World* (Lanham, MD: Rowan & Littlefield for the Carnegie Commission on Preventing Deadly Conflicts, 2000); David Carment and Frank Harvey, *Using Force to Prevent Ethnic Violence: An Evaluation of Theory and Evidence* (Westport, CT, and London: Praeger, 2001), especially chapter 6, "NATO and Postconflict Resolution in Bosnia and Kosovo;" Fen Osler Hampson and David M. Malone, eds, *From Reaction to Conflict Prevention: Opportunities for the UN System* (Boulder, CO and London: Lynne Reinner for the International Peace Academy, 2002); and Gareth Evans, *The Responsibility to Protect: Ending Mass Atrocity Crimes Once and For All* (Washington, DC: Brookings Institution Press, 2008).

26 See Walter A. Kemp, ed., *Quiet Diplomacy in Action: The OSCE High Commissioner on National Minorities* (The Hague: Kluwer Law International, 2001). The OSCE currently has 56 member states. For an overview of OSCE conflict prevention activities, see Alice Ackermann, "OSCE Mechanisms and Procedures Related to Early Warning, Conflict Prevention, and Crisis Management," *OSCE Yearbook 2009, Volume 15* (Baden-Baden: Nomos, 2010), pp. 223–34, also at http://www.core-hamburg.de/documents/yearbook/english/09/Ackermann-en.pdf [accessed 12 March 2012].

27 Ackermann, "OSCE Mechanisms and Procedures Related to Early Warning, Conflict Prevention, and Crisis Management," p. 204.

28 Michael Johns, personal correspondence. See http//www.osce.org/hcnm/49382 for specifics.

29 Kemp, *Quiet Diplomacy in Action*, pp. 183–99; and Michael S. Lund, "Preventive Diplomacy for Macedonia, 1992–1999: From Containment to Nation Building," in Jentleson, ed., *Opportunities Missed, Opportunities Seized*, pp. 173–208.

30 Soerensen, *State Collapse and Reconstruction*, p. 30.

31 Ibid., pp. 33–4.

32 *A Strategy for EU Foreign Policy*, pp. 38–9.

33 Ibid.

34 Ibid., p. 40.

35 Rausch, ed., *Combating Serious Crimes*. The contributors describe international efforts in many post-conflict settings but with particular attention to lessons learned in Kosovo and their application to Bosnia. The continuing security challenges for local and regional governments in the former Yugoslav republics are analyzed by local researchers in Iztok Prezelj, ed., *The Fight Against Terrorism and Crisis Management in the Western Balkans* (Amsterdam: IOS Press, NATO Science for Peace and Security Studies, 2008).

36 An analysis that remains relevant more than a decade later is Henri J. Barkey and Graham E. Fuller, *Turkey's Kurdish Question* (Lanham, MD: Rowan & Littlefield for the Carnegie Commission on Preventing Deadly Conflict, 1998).

37 Algeria now has more than 40 legal parties. The two cited here together won 13 per cent of the vote in 2007 elections for the national assembly.

38 The trend among European states is to decriminalize private possession and consumption of drugs. But as long as production and marketing remain illegal it would be impossible for, say, international corporations to take over and rationalize the markets – even though this might gradually put an end to "narco-terrorism" and eliminate most of the illicit income of Albanian and Kurdish networks, the Taliban in Afghanistan, etc.

39 Peter Andreas, "Symbiosis between Peace Operations and Illicit Business in Bosnia," *International Peacekeeping*, vol. 16, no. 1 (February 2009), p. 33.

Select bibliography

Adams, James. *The Financing of Terror: How the Groups that are Terrorizing the World Get the Money to Do It.* New York: Simon & Schuster, 1986.

Aliza, Marcus. *Blood and Belief: The PKK and the Kurdish Fight for Independence.* New York and London: New York University Press, 2007.

Andreas, Peter, and Ethan Nadelmann. *Policing the Globe: Criminalization and Crime Control in International Relations.* Oxford and New York: Oxford University Press, 2006.

Argomaniz, Javier. *The EU and Counter-Terrorism: Politics, Polity, and Policies after 9/11.* London and New York: Routledge, 2011.

Attanassoff, Velko. "Bosnia and Herzegovina – Islamic Revival, International Advocacy Networks and Islamic Terrorism," *Strategic Insight*, vol. 4, no. 5 (May 2005).

Bryden, Alan, and Marina Caparini, eds. *Private Actors and Security Governance.* Geneva: Centre for the Democratic Control of Armed Forces, 2006.

Cagaptay, Soner. "Can the PKK Renounce Violence? Terrorism Resurgent," *Middle East Quarterly*, vol. 4, no. 1 (Winter 2007), pp. 45–52.

Center for the Study of Democracy. *Partners in Crime: The Risk of Symbiosis between the Security Sector and Organized Crime in Southeast Europe.* In Bulgarian and English. Sofia: author, 2004. URL http://www.csd.bg/artShow.php?id=9626

Center for the Study of Democracy. *Organized Crime in Bulgaria: Markets and Trends*, by Tihomir Bezlov, Emil Tzenkov, Marina Tzetkova, Filip Gounev, and Georgi Petrunov. In Bulgarian and English. Sofia: author, 2007. URL http://www.csd.bg/artShow. php?id=9120\

Cockayne, James, and Adam Lupel. "Introduction: Rethinking the Relationship Between Peace Operations and Organized Crime." Special Issue of *International Peacekeeping*, vol.16, no.1 (February 2009), pp. 4–19.

Cohen, Lenard. *Broken Bonds: Yugoslavia's Disintegration and Balkan Politics and Transformation.* Boulder, CO: Westview Press, 1995.

Council Framework Decision of 13 June 2002 on combating terrorism. *Official Journal L 164, 22/06/2002 P. 0003–0007* URL http://eur-lex.europa.eu/LexUriServ/LexUriServ. do?uri=CELEX:32002F0475:EN:HTML

Council Framework Decision 2008/978/JHA of 18 December 2008 on the European evidence warrant for the purpose of obtaining objects, documents and data for use in proceedings in criminal matters. URL http://eur-lex.europa.eu/LexUriServ/LexUriServ. do?uri=OJ:L:2008:350:0072:0092:en:PDF

Curtis, Glenn, and Tara Karacan. "The Nexus among Terrorists, Narcotics Traffickers, Weapons Proliferators, and Organized Crime Networks in Western Europe." Washington, DC: Library of Congress, 2002. URL http://www.loc.gov/rr/frd/

216 *Select bibliography*

Ehrenfeld, Rachel. *Funding Evil: How Terrorism is Financed – and How to Stop It*. Chicago: Bonus Books, expanded edition, 2005.

European Parliament and Council. Directive 2005/60/EC of the European Parliament and of the Council of 26 October 2005 on the prevention of the use of the financial system for the purpose of money laundering and terrorist financing. URL http://eur-lex.europa.eu/LexUriServ/LexUriServ.do?uri=OJ:L:2005:309:0015:0036:en:PDF

Evans, Martin, and John Phillips. *Algeria: Anger of the Dispossessed*. New Haven, CT and London: Yale University Press, 2007.

Farah, Douglas. "Terrorist-Criminal Pipelines and Criminalized States: Emerging Alliances." PRISM (National Defense University), vol. 2, no. 3 (2011). URL http://www.ndu.edu/press/emerging-alliances.html

Forest, James J. F., ed, "Special Issue: Intersection of Crime and Terrorism," *Terrorism and Political Violence*, vol. 24, no. 2 (2012).

Friman, H. Richard, and Peter Andreas, eds. *The Illicit Global Economy and State Power*. Lanham, MD: Rowman & Littlefield, 1999.

Giatzidis, Emil. "The Challenge of Organized Crime in the Balkans and the Political and Economic Implications." *Journal of Communist Studies and Transition Politics*, vol. 23, no. 3 (September 2007), pp. 327–51.

Glenny, Misha. *McMafia: A Journey through the Global Criminal Underworld*. New York: Alfred A. Knopf, 2008.

Grabosky, Peter, and Michael Stohl. *Crime and Terrorism*. Los Angeles, London, and New Delhi: Sage, 2010.

Gupta, Dipak K. *Understanding Terrorism and Political Violence: The Life Cycle of Birth, Growth, Transformation, and Demise*. London and New York: Routledge, 2008.

Gurr, Ted Robert. *Peoples Versus States: Minorities at Risk in the New Century*. Washington, DC: United States Institute of Peace Press, 2000.

Harff, Barbara and Ted Robert Gurr. *Ethnic Conflict in World Politics*, 2nd edn. Boulder, CO: Westview Press, 2004.

Haut, Francois. "Kurdish Extremism and Organized Crime: The Kurdistan Workers Party." URL http://www.drmcc.org/IMG/pdf/41b3a3abccc0f.pdf

History Channel. Arkan War Criminal 1/5 and 2/5. http://www.youtube.com/watch?v=Hli-0cJQoSg&feature=related

History Channel. Arkan War Criminal 3/5 and 4/5. http://www.youtube.com/watch?v=L1576qHHtXs&feature=related

Hoare, Marko Attila. "The Serbia–Kosovo Dispute as a Factor of Instability in the Balkans." URL http://www.humsec.eu/cms/fileadmin/user_upload/humsec/Workin_Paper_Series/WP_Hoare.pdf

Hristov, Hristo. *The Secret Bankruptcies of Communism*. In Bulgarian. Sofia: Siela, 2007.

Jelavich, Barbara. *History of the Balkans: Eighteenth and Nineteenth Centuries*, vols I and II. New York: Cambridge University Press, 1983.

Jenkins, Gareth. "The PKK Insurgency Enters a New Era." *The Central Asia Caucus Institute Silk Roads Studies Program*, vol.3, no. 12 (21 June 2010). URL http://www.silkroadstudies.org/new/inside/turkey/2010/100621A.html

Jojarth, Christine. *Crime, War, and Global Trafficking: Designing International Cooperation*. New York and Cambridge: Cambridge University Press, 2009.

Jordan, David C. *Drug Politics: Dirty Money and Democracies*. Norman, OK: University of Oklahoma Press, 1999.

Kalayvas, Stathis N. "Wanton and Senseless? The Logic of Massacres in Algeria." *Rationality and Society*, vol. 11 (August 1999), pp.243–85.

Select bibliography 217

Kalinova, Evgenia and Iskra Baeva. *The Bulgarian Transitions 1939–2005*. In Bulgarian. Sofia: Paradigma, 2006.

Kemp, Walter A. "The Business of Ethnic Conflict." *Security Dialogue*, vol. 35, no. 1 (2004), pp. 43–59.

Kepel, Gilles. *Jihad: The Trail of Political Islam*, trans. Anthony F. Roberts. Cambridge, MA and London: Harvard University Press, 2002.

Kepel, Gilles. *Beyond Terror and Martyrdom: The Future of the Middle East*, trans. Pascale Ghazaleh. Cambridge, MA and London: Harvard University Press, 2008.

LeSueur, James D. *Between Terror and Democracy: Algeria since 1989*. Halifax and Winnipeg: Fernwood Publishing, and London and New York: Zed Books, 2010.

Lilly, Peter. *Dirty Dealing: The Untold Truth about Global Money Laundering, International Crime and Terrorism*, 3rd edn. London and Philadelphia, PA: Kogan Page, 2006.

Lowi, Miriam R. "Algeria, 1992–2002: Anatomy of a Civil War," in Paul Collier and Nicholas Sambanis, eds., *Understanding Civil War: Evidence and Analysis*, Volume 1: *Africa*. Washington, DC: World Bank, 2005, pp. 221–46.

Madsen, Frank G. *Transnational Organized Crime*. New York and London: Routledge, 2009.

Makarenko, T. "The Crime–Terror Continuum: Tracing the Interplay between Transnational Crime and Terrorism." *Global Crime*, vol. 6, no. 1 (2004), pp. 129–45.

Malcolm, Noel. *Kosovo: A Short History*. London: Macmillan, 1998, and Pan Books, 2002.

Martinez, Luis. *The Algerian Civil War 1990–1998*, trans. Jonathan Derrick. New York: Columbia University Press, 2000.

Migdalovitz, Carol. "2010 Congressional Brief Turkey: Selected Foreign Policy Issues and U.S. Views." 28 November 2010. URL www.crs.gov

Mincheva, Lyubov G., ed. *Comparative Balkan Parliamentarism*. Sofia: International Center for Minority Studies and Intercultural Relations, 1995.

Mincheva, Lyubov. "The Albanian Ethnoterritorial Separatist Movement: Local Conflict, Regional Crisis." *Nationalism and Ethnic Politics*, vol. 15, no. 2 (April–June 2009), pp. 211–36.

Napoleoni, Loretta. *Terror Incorporated: Tracing the Dollars Behind the Terror Networks*. New York: Seven Stories Press, 2005.

Pargeter, Alison. *The New Frontiers of Jihad: Radical Islam in Europe*. London: I.B. Tauris, and Philadelphia, PA: University of Pennsylvania Press, 2008.

Rausch, Colette, ed. *Combating Serious Crimes in Postconflict Societies: A Handbook for Policymakers and Practitioners*. Washington, DC: United States Institute of Peace Press, 2006.

Reuveny, Rafael, and William R. Thompson, eds. *Coping with Terrorism: Origins, Escalation, Counter strategies, and Responses*. Albany, NY: State University of New York Press, 2010.

Reveron, Derek S., and Jeffrey Stevenson Murer, eds. *Flashpoints in the War on Terrorism*. New York and London: Routledge, 2006.

Richardson, Louise, ed. *The Roots of Terrorism*. New York and London: Routledge, 2006.

Roth, Jürgen. *Die Neuen Daemonen: Das Bulgarische Mafianetzwerk*. Sofia: Slance, 2009. This book was published in Bulgarian only; no German edition exists.

Roth, Jürgen. *Gangsterwirtschaft [Gangster Economics]: Wie uns die organisierte Kriminalität aufkauft*. Berlin: Eichborn, 2010.

Schindler, John R. *Unholy Terror: Bosnia, Al-Qaida, and the Rise of Global Jihad*. St Paul, MN: Zenith Press, 2007.

Shelley, Louise. *Human Trafficking: A Global Perspective*. New York and Cambridge: Cambridge University Press, 2010.

Sørensen, Jens Stilhoff. *State Collapse and Reconstruction in the Periphery: Political Economy, Ethnicity and Development in Yugoslavia, Serbia and Kosovo*. New York: Berghahn Books, 2009.

218 Select bibliography

Strazzari, Francesco. "L'Oeuvre au Noir: The Shadow Economy of Kosovo's Independence." *International Peacekeeping*, vol. 15, no. 2 (April 2008), pp. 155–70.

Tremonti, Giulio. *La paura e la speranza – Europa: la crisi globale che si avvicina e la via per superarla* [*Fear and hope –Europe: The approaching global crisis and how to overcome it*]. Milano: Mondadori, 2008.

United Nations Office on Drugs and Crime (UNODC). *Crime and its Impact on the Balkans and Affected Countries*. Vienna: author, March 2008. *Note:* UNODC is an excellent source of carefully researched global and regional reports on organized crime and trafficking.

United Nations Office on Drugs and Crime (UNODC). *The Globalization of Crime: A Transnational Organized Crime Threat Assessment*. Vienna: author, 2010.

Velikonja, Mitja. *Religious Separation and Political Intolerance in Bosnia-Herzegovina*. College Station, TX: Texas A & M University Press, 2003.

Viano, Emilio C., José Magallanes, and Laurent Bridel. *Transnational Organized Crime: Myth, Power, and Profit*. Durham, NC: Carolina Academic Press, 2003.

Additional websites

Federation of American Scientists (FAS). This is an independent, nonpartisan think tank dedicated to providing objective, evidence-based analysis and practical policy recommendations on national and international security issues connected to applied science and technology. URL http://www.fas.org/about/index.html

The *Global Terrorism Database (GTD)*. URL http://www.start.umd.edu/start/data_collections/GTD includes information on international as well as domestic terrorist events around the world from 1970 through 2010. GTD currently provides information on over 98,000 cases. For each GTD incident, information is available on the date and location of the incident, the weapons used and nature of the target, the number of casualties, and – when identifiable – the identity of the perpetrator.

The *Jamestown Foundation*: *Global Terrorism Analysis*. The Jamestown Foundation website provides political news, analyses, and featured articles on politics and violence in Eurasia, China, and the World of Terrorism. URL http://www.jamestown.org/programs/gta/

The *Minorities at Risk* project (*MAR*). URL http://www.cidcm.umd.edu/mar/ The MAR project monitors and analyzes the status and conflicts of up to 287 politically active communal groups globally. Depending on the group and variable, annual or decennial data have been coded from 1945 through 2006. Data on an additional 100 groups have been coded and will be posted for analyses of selection bias issues. The MAR database and code book as well as detailed historical chronologies are available through this site.

The *Minorities at Risk Organizational Behavior* project (*MAROB*). URL http://www.cidcm. umd.edu/mar/The MAROB dataset is a subsidiary of the *Minorities at Risk* Project. Initiated in 2005, the project seeks to identify factors that motivate some members of ethnic minorities to become radicalized, and form activist organizations, using violence and terrorism. The project has collected data on 118 ethno political organizations representing MAR groups in the Middle East and North Africa and 271 such groups in the post-Communist Eurasian states.

Index

In this index names starting with the al- prefix are sorted under the following letter; e.g al-Haili will be found under H.

Abashidze, Aslan 157
Abderahman, Yusuf 75
Abdic, Fikret 76
Abu-Sayyaf group 6
Active Islamic Youth (AIY) 78
activism, Islamic in Algeria 91
actors, criminal 10
Adams, Gerry 151
Adams, James 144, 151, 158
Adana Memorandum 58
Adjara 156, 157, 177
Adzharia *see* Adjara
Afghanistan: and Algerian fighters 91, 96; drug trade xviii, 148, 153, 179n.4; and Pakistan 146; as weak state 16 *see also* Taliban
Agrokomerc foods 76
Ahmadi, Haji 48
aid: development projects 21, 165; Kosovo 38; and trans-border political/criminal networks 165
AIS (Islamic Salvation Army) 89, 94
Aksamija, Azra 79
Albania: clans 25, 26, 35; criminal networks 24, 35, 105; drug trade 31, 32; economy 40; ethnic militancy 29; ETSM 26–31, 107; KLA in 32; nationalism 29, 34, 163; people/traditions 25–6; political-criminal syndicate 5; separatism 30, 35, 39; Spring uprising 27, 29; terrorism 39, 160
Albanian National Army (ANA) 30, 154
Albanian nationalist movement 1, 5, 29, 34, 148, 176, 177
Albright, Madeleine 105–6
Alema, Massimo D' 60
Alexander, King of Yugoslavia 108
Algeria: al-Qaeda in 87, 88, 89, 98; and Arab Spring 18; assassinations 96, 97–8; background to Islamist revolution 88–9; as black hole 17; civil war 102, 148, 161; corruption 18, 88, 92, 93, 102, 161; drug trafficking 100; economy 92, 93, 95, 96, 98; funding of Islamist movement 93–4; gas revenues 88, 92, 203n.63; government complicity in violence 97; human rights 89, 175; identity networks 87; ideological interactions 6; Islamists in 6, 17, 161, 163; Islamist terrorism in xviii, 94–8, 175; jihadism 91–2, 95–6, 98–101, 102, 177; massacres 87, 89, 97; oil 87, 88, 92, 161, 203n.63; poverty 88, 93, 98; predatory networks 7; smuggling 89, 95, 96, 100; socialism 88, 91; unemployment 88, 92, 93, 102; as weak state 16
Algerian Brotherhood in France (FAF) 94
Algerian revolution, political economy of 92–3
Alliance for the Future of Kosovo 37
All-National Congress of the Chechen People 155
al-Qaeda: Algeria 87, 88, 89, 98; and Bosnia 84, 86, 197n.22, 199n.58; and al-Gama'at Islamiya 85; and Sierra Leone 14
al-Qaeda in the Islamic Maghreb (AQIM) 89, 92, 98, 98–100, 102
Amal 152
amphetamine production, Bulgaria 135, 136, 139
Anastasievic, Dejan 115
Andreas, Peter 72, 75
al-Anfal genocide campaign 48, 49
Ankara 56
Al-Ansar 96

220 Index

Antalya 56
Anti-Corruption Agency, Serbia 120
Anti-Mafia Investigation Directorate
  (AID) 34
anti-terrorism policy strategies, EU 22, 39,
  166, 167, 168, 169
Apo's Revenge Hawks 55
Apo's Youth Revenge Brigade 55
Arab Spring: and Algeria 18; as regional
  opportunity factor 52; and Syrian
  Kurds 46
Arafat, Yasser 151
Arkan 106, 111–14, 114–15, 116, 118, 158
armed conflicts: and ethnic minorities 9;
  and identity networks 89–92
Armed Islamic Group (GIA) see GIA
Armenian Secret Army for the Liberation of
  Armenia (ASALA) 61
arms trafficking 4, 10; Bosnia/Kosovo
  militants 31; Bulgaria 129, 138;
  Chechnya 155; and funding of militant
  groups 149; KOS 116; PKK 65; post-
  conflict 176; Transdniestria 156
Army of National Liberation (ANL) 88
assassinations: Algeria 96, 97–8;
  Arkan 115; Bulgaria 136, 141; and
  Serbs 205n.27
Association of Algerian Ulema (AAU) 90
Ataturk, Mustafa Kemal 52
atrocities, Bosnian civil war 70–2 see also
  ethnic cleansing, genocide; violence
Attanassoff, Velko 78–9
autonomous governments 17–18
Autonomy Accord, Iraqi government/
  Kurdish leaders 49
Aziz, Abu Abdel 74

Bahara Valley, cannabis farms 65
Baie Mille 129, 138, 139
Balkan Center in Zenica 78
Balkan route, heroin trade 31, 38–9, 148
Balkans: contraband trade 138;
  corruption 160, 164; criminal
  entrepreneurs 33; criminalized
  states 103; criminalized transitions 20;
  criminal networks 31; and ETSMs 107,
  111; EU policy 172–3; trans-border
  identity networks 103; as protracted
  conflict region 8; smuggling 138
Balkan wars 20, 160
bandits: social 7; stationary bandits 15, 18
Banja Luka 110, 113
banking sector: bank credit frauds 14;
  Bulgaria 7, 133; criminal banks 13;
  criminal lobbies in 15

Bardos, Gordon 26
Barzani, Masrour 189n.26
Barzani, Mustafa 47, 50, 190n.37
Basayev, Arbi 155, 156, 158
Bayik, Cemil 48
Becktein, Gunter 64
Belcacem, Bensayah 84, 199n.64
Belgrade Red Star soccer team 112, 115
Belhadj, Ali 88, 91
Belli, Roberta 150
Bell, Martin 112
Belmokhtar, Mokhtara 100
Ben Badis, Abdelhamid 90
Bendjedid, Chadli 88, 91, 93
Benevolence International Foundation
  (BIF) 85
Bentalha 97
Berber minority, Algeria 92
BiH 80, 81, 83
Bihać triangle 76
Bijelina 113
bin Laden, Osama 150–1; and Albania 34;
  Algeria 98; and Bosnia 197n.22,
  199n.58; and Sierra Leone 14
Birler, Hayri 65
black holes 17–18
black lawyers, Bulgaria 136, 137
black markets: and Arkan 113; Bosnian civil
  war 68, 75–6, 197n.30; Bulgaria 127–8;
  Serbia 117
Black Shadow, The 29
blood diamonds, Sierra Leone 14
blood feuds, Albanians 25
Bobovic, Budimir 112
Bokan, Vanja 148
bombings: Bulgaria 128, 129; Madrid 168,
  199n.64; Morocco 199n.64;
  Turkey 191n.63; US/UK embassies
  in Bosnia 84 see also suicide bombings;
  terrorism
Bonev, Milcho see Baie Mille
Bosnia: and al-Qaeda 84, 86, 197n.22,
  199n.58; arms trafficking 31; as
  black hole 17; civil war 6, 68–80,
  154; corruption 68, 76, 80, 81–3, 86;
  and crime–terror networks 68, 75,
  83–5, 86; criminalization of 72–6,
  116; demographic structure 79–80;
  economy 82; ethnic cleansing 70,
  79–80; genocide 71–2; ideological
  interactions 6; indoctrination of
  youth 78; and international Islam 76–
  80; Islamists 6, 163; mujahedeen 68,
  69, 72, 74–8, 81, 83, 84, 86; official
  corruption 76; peacekeepers/and

Index 221

crime 176, 179n.2; post-conflict 174;
post Dayton 68, 80–3, 105; as
protectorate 173–4; Saudi Arabia
financing of 69, 72, 76, 77, 79, 85;
security in 82–3, 174; and Serbia 105;
smuggling 68–9, 116, 120; terrorism 79–
80, 81–3; unholy alliances 161
Bosnia-Herzegovina 69
Bosniak atrocities, Bosnian civil war 71
Bosniaks 196n.4; identity 78–9
radicalized 84
Bosnian Finance Police 85
Bosnian Interior Ministry 85
Bosnian jihad 74
Bosnian Muslims 77, 86
Bosnian Serbs 69–70, 71
Bougarel, Xavier 83
Bourghezoul barracks attack 96
Bouteflika, Abdelaziz 89
Bozinovich, M. 33
Bratislav, Ojrubadic 113
Bretton Woods system 13
British National Service of Criminal
Intelligence 64
Brookings Institution 16
brothels, Kosovo 34
Bulgaria: amphetamine production 135,
136, 139; arms trafficking 129, 138;
assassinations 136, 141; banking
sector 7, 133; cocaine market 136, 139;
contraband trade 129–30, 139–40;
corruption 124, 125, 130–4, 140,
162; as criminalized state xvii, 103,
122–3; criminal networks 122, 162,
163, 164, 205n.27; democracy 140;
drug trade 135, 136, 139, 141;
economy 7, 123–4, 124; economic
crisis of socialism 123–4; market
fundamentalism 20; market of
violence 126–30, 131, 133–4; money
laundering 131, 132, 136; narco-
criminalization 125–6, 134–7, 140;
oligarchs 130, 131, 132, 138, 141;
post-communist transition 124–6,
206n.3; poverty 124; predatory
networks 7; smuggling 129–30,
138, 139, 140, 162; socialism 123–4;
structural corruption 137; trans-border
criminal networks 122, 125, 137,
138; and transition from illicit/licit
enterprise 150; unemployment 124;
unholy alliances 162; as weak state 16;
wrestlers/security groups 139, 142,
162
Bulgarian Black Sea Fleet, London 133

Bulgarian Communist Party 131
Bulgarian Merchant Fleet 133
Bulgarian Socialist Party (BSP) 139
Business of Ethnic Conflict, The 76
business, transition from illicit to licit 150,
151

Caco 80
Cagaptay, Soner 53, 64, 66
Call to Global Islamic Resistance 98–9
cannabis production 17, 65, 136
capital flow, and global illegal
economy 12–13
captagon production 135
car crime 65, 117, 120, 139–40, 154
CARDS programs 173
Ceca 113, 118
Center for the Affirmation of Islamic
Science 78
Center for the Study of Democracy
(CSD) 20, 119, 125, 129
Cesme 56
charities, Islamic/finance of terrorism 85
Charter for an Islamic State, A 91
Chechen nationalists 177
Chechen Wars 155
Chechnya 154, 155–6, 158
chemical weapons, Saddam Hussein 49
Chetnik movement 108, 109
children, abduction of/PKK 65
China, money laundering 117
Cilluffo, Frank 64
Cilluffo, Frank & Salmoiraghi, George 35
Citizenship Review Commission, Bosnia
81
civil societies: and crime/politics 40;
Kosovo 38; and post-conflict
development projects 21
civil war: Algeria 102, 148, 161; Bosnia 6,
68–80, 115
clan-based networks: Albanian 25, 26, 35;
and drug trade 32; Kosovar Albanian
nationalists 5; Kosovo 18, 24, 26, 105,
158, 186n.50 *see also* clans; *fis*
clans: Albania 35; Albania/Kosovo 33,
38, 39; criminal in Turkey 65;
Kosovar/international political-criminal
syndicates xv, 32–3; Kosovo 31–2, 33,
37, 38, 105, 160; and Kosovo Liberation
Army 27; Kurdish/smuggling 65;
political killings 33; Serbia 117; and
urbanization 38 *see also* clan–based
networks; *fis*
clientism, Algeria 88
Club 777 129

222 *Index*

cocaine market, Bulgaria 136, 139
coca leaf production 134
Cockayne, James & Lupel, Adam 164
coercion, protracted conflict regions 8; and terrorists xvii
coercive diplomacy 171
Cohen, Lenard 109
Cold War era 21, 61
Collier, Paul & Hoeffler, Anke 3
Colombia 3
Combating Serious Crimes in Postconflict Societies 174
Commission of the European Communities 36
Committee for State Security (CSS), Bulgaria 126
Common Foreign and Security Policy (CFSP), EU 166, 167
communist party: Bulgaria 131; Yugoslavia 109, 121
complex dependent variable 2–8
concentration camps, Banja Luka 113
Conceptual Framework on the ESDP Dimension of the Fight Against Terrorism 169
Confederation of Kurdish Organizations of the Commonwealth of Independent States (CIS) 59
conflict management 145, 171–4
Congress for Freedom and Democracy in Kurdistan (KADEK) 55
constraints, criminal market 12–15
Contact Group Peace Plan for Bosnia 111
contraband trade: Balkans 138; Bulgaria 129–30, 139–40 *see also* smuggling
cooperation, and trust 4
cooperatives, criminal 10, 11
corruption: Algeria 18, 88, 92, 93, 102, 161; Balkan states 160, 164; Bosnia 68, 76, 80, 81–3, 86; Bulgaria 124, 125, 130–4, 140, 162; of Croat officials 73; and elites 19; Kosovo xv, 36, 37, 40; Milošević government 117; official xvi, 178; and peacekeepers 176; public sector 18, 34, 40, 76; Serbia 120, 121; state/organized crime 18–21; structural 19–20, 21, 125, 130–4, 137, 140
Council for Mutual Economic Assistance (COMECON) 123
Council Framework Decision, EU 170
Council of Ministers of Bosnia 82
Council of the EU 167
counter-intelligence/insurgency 178

Counter Terrorism Coordinator, EU 168, 169
counter-terrorism/crime policies/ legislation 166, 167, 168, 170, 178
counter-terrorism, global 210n.13
credit millionaires, Bulgaria 7
crime: Bosnia 81–3; Chechnya 155; domestic profit-driven 12; Middle East 152–3, 157; and militant movements xviii, 3; organized economic 19; post-communist states 153–4; and terrorism 3, 5–6; trans-border/Serbia 111–14
crime–terror alliances xxi, 72–6
crime–terrorism interactions, trans-border 103
crime–terror networks: Bosnia 68, 75, 83–5, 86; and Milošević 104
Criminal Code of Bosnia and Herzegovina 82
criminal enclaves 17
criminal enterprise(s) 3; and control of resources 11; international 3, 12, 39, 63–6; as social networks/cooperatives 11; and state officials 15
criminal groups: goals of 3; international 3, 12, 39, 63–6
criminalized states 15, 135, 141; Balkans 103; Bosnia 72–6, 116; Bulgaria 103, 122–3; and corruption 19–20; Kosovo 25; Serbia 106, 114–21, 162
criminally exploitable ties 11, 38, 140
criminal-militant networks, hybrid xvi, xvii
criminal networks 11–12; Albanian 24, 35, 105; Bulgaria 122, 162, 163, 164, 205n.27; and economic crime 158; Italy/Kosovo 32; Kosovo 24, 31–4; and militant networks 4–5; and nationalist movements 1; and politics/the state 37; and public sector corruption 18; and terrorist movements 146
criminals, amnestied 139
Criss, Nur Bilge 59
Croatia: and Bosnian civil war 71, 73; corruption of officials 73; independent state of 108–9; and Serbia 105; Serbs 110
cross-border identity networks *see* identity networks
cross-border movements 8–9, 11
cultural cohesion, and trust 4
Curtis, Glenn & Karacan, Tara 5–6, 64–5, 66

Index 223

Customs Bureau, Serbia 116, 117, 119
Cvetković-Maček Agreement 108
Cyprus 117

Dayton Peace Accords: Bosnia since 68,
80–3, 105; and ethnic cleansing 113;
EUFOR-ALTHEA mission 173;
and Kosovars 27; and Kosovo
judiciary/crime 164
debts, Bulgaria 124
Declaration on Combating Terrorism 168–9
DEHAP, Turkey 53
Demirel, Suleyman 58
democracy: Bulgaria 140; and
criminalization of Bulgaria 122; and the
Umma 91
Democratic League of Kosovo 26
Democratic Party of Iranian Kurdistan 47
Democratic Party of Kosovo 37, 154
Democratic Society Movement (DTH) 53
Democratic Society Party (DTP) 53
Denmark, and PKK 58, 62, 193n.100
DEP (Turkey) 53
Departement de Recherche sur les Menaces
Criminelles Contemporaines 62
development projects, post-conflict 21, 165
diasporas: Albanian 25, 32, 39;
Algerian 87, 94; Balkan 160; crime
networks 160; funding of militant
groups 147; and identity networks 165;
Kosovars 27; Kurdish 61–3, 160;
Muslim in Europe 93; radicalization
of 94; and trans-state/cross-border
identities 8
Dillman, Bradford 93
Dimitrov, Konstantin 136
diplomacy, coercive 171
Directive on Money Laundering, EU 169
Directives, EU 168
discrimination: Iranian Kurds 47; and
OSCE 175; Syrian Kurds 45
Divjak, Jovan 80, 198n.42
Djindjić, Zoran 106, 118, 119, 121
Dlouhy, David 81–2
Doctora 139
donation, and militant groups 146–7, 158
Drenica group 33
Drina River campaign 111
DRS, Algeria 97
drug markets: Bulgaria 135, 136, 139;
European 148, 160, 176
drug production: amphetamines 135, 136,
139; cannabis 17, 65, 136; captagon
production 135; coca leaf 134; and
international crime 12; Kurdistan/

PKK 65; poppy production 134, 153
drug trade 134; Afghanistan 148, 153,
179n.4; Albanian 31, 32; Balkan
route 31, 38–9, 148; and clan-based
networks 32; in France 64; and global
financial crisis 14; and international
crime 12; and KLA 32, 33; and
organized crime 19; and PKK 64; post-
conflict 176; and the Taliban 153, 177,
179n.4; trans-border 20; transnational/
Bulgaria 139; Turkey 191n.55 *see also*
heroin trade; narco–criminalization
drug trafficking: Afghanistan 179n.4;
Albania 32; Algeria 100; Bulgaria 141;
Chechnya 155; and criminalized
states 20–1; and funding of militant
groups 148; and Kosovo 24; and
militant groups 4; and PKK 51, 64, 148
Dugagjini group 33

economic crime, and criminal networks 158
economic deprivation, Iraqi Kurds 49
economic embargoes: Bosnian civil war 75,
85; Iraqi Kurds 49, 50; Yugoslav and
Bulgaria 72, 124, 129–30, 162
economics, globalization of 19
economic transitions, criminalized 20
economy: Albanian 40; Algerian 92, 93,
95, 96, 98; alternative global 14–15;
Bosnian 82; Bulgaria 7, 123–4,
124; global illegal 12–13; illiberal/
Yugoslavia 164; Iraqi Kurdistan 51;
Kosovo 24, 32, 34, 37–8; Turkish 56, 57
educational institutions, Bosnia 79
education, Bosnian students/Islamist
institutions abroad 78–9
elites: Algeria 87, 88, 92, 93, 102, 161;
Bulgaria 7, 20, 131, 132; corruption 19,
178; hybrid terror-crime networks 67;
Iraqi Kurds 49; Kurdish 47, 51;
oligarchs/Bulgaria 130, 131, 138,
141; post-communist governments 35;
Serbian 104; Serbia/Yugoslavia 20;
Syrian Kurdish 46; and trans-state/cross-
border identities 8
El Mujahid (Holy Warrior) Battalion 74–5
Elwert, Georg 125
embargoes: Bosnian civil war 75, 85; Iraqi
Kurds 49, 50; Yugoslav and Bulgaria 72,
124, 129–30, 162
Emerson, Stephen 101
ENA (Etoile Nord-Africaine) 90
enemies, near and far/Albanian jihadists
99
energy sector, PKK targeting of 56

224 *Index*

entrepreneurs: criminal 33, 40; militants
 as 149; moving to licit economy 175, 176
entrepreneurship, and funding of militant
 groups 148–51, 152, 158
Erdogan, Recep Tayyip 59
Erdogan, Turkish Prime Minister 193n.100
ethnic cleansing: Bosnia 70, 79–80;
 by ethnic Albanians 30; Milošević
 government 106; and Red Berets 116;
 Serbia 109, 111–14, 116, 121, 162; by
 Serbian forces 28, 105
ethnic division, Algeria 92
ethnic minorities, and armed conflicts 9
ethnic movements, and militant-criminal
 interactions 1
ethnic networks, Albanian 25
ethno-kleptocratic societies 156
ethno-national identifications, and trust 4
ethnonational movements 161
ethnopolitics, Kurdish 53
ethnoterritorial separatist movement *see*
 ETSM
Etoil Nord-Africaine (ENA) 90
ETSMs (ethnoterritorial separatist
 movements): Albanian 26–31, 107;
 Balkan 107, 111; Iranian 47–8;
 Iraqi 48–50; Kurdish 43–52, 61–2, 160;
 Serb 106–10, 111; Syrian 45–7, 67;
 Turkish 52–8
EUFOR-ALTHEA mission 173
Eurojust 166
Europe: drug markets 148, 160, 176;
 jihadist cells in 100; Muslim diaspora 93;
 organized crime networks 64–5
European Agency for Reconstruction 173
European Arrest Warrant 168, 170
European Commissioner for External
 Relations and European Neighbourhood
 Policy 167
European Community, and international
 terrorism policies 39, 167
European Council 167
European Evidence Warrant 169, 170
European Police College 166
European Security and Defense Policy
 (ESDP) 166, 168, 173
European Security Strategy 168
European Union: Bosnian membership 86;
 Bulgarian membership 142; counter-
 terrorism/crime policies 22, 39, 166,
 167, 168, 169; foreign policy 167; Justice
 and Home Affairs Council 166; and
 Kosovo 38; Kurdish organizations in 62,
 63; security policy 174; and Serbia 121;
 and unholy alliances 165–71, 177
European Union Common Foreign and

Security Policy (CFSP) 166, 167
European Union Council Framework
 Decision 168, 170
European Union Counter-Terrorism
 Coordinator 168, 169
European Union Counter-Terrorism
 Strategy 169
European Union Directive on Money
 Laundering 169, 170
European Union Directives 168
European Union Military Committee 166
European Union Police and Judicial
 Cooperation in Criminal Matters
 (PJC/PJCC) 166
European Union Police Mission 173
European Union Police Mission in Bosnia
 (EUPM) 173
European Union policy, Balkans 172–3
European Union Political and Security
 Committee 166
European Union reform package,
 Bosnia 82
European Union Rule of Law Mission in
 Kosovo (EULEX) 24, 30, 38, 40, 173,
 187n.59
Europol 63, 166–7, 170
Evans, Martin & Phillips, John 96
extortion 147

FAF (Algerian Brotherhood in France) 94
Fahd, King of Saudi Arabia, and Bosnia 72
failed states 15
Farah, Douglas 17
FARC, Colombia 63
fares' networks *see fis*
FARK (armed forces of the Republic of
 Kosovo) 26
Fatah 61, 151
Fatah Revolutionary Council 152
Federation of Bosnia and Herzegovina (BiH)
 see BiH
Felhab-Brown, Vanda 153
al-Filistini, Abu Qatada 96–7
finance, globalization of 13
Finance Ministry, Bulgaria 138
Financial Action Task Force on Money
 Laundering 169
financial capital, and national wealth 19
financial power, elites 7
financial systems, criminalization/
 liberalization of 13
Financing of Terror, The 144
Finsbury Park Mosque 96–7
fis 25, 32, 33, 35, 105
FIS (Islamic Salvation Front) 88–9, 91, 93,
 94, 95, 102, 175

Index   225

FLN (National Liberation Front) 88, 90–1, 92
foreign investment, Iraqi Kurdistan 49
foreign policy: EU 167; and support of terrorist organizations 146
Framework Decision on Combating Terrorism 168
Framework Decisions, EU 168, 170
France: and Algeria 87–8, 90; and Algerian jihadists 100–1; drug trade in 64; Muslims in 93–4; terrorism in 101, 102, 203n.69
Franz-Ferdinand, Archduke 108
fraud, Bosnia 81
Freedom-for-Ocalan.com 62
fuel smuggling, Bulgaria 129, 130
funding: Arkan/Tigers 112; countering terrorist funding 169; criminal/Middle East 152–3; GSPC/AQIM 100; jihadist organizations in Algeria 93–4, 95; of jihadist terrorism 147; of KLA 31, 33, 39, 147; militant groups by diasporas 147; of militant movements 4, 85, 143–51, 176; of paramilitary forces/Serbia 116; of PKK 51, 63–6, 145–6; Saudi Arabia of Bosnia 69, 72, 76, 77, 79, 85; Saudi Arabia of militant groups 147, 158; war in Algeria 87–8

al-Gama'at Islamiya 85
games in multiple arenas 46
Garăsanin, Ilija 106, 107
gas revenues, Algeria 88, 92, 203n.63
General Dudaev's Army 154
genocide: Bosnian civil war 71–2; Iraqi Kurds 48, 49; Kosovo 160; Serbia 109, 110; Srebrenica 113
Georgia 157, 171
Germany: drug trade in 31, 64; money laundering 117; and Ocalan 60
Ghegs 25
GIA (Armed Islamic Group): defeat of 161; financing of 95; in France 203n.69; jihad of 92, 94; principles of 96; violence of 89, 97, 98, 175
Giatzidis, Emil 25
Gjonir, Ilir 34, 40
Glenny, Misha 112, 122, 131
Global Corruption Barometer 82
global financial crisis 14
Global Integrity 2007 82
global Islamist movement, Saudi Arabian funding 158
globalization: and criminal enterprise 12; of economics 19; and illicit financial transactions 125; and structural corruption 130

Globalization of Crime report 145
global jihadist movement, and Bosnia 84
Global Relief Fund 85
goals, international criminal groups/militant political movements 3, 4–5
Golden Sands resort 132–3
Good Friday Agreement 1998 151
governance, Kosovo 35–8
Government of Democratic Forces, Bulgaria 133
governments, as stationary bandits 15
Grabosky, Peter & Stohl, Michael 143, 149
Greece 58, 60, 117
Gross Criminal Product 12
Groupe Islamique Combattant Morocain 199n.64
GSPC (Group for Preaching and Combat) 89, 96, 98–100, 175, 199n.64, 202n.57, 203n.69
Guantanamo Bay, Bosnian detainees 84
guerrilla warefare, PKK 56
gun running *see* arms trafficking

HADEP, Turkey 53
Hadzic, Goran 120
Hadzic, Mehmet 113
Hague Program 169, 213n.19
Hague, The 105, 106, 119, 120 *see also* International War Crimes Tribunal at The Hague
Al-Haili, Al-Zubair 74
Hamas 98, 152
Haradinaj clan 30
Haradinaj, Ramush 33, 37
Haramain Islamic Foundation 85
al-Hasayan, Fatih 72, 73
Haut, Francois 62, 63, 66
Haviv, Ron 7, 113
Hawks of Thrace 61
Hekmatyar, Gulbuddin 153
HEP (People's Labor Party) 53
heroin trade: 134; Afghanistan 134; Albanian 32; Balkan route 31, 38–8, 148; Bulgaria 136, 139; and Kosovo clans xv; and PKK 64; and the Taliban 153, 177, 179n.4; Western Europe xx *see also* drug production/trade/trafficking
Hewitt, Joseph 22
Hezbollah, Turkish (KH) 152–3, 193n.96
High Commissioner on National Minorities 171
High Committee of the State (HCE), Algeria 88
High Islamic Council, Algeria 91

226 *Index*

High Representative for the Common
  Foreign and Security Policy 166, 167
Hizb-i Islami Afghanistan 152–3
Hoare, Marko Attila 104
Hobsbawm, E.J. 7
Hoffman, Bruce 63
holy war, Bosnian civil war as 77
homicide rates, Albania 25
Hoxha, Enver 25–6
humanitarian aid/workers, Bosnia 72, 75
human rights: Algeria 89, 175; ethnic
  Kurds 45, 47
Human Rights Watch 37
human trafficking: Chechnya 155;
  and funding of militant groups 149;
  Kosovo xv, 24, 179n.2; PKK 65, 66
Hussein, Saddam 49, 59, 190n.34
HVO casualties, Bosnian civil war 71
hybrid networks 17
hybrid terror-crime networks xvi, 42, 43,
  53, 66–7, 87, 160
hybrid trans-border networks 159
hyperinflation, Bulgaria 7

identity: Algerian 90; Bosniak 78–9;
  Bosnian national 77–9; communal 110–
  11; Islamic 10, 87
identity conflicts, and hybrid crime–terror
  networks 53
identity networks 1; advantages
  of 164–5; Algeria 87; and armed
  conflicts 89–92; cross-border/trans-
  state 8; and diasporas 165; Islamic 10,
  83; Serb trans-border 107–8; trans-
  border 6, 22, 43, 44, 45, 103, 109;
  trans-republican 110
ideological movements, militancy–crime
  linkages 6
IFOR (Implementation Force) 173
Iliev, Vassil 129
illegal collective behavior, organized crime
  as 10, 11
illiberal economy, Yugoslavia 164
Information Agency, Serbia 119
Inside Rebellion 144
instability, countries at risk of 22
institutional design, and opportunities 51
insurgencies: ethnic base of 9; PKK in
  Turkey 53, 54, 56, 57, 67
insurrectory networks, Serb 107
interdependence, opportunistic 5–6
international actors, and KLA 39
international criminal groups 12; and
  international actors 39; PKK 63–6;
  profit maximization/risk reduction 3

International Criminal Tribunal for the
  former Yugoslavia (ICTY) 71, 173
international organizations, and trans-
  border violence/crime 21–2
International War Crimes Tribunal at The
  Hague 105, 115, 116, 118, 120 *see also*
  Hague, The
Interpol 65, 112, 156
Iran: and Bosnian civil war 73, 77;
  ETSM 47–8; intelligence/security
  presence in Bosnia 72, 75, 84; and
  PKK 58, 59
Iranian Kurds 47
Iranian Ministry of Intelligence and
  Security 75
Iraq: as black hole 17; ETSM 48–52;
  invasion of Kuwait 190n.35; and
  PKK 19, 57, 58, 59, 195n.138;
  and PKK/Turkish war 56; and
  Turkey 192n.81; war on 190n.36
Iraqi Kurdish Civil War 195n.138
Iraqi Kurdish Regional Government 161
Iraqi Kurdistan 48, 49, 51
Iraqi Kurds: genocide 48, 49; Iraqi
  Kurdish ETSM 48–52; and PKK 41;
  political agenda 48–9, 50 *see also* Kurdish
  Democratic Party
Irish Republican Army (IRA) 147, 149,
  151, 176
Islam: Algeria xviii, 90; and Bosniak
  identity 78–9; financing of militant 4,
  85; and FLN government 91;
  international and Bosnia xviii, 76–80;
  militant/Algeria 98–9; militant/war in
  Kosovo 34–5; political uses of 90; third
  phase of militant 98–9
Islamic Balkan Center in Zenica 84
Islamic charities, Bosnia 68
Islamic Community (Islamska Zaednica),
  Bosnia 78–9
Islamic Declaration 69
Islamic fighters 74
Islamic identity 10, 87
Islamic identity networks 10, 83
Islamic Jihad 9
Islamic Movement Army (MIA) *see* MIA
Islamic movements, trans-state 161
Islamic Regiment, Chechnya 155, 158
Islamic Salvation Army (AIS) *see* AIS
Islamic Salvation Front (FIS) *see* FIS
Islamic state, and jihad in Algeria 94
Islamic Umma 10, 90, 91
Islamist advocacy network 79
Islamist crime–terror network, and
  Bosnia 83–5

Islamist institutions, Bosnia 83
Islamist mobilization 83
Islamist movement: financing of/
Algeria 93–4, 95; global in Bosnia 83
Islamist networks, training camps 17
Islamists: Algerian 6, 17, 161, 163;
Bosnian 6, 163
Islamist terrorism, in Algeria 94–8, 175
Islamization, Bosnia 78–9
Italy: Albanian organized crime groups 34;
and Algerian jihadists 100; criminal
networks 32; and Montenegro/
smuggling 31, 149; and PKK 60; Red
Brigade 151
Ivanov, Dimiter 131
Izetbegović, Alija 31, 69, 70, 77, 81,
198n.42

Jahic, Edin 83
Jashari, Adem 27, 33
Jashari clan 28
Al-Jazareiri, Abd el-Kadr 90
Jihad, economy of global 14
jihadist networks, Bosnian civil war 72
jihadists: Algeria 91–2, 95–6, 98–101, 102,
177; Bosnia 161
jihadist terrorism, funding of 147
jihadist units, Bosnian civil war 71
JNA (Yugoslav National Army) 26, 70, 105,
111, 115, 116, 117
Joffee, George 92, 93
Jordan, David C. 13, 19, 21, 134
Josic, Sreten 139
Joulwan, George 113, 114
Judah, Tim 120
judicial systems: Bosnia 164; Bulgaria 126,
136, 137; Kosovo 36–7, 164;
rebuilding 174, 175
Justice and Home Affairs Council, EU 166

Kabylia Berbers 92
Kabylia mountains, jihadists 99, 100
Kalyvas, Stathis 87, 97
Kamenov, Ivo 141–2
Kanun of Lek Dukagjini 25
Karadžić, Radovan 106, 110, 112
Karayilan, Murat 54, 57
Kasar, Monser al 138
Kemp, Walter 76, 81, 145, 156, 157
Kepel, Gilles 94, 98
Kertes, Mihalj 116
Khatami, Mohammad 47
kidnappings 89, 100, 155
Kingdom of Serbs, Croats and
Slovenes 108

Kingdom of Yugoslavia 108 see also
Yugoslavia
King Fahd mosque in Sarajevo 79
kin groups 164 see also clans; fis
Kintex 138
Komala (Revolutionary Organization of
Kurdish Toilers) 47
KONGRA-GEL 55, 65
KOS, Yugoslavia 116
Kosovar nationalists 1, 5, 148, 176, 177
Kosovar networks, predation by 148
Kosovars: and Dayton Peace Accords 27;
and Italian criminal networks 32
Kosovar Stability Initiative (IKS) 40
Kosovo 24; as black hole 17; clan-
based networks 18, 24, 26, 105, 158,
186n.50; clans xv, 31–2, 33, 37, 38, 105,
160; corruption 36, 37, 40; criminal
networks 24, 31–4; as criminalized
state 25; drug trade 24, 32; and drug
trafficking 24; economy 24, 32, 34,
37–8; genocide 160; governance
in 35–8; human trafficking 24,
179n.2; independence 26–31; money
laundering 36, 37; mujahedeen 34;
and OSCE 172; post-conflict 174;
as protectorate 29, 105, 174; and
Saudi Arabia 34–5; and Serbia 105;
terrorism 29, 30, 105; and transition
from illicit/licit enterprise 150;
unholy alliances 160; war/and crime
networks 24, 31–4; war and militant
Islam 34–5 see also KLA
Kosovo 2008 Progress Report 36, 37
Kosovo C 34
Kosovo Force (KFOR) 39, 187n.59
Kosovo Liberation Army (KLA) xv, 27–9,
105; Albania/Macedonia 32; conversion
to police force 35–6, 177; and drug
trade 32, 33; and fis 5, 27, 33; funding
of 31, 33, 39, 147; and international
actors 39; post conflict 160; trade in
human organs 148
Kosovo Police Force (KPF) 35
Kosovo Police (KP) 36, 37
Kosovo Police Service (KPS) 32, 177
Kosovo Protection Corps (KPC) 28, 36, 39,
160, 177
Kosovo Protection Force (KPF) 35
Kosovo Protection Service 36
Kostov, Ivan 133, 206n.3
Kravica 71
KRG (Kurdistan Regional
Government) 50, 51
Kudistan Democratic Confederation 48

228 *Index*

Kuiovic, Budimir 139
Kurdish Autonomous Region, Iraq 48–9
Kurdish cultural centers, Europe 63
Kurdish Democratic Initiative 57, 192n.69
Kurdish Democratic Party (KDP), Iraqi 48,
  49, 50, 51, 146, 190n.37, 195n.138
Kurdish Democratic Party of Syria 45
Kurdish ETSM 43–52, 61–2, 160
Kurdishin for.com 62
Kurdish liberation movement, Iraqi 48–9
Kurdish liberation movement, Turkey 41
Kurdish Parliament in exile 62
Kurdish Workers Party (PKK) *see* PKK
Kurdistan Freedom Falkans 56
Kurdistan Freedom Hawks (TAK) 56
Kurdistan, Iraqi 49
Kurdistan National Assembly of Syria 45
Kurdistan People's Conference 55
Kurdistan People's Congress (KONGRA-
  GEL) 55, 65
Kurdistan Regional Government
  (KRG) 56, 59, 195n.138
Kurds: human rights/discrimination 45,
  47; Iranian 47; people/traditions 43–52;
  Syrian 45–6; in Turkey xviii, 1, 42, 52–
  3, 175; Turkish/nationalist movement 1
Kusadasi 56
Kuwait 72, 190n.35
Kvadrat (Quadrant) 84
Kyulev, Emil 132

Lamari, Smain 92
Law on Information about Nonperformance
  Loans, Bulgaria 133
Legija 106, 118, 119
legislation, crime 167
Liberation Army of Preshevo, Bujanovac
  and Medvedja (UCPMB) 29
Lisbon Treaty 170
loans, Bulgaria 133
London mosques 96–7, 99
Lord's Resistance Army (LRA) 146
Loukanov, Andrei 131
Lowi, Miriam 87, 96
Lukovic, Milorad *see* Legija

Maastricht Treaty 167
Macedonia 29, 32, 105, 171, 172
Macedonian crisis 2001 29
Madani, Abbassi 88, 91
Madelenat, Paul 113
Madrid bombings 168, 199n.64
Madzho 129, 138
mafia: Albanian 26; Bulgarian
  Communist 131; and global financial
  crisis 14; Sicilian 7

Mafia Borguesse 19, 136–7, 183n.59,
  208n.67
Majine 71
Malaysia 73
al-Maliki, Nouri 59
Maoist theory of the people's war 54, 56
Marc 93 (Bulgaria) 129
Marcus, Aliza 59
market economy, Bulgaria 7
market fundamentalism, Bulgaria 20
marketism 20, 131
market of violence 125, 126–30, 131,
  133–4, 138, 162
market opportunities, criminal 12–15
markets, illicit 15
Markov, Dancho 129
Marmaris 56
Marshall, Monty 8
Martinez, Luis 93, 95
Marxist-Leninism of PKK 54, 59
al-Masri, Abu Hamza 97
massacres: Algeria 87, 89, 97; Raćek
  massacre 28; by Serbian forces 105;
  Srebrenica 71–2
material gain, predatory networks 7
Mauritania 99
Maxwell, Robert 131
*McMafia: A Journey through the Global Criminal
  Underworld* 122
media, and PKK 62, 66, 193n.100
Mediene, Mohammed 92
Med TV 66
Memorandum of Understanding (MOU),
  Iraq/Turkey 51, 59
Merchant Fleet, Bulgarian 133
Merdan, Jasmin 83
Metohija group 33
Mexico, state/drug networks xvi, 21
MIA (Islamic Movement Army) 91, 95
Michaletos, Ioannis 34, 37
middle class, Bulgaria 131
Middle East, groups engaged in political
  violence/crime 152–3, 157
Mihalev, Mladen *see* Madzho
Milerici 71
militancy–crime linkages 5–8
militant clerics, justification of killings 97
militant-criminal interactions 1, 3
militant-criminal networks 4–5, 165, 176,
  177
militant networks 1; and public sector
  corruption 18
militant political movements 3–4
militants: funding of 4, 85, 143–51, 176;
  legitimacy of 148; objectives of 145 *see
  also* terrorists

military supplies, Bosnian civil war 73–4
militia, private/Bulgaria 129
Milošević government: and Bosnian
war 115; corruption 117; and
criminalization of Serbia 114, 121, 158;
ethnic cleansing 106; and Kosovo 28,
107; and Serbian nationalism 26, 68, 69;
and terror networks 7, 103–4
Milošević, Slobodan: and Arkan 118; and
crime/terrorism 104, 117; finances
of 116; and OSCE 172; and radicalism
of Serb ETSM 111; removal of 105,
118; territorial objectives 162
Milward, Alan 170
Mincheva, Lyubov 8
Mini, Fabio 36
Ministry of Interior, Bulgaria 126, 138
Ministry of Interior, Serbia 117, 119
minorities: Albanian/Kosovar violence
towards 30; and OSCE 171; trans-
border networking 9
Minorities at Risk Organizational
Behavior (MAROB) project xvii–xviii,
152–3
Minorities at Risk project 9, 10, 22, 42,
181n.25, 188n.7
Mitrovica 30
Mladić, Ratko 71, 106, 112, 113
Moldova 156
money-dirtying 150
money laundering: al-Qaeda 14; and
alternative global economy 15;
Bulgaria 131, 132, 136; EU Directive on
Money Laundering 169, 170; global 13–
14; Kosovo 36, 37; and PKK 64, 66;
Serbia 117; and transition from illicit/
licit enterprise 150–1
Montenegro 149
Morocco 199n.64
mosques, London 96–7, 99
Movement for Rights and Freedon
(MRF) 139
movements for national liberation and
unification (MNLU) 44
mujahedeen 196n.4; Algerian 203n.69;
Bosnia 68, 69, 81, 83, 84, 86; Bosnian
civil war xviii, 72, 74–5, 76–7, 78;
Kosovo 34
multidimensional economy 134
Multigroup 130, 131–2, 138
multinational systemic crime 3
Musaj clan 30
Muslim Brotherhood: Bosnia 84; Egypt 69
Muslims, Jihadist 1
Muslim World League Journal 72
Mustafa, Rustem *see* Remi

Nacertanije 106
Nahnah, Mahfoudh 91, 98
Napoleoni, Loretta 12, 14
narco-criminalization: 21; Bulgaria
125–6, 134–7, 140 *see also* drug markets;
drug trade
narco-economies 20, 134–5
narcostatization 20
narco-terrorism 3
narco-trafficking *see* drug trafficking
Narodna Odbrana 108
national identity: Algerian 90;
Bosnian 77–9
nationalism: Albania 29, 34, 163;
Ataturk's 52; Kurdish 44–5, 47, 52;
Serb 26, 103, 104–5, 111, 114–21, 162,
163; violent/Kosovars xv, 25
Nationalist Kurdish Revenge Teams 55
nationalist movements 161; Albanian 1, 5,
29, 34, 148, 176, 177; Turkish Kurds 1
National Liberation Army (NLA) 29–30
National Liberation Front (FLN) *see* FLN
National Liberation Front of Kurdistan
(ERNK) 54
National Movement, Bulgaria 133
National Security Agency 130
National Unification Front (NUF) 28
NATO: air strikes Serbia/Kosovo xv,
28; Bosnia's membership 82, 86; and
Dayton Accords 114; and KLA 39;
in Kosovo 24, 160; Partnership for
Peace program 120; and Serbia 120;
and Srebrenica 113; Stabilization
Force/Bosnia 84
nested games 46
nested games within spillover crises 49, 51,
66–7
Netherlands 58, 60–1
New Ways to Make Big Money 93
NGO humanitarian workers, Bosnia 72
Nicovic, Marko 117
no-fly zone, Northern Iraq 49, 195n.138
NORAID 147

objectives, of militants 3, 4–5
Ocalan, Abdullah 41; capture of 6, 60,
66; Freedom-for-Ocalan.com 62;
imprisonment 191n.56; in Iraq 50; and
PJAK 48; and Russia 59; and Syria 58;
and Turkey 56; violence of 54, 55
Ochite, Mitio 136
Office of the High Representative,
Bosnia 81
Officio de'Informazione del Kurdistan 62
offshore zones, global finance 13
Ohrid Agreement 2001 30

230 *Index*

oil: Algeria 87, 88, 92, 161, 203n.63;
  and funding of militant groups 147;
  Iraqi Kurdistan 48, 49; piracy/
  Chechnya 154; PKK targeting of
  Iraqi 56; smuggling/Bulgaria 138
oligarchs, Bulgaria 130, 131, 132, 138, 141
Operation Saber 119, 120, 139
opium trade xviii, 32, 177 *see also* drug
  production/trade/trafficking
Organization for Security and Cooperation
  in Europe (OSCE) 171–2, 175
organizations, regional/international post
  Cold War 21
organized crime: Bulgaria 128, 162;
  Europe 64–5; and Kosovo economy 37;
  and PKK 6; and state corruption 18–21;
  transnational/narco-trafficking 20–1;
  and UN employees 34; and unholy
  alliances
  10–15; and UNMIK 36
Organized Crime in Bulgaria 125
Orić, Naser 71, 197n.30
Ottoman Empire 107
Özal, Turgut 55

Pahlavi Dynasty 47
Pakistan: and Bosnian civil war funding 72;
  support of Taliban 146
Palestine Liberation Organization
  (PLO) 61, 144, 146, 150, 176
Pantev, Poli 136
paramilitary alliances, Serb
  trans-border 110–11
paramilitary forces: Bosnia 70; funding
  of 116; Serbia 103–4, 105, 107–8, 109,
  121; training camps Croatia 114
Pargeter, Alison 74
Partnership for Peace program 120
Party of Democratic Action *see* SDA
Party of Free Life of Kurdistan (PJAK) 47–
  8, 59
Patriotic League, SDS 70
Patriotic Union of Kurdistan (PUK) 48, 49,
  50, 51, 190n.37, 195n.138
Pavkovic, Nebojsa 120
Pavlov, Ilya 131–2, 134, 138
Peace and Democratic Party (BDP) 53
peacekeepers/and crime 176, 197n.30
peacekeeping xv, 21, 72, 76, 166, 171, 176
Pelović, Borislav 114
People's Defense Forces, Turkey 57
People's Liberation Army of Kurdistan
  (ARGK) 54
People's Movement of Kosovo (LPK) 27
Peru 3
Petersberg tasks 166

Philippines 6
Pinarcik 55
PKK: 5–6, 41–2; cannabis farms/
  Iraq 17; drug trafficking 51, 64, 148;
  and DTP 53; funding of 51, 63–6,
  145–6; group-state alliances 50; guerrilla
  warefare 56; human trafficking 65,
  66; international support for 58–63;
  and Iraq 19, 57, 58, 59, 195n.138; and
  Iraqi Kurdish parties 50; and KDP/
  PUK 51; and Kurdish Democratic
  Initiative 192n.69; leadership 165; and
  media 62, 66, 193n.100; and money
  laundering 64, 66; objectives of 41,
  54; and Party of Free Life of Kurdistan
  (PJAK) 48; radicalism of 52; territorial
  objectives 190n.46; trans-border
  activities 152; and Turkish ETSM 52–8;
  and Turkish Hezbollah 193n.96; unholy
  alliances 160, 163 *see also* Ocalan,
  Abdullah
police: Bosnia/Kosovo 174; Bulgaria/
  heroin market 136; Serbia 117
Police and Judicial Cooperation in Criminal
  Matters, EU 166, 167–8
Political and Security Committee, EU 166
political economy, PKK war on
  Turkey 58–66
politically exploitable ties 38
political militants, goals of 3
political networks, based on Islamic
  identity 87
political parties, corruption in/ Bosnia 82
political upheaval, and unholy alliances 16
political violence, and black holes 17
politicide, by Serbian forces 28
politics, and criminal networks 37
Popov, Dimiter 131
poppy production 134, 153 *see also* drug
  production/trade/trafficking
post-Cold War conflicts 17
post-Cold War reconstruction 165
post-communist transitions: Bulgaria 124–
  6; criminalized 20
post-communist world, groups engaged in
  political violence/crime 153–4, 158
post-conflict reconstruction 21, 165, 171–4
poverty: Algeria 88, 93, 98; Bulgaria 124;
  Sahara region 101
power, and criminalized rebels 2–3
predation, and funding of militant
  groups 147–8
predatory networks 5, 7–8, 140–2, 158
predatory states 15
predatory trans-border networks 127, 131,
  137–40

Pridnestrovian Moldovian Republic
(PMR) 156–7
private sector corruption, Algeria 93
privatization schemes, Bulgaria 132, 133,
162
profit, and criminalized rebels 2–3
profit maximization, international criminal
groups 3
propaganda machine, of PKK 62
protection money, and PKK 63
protection rackets 15
protection services, private/Bulgaria 126
protectorates 173
protracted conflict regions 8, 10, 189n.9
public sector corruption 18, 34, 40, 76

racketeering 33, 95
radicalization of Muslim youth, France 94
Raćek massacre 28
Raikovic, Dragomir 139
Rambouillet Accords 1999 28
RAND Corporation 63
Rašković, Jovan 110
Ratzel, Max-Peter 63
Raufer, Xavier 5, 32–3
Ražnatović, Ceca 113, 118
Ražnatović, Zeljko see Arkan
RDB 115–17, 119
rebellion 3
rebels, criminalized 2–3
Reconciliation Councils, Albania 35
reconstruction, post-conflict 165, 172–4
Red Army Faction, and PKK 61
Red Berets 106, 112, 116, 119, 120
Red Brigade, Italian 151
Red Star soccer team 112, 115
Regulations, EU 168
religion: and identity groups 10; and
Kosovar Albanians 34; SDA use of 78
religious movements, and militant-criminal
interactions 1
Remi 33
rent seeking, Algerian elites 92, 93
repression: Algeria 89; Iraqi Kurds 49
Republica Serpska 70
Republic of Kosovo 26–7 see also Kosovo
Republic of Mahabad 47
Republika Srpska (RS) 154
resources, and criminal enterprise 11
Reveron, Derek S. & Murer, Jeffrey S. 9
*Revised EU Plan of Action to Combat
Terrorism* 168
Revival of Islamic Heritage Society 85
Revolutionary Guard 75
Revolutionary United Front (RUF), Sierra
Leone 14

rioting, Algeria 88, 92
risk reduction, international criminal
groups 3
Riyadus-Salikhin Reconnaissance and
Sabotage Battalion 154
Roj TV 62, 193n.100
Roth, Jürgen 14, 131, 134, 138
Rugova, Ibrahim 26, 27, 28, 31, 172
Russia: invasion of Chechnya 155; and
PKK 58, 59 see also Soviet Union

Sahara base, jihadists 99, 100
Sahraoui, Nabil 98
Sakik clan 65
Salafism 196n.4; Algeria 202n.44;
Bosnia xviii, 78, 83
Salafist Group for Preaching and Combat
(GSPC) see GSPC
Samokovetza 136
sanctions: and smuggling 160;
Yugoslavia 164
Sarajevo 70, 77; ethnic cleansing/
terrorism 79–80, 112; Iranian agents
in 75
Saudi Arabia: financing of Bosnia 69,
72, 76, 77, 79, 85; funding of militant
groups 147, 158; and Kosovo 34–5; and
Wahabism 147
Saudi High Commission for Relief 85
Schengen Information System (SISII) 169
Schindler, John R. 34, 71, 73
Schook, Steven 34
SDA (*Stranka Demokratske Akcie*) 68, 69, 70,
78
SDS (Serbian Democratic Party)
government 70, 72, 73, 75, 77
SDS Patriotic League 80
sectarian identification, and trust 4
secularism, Algeria 90
security: in Bosnia 82–2, 174; and EU 166,
168, 173; and EU/individual states
responsibility 170; European and Muslim
Bosnia 68; Kosovo 174
security forces, and atrocities 202n.50
security services, private in Bulgaria 125
seperatist movement, Albanian 26–31
September 11th, anti-terrorism measures
following 84, 101, 147, 168 see also war
on terror
Serb Communist Party 110
Serb Confederation 110
Serb Council 110
Serb Democratic Party 110
Serbia: corruption 120, 121; criminal
clans 117; criminalization of state 106,
114–21, 162; de-criminalizing the

232 *Index*

Serbia: corruption (*cont.*):
  state 118–21; and disintegration of
  Yugoslavia 104; ethnic cleansing 109,
  111–14, 116, 121, 162; ETSM 106–10,
  111; genocide 109, 110; history
  of 107–9; illiberal economy of 20;
  nationalists 26, 103, 104–5, 111, 114–21,
  162, 163; paramilitary forces 103–4, 105,
  107–8, 109, 121; predatory networks 7;
  recent history of 104–6; state sponsored
  terrorism 112, 114; trans-border
  identity networks 106, 108, 109, 110;
  ultranationalists 26; unholy alliances 162
Serbian Democratic Party 154
Serbian Security Information Agency 27
Serb National Assembly 110
Serb Republic of Bosnia-Herzegovina 110
Serb Republic of Krajina 110
Serbs, and assassinations 205n.27
Serb State Security Bureau (RDB) *see*
  RDB
Serb Unity Party 114
Serhildan 55
7th Muslim Brigade 74
sex trade, West European 160; *see also*
  human trafficking
SFOR (Stabilisation Force) 173
Sghouridhis, Panayiotis 60
al-Shabaab 145
Shaban, Anwar 74
al-Sharhan, Muhammad 77
sharia state, and Algerian jihad 94
Sheriff group 156
Shqiptarë 25
SIC, Bulgaria 129, 130, 132–3, 138, 139,
  141
Sicilian Mafia 7
Sidik, Abu Bekir 34
Sierra Leone 14
Silajdzic, Haris 80
Simatović, Franko 116
Simeon II 133
Sinn Fein 151
Siptar 118
Smirnov, President 156
smuggling: Algeria 89, 95, 96, 100;
  Arkan 113; Balkans 138; Bosnia 68–9,
  116, 120; Bulgaria 129–30, 138, 139,
  140, 162; and funding of militant
  groups 149; and KLA xv, 33; Kurdish
  clans 65; Montenegro/Italy 31, 149; and
  sanctions 160; Serbia 117
social bandits 7
socialism: Algeria 88, 91; Bulgaria 123–4;
  collapse of state 160

Socialist Federation of Yugoslavia 104
  see also Yugoslavia
social movements, ETSMs as 43
social networks, criminal enterprises as 11
social ties, and criminal cooperation 11
Sofia, heroin market 136
Solana, Javier 168
Solidarity clause 169
Somalia 16, 145, 209n.8
Sørensen, Jens S. 26
South Africa 117
sovereign-free zones 17
Soviet Union: and Bulgaria 123; and
  PLO 146 *see also* Russia
spaces, ungoverned 15
Spain 100
Special Purpose Islamic Regiment 155,
  158
Spider Traps, Bulgaria 132
spillover crises, PKK-Turkish conflict 57,
  67
sponsorship, of militant groups 145–6
Srebrenica 71–2, 113
Sri Lanka 147
Stability Pact for South Eastern
  Europe 165, 172
Stabilization and Association Process
  (SAP) 173
Stamatovic, Franko 120
Stanisic, Jovica 115–16, 118–19, 120
state agencies, and global illegal
  economy 13
State Agency for Protection and
  Investigation (SIPA) 81
state criminalization, Bulgaria 126–7
state officials, as stationary bandits 18
states: corruption/organized crime 18–21;
  and criminal networks 37; failure
  of/instability 16–17; predatory 15;
  and territory/wealth 19; and unholy
  alliances 15–21; weak 16; *see also*
  individual countries
state sponsorship, of militant groups 145–6
stationary bandits 15, 18
Steiner, Michael 30
Stockholm Program 170
Stop the Hague conspiracy 119
Stranka Demokratske Akcie (SDA) 31
Strategy for EU Foreign Policy, A 166, 173
Strazzari, Francesco 31, 36, 38
structural corruption 19–20, 21, 125,
  130–4, 137, 140
Sudan 146
Sufism, Bosnia 78
suicide attacks, French

embassy/Mauritania 101
suicide bombers 55, 99
supra-national institutions, and unholy
  alliances 21–2
Surcin clan 117
al-Suri, Abu Musab 98–9
Susak, Gojko 73
Switzerland 117
Syria, and PKK 58
Syrian Arab opposition movement, and
  Turkey 46
Syrian ETSM 45–7, 67
Syrian National Council (SNC) 46

Tajik minorities, and radical Islam 10
takfir, and GIA 97
Talabani, Jalal 50, 51, 190n.37
Taliban: and heroin trade xviii, 153, 177,
  179n.4; and Pakistan 146; resurgence
  of 63, 177
Tamil Tigers 147
Tarrow, Sidney 43, 44, 108
temporary village guards, Turkey 54
10th Mountain Brigade, Bosnia 80
terrorism: Albania 39, 160; Algeria 89,
  94–8, 99, 102, 175; Bosnia 79–80, 81–3;
  Chechnya 155; and Cold War era 61;
  and crime 5–6; as criminal behavior 3;
  in France 101, 102; funding of 85,
  143–51; Kosovo 29, 30, 105; narco-
  terrorism 3; and PKK 55, 56; post-
  Communist Bulgaria 140–1; Serb 107,
  109, 111–14, 121, 162; state sponsored/
  Serbia 116; terrorist groups as allies 61;
  training camps Albania 34; US/UK
  embassies in Bosnia 84
  see also anti–terrorism; suicide
  attacks/bombers
terrorist movements, and crime
  networks 146
terrorists xvi–xvii, 143 *see also* militants
terror, new economy of 14, 15
Thaqi, Hashim xv, 33, 37, 179n.1
Third World Relief Agency (TWRA) 72–3
Tigers 106, 112, 113, 115, 116, 158
TIM group 141–2
Tito, Marshal 26, 104, 109
tobacco trade, Bulgaria 139
Todorov, Ivan *see* Doctora
Topalovic, Musan *see* Caco
Tosks 25
tourism, as PKK target 56
trabendo networks 95
training camps: Albania 34; Islamic 17;
  paramilitary/Croatia 114

trans-border alliances: identity conflicts
  8–10; predatory networks 7
trans-border crime–terrorism
  interactions 103
trans-border criminal networks:
  Bulgaria 122, 125, 137, 138; EU security
  initiatives 173, 174
trans-border identity networks: Balkan
  region 103; Bosnia/Algeria 6; and
  ETSMs 43, 44; Islamist 69; and
  Minorities at Risk project 22; Serb 106,
  108, 109, 110
trans-border nationalist terror networks 103
trans-border networking 9
trans-border terrorism-crime networks 116,
  162
trans-border terrorist networks 152
Transdniestria 156–7, 177
transnational Islamist network 86
Transparency International (TI) 18, 22,
  82, 124
trans-republican identity networks 110
Trans-Sahara Counterterrorism Initiative
  (TSCTI) 101
Trans-Sahara Counterterrorism Partnership
  (TSCPI) 101
trans-Sahara region 101
trans-state identity groups xv–xvi, 9, 11, 86
trans-state Islamic identity networks 6
trans-state movements 1, 8–9, 165
trans-state networks xvii, 4
Treaty of Amsterdam 167
Treaty of Lausanne 52
Treaty of Lisbon 167
Tremonti, Giulio 19, 20, 131
Triple Alliance 108
troikas 27
trust: and cooperation 4; and shared
  identity 149; and social affiliation 11
Tsebelis, George 46
Turkey: bombings/tourism 191n.63;
  and Bosnian civil war 73; clans 65;
  drug trade 191n.55; economy 56,
  57; ETSM 52–8; history of 52; and
  Iraq 192n.81; and Iraqi Kurdish
  Regional Government 161; and
  organized crime 191n.55; and PKK
  see PKK; public sector corruption
  18–19; and Syrian Arab opposition
  movement 46; as weak state 16
Turkish Kurds xviii, 1, 42, 52–3, 175
Turkish Ministry of Foreign Affairs 60, 64,
  65
Turkish State Planning Organization 53
TWRA (Third World Relief Agency) 74

234   *Index*

Uganda 146
Ukraine 76
Ulemek, Milorad *see* Legija
ultranationalists, Serbia 26
Umma, the 10, 90, 91
UN employees, and organized crime 34
unemployment: Algeria 88, 92, 93, 102;
  Bulgaria 124
UN General Assembly 70
ungoverned territories 17, 101
unholy alliances xvi, 1, 2, 4; hybrid trans-
  border networks 159; and organized
  crime 10–15; and states 15–21; and
  supra-national institutions 21–2;
  territorial bases of 154–7; trans-border
  identity conflicts 8–10; why they come
  apart 174–7
Unholy Alliances project xiv, 42
UN humanitarian workers, Bosnia 72, 75
Unification or Death 108
UN Interim Administration Mission in
  Kosovo (UNMIK): and ANA 30;
  and corruption 39; and crime 33;
  criminal justice system 35; and drug
  trade 32; institution building of 24;
  and organized crime 36, 37; post-war
  administration 28–9, 33, 173, 187n.59;
  and regulation 174; and terrorism 28–9
UN International Police Task Force 173
United Arab Emirates 72
United Nations Office on Drugs and Crime
  (UNODC) 14, 21, 32, 135, 179n.4
United States: Albanian criminal networks
  in 24; and ANA 30; anti-terrorist black
  list 85; and Bosnia 73, 81–2, 84; and
  KLA 28; money laundering in 150; war
  on terror 87, 101, 102
UN Office on Drugs and Crime 64, 145
UN peacekeepers, Bosnia 72 *see also*
  peacekeeping
UN personnel, involvement in crime 75–6
UN safe haven, Srebrenica 71–2, 113
UN Secretary-General's 2005 report to the
  General Assembly 71
UN Security Resolution 688 49
urbanization, and clan-based structures 38
urban terrorism, PKK 55, 56
Uståshe 109
Uzbek minorities, and radical Islam 10

Van der Stoel, Max 171, 172
Varna, police/drug trade 136
Vasilijevic, Aleksandar 116
Vazir 85
Vetevendosja (Self-Determination) political
  group 30

violence: Albanian Kosovar 30; Algeria 94,
  98; clans 33; and criminal groups/
  political militants 3; cross-border 57, 67;
  GIA 89, 97, 98, 175; homicide rates in
  Albania 25; illegal 3; justification of 97;
  market of 125, 126–30, 138; PKK 53,
  55, 57; protracted conflict regions 8;
  Serb 28; state-sponsored/Serbia 107 *see
  also* ethnic cleansing; genocide; terrorism
VIS, Bulgaria 129, 130, 136, 139, 141
Visa Information System (VIS) 169
von Lampe, Klaus 11
Vukovar 113, 120
vulnerable states 16

Wahabism: Bosnia 83, 161; Saudi Arabia's
  support of 147, 196n.4
Waple, Mark 74
war crimes, Bosnia 70
war economies, and alternative global
  economy 14
war on terror 87, 101, 102 *see also*
  September 11th
Washington Agreement 49
weak states 15, 16
weapons *see* arms trafficking
weekend warriors, Serbia 109
Weinstein, Jeremy 144, 158
women, trafficking in/Kosovo xv, 24
  see also human trafficking
World War I 108
wrestlers/security groups: Bulgaria 139,
  142, 162; Bulgaria/markets of
  violence 128, 129, 130, 131, 133–4

Yoshihara, Susan F. 27, 28
Young Bosnia 108
Yugoslav Federal Army (JNA) *see* JNA
Yugoslavia: criminals 205n.27; dissolution
  of 8, 104, 109, 160; illiberal economy
  in 164; Kingdom of 108; and political
  economy of war 20; transitional
  years 104–6; wars and crime 31–2
Yugoslav National Army (JNA) *see* JNA
Yugoslav People's Army 109
Yugoslav state security agency 115

al-Zarqawi, Abu Musab 202n.57
al-Zawahiri, Ayman 98
Zemun clan 117, 118, 119, 120
Zeroual, President 98
Zeroul, Liamine 89
Zhivkov, Todor 123
Zogiani, Avni 36, 37, 38, 40
Zonoozi, Manouchehr Tahsili 62
Zvornik 113